I0825361

Advance Praise for

The Education of a Senator

"To read Lamar Alexander's vivid and surprising memoir is to be in conversation with a man who knows how to tell a great story—and who has given his life to a country that needs to hear what he has to say."

—**Jon Meacham**, author of *Destiny and Power*

"What a wonderful and refreshing memoir! It reminds us of the not too distant past when people got to know opposing politicians and their views, searched for ways to compromise, and never forgot the profound responsibility of citizenship in a democratic society. Lamar Alexander has been that gift to us—a dedicated, civil servant more interested in getting things done and improving the lives of others than in grabbing the headlines, bashing an opponent, or participating in the partisanship that seems to suffocate today's politics. This is a reminder of what a great man, committed to virtue and reason, can accomplish. Bravo!"

—**Ken Burns**, filmmaker

"For decades, Lamar Alexander was not just an astute observer of some of the most important moments in our nation's history, but an important participant in them. In this revealing and highly entertaining memoir, he takes us inside those vital times. Historians will long rely on his insights to understand these critical years for America."

—**Karl Rove**, senior advisor and deputy chief of staff
to President George W. Bush

"For eighteen years, there has been Lamar Alexander, and there's been the rest of us ... [he is] hands-down one of the most brilliant, most thoughtful, and most effective legislators any of us have ever seen."

—**Mitch McConnell**, US Senate Majority Leader

THE EDUCATION OF A SENATOR

THE EDUCATION OF A SENATOR

From JFK to Trump

LAMAR ALEXANDER

Foreword
by JON MEACHAM

A POST HILL PRESS BOOK

The Education of a Senator:
From JFK to Trump

ISBN: 979-8-89565-648-8
ISBN (eBook): 979-8-89565-649-5

Cover design by Conroy Accord
Cover photo by Robin Hood
Interior design and composition by Greg Johnson, Textbook Perfect

Photographs used on the inserts are the personal property of Lamar Alexander, unless credited otherwise.

Post Hill Press
New York • Nashville
posthillpress.com

Published in the United States of America
1 2 3 4 5 6 7 8 9 10

For Honey

"I woke up every morning thinking that I might be able to do something good for my state or country, and went to bed most nights thinking that I had."

—LAMAR ALEXANDER

Contents

PART FIVE: A'swiveling in the Governor's Chair 1979 to 1987

PART SIX: Where Now? 1987 to 1989

PART SEVEN: Back to Washington, DC 1990 to 1993

PART EIGHT: The Ultimate Startup 1993 to 2000

PART NINE: The Most Exclusive Club 2001 to 2008

PART TEN: Working with Obama
2009 to 2017

PART ELEVEN: Finest Hour or Lack of Spine?
2017 to November 2020

PART TWELVE: Heartbreak
November 2020 to December 2022

Foreword

By Jon Meacham

THE STORY HAD NOT BEGUN AS HE HAD HOPED.

In 1974, after working for Howard Baker in the United States Senate and President Nixon in the White House, Lamar Alexander—at the tender age of thirty-three—launched a campaign for governor of his native Tennessee. According to contemporary newspaper reports, Alexander, a graduate of Vanderbilt and New York University's School of Law, had seemed aloof on the trail. And on election day, he lost.

Most importantly, however, he had *learned*. Four years later, in 1978, Alexander jettisoned his suits and announced that he would traverse the state on foot, inviting Tennesseans to "Come On Along." "Some people thought Lamar Alexander, an Eastern-educated lawyer, was a stuffed shirt when he ran for governor four years ago," the *Jackson Sun* observed in the spring of 1978. "This time, he's going to be better known by his red plaid shirt that he is wearing on a 1,000-mile walk across Tennessee from Mountain City to Memphis."[1] Only bad dogs and lightning would knock him off schedule.

Across the state that had given the nation Andrew Jackson, Dolly Parton, and Cordell Hull, the young Republican would stretch out his hand again and again and again. "I'm Lamar Alexander," he'd say. "I'd like to be your next governor."

The reaction was not always what the candidate hoped for. "Oh, you are, are you?" people would reply. "And you would, would you?" Out on the road, a reporter for Memphis's *The Commercial Appeal* thought voters really had a more fundamental question. "Who is this guy, some kind of nut? The sensation that one is being put on is strong."[2]

But as history and this wonderful memoir will show, Lamar Alexander was no nut—at least not in a disqualifying way—and he wasn't putting anyone on. The powerful blend of curiosity, service, and ambition that propelled him across Tennessee nearly half a century ago was real, deep, and enduring. Alexander won that 1978 campaign, and the story went on.

His has been a great American life. As a young aide in a now-distant Washington, as a governor, as a member of the Cabinet of George H.W. Bush, as a university president, as a presidential contender, and as a United States senator, Alexander has been a thoughtful, observant, and effective participant in what Oliver Wendell Holmes Jr. once called the "passion and action"[3] of the time. From the foothills of the Smoky Mountains to the highest levels of American politics, Lamar Alexander has always been *learning*.

In this, he was his mother's son. She made sure he had a library card and took piano lessons, thus introducing him to the panoply of human experience. Never doctrinaire, Alexander has long been attuned to the vagaries of the character of both the leaders and the led. Governance is about politics, and politics is about people—our fears and our hopes, our selfishness and our generosity. The great, constructive politicians—and Lamar Alexander is a great, constructive politician—appeal not only to our basic instincts but also to what Lincoln called "the better angels of our nature."[4] To do so, one must not merely be a vote-getter (though vote-getting is essential) but a student of souls and a shaper of minds as well.

Alexander is all three. He is, perhaps, the rarest of hat tricks. One need not agree with, nor approve of, everything he did in his public life to appreciate that he embodies the depressingly scarce virtues of democracy and decency. In these pages, we are given a privileged seat to a life lived in full; a life given to the service of state and of country; a life reminding us that good and thoughtful people like Lamar Alexander have stood watch over our flawed and frustrating, yet noble and glorious, national experiment. This is his story—one that has much to teach a country struggling to write its next chapter. We are fortunate, indeed, that he is inviting us to come on along once more.

Author's Note

Maryville, Tennessee. December 15, 2025.

When I was a student at Vanderbilt University in 1961, Robert Frost read poetry to an audience in Alumni Hall.

An English professor asked Frost to explain one of his poems.

"Why should I, in other and worse words?" Frost said.

I have relied on Frost's reply in gathering sources for this book. If I was happy with what I wrote years ago, I saw no need to write it again. In any event, I have found that, when I borrow words from earlier writings, they live in a new context and have a different meaning, just as *Huckleberry Finn* seemed different when I read it in my forties than when I read it as a child.

Among my sources are nine books that I wrote.[1] Four were about my time as governor during the 1980s, my walk across Tennessee, my early swearing-in as governor, a scrapbook of stories, and a book with photographs of Tennessee's friendship with Japan.

In 1986, during my last year as governor, I asked Peter Jenkins, an author of bestselling books about walking across America, to introduce me to publishers.

"Lamar would like to write a book about what a great governor he has been," Peter would say.

"His mother might read it," the first publisher said.

"Boring," said Number Two.

I forget what the third said.

"Anything else you could write about? Doing anything interesting after you leave office?" Number Four asked.

"Not really. The whole family's moving to Australia for six months. I'm going to do absolutely nothing," I said.

"Six months off... now that might be interesting," Number Four said.

"Six months off," said Peter Jenkins. "That's exactly the book we had in mind."

William Morrow paid me an advance to write *Six Months Off*, a book that the Michigan State professor with a national radio show, Dick Estell, read in its entirety over NPR.

During the 1990s, I wrote three more books in connection with my campaigns for president, including an account of my driving tour of America and essays describing *The New Promise of American Life*. I wrote *Lamar Alexander's Little Plaid Book: 311 Lessons, Rules, and Reminders About Running for Office and Making a Difference Whether It's for President of the United States or President of Your Senior Class.*

The inspiration for my little plaid book came from H. Jackson Brown Jr.'s *Life's Little Instruction Book*. The big difference was that Jack's book sold five million copies and I gave mine away. My book did produce many laughs. Senator Trent Lott told me he keeps it in his bathroom for reading. I have included many of the little book's rules—and other maxims—in this volume.

After years of entertaining our children and grandchildren with tales of *Chief Waki Waki Poo & the Swimming Pool Monster*, I wrote that story in a children's book for family members and friends.

Other helpful sources have been a half-century of my articles, columns, and speeches, which are online at the Vanderbilt University Archives. There is one other source that is not yet online. That is my diary. In 2008, after a visit to the home of President James K. Polk in Columbia, Tennessee, I read his four-volume diary. This inspired me to resume writing my own diary, a project that I had attempted for a few months in 2005, my third year in the Senate.

I restarted my diary on Thursday, November 12, 2009, when I wrote 2,800 words. I continued almost every day until I retired from the Senate on Sunday, January 3, 2021. On that day, my diary entry contained 38,320 words, including attachments. I spent about forty-five minutes writing each entry, either at night or early in the mornings. I have given the diary to the Vanderbilt Archives to be sealed until twenty years after my death, so as not to complicate the lives of my contemporaries. The diary, with attachments, contains seven million words.

This is what I wrote on the first day:

Polk began his diary on August 26, 1845 in the first year of his presidency with a memorandum of events concerning the contest with Great Britain for the Oregon Territory. He continued every day thereafter. He wrote in longhand and he must have done this by gaslight lamps at the end of exhausting workdays.

The details of his daily life are the most interesting to me. Cabinet meetings were every Tuesday and Saturday. Dinner was at 4 p.m., after which he took a walk. He had only one staff member, a private secretary. In the morning the butler would open the White House door to anyone, most of whom asked for jobs and money. Senators Sam Houston and Thomas Hart Benton might come by at 9 p.m. for an hour "interview."

I am aware that my notes are much less significant than his. But I do see things on many days that may one day be of some interest to others.

PROLOGUE

The Republic Will Survive

"Aren't we privileged to serve our country in such serious times."

—**JOHN ADAMS TO THOMAS JEFFERSON,**
in a letter, August 1788

"I'd a lot rather have my job any day crawling under your house to find a dead rat than your job working up there in Washington, DC."

—**DELMAR CAYLOR, HOME BUILDER,**
Townsend, Tennessee, 2006

ON A FEBRUARY MORNING IN 1994, I was preparing to run for president when a doctor who had rarely even voted came by my Nashville office.

"I'm going to run for the United States Senate," he said.

"Why would you do that?" I asked. "Why would you give up being one of the world's leading heart transplant surgeons?"

He said, "Today, I can fly to Chattanooga, cut out a beating heart, put it on ice in an Igloo® cooler, make sure I get back to Vanderbilt Hospital within four hours, and perform an eight-hour operation. A year later, I might meet one person on the street who will thank me for saving his or her life. If I'm a senator, maybe I can save a million lives."

At age forty-two, Dr. Bill Frist won that Senate race and, working with President George W. Bush, created PEPFAR (President's Emergency Plan for AIDS Relief), investing $120 billion to combat HIV/AIDS.[1] That saved *twenty-six* million lives. When he retired after two terms, he chaired the global board of The Nature Conservancy, but never again will he be able to help as many people as he did as a senator. No one doubts that private citizens—from Edison to Einstein to Billy Graham—can make a huge difference. But Dr. Frist learned that public service is the surest way to unleash our country's potential to help the most people.

The stories in this book are about that lesson, along with others that helped me, as both a governor and United States senator, to wake up every morning thinking that I might be able to do something good for my state or country, and to go to bed most nights thinking that I had.

My serendipitous journey in and out of public life spanned fifty-eight years, from the Cold War to the "Digital Democracy." Imagine if a senior White House aide during John F. Kennedy's 1,000 days had written an eyewitness account of working with presidents, senators, and governors since serving as a young assistant to Teddy Roosevelt. I've worked with ten presidents. I've been onstage with three hundred US senators and one hundred governors. Not many living Americans have participated in public life for so long and have seen it from as many angles.

My journey started where it ended, behind a desk in Washington, DC. It began on Monday, June 17, 1963, when, as a summer intern for Attorney General Robert F. Kennedy, I took a seat behind a heavy desk crammed into a basement office of the United States Department of Justice. It concluded on Sunday, January 3, 2021, when I stepped away from my desk on the floor of the Senate and went home to Tennessee—three days before a mob stormed the Capitol trying to overturn Joe Biden's election as president.

I wrote this book to persuade, and hopefully to inspire, the reader to believe what Bill Frist and I and countless others have learned: despite the indignities that come with it, the most reliable way to help the most people—and to keep the republic from falling apart in our new and contentious "Digital Democracy"—is to be elected to office or to go to work for someone who has been.

* * *

My first teachers were my parents.

"We had little money," my mother said. "We hardly had anything, but you had a piano lesson from the day you were three and a library card from the day you were four. You had everything you needed that was important."

Mother offered a useful Rule of Life when, at age four, I climbed too high in the willow tree.

"You got yourself up there, you can get yourself down," she said.

Somewhere along the way, I caught the political virus. At sixteen, I arrived at American Legion Boys State with posters announcing my candidacy for governor.

Next came three wise mentors.

Federal Judge John Minor Wisdom showed me what courage looked like when he ordered Ole Miss to admit its first African American student.

Senator Howard Baker taught me that "the other fellow might be right."

Fifty feet from the Oval Office, I sat next to Bryce Harlow as he asked other White House aides, "What would be the *right* thing to do?"

When I ran for governor, my wife, Honey, reminded me of the most important—and hardest—question in politics.

"Wait a minute," she said. "I want to know why you want to be governor. You're going to have to convince me first. I have to be convinced that this is the very best thing for the state and for you and for us."

I learned that working county by county with political "rats in the barn" was often more important than having a well-organized campaign. The truck driver who hit me early in my six-month walk across the state taught me to keep my eyes on the road. Spending the night with seventy-three families during that walk helped me be a better candidate and a better governor.

When Democrat legislators swore me in three days early to oust a corrupt governor we learned to work together in a kind of bipartisan boot camp. A lesson from President Carter at my first White House dinner led to Japan recruiting auto jobs to Tennessee. Dealing with a Democrat-dominated legislature taught me that if I wanted to pay teachers more for teaching well, I needed votes from the other political party. I learned to be bipartisan—but also that bipartisanship is only a tactic. Accomplishing a result is the goal.

My grandfather instructed me to aim for the top, so I ran for president—twice. In 1996, I came close in the New Hampshire primary, but my second try lasted about as long as the Wright brothers' first flight. Yet, those experiences taught me perseverance and humility. The next thing I knew, I was on the faculty of Harvard's John F. Kennedy School of Government and then in the United States Senate.

Along the way I learned about leadership. Being governor is like being Moses—see a need, develop a strategy, and persuade at least half the people you're right. Accomplishing something as a senator is more like being a drum major in a marching band. To end up where you want to go, you must select the music, recruit musicians, line them up, make sure they don't wander into the ditch, and usually allow one or two of them to march out front. Both governors and senators need the leadership skills of Count Basie, who could sit with a new group of musicians, tinkle a few keys, and soon, they would be playing better than they'd ever had before.

I learned to make a speech. The best suggestion came from Alex Haley, the author of *Roots*, who once said after hearing me speak, "If you would start by saying, 'Instead of making a speech, let me tell you a story,' someone might actually listen to what you have to say."

After four years in the Senate, I won the Number Three spot in the Republican leadership. Four years later, I stepped aside from leadership to spend more time on the issues I cared about most. Working on those issues reminded me that *I* didn't elect the president, the *people* did, and that to make a law, the president had to sign it.

So, I learned to work with President Obama, with whose liberal policies I disagreed.

"If it had just been you and me these eight years, everything would have been fine," Obama told me when he signed the "21st Century Cures Act," a law he called "a Christmas miracle" on which we had worked together.

Then, I shifted gears and learned to work with President Trump, with whose views I mostly agreed—but with whose behavior and temperament I disagreed. A surprising—some said unholy—alliance that I helped engineer between Trump and 800 outdoors groups produced the most important conservation law since Teddy Roosevelt—or, as Trump said, "Wouldn't you say *ever*?"

"Everyone in Tennessee loves me—except you, Lamar," Trump told me when he agreed to add all public lands to the "Great American Outdoors Act."

Nevertheless, I developed an excellent working relationship with Trump—and with Obama—because they may have come to the same conclusion I did: after the people decide who is president and who is senator, we should respect each other's offices and do things together when we can.

Some lessons were more important than others. A governor who throws himself into something important with everything he's got for as long as it takes can usually wear everybody else out and get what he wants. A senator's most important lesson is that it's hard to get here and hard to stay here, so while you're here, you might as well try to accomplish something good for our country. In other words, make every day count.

Perhaps most importantly, in public life, it helps to have a sense of purpose—and a sense of humor.

* * *

I detested being described as a "moderate." That's a lazy brand applied to those who speak without shouting, work across the aisle to achieve results, and don't always toe the party line. In truth, "moderate" describes one's style better than philosophy. The greatest division among Republicans is not one of moderates versus conservatives, but between conservatives who think their job is finished when they make a speech and conservatives who want to govern.

I especially resented self-righteous political pharisees who claimed to be a better Republican than I am, in the same way someone might wander into my Sunday school class and claim to be a better Christian. I am a very Republican Republican, a bona fide Abraham Lincoln-mountain Republican descended from Union soldiers who voted like they shot. In over forty years in a conversative state, I won six statewide Republican primaries and lost none.

I was a small-town, anti-gambling, culturally-conservative, prayer-breakfast-sponsoring governor who fought the teachers' union, twice vetoed photo driver's licenses for smacking of too much government, and urged President Reagan to get the federal government entirely out of K–12 education. I supported gun rights and opposed abortion, although back then, those issues rarely came up.

When I ran for the Senate in 2002, I'd said, "I have conservative principles and an independent attitude." For three terms, I voted that way.

I discovered that the greatest challenge in public life is leaving it with your family and your reputation intact. After eight years in the governor's residence, Honey said, "We've got to get out of here. A long way away and for a long time. We need to get to know each other again." So, with three teenagers and a seven-year-old, our family took six months off in Australia.

After eighteen years in the Senate, I retired at age eighty, preferring the example of Ted Williams, who hit a home run in his last at bat instead of waiting until he had to be carried off the field. I had served in Washington, DC, long enough to get vaccinated, but not infected.

I thus avoided what Senator Jeff Bingaman had warned me were the "Three Ds of Public Life: death, disgrace, and defeat."

* * *

My years in public life, from 1963 to 2021, roughly coincided with an era of American Democracy.

After the Eisenhower presidency, an interlude offering the chance to catch one's breath, here came the Kennedys with a boisterous, coat-thrown-over-the-shoulder, touch-football-playing, ask-what-you-can-do-for-your-country, join-the-Peace-Corps appeal that fired the imagination—especially of those of us in college. This elation soon descended into a half-century of turmoil, with aggrieved Americans demanding justice in ways that aggrieved other Americans.

The year 2008 changed everything. Barack Obama's election helped atone for slavery but created anxiety. The Great Recession produced panic. Facebook and iPhones distributed extremism. Then, down the escalator rode Donald John Trump. Next came a pandemic and artificial intelligence. This combustible brew created the "Digital Democracy." The nation polarized. Public discourse turned nasty. In most states, two-party political competition disappeared, and good government suffered. The era JFK had launched careened to a conclusion.

Since the fall of the Berlin Wall in 1989, the United States has gone from being the world's example to an uncertain beacon.[2] American failures in Iraq, the Great Recession, the rush out of Kabul, and the January 6 insurrection at the Capitol have caused countries to look to other places as models of military strength, economic success, and political institutions. Americans tell pollsters that our government is corrupt and that we don't trust our most basic institutions.

That is where we are today.

And that is why I have had a hard time persuading friends that serving in public office is worth it.

"How can you stand to be there? How do you ever get anything done?" they demand to know.

One of these friends, homebuilder Delmar Caylor, showed me a large dead rat he had found under our log house. The rat had been causing a stink.

"I stuck my arm up there and felt something furry and knew I had something. I found another one behind the sofa," he said.

"I wouldn't want your job," I said.

"I'd a lot rather have my job any day crawling under your house to find a dead rat than your job working up there in Washington, DC," Delmar said. "If I'd had your job, I would've had a fist fight every day."

I suggested to Delmar that he look at the Senate as a split screen television. On one side is the "dysfunction screen," where headline seekers spread controversy. Instead, watch the "function screen" on the other side, where senators create laws that most of them can vote for and most voters will accept. Senators on the "function screen" produce a better outcome but make less news, just as a plane landing safely makes less news than a plane crashing.

* * *

"Can we survive this?" worried friends ask.

I remind them that Americans have asked this question ever since the nation was founded in times even more troubling than today's—through wars, economic panics, pandemics, and social upheaval. After colonists won a brutal eight-and-a-half-year war against the British Empire that was also a civil war, the question was, "Okay. Now what do we do?" The greatest uncertainty was regarding the new form of government. On September 17, 1787, at the end of the constitutional convention, a woman asked the oldest delegate, Benjamin Franklin, "Well, Doctor, what have we got, a republic or a monarchy?"

"A republic, if you can keep it," Franklin replied.[3]

He could have said, "A democracy, if you can keep it." There is a difference. Democracy is government by the majority, and something Americans could do today if everyone voted on everything on the internet. A republic is a government of elected officials exercising their judgment according to a constitution. This is a messier operation, with checks and balances on the branches of government—and on the people themselves.

The founders did not want a king, and they did not want too much democracy either. In the 1830s, after seeing it in person, the Frenchman Alexis de Tocqueville wrote a book, *Democracy in America,* in which he warned of the "tyranny of the majority." In the 1930s, Germany showed that elections can produce a demagogue. The source of our freedom is a constitutional framework of checks and balances, as the late former Supreme Court Justice Antonin Scalia reminded us. That is why Americans pledge allegiance to a republic.

In *Team of Rivals,* Doris Kearns Goodwin describes other uncertain times. "As a young man, Lincoln worried that the 'field of glory' had been harvested by the founding fathers, that nothing had been left for his generation but modest ambitions. In the 1850s, however, the wheel of history turned. The ... threatening dissolution of the nation itself provided Lincoln and his colleagues with an opportunity to save and improve the democracy... creating what Lincoln later called a 'new birth of freedom,'" she writes.[4]

The wheel of history has turned again, and there is plenty left to fix. Our "Digital Democracy" is splintering the nation and providing an opportunity for Americans to be a part of a great project to save and improve our republic. Fortunately, we have more capacity than any other country to put things back together and to keep it going.

The United States produces 26 percent of the world's money for only 4 percent of the world's people, has the strongest military and most of the best universities, creates the most advanced vaccines and cures, and leads in AI and hundreds of other technologies. Its constitutional guarantees of liberty are the envy of the world. Millions want to come here, not leave here. This is no recipe for despair.

The republic will survive—*if* we remember the lessons of the last 250 years.

Franklin's advice to the other convention delegates still is good. "[I urge] that every member... would with me, on this occasion doubt a little of his own infallibility, and... put his name to this instrument," he said.[5]

Filmmaker Ken Burns suggests paying more attention to the country's original motto, *E pluribus unum,* meaning "Out of many, one."

"Today we have too much *pluribus* and not enough *unum,"* he says, quoting the late historian, Arthur Schlesinger Jr.[6]

It would help to find more ways to work together, as we did when the nation survived Reconstruction, wars, economic panics, marches, assassinations, Watergate, controversies over women's rights and sexual orientation, the collapse of the Soviet Union, terrorist attacks, and pandemics. As we did when Congress and several presidents created social security, Medicare, civil rights laws, national parks, national laboratories, the National Institutes of Health, and national defense. And when we created a country where people of many backgrounds could say, "We are all Americans."

Keeping the republic will take builders. "Any jackass can kick down a barn, but it takes a good carpenter to build one," House Speaker Sam Rayburn once said.[7]

The stories and lessons in this book are a reminder that the surest way to become a part of saving and improving our republic—and to unleash the country's potential to help the most people—is to be a public-spirited builder who is elected to office or who goes to work for someone who has been.

* * *

On Saturday evening, November 25, 2006, as I was completing my fourth year as a senator, I wrote in my diary:

"I often think of John Adams' letter to Thomas Jefferson in 1788 when the United States of America barely existed.

"'Aren't we privileged to serve our country in such serious times?' Adams asked.

"I feel that same way today," I wrote.

You may feel that way too. You may even be one of the 2 percent of all Americans[8]—from school board members to the president—who say they have run for elective office. Or perhaps you could be one of the millions who work for those elected officials. Or a student or someone on the sidelines itching to serve. Or just one of tens of millions who admire those who do. This, then, is a book for and about you.

The book opens with a legal coup in the Tennessee Capitol, on Wednesday January 17, 1979, when legislative leaders swore me in early to oust a governor who was releasing prisoners in exchange for cash. It concludes with an illegal attempted coup forty-two years later, when a mob stormed the US Capitol trying to stop Congress from certifying the duly elected president of the United States.

At the time of this writing, Donald Trump is president again. A rowdy new era is in full swing. The stories in this volume are a reminder of what Adams wrote to Jefferson during even more uncertain times, and of how that spirit still can succeed. Technology advances, but human nature does not change.

And so, our tale begins on a gloomy winter morning in Nashville.

PART ONE

We Did What We Had to Do

January 17, 1979

"The peaceful transition of power is what will separate this country from every other country in the world."

—ATTRIBUTED TO GEORGE WASHINGTON

CHAPTER 1[1]

The Coup

"I can't believe you would decide to replace the most important celebration of your life with an event that's more like a funeral."

—HONEY ALEXANDER, January 17, 1979

"Rule 153. If you're going to back someone into a corner, make sure you leave them some way out that doesn't run over you."

—LAMAR ALEXANDER'S LITTLE PLAID BOOK

Nashville. Wednesday, January 17, 1979, 10:00 a.m.

I WAS WRITING MY INAUGURAL ADDRESS when the United States attorney called.

"The FBI has information that Governor Blanton is about to pardon inmates who have paid cash for their release," he said. "As a Tennessean, and not as United States attorney, I am calling to ask that you take office as governor as soon as you can, today, to stop him."

The caller was Hal Hardin, a Democrat about my age who some said might be governor one day.

Every bone in my body told me that I did not want to do what he was asking—but that I would have to do it. I took a deep breath.

Finally, I said, "I'll call you back in a few minutes."

I wanted to telephone the US attorney's office myself to make certain that the caller really was Hardin and not some crank. And, I wanted time to think.

Out my office window, I watched freezing rain splatter on the sidewalks. I thought about the trouble that had erupted since Monday, two days earlier, after State Senator Victor Ashe announced that he had an opinion letter from State Assistant Attorney General William "Tripp" Hunt saying that I could be sworn in as early as midnight on that same Monday.

The state attorney general himself, William Leech, was in Washington, DC, on that day, January 15, preparing to argue a case before the Supreme Court. When Leech learned about Hunt's opinion letter, he was livid—first, because he had not known about it, and second, because he believed it was wrong.

So did I. The legislature had set the inaugural ceremony for five days later at noon on Saturday, January 20.

"The opinion has to be wrong. A newly elected governor can't assume office whenever he wants," I told reporters.

But there was no way to ignore it. So, as Leech scurried about in Washington, DC, revising his junior staff member's surprise opinion, it was producing dramatic consequences in Nashville.

At 7:00 p.m., only a few hours after Senator Ashe's announcement, Governor Ray Blanton's familiar black Lincoln appeared at the state Capitol, gleaming in the streetlights and rain. Blanton rushed up the concrete steps and disappeared into the governor's office. His legal counsel had spread stacks of files on the governor's desk, on the oak conference table, and even on the carpet.

"I suppose you'll want to start with this case," the counsel said, handing over a thick file.

"Well, I've given this one more consideration than you can imagine. I've made up my mind," Governor Blanton said, and signed a pardon for Roger Humphreys, a convicted double murderer.

Secretary of State Gentry Crowell had been summoned to authenticate the governor's signature.

"This takes guts," the governor said to Crowell, who was also a Democrat.

"Yeah. Well, some people have more guts than brains," the secretary of state replied.

Blanton had Humphreys's clemency papers delivered to the prison immediately after he signed them. The prisoner was waiting in the warden's office with his suitcase packed when his lawyer arrived to pick him up. He had served two months of a twenty- to forty-year sentence.

That same night, Blanton signed fifty-one other pardons and commutations for some of Tennessee's most notorious prisoners, murderers, rapists, and robbers. Many of them, the US attorney believed, had paid cash in exchange for their release from prison.

* * *

Blanton's promise fifteen months earlier to pardon Humphreys had become the most prominent of many controversies surrounding the governor.

Six years earlier, Humphreys, the son of a Blanton county patronage chairman, had found his former wife in bed with her lover. After having breakfast with the two in his ex-wife's apartment, he used a double-barrel derringer pistol "to stitch an eleven-shot circle in her back," and to shoot the boyfriend six times. To accomplish the murders, he had to reload the pistol at least eight times, according to court documents.

"I am the most persecuted governor in the anals [sic] of history," Blanton had complained during a wide-ranging television interview in late 1977.

He promised then and there that he would pardon Humphreys.

On many days, Blanton began drinking vodka at 10:00 a.m. according to the governor's attorney—who then told the US attorney.

"After that, he listens to nobody," Blanton's attorney had continued.

Apparently, the day of the television interview had been one of those days.

When the governor played golf, a state trooper drove him in one golf cart while another followed in a second cart with his bar. Blanton would literally drink himself around the course. On some days, Blanton and his cronies played checkers using whiskey bottles on the black-and-white squares of the marble foyer in the governor's residence. Some nights, three highway patrol cars would leave the mansion with Blanton crouched on the floor of the back seat. To avoid detection by the FBI or media, the three cars would then head in different directions, with one taking the governor to see his girlfriend.

Blanton's promise to pardon Humphreys made Humphreys the most famous double murderer in Tennessee history—and helped make me Blanton's successor. Blanton changed his mind two weeks before the November election. Then, two weeks after the election, he reversed course again, saying Humphreys was "a fine young man" who deserved a pardon.

One month later, on Friday, December 15, 1978, FBI agents arrested Edward "Eddie" Sisk, the governor's legal counsel. On that same morning, Tennessee's retiring first lady, Betty Blanton, was giving a tour of the governor's residence to her successor, Honey Alexander.

"I'm sorry. There is no way I can take you to look at the master bedroom upstairs because the governor and his advisers are meeting in there," Mrs. Blanton had said to Honey.

The governor had much to discuss in that meeting. The indictments accused Blanton's chief of security and his extradition officer, as well as Sisk, of twenty-six instances of selling clemencies for cash. There were videotapes to prove it.

"How much would it cost to spring James Earl Ray?" an FBI informant had asked Blanton's chief of security on one videotape as they sat under surveillance in a Memphis motel room.

Ray was serving ninety-nine years in Brushy Mountain State Penitentiary for the murder of Dr. Martin Luther King Jr. US Attorney Hardin, who was overhearing the taping in an adjacent room, had suggested the informant try a Hail Mary to test how far the governor's corrupt aides were willing to go.

"Whew, I don't know. That's pretty hot. What about $75,000 for an escape?" the chief of security said, according to Hardin.

These events reached a crescendo on Monday, January 15 (the day of the surprise opinion) prompting the governor to drive to the Capitol to pardon Humphreys and fifty-one others.

As Tennesseans awoke to Tuesday's news, you could almost hear explosions of anger popping, house by house.

"BLANTON GRANTS CLEMENCY TO 52 TENNESSEE CONVICTS," headlines screamed.

The storm of protest was unmatched by anything since the Civil War.

"He makes Nixon look like a choir boy," said one Democrat state senator.

Also on Tuesday, the governor's new counsel, Robert Lillard, said that there would be as many as eighteen more pardons before the governor left office, and that there was one big name in the group.

Rumors spread that the one big name was James Earl Ray.

* * *

While I waited on that gloomy Wednesday morning to call the United States attorney back, I thought about the enormity of what he was asking me to do. It would amount to a coup—a Republican ousting an elected Democrat governor before his term expired.

I had attended the inaugurations of Presidents Johnson, Nixon, Ford, and Carter, and had witnessed the peaceful transfer of great power from one elected president to the next, our country's constant practice since John Adams succeeded George Washington. As a college student, I had toured Latin American capitals where overthrowing governments seemed routine. I was confident nothing like what Hardin was proposing had ever happened before in American democracy.

Questions began popping up. What if Governor Blanton orders the National Guard to surround the Capitol or mobilizes the highway patrol? Tennessee would become a laughingstock. How could I launch a successful administration in such a mess?

I also needed to think about what might happen if I *didn't* do it. That morning, sources in the governor's office had reported to the FBI that more pardons were coming.

"Does the Constitution give the governor authority literally to empty the prisons?" I once asked William Leech, the state attorney general.

"Yes. His power to pardon is absolute," Leech had replied.

What about the campaign supporters who had saved money for hotel bills and bus tickets? The band members who had been practicing in cold weather for the inaugural parade? The campaign staff who had worked so hard? My parents would not know about it.

I called home to tell Honey about Hardin's call. She was packing boxes so that later that day, we could move across town and into the governor's residence. When I left that morning, the house looked like a tornado had swept through it.

"Why let Blanton ruin two inaugurations in a row? He beat you in 1974. That ruined one. And now, because of the way he's acting, they want you to let him ruin a second one," she said.

The intrigue and the foul weather created a day Honey always remembered as "cold, gray, and horrible."

Above all, the inauguration was supposed to put a big exclamation point at the end of my campaign, and a big capital letter at the beginning of my new administration. I wanted Tennesseans to feel good about their government, to want to be a part of it, to have pride in it. This coup could blow all that up.

But it did not blow up. About a half hour after Hardin first called me, I telephoned the United States attorney's office. Again, he urged me to be sworn in early.

"Will you ask Bill Leech to tell Wilder and McWherter what you want me to do?" I asked Hardin.

John Wilder was lieutenant governor and Speaker of the Senate. Blanton's home was in Wilder's state senate district. Ned Ray McWherter was Speaker of the House. Like Hardin and Leech, they were Democrats.

Leech had returned from Washington, DC. Hardin decided that he and Leech needed to be face to face.

"The press was everywhere," Hardin told me later. "To avoid encounters, I went down the stairs in the federal building to the garage where I was parked, and drove across Broadway two blocks to the Sheraton Hotel."

* * *

For the next eight hours, the state's leading Democrats and I swiftly and effectively did what none of us wanted to do—but what we all knew we had to do.

Leech, who was forty-three, was a forceful advocate, and a self-described "yellow dog" Democrat who relished hunting and fishing. He first briefed forty-eight-year-old McWherter, whose 270-pound, barrel-chested presence bore a startling resemblance to Hoss Cartwright on television's *Bonanza*.

Earlier, McWherter had privately told *Tennessean* reporters that an early swearing-in "might be the thing to do." Nevertheless, he found the idea troubling. He'd already had his eye on being the next governor. To do that, McWherter would have to win a Democrat primary whose voters included many of Blanton's friends.

Then, Leech called Speaker Wilder, a fifty-seven-year-old soybean farmer.

"The Speaker doesn't like to hunt. The Speaker doesn't like to fish. The Speaker doesn't play golf. The Speaker likes to be Speaker," Wilder would say to explain why he had served thirty-six years as lieutenant governor.

Leech's deputies, Hayes Cooney and Bill Koch, arrived at the Sheraton between 10:00 a.m. and 11:00 a.m. The room was filled with cigarette smoke and intrigue. Meanwhile, at the Capitol, the Speakers excused themselves from a State Building Commission meeting and met in Wilder's office. I remained in my temporary office in the Green Hills neighborhood near our home. My two most senior staffers, Lewis Donelson and Tom Ingram, soon joined me. Telephone lines began to buzz.

I had asked Donelson, sixty-three, to leave a lucrative Memphis law practice to become chief operating officer of state government.

"You're the best person for the job, and you have a duty to do it. If someone of your stature will come into state government, I can attract others and begin to restore its reputation," I had told Donelson.

He was a descendant of Nashville founder John Donelson, whose daughter Rachel had married Andrew Jackson. "Lewie," as everyone called him, was five-foot-six, but pugnacious. His idea of negotiation was to knock his adversary backward, and if the adversary was able to get halfway back up, both might consider that a victory.

"Lah-mahh said to me, 'Lewie, you run the state and I'll be the guvnahh,'" was the way Lewie described my invitation to him.

Some thought I was asking for trouble by recruiting a strong-minded older aide, but I liked having Donelson's experience and ability to operate the 40,000-person state government while I led it.

Ingram was a thirty-two-year-old former reporter for both Nashville newspapers. He was tall, genial, and an excellent tennis player who thrived in the camaraderie of legislators, lobbyists, and journalists who swarmed the state Capitol. He had been my campaign manager. I asked him to become deputy to the governor and to supervise politics, policy initiatives, and strategy.

"You'll be governor by tonight," Herchel Winstead, the ex-Marine state trooper, said as he drove me home for lunch at 1:00 p.m.

When I returned to the office, telephone lines began buzzing again. But by midafternoon, negotiations had lurched to a stalemate. None of us were willing to take the lead. It was getting late. The Speakers were saying, "You go ahead and we'll back you up."

I telephoned Honey. She was entertaining three children—two bored and one sick—in an empty, cold, depressing house filled with boxes packed for moving.

"Why doesn't somebody make up his mind? It's such a bad idea to begin with. At least make some decision," she said.

At about 3:00 p.m., I called Leech at the Sheraton.

"Can't they understand?" I shouted at Leech. "There is no way in the world I'll take the initiative by myself. Tell the Speakers this is not my idea. I don't want to do it. I will do it only if we do it together."

CHAPTER 2

In a Pickle

"I knew that if I urged you to do it, you would have to do it."

—HAL HARDIN, former US attorney, March 21, 2023

Nashville. Wednesday afternoon, January 17, 1979.

I WAS NOT THE GOVERNOR—yet—but I had to act as if I were, or we were likely to have an even bigger mess on our hands.

I proposed decisions to the Speakers for our joint agreement. When would the ceremony be? (6:00 p.m.) Where? (The Tennessee Supreme Court Building.) Who would be present? (Every leading Democrat I could think of.) Who would swear me in? (The chief justice, if he would agree.) Would I take the initiative with the Speakers' support, or would we do this together? (Together, or not at all.) Who would speak at the swearing-in? (I would read a joint statement for the Speakers and myself.) When would we tell the public? (A half hour before the ceremony.)

I made other decisions. Would all fifty-two prisoners whose documents Blanton had signed on Monday night go free? (I instructed Koch to tell the warden to keep them locked up unless the clemency documents had been delivered, but later the courts overruled me.) Would I go ahead with Saturday's scheduled inaugural? (Yes.) Would I go to the governor's office tomorrow? (No. I waited until Saturday.)

The roomful of lawyers agreed that I could legally be sworn in early. Leech said he would defend the position. I drafted a joint statement that I would read at the swearing-in. Leech telephoned the Speakers and read it to them. Then, at 3:30 p.m., to guard against misunderstanding, I telephoned the Speakers and read it to them myself:

> The state Attorney General has informed us that he has substantial reason to believe that Governor Blanton is about to release one or more persons who are targets of a US investigation into alleged payoffs for pardons and commutations of sentences. That information, taken with other recent events, causes each of us to believe it is in the best interests of the people of Tennessee for the Governor-elect to take office immediately. We believe the taking of the oath should be done publicly and with each of us present. The state attorney general has assured each of us that, in his opinion, the assumption of the office in these circumstances is constitutional.

For the swearing-in, I wanted Chief Justice Joe Henry, sixty-two, as a conspicuous symbol of bipartisan action. No one's Democrat credentials exceeded his. He had once compared Republican Governor Winfield Dunn's election to the "arrival of a plague of political locusts."[1] I dispatched Bill Koch to Henry's apartment, where the justice was recovering from congestive heart failure. Henry did not want to be left out. He had a penchant for drama. When he was adjutant general, he had confronted a mob of anti-desegregation protestors while riding in an Army National Guard tank with a pair of silver-plated pistols on his belt.

At 5:15 p.m., our family of five, plus Ingram, stuffed ourselves into an unmarked patrol car. Trooper Winstead drove us from home to the basement parking garage of the Supreme Court building near the Capitol. Honey and the children wore mostly borrowed clothes. I wore a tie and belt borrowed from Ingram. We took the elevator to the first floor and waited in the robing room adjacent to the Court chamber with Henry, Wilder, McWherter, Leech, Secretary of State Crowell, Koch, Ingram, and Donelson. I outlined how the short ceremony would proceed.

Just before we entered the courtroom, McWherter telephoned Blanton at his personal residence and handed the telephone to Leech.

"Governor Blanton. I wanted to let you know that in a few minutes, Lamar Alexander will take the oath of office, and he will be the new governor of Tennessee," the attorney general said to his about-to-be former client.

"The hell, you say! I hate to go out of office like this," Blanton said.

The ceremony was over in six minutes.

Somehow, amidst the confusion, Honey had remembered to bring the family Bible that my great-grandparents had used in their marriage in 1868.

"I had saved it back. I know how things get lost in the move. That was one thing I was going to move myself, because I know how important it is to you," she said.

I opened it to my father's favorite verse, 2 Timothy 2:15: "Study to shew thyself approved unto God, a workman that needeth not to be ashamed, rightly dividing the word of truth."

I placed my left hand on the Bible and repeated the oath of office.

Tears streamed down Honey's cheeks.

"I just had a cold," she said, but it was more than that.

I dispatched Donelson, Ingram, and Koch to secure the Capitol, a task that the feisty Donelson's friends said he had been waiting his entire life for someone to ask him to do.

Blanton phoned and asked to retrieve his papers.

"No," Donelson told him.

"You mean I'm not allowed to come to the Capitol to get my papers?" Blanton asked.

"That's right," Donelson replied.

"By whose authority?"

"By the governor's authority."

"I am the governor."

"Not anymore," Donelson answered.

Blanton did not participate in Saturday's swearing-in. Ten thousand well-wishers did attend, transforming the legislative plaza into a sea of brightly colored umbrellas. Freezing rain stopped just before the ceremony began at noon. That night, 4,000 attended the inaugural ball at Opryland, one of three that night.

On Sunday, when we crawled out of bed at the governor's residence, Honey was happy to see a blanket of snow on the lawn.

"It is a clean, sweet snow. Everything is washed clean again," she said.

Hardin had handed off his dilemma to me, but told nobody—not the FBI, not his staff, not his Justice Department superiors.

"I didn't want to compromise the investigation in any way by involving them. I didn't think about calling you until that morning," Hardin later told me.

"You put me in a pickle," I said.

"We were both in a pickle. I was in one, and I put you in one. I knew that if I urged you to do it, you would have to do it," he said.

Until we participated in a forum thirty-five years later, Hardin and I never talked about that wintry Wednesday. For eight years, I worked almost daily with McWherter and Wilder. We never discussed it.

* * *

The early swearing-in was not the only unprecedented event on January 17, 1979. The preceding eight hours of intrigue became a bipartisan boot camp that taught participants lessons about working together.

Lesson number one: no second-guessing.

Immediately after the ceremony, a reporter challenged McWherter.

"The man you just swore in is a Republican. You are a Democrat and most of the people who participated in the decision to swear him in early are Democrats. The man—"

McWherter cut off the reporter.

"Let me say to you, first, I'm a Tennessean. I think this is in the interest of Tennessee, regardless of party," the Speaker said.

Wilder told reporters, "We had to do what we did. We wished we had not, but we had to do it."

Attorney General Leech defended the state against lawsuits brought by the prisoners Blanton had pardoned.

Hal Hardin was thirty-five at that time and on anyone's list of most promising Democrat candidates. At six-foot-three, he was handsome and personable. However, after his role in my early swearing-in, he never sought elective office.

"Attorney General Griffin Bell later told me I did the right thing. So did President Carter," Hardin told me.

The participants' discretion did not keep outsiders from second-guessing.

A videotape of NewsChannel 5's live coverage of the Wednesday night ceremony shows a conversation between the station's weatherman and anchorman. It was during a commercial break, so no one but the tape machine was listening.

"How can he do that? What recourse does Governor Blanton have?" the anchor asked the weatherman.

Justice Henry might have backed out of the early swearing-in if he had first consulted his colleagues.

"Wilder, McWherter, and Chief Justice Henry—really [none] of them had the power to terminate Blanton's power. The only group of people who can remove a governor is the legislature," Associate Justice Robert Cooper later told Keel Hunt.

The participants in the bipartisan boot camp learned other lessons.

We communicated carefully, repeating conversations or rereading a joint statement out loud to one another. We relied on the advice of senior state attorneys and the local federal attorney. We tried to put the best interests of citizens before our own. We avoided placing each other in awkward political positions.

"That's one time I've seen a pure example of people taking politics and throwing it aside," said Hayes Cooney, the state deputy attorney general.

Our actions encouraged our successors in both political parties to work together over the next forty years. Neighbors took notice.

On Friday evening, October 26, 2018, United States Senator Doug Jones, an Alabama Democrat, addressed a national convention of US attorneys in Nashville.

"Our challenge . . . is to demand . . . that our public officials and candidates do . . . as Hal [Hardin] did and as . . . Lamar Alexander and the cadre of Tennessee Democrats did that January afternoon in 1979—to put state and country above political party. As you can see . . . in this incredible city of Nashville, the results can be downright amazing."[2]

Will there be leaders willing to participate in future bipartisan boot camps? I believe the answer is "yes"—*if* the next generation is nourished in communities where children learn to work well together, to respect public service—and that, for them, anything is possible.

The search for such an environment leads to a quiet town in the foothills of the Great Smoky Mountains, and to the story of a formidable woman who expected every one of the hundreds of preschoolers she taught over thirty years to one day amount to something—including her own son and two daughters.

PART TWO

If Mozart Could Do It

1940 to 1965

"Rule 220. Remember that governing is a lot like playing the piano."

"Practice. Get it right. Play nice and even. Keep it under control. Always play it just a little slower than you actually can play it."

—MISS LENNIS TEDFORD,
in *Lamar Alexander's Little Plaid Book*

CHAPTER 3

Maryville

"Rule 28. If you grew up in a small town, be grateful. There is something about it that encourages achievement and adventure."

—*LAMAR ALEXANDER'S LITTLE PLAID BOOK*

Maryville, Tennessee. 1940–1958.

DURING MY 1996 PRESIDENTIAL CAMPAIGN, a reporter wrote that "Lamar Alexander grew up in a lower middle-class family at the edge of the Great Smoky Mountains."[1]

When I called home that weekend, my mother was reading Thessalonians to gather strength to deal with what she called "this slur on the family."

"Son, we never thought of ourselves that way," she said. "We had little money. We hardly had anything. But you had a piano lesson from the day you were three and a library card from the day you were four. You had everything you needed that was important."

In 1944, my mother took me to get a library card.

"Mrs. Alexander, we don't give library cards to four-year-olds," the librarian said.

"Well, you should," Mother said. And so, the librarian did.

What Maryville did *not* have in those days was a good hospital, and my parents had no car. That is why on Wednesday afternoon, July 3,

1940, Mother's cousin drove her to Fort Sanders Hospital in Knoxville, where I narrowly missed being born in the midst of Independence Day celebrations.

"I tried, son. It was close. The fireworks were popping," Mother later said.

I was eight pounds and three-quarters of an ounce, twenty-one inches long, and had reddish hair and a fair complexion, according to the baby book that she meticulously kept.The fireworks that mattered on Independence Day 1940 were popping in Europe. The British Royal Air Force and the German Luftwaffe were lighting up the skies above London. Uncle Joe, my father's brother, left for a US Army field artillery unit in North Africa. Dad stayed home because of his age (thirty-four), my birth, and a heart issue.

It seemed like every man not overseas was among the 14,000 workers at three Alcoa plants making aluminum for war material. Dad was one of them. Alcoa had offered a salary twice what he was making as the principal of West Side Elementary School. He reluctantly left teaching and studying for a master's degree after being assured that he could continue "teaching" as a safety director at the aluminum smelting plant.

With so many men fighting the war, aluminum company buses picked up mostly women workers from surrounding counties at 4:00 a.m. and hauled them to the plants. Friends not working at Alcoa drove forty miles to work in a new secret city that would later be called Oak Ridge. None of them knew that they were making the "atom bomb" that would win World War II.

The war seemed remote from my growing up because Mother kept me busy. When I was eleven months old, she included me in her first nursery school session in the living room of our new, white frame family residence at 121 Ruth Street.

"He enjoyed the children, played in the sand, climbed on the boards, and the children were very tolerant of him," she wrote in the baby book.

During the next five years, my education continued in "Mrs. Alexander's Nursery School and Kindergarten," because she, the teacher, had nowhere else to put me.

I began piano lessons at age three in classes at Maryville College.

"Learned quickly and was interested," the baby book records.

During visits to Newton, Kansas, my grandmother taught me to read music. In 1946, in first grade, weekly lessons began with Miss Lennis Tedford. I was fascinated with Mozart and played his variations on "Twinkle, Twinkle, Little Star" as rapidly as my little fingers would allow. When I was six, a friend drove Mother and me to Johnson City to compete in my first Tennessee state festival of the National Federation of Music Clubs. At age seventeen, I won the Haworth Cup in a statewide piano competition at Peabody College in Nashville. I performed Rachmaninoff's "Prelude in G Minor," a showy and spirited piece.

"But he made mistakes," protested the teacher of a student who did not win.

"He played with such a nice flourish," said the judge, providing an early lesson in performance.

One reason I sometimes made mistakes was that when I was six, I discovered that I could pick out melodies on the keyboard as Mother sang them. I could play "by ear," a gift Mother's Aunt Clara also had. And since most of what I heard was on the radio, that meant that as time went on, I could play Elvis's "Love Me Tender" and Jerry Lee Lewis's "Great Balls of Fire," plus gospel hymns and just about anything else I heard.

Being able to play what I heard without having to read notes had its downsides, though. When sight-reading a difficult Bach passage, I might invent an easier version that Bach never imagined, but that sounded just fine to me. However, such inventions did not sound just fine to Miss Tedford, a kind, crumpled woman whose arthritis prohibited her from playing a note, herself. She had a keen ear, though. Sometimes she would strike her ruler on the tabletop to stop me during a lesson and instruct me to use the metronome.

My parents purchased a used upright Kimball piano for twenty-five dollars, which sat against the wall in our dining room. The alarm clock would ring at 4:30 a.m. so I could pick up seventy-five copies of the *Knoxville Journal* at Broadway Food Market. Then, I would speed along my paper route, expertly extracting each paper with one hand from my bicycle basket, folding it, and tossing it on a front porch. I could be home by 5:15 a.m. to take a nap, then practice the piano for forty-five minutes before walking to school.

This early morning piano practicing routine was the result of negotiations with my mother. It left afternoons free for sports and other activities. My favorite activity had been football, until a teammate kicked me in the face, paralyzing a muscle in my right eye, causing it not to move up or down. This led me to basketball, which, because I had one stationary eye, required a sort of trigonometry to make a shot.

* * *

I never learned to say "Ruth Street" correctly. I would say the word "Ruth," and my tongue would still be out like a snake's when I tried to say "Street." It was easiest just to say "the corner of Ruth and Oak Park," which is what I said whenever anybody wanted to know where I lived—which was not often, because in a small town like Maryville, almost everybody knew where you lived anyway. They knew at least *that* about you.

Ruth Street ran from the Blount County Fire Hall on Broadway to Pistol Creek at the bottom of the hill. The supreme afternoon activity was riding my bike down to Pistol Creek, where the woods provided a hospitable den for hiding bicycles and smoking Indian "see-gars." It also provided a good supply of the see-gars themselves.

Indian see-gars did not grow as see-gars, and you could not buy them at Broadway Food Market. They had to be cut at some considerable risk from grapevines hanging high in the poplars and oaks. Nothing was more satisfying than lying on the banks of Pistol Creek with friends, protected by trees, cutting and smoking a dozen or so of these top-quality see-gars, lighting one on the end of the last one.

I had never smoked an Indian see-gar before I was ten. The only actual smoking I ever did before age ten was picking up cigarette butts off the street and finishing them off. They were often Camels, when I could find them, because my grandad, R.R. Rankin, smoked Camels. I had to rewrap most of the butts because the first smokers had usually dropped them while they were lit, then stepped on them, leaving them in sorry shape.

This was not much of a problem, though, since cigarette paper for rewrapping was available at Broadway Food Market. We pooled our allowances, and one of the other boys would buy the cigarette paper, explaining to Mr. Nicely that the paper was for a father who rolled his own. My allowance was fifteen cents a week—a nickel for my bank, a nickel for the church, and a nickel for things I might purchase at Broadway Food Market.

On summer days, we would pedal our bikes to the end of Maple Street, where our gang would gather under a towering white oak. Our gang was not large. There were three of us, and, like Tom Sawyer's, it was not dangerous. Nevertheless, it was our gang. I named it "Vogel's Vicious Villains" in honor of the Reverend Bill Vogel, youth pastor of our church. This seemed appropriate since the reverend spent most of his time suppressing the mischief we aimed at him, and the gang was our highest form of mischief.

From a catalog, we ordered tie clasps, from which dangled three shiny "Vs"—even though we were not old enough to wear ties. But these ornaments served well as badges of membership. Demonstrating an early grasp of civics, we organized ourselves into three branches of government—legislative, executive, and judicial—and each of us took charge of one branch. Much like the real United States Senate, we "VVV's," as we called ourselves, deliberated at length under the white oak tree and rarely came to a conclusion.

Early morning piano practice also taught discipline. Using the metronome when playing Czerny exercises taught precision. I would practice pieces slowly, then speed up the tick-tocking of the metronome to as fast as I could play. By the time I was at Maryville High School, I could entertain friends with anything Elvis sang. I played at school assemblies and at the New Providence Presbyterian Church. I saved enough money from paper routes and lawn mowing to buy a Reynolds Contempora trombone, which I played well enough to join the all-state band.

I also learned to play the sousaphone, which created new opportunities for mischief. Marching at the end of the row during parades, I would dip the wide bell of the sousaphone to the left as our band moved down Broadway, banging heads of startled onlookers who were standing too close to us on the street.

* * *

"I believed God gave me the tuition money (twenty-five dollars, per child, per semester) to spend on you children. Dad did the tithing," Mother wrote to me in a 1993 letter.

She used her tuition money to pay for my piano lessons, and to buy inexpensive reproductions of Van Gogh paintings and Metropolitan Museum of Art publications. She purchased records of *Brigadoon, Oklahoma,* and Oscar Levant playing George Gershwin. She bought tickets to hear Dame Myra Hess, who pounded the Steinway so fiercely that I was certain it would crash through the stage floor. At Eagles Dime Store, she bought a ten-cent item each year until she had a complete Christmas manger scene. I wore hand-me-down suits from an older cousin. We had no television until 1955, when I was fifteen.

She did not think it was worth the money to have my name inscribed on the trophies I won in piano competitions.

"We know, and he knew, that they were given to him for his outstanding achievements, and that's all that mattered," she'd said.

Dad rode in carpools to the aluminum plant each day until I was ten, when he bought a white, 1940 two-door Chevy. A couple of classmates smirked because their fathers had nicer cars. But nobody in Maryville smirked much because it was hard to tell who was poor or rich. Most people had enough money due to the thousands of Alcoa jobs available or from farming—or both. The few who were rich, relatively speaking, were careful not to act rich, and most people who were poor did their best to neither feel nor act that way.

"What kind of youngster was he?" an interviewer asked mother in 1996.

"Quick. Quick in everything. You couldn't stay ahead of him, but I did a pretty good job. We knew he would always be around people, and we tried to see that he was around the right kind of people," she said.

To accomplish this, Mother had a gift for handing down Rules of Life, most of which were designed to keep me busy and out of mischief. For example, piano playing was how she interpreted the First Catechism of the Presbyterian Church.

"Man's chief end is to glorify God, and the reason you play so much music is that God gave you that gift," she would say.

She was also good at announcing rules that meant more than they seemed to mean.

"Finish what you start; your dad always does," did not mean that you should finish something, but that you should *start* something—and respect your dad.

Dealing with these extra rules—and side yard football, softball, and basketball—kept my afternoons full until 5:30 p.m., when I would rush to the Broadway Food Market for my package of the afternoon *Knoxville News Sentinel*. While it was still daylight, I could run the Ruth Street route in half the time it had taken to deliver the morning *Journal* and still arrive home in time for supper at six.

Then, at 6:30 p.m. on Mondays, Wednesdays, and Fridays, Dad and I would flop on the living room floor in front of the tall mahogany Zenith radio, eager for the staccato trumpet announcing the beginning of another adventure of *The Lone Ranger*. On warm autumn Saturday afternoons, we'd carry the big radio to the front porch and turn it up loud to hear University of Tennessee football games while we worked in the yard. In winter, the radio stayed inside on Saturday afternoons so we could hear Milton Cross and the Metropolitan Opera—something I never got used to.

Despite her penchant for issuing Rules of Life, Mother never told me what she thought I should do with my life. One college offered a music scholarship. But after listening to Vladimir Horowitz's and Arthur Rubinstein's records, and attending concerts by Dame Hess and Leonard Pennario, I concluded that, while I might play the piano better than most, I was not good enough to go on tour. To shock Mother, I would sometimes say that I had the skills to be a politician, a preacher, or a criminal. She never took the bait.

"I didn't have any particular expectation for Lamar. I wanted him to achieve. I wanted what he wanted to do to be of service and decent and helpful, but I didn't know which way it would go and I never tried to interest him in any certain course of anything, just so long as it was something that was good," she told the *Daily Times*.

I studied the careers of famous men, trying to determine what had made them successful. I read biographies of Clarence Darrow, Sam Houston, Thomas Edison, Albert Schweitzer, Peter Marshall, Daniel Webster, Daniel Boone, Davy Crockett, Mozart, Bach, Horowitz, and several presidents of the United States, among others, trying to discover within each life some common denominator, some trait that helped them all succeed. Finally, I concluded that what they had in common was that they all were different; that each man was his own unique person and stayed true to himself—which was, in itself, another Rule of Life.

* * *

New Providence Presbyterian Church was the center of much of our lives. In addition to Sunday school and singing in the choir, there was Westminster Fellowship on Sunday night, Boy Scouts on Monday night, choir practice on Tuesday, prayer meeting on Wednesday, weekend rallies, and Vacation Bible School and church camp in the summer.

And there were weddings, baptisms, and memorial services. On Sunday evening, May 27, 1984, fifteen hundred people filled the sanctuary at New Providence after Dad, Andrew Alexander, who everyone called "Andy," died of kidney failure at Vanderbilt Hospital. He was seventy-six. I could not bring myself to speak, so I played his favorite hymns on the piano, including "In the Garden," which Grandad Rankin always sang as "Andy walked with me, Andy talked with me, Andy told me..."

Mother suffered a cardiac arrest in May 1996, but lived until Saturday, July 1, 2000—a month before her eighty-sixth birthday. She had spent her last four years at a Presbyterian home in Dallas near my sister, Janie, who earned sainthood caring for her. At her New Providence memorial service nine days later, the sanctuary was filled with former students and mothers whose names had once been on the waiting list for "Mrs. Alexander's Nursery School and Kindergarten."

Janie's husband, the Reverend Bill Carl, reminded the congregation that Flo Alexander had not minced words, and repeated some of her lessons.

"Be a lady," was Mother's advice to Janie.

"It was *I*," was her instruction to me—loud enough for a large audience to hear—after I'd said, "It was me," while being sworn in as president of the University of Tennessee.

She agreed with state historian Wilma Dykeman, who once told her, "We East Tennesseans sometimes sound like we live south of the Mason-*Diction* line."

She also agreed with my senior year English teacher, Mrs. Martin Badgett, who made me stand in front of my classmates and write the word "just" on the blackboard one hundred times.

"You are always saying 'jist' and if you grow up saying 'jist,' you'll never amount to anything," she'd say.

"Flo believed that no one could chew gum without looking like a cow chewing her cud," Reverend Carl said.

"Honey, if your jaw is getting tired, there's a wastebasket right over there," she once said after a friend of my sister, Ann, had chewed gum for as long as Mother could stand.

After an interview, a reporter described her as very opinionated. This infuriated her.

"He asked me all my opinions on all sorts of things for nearly two hours, and if I had an opinion, I gave it to him. Then, he had the audacity to call me opinionated," she said.

She never consented to another interview.

After Mother's death, Mary Jane Rose summed up her older sister's life.

"She was such a complex person. Outgoing, yet reserved and private. Generous to a fault, yet self-preoccupied. A pacifist, yet fiery. Often fun, with sharp wit, but gloomy and morose. Thoroughly modern, yet living a traditional lifestyle. Always fiercely loyal to family. Careless in many of her habits, yet a perfectionist. Critical of others, but even more critical of herself. Extremely competitive. A woman of many, many talents, yet very unsure of herself. She probably lived out her great possibilities in the lives of her children," Mary Jane wrote.

* * *

Growing up in Maryville wound me up and thrust me on my way, too naïve to know what was impossible to achieve. During my teenage years, I watched Tennessee play Alabama in their first televised college football game, wore pink and black T-shirts with sleeves rolled up to show my muscles, and listened to Pat Boone and the Everly Brothers. During summers, I kept busy as a counselor at a Florida dude ranch and a Boy Scout Camp, where I blew the bugle, provoking one camper to shoot me with a BB gun when reveille woke him up.

There were plenty of opportunities to taste success—to become an Eagle Scout; to achieve superior ratings in piano competitions; to win in sports, and sing well enough at choir practice to appear on Sunday. There were contests to see who could read the most books. From first grade on, elections were a big part of the system of mischief control. Almost everyone was elected to something, and accorded the applause of the community. You might find your photograph in the *Daily Times* for almost any accomplishment.

Of course, not everyone always succeeded, but to pick us up and encourage us, there were scoutmasters and Sunday school teachers, neighbors and friends who we called "Aunt Betty" or "Uncle Connor" or "Aunt Maxey," even though there was no blood relationship. If we wandered off-track, these surrogates would notice, help us back on track, then usually inform our actual parents. By the time I graduated from Maryville High School, I was motivated, applauded, well-trained, and launched on a trajectory that would seem to have no limit.

Growing up in Maryville, anything seemed possible.

Thirty-five y [illegible] after being propelled by such an upbringing, I ran for president of the United States, telling stories of how I grew up.

"You talk too much about Maryville. Not every town is like that," my campaign chairman, William Bennett, the former US secretary of education, said.

"Well, they should be," I told him.

CHAPTER 4

Flo and Andy

"You got yourself up there. You can get yourself down."

—**MY MOTHER,**
when, at age four, I climbed too high in the willow tree

Maryville. 1940–1958.

"I WAS IN YOUR MOTHER'S NURSERY SCHOOL," Melissa Goddard's email to my Senate office said in 2020.

"One evening, I got a phone call late at night," she wrote. "After answering, here is *exactly* what I heard. 'Melissa, this is Flo Alexander. I am in Dallas visiting. I always thought you would amount to something, and I am just calling to see if you did.'"

Genevra Floreine Rankin Alexander, my mother, had established her own high standards and expectations for "Mrs. Alexander's Nursery School and Kindergarten." She expected every one of the 1,100 children she taught over thirty-one years to amount to something, including my two sisters and me. These were the days before public kindergarten. Families moving to Maryville and expectant mothers clamored to add their children to a waiting list.

After four years in her living room, Flo's preschool moved to four rooms in a converted garage in her backyard. Each Tuesday through Friday, promptly at 9:00 a.m., between ten and a dozen mothers would deposit their three- to four-year-olds at 121 Ruth Street, then pick them up promptly at 11:30 a.m. Ninety minutes later, other mothers would drop off twenty-five five-year-olds, and pick them up at 3:30 p.m. A late-arriving mother would receive a stiff admonition, because Flo managed this daily assemblage of preschoolers with only one helper or sometimes, just by herself.

She never taught on Mondays.

"I just thought—this is a Bible town. This is a church town," she said. "Children often went to evening services with their parents, and children would be tired on Monday.

I never kept them more than two-and-a-half hours. I had a program for the children. It was not a babysitting service."

Charles Wright, who became a New York City television executive, recalled his kindergarten days.

"She took us to do and see things. We made cookies in the kitchen, or rode the train from Loudon to Knoxville so we could have those experiences before passenger trains went away. She taught us about farming, and how to make bread, before she took us to Kern's Bakery," he said.

Judge Henry Callaway, another former student, said, "Parents all over town were telling their children [to] 'use [their] inside voices the way [they] learned in Mrs. Alexander's nursery school.'"

Flo often discovered disabilities before parents did. Parents became accustomed to finding a note about their child's progress.

"I would put the notes on their caps where the parents couldn't miss it," Mother said.

Flo taught children to share, take turns, clean up their messes, and put things back where they found them. After a lunch snack, kindergarteners would take a rest.

"If all of us, every afternoon, after lunch, or after a snack, could take our blankets and take a nap, how much better... how much less stress there would be in the world," she said.

She racially integrated her classes several years before public schools did.

"The parents simply asked, 'Would I?' and I said, 'Why of course, if I have room I will.' And so, I did," she said.

"What is the most important thing in education?" the *Daily Times* asked her.

"Learning to get along with your peers... with other people. An exceptional IQ is not going to do you much good if you can't get along with other people," she said.

* * *

Flo had arrived in Maryville in September 1939, a newlywed, and credentialed by training and heritage to open the town's first preschool program. She was an outsider, but for 150 years, her forebears had lived in the foothills of the Great Smoky Mountains. When the Revolutionary War ended, her immigrant ancestors migrated down Virginia's Great Valley finally settling in the "Tennessee country" at the head of Dumplin Creek, in what is now Jefferson County.

A century later, in 1897, Flo's father, Reu Raymond Rankin, at age eleven, fled a dysfunctional family with eighteen children, headed west to become a cowboy and eventually a switch engineer on the Santa Fe railroad. He finally settled and raised a family in Newton, Kansas. In 1931, her father sent Flo "home" to East Tennessee to attend Maryville College.

At age seventeen, she was five feet, seven inches tall, with chestnut hair and a pretty face—presenting a striking presence. To help pay her way, she set tables in the college cafeteria seven days a week. After one semester, she arrived home wearing Andrew Alexander's letter sweater. Andy was handsome. He was five-foot-eleven with wavy black hair—and seven years older. He had a friendly disposition, a pure tenor voice, and movie-star good looks. His Alexander ancestors had arrived in Maryville in 1817.

"There was *nothing* about Andy not to like," Flo's younger sister, Mary Jane, later wrote.

But the Christmas of 1931 was the depth of the Great Depression, and the Rankins could not afford to send Flo back to Maryville College. During the next eight years, she earned a teaching certificate, taught at country schools, and spent summers teaching at a settlement house in Chicago and the Junior League of Wichita preschool program. Meanwhile, Andy was back in Tennessee, working to pay off the debts of his father, who'd died in 1931, and to support his widowed mother. After graduating from college in 1934, he walked a ten-mile round trip each day to and from Alnwick Elementary School, where he was the principal.

Andy and Flo were married in Newton on a Thursday evening, June 1, 1939, that Mary Jane described as "terribly hot." Flo wore her mother's silk wedding dress.

* * *

In September 1939, the young couple moved into an apartment on High Street in Maryville, a town with a population then of 5,609.

The town had come a long way since the pioneer days, when every able-bodied man, aged twenty-one to fifty, belonged to the militia. Back then, there were ferries across the rivers. The few bridges were covered. Chestnut trees grew so large that six men extending their arms could not circle one of them.

But Maryville still had a ways to go. It was located in the mountainous region that the rest of the country called Appalachia.

"This section of Tennessee was first settled by a very low, ignorant, and immoral class of people. This made it difficult to form churches and schools," wrote the Reverend John Rankin, a Jefferson County ancestor of Flo's, and an abolitionist preacher who, in 1817, moved to Ohio, where he became known as "The Conductor" of the underground railroad.[1]

After the Civil War, missionaries, government workers, and others seeking to do good or to tell a good story, discovered mountain people, and began to portray the entire region as populated with shiftless, backward, peculiar characters.

"Culturally backward, violent and in need of help," was how John Fox Jr. a Harvard-educated Kentuckian, depicted Appalachian people in his books and stories.

East Tennesseans resented such stereotyping.

"It is so easy...for sensational writers to take exceptional or rare characters and clothe them with fictitious and exaggerated qualities and present them as representatives of whole communities," Knoxville businessman Oliver P. Temple said in 1899. Hurt feelings among those who were labeled as hillbillies created low self-esteem, and therefore, low aspirations.

But Maryville was different. In 1819, the Reverend Isaac Anderson, a circuit-riding evangelist, founded a Presbyterian seminary—later Maryville College—to educate ministers for the frontier. Then, in 1914, to take advantage of cheap hydropower created by rivers running down mountains, the Aluminum Company of America (Alcoa) built three plants just outside Maryville. As world wars consumed aluminum, the plants hired thousands of mountaineers and began paying them union wages that were negotiated in Pittsburgh. When Alcoa first arrived in East Tennessee, family incomes were one-third the national average. For the new, high-paying aluminum plant jobs, men would drive 200 miles a day out of the hills.

Good incomes, Maryville College, and the coming and going of executives who lived at Alcoa operations in other states and countries created a cosmopolitan quality of life in Maryville—and more demand for preschool education. With her background in Kansas and Chicago preschool programs, Flo's arrival in 1939 fit Maryville better than it would have fit most of Appalachia—but still, it created a stir.

"Mrs. Alexander's Institution of Lower Learning," as I would call it to tease Mother, attracted dozens of students, who were often put on a waiting list. Andy was elected to the city school board, and served twenty-five years with the goal of making Maryville schools among the best in the state. At Flo's urging, he worked to build kindergarten classrooms "to put [her] out of business" before there was a state program.

After eight years of being apart and struggling to make ends meet, Flo and Andy began to build a family within fifty miles of where six generations of their ancestors were buried.

CHAPTER 5

"Aim For the Top. There's More Room There."

"Rule 210. Remember that the higher an ape climbs in a tree, the more his rump is exposed."

—LAMAR ALEXANDER'S LITTLE PLAID BOOK

Maryville. 1957–1958.

THE FIRST GUBERNATORIAL INAUGURATION I ever attended was my own.

It was in the summer of 1957, before my senior year at Maryville High School. I sat in the hot sun on the platform at Castle Heights Military Academy in Lebanon, reviewing the inaugural parade at American Legion Volunteer Boys State. Having already learned the political Rule of Life, "you can start too late, but never too soon," I had boarded the chartered school bus in Maryville to travel to Lebanon, my bag stuffed with campaign posters announcing my candidacy for governor.

At stops in Knoxville and Oak Ridge, I gathered support from boys who were surprised to learn that only four Boys State governors had ever been elected from East Tennessee, an injustice that I argued must be corrected. Two Knoxville delegates I had known from Key Club conventions formed "The Singing Waiters," and with their ukulele and banjo, we cooked up a jingle to the tune of a Brock candy commercial. I won a three-man race for governor in a four-vote landslide.

Just as the inaugural ceremony began, squealing sirens announced the approach of the *real* governor of Tennessee. The police chief's Ford arrived first, flashing its red light, followed by a black limousine that swerved through iron gates and sped to a dramatic stop in front of the steep concrete steps where we sat. A state trooper opened the right rear door.

Governor Frank Goad Clement emerged, wearing a big smile and a bigger western hat. He walked quickly up the steps to the reviewing stand. The governor was a celebrated orator. Before an address, he would turn up the volume on his car radio and listen to gospel music. This allowed him to infuse the gospel beat into the rhythms of his speech.

At our ceremony, Governor Clement spoke earnestly, with frequent appeals for divine help. Then, I delivered my inaugural address, calling for a right-to-work law, enacting civil rights laws, and outlawing the Ku Klux Klan. Civil rights were in the news then. Our Boys State was all White, but three years earlier, on Monday, May 17, 1954, the Supreme Court had said that racial segregation in public schools must end. In 1956, in an action I admired, Governor Clement had ordered National Guardsmen into Clinton, only thirty-six miles from Maryville, to enforce the admission of twelve Black students into the local school. The next year, shortly after my week at Boys State, President Eisenhower sent the 101st Airborne Division to integrate Little Rock Central High School.

When the inaugural ceremony ended, I plunged into the back seat of my parents' 1955 Ford, thinking of the one sentence Governor Clement had said that stuck in my mind. "Someday, one of you boys is going to grow up to be the real governor of Tennessee."

* * *

The next time I met a real governor was two years later, in 1959, when I was a Vanderbilt University freshman. The father of my then-girlfriend, Jane McDade, took me to breakfast with his friend, Governor Buford Ellington. "Mr. Mac" (which is what I respectfully called Jane's father) was an important executive at the Alcoa aluminum plant. He was so important that he knew the way to the state capital in Nashville almost without having to look—which was the way he drove that day, slumped low behind the steering wheel in his new 1959 Oldsmobile 98, inhaling Winstons, and occasionally waving one arm and instructing me on some crucial Rule of Life.

When we reached the gate outside the governor's mansion, we paused to admire the three-story Georgian home that sits on ten well-shrubbed, tall-treed, blue-grassed acres, and that symbolizes political victory, the prize of battle, the real spoils.

Then, it was The Mansion. Now, it is called The Residence.

"I expect you'll live here one day," Mr. Mac said in that low growl I always envied.

A trooper led us through the black-and-white, marble-floored foyer to the breakfast room where the governor was sitting at the head of the table, reading the morning newspaper, the *Tennessean. This must have been an unpleasant exercise,* I thought, since the newspaper constantly criticized Governor Ellington, accusing him and Governor Clement of playing "leapfrog" with the governorship. Since governors at that time could not serve more than one consecutive four-year term, Democrats Ellington and Clement had been swapping the office between themselves for sixteen years. There were no serious Republican nominees to worry about.

Mr. Mac and I took seats. Mr. Mac lit a Winston. The governor smoked a DFT (Dual Filter Tareyton). What impressed me most about the breakfast was the way the two of them carried on. They were soul brothers—two Mississippi White boys grown up. Once, they had both been skinny, creek-smart, and sweaty, scratching out a rock-hard barefoot living at the bottom of the heap in black-and-white, cotton-quilted, little Delta towns. Now, they were fleshed out, air-conditioned, Oldsmobile-98-luxuriating, cleated-rubber-golf-shoe, high-powered-fishing-boat Tennesseans—happily splashing in new ponds where the governor was the biggest frog of all and Mr. Mac had pretty nice lily pad for himself.

"Be the big frog in the smaller pond," was one of Mr. Mac's Rules of Life.

The two men even spoke in Mississippi, a language of growling and nudging, elbowing and foot-stomping (if standing), shuffling around in your chair and table slapping (if sitting down, as we now were), undulating belly laughs and good-natured cussing, and hugely glorified stories about happiness in the rock-hard days.

Seeing the prisoners who served as staff at the Mansion made me uneasy. The "outside" prisoners clipped the putting greens, cleaned the paddock and stable, raked leaves, tended azaleas, washed the cars of the governor's political supporters, and shot basketballs at a hoop above one of the doors of the six-car garage.

The "inside" prisoners cleaned the nine bathrooms, changed sheets in the six bedrooms, scrubbed the marble floor in the foyer, and polished the walnut railings. Some "inside" prisoners played cards in the basement. Still others cooked and served our ham and eggs, grits, coffee, and toast.

The governor left before 8:00 a.m. to go to his Capitol office, where, according to his critics in the morning newspaper, by noon, he was often able to have the state on such an even keel that he could spend the rest of the day on the golf course. On the way back, I pondered what the governor had told me about the prisoners.

"Murderers are the best, better than thieves. Murderers' crimes are crimes of passion," he had said.

* * *

Mother was my sparkplug.

Left to my own devices, I would have spent more time playing basketball and smoking Indian see-gars. On my own, I would never have imagined that 2 Timothy 2:15 required filling up every spare moment with work. That level of example, encouragement, and inspiration wound me up like a spinning top, but it also grated, creating a relationship that was not always easy. Mother and I were independent forces with minds of our own, often colliding.

Dad and I rarely had a conflict. He was softspoken, frugal, and the kind of man everyone was happy to see coming down the street.

And he was a man of routine.

At breakfast, he would crush cornbread into his buttermilk, drink two cups of black coffee, and study the *Knoxville Journal's* Republican version of the news.

"Did you hear what Ike said yesterday?" he would ask.

"Yes," I would always answer, because I had read the same stories at 6:00 a.m. after completing my paper route.

On Saturday mornings, he examined political trends with the postmaster. Saturday nights, after I had gone to bed, he shined his Sunday shoes—and mine.

Dad set examples too. Because he had to pay off his father's debts, he stayed away from debt himself. He kept detailed accounts and lists of what he had done and needed to do, as I do today. In 1983, when Honey and I turned a nineteenth-century log cabin into our mountain home, Dad said, "I spent a long time trying to get out of houses like this and you're spending all this money trying to get into one."

Like Mother, he was culturally conservative—but no ideologue. My love of sports and Republican politics comes from him. So does most of my music. While Mother made sure I practiced the piano, it was Dad who sang in the glee club, choir, and college plays. He led the singing while I played gospel hymns. When we listened to news broadcasts and national political conventions on the Zenith radio, it was because both parents wanted me to respect public life.

My closest family relationship was with Mother's father. If I had to trace to a single source my boldness bordering on impertinence—the kind of rule-breaking, reckless spirit that everyone who eventually runs for president of the United States seems to possess—it would be Reu Raymond Rankin, the railroad engineer.

Grandad Rankin was six-foot-four and not the kind of fellow to argue with. He was typical of Presbyterian immigrants from Northern Ireland—stiff, angular, liberty-loving, and stubborn.

"Lord, grant that I may always be right; for thou knowest I am hard to turn," is a Scotch-Irish prayer[1] that described him well.

When Mother contracted undulant fever in the fall of 1944, she shipped my sister Ann and me to Newton, Kansas to live with our grandparents for six months. I walked to public kindergarten there, a benefit not yet available in Maryville. In the afternoons, while Granddad was railroading and Grandmother was cooking and singing in the kitchen, I would slip into his second-floor study where his tobacco stand was and, after opening all the windows, puff away on his Camel cigarettes until my mouth tasted like burnt cardboard.

I was certain that being a railroad engineer made Granddad one of the most important men in all of Kansas. He took me to the roundhouse where the Super Chief and other giant locomotives were turned around and repaired. I sat next to him in the engineer's cab. He gave me a watch that worked and showed me a real one-hundred-dollar bill. He taught me hunt-and-peck, writing letters on his Royal typewriter—a method I still use on computers today.

When I was a teenager, Granddad retired to a farm near Cassville in the southwest corner of Missouri where Grandmother had grown up. That part of Missouri had been settled by the same wild and ornery Scotch-Irish frontiersmen—like the Rankins and Alexanders—who had pioneered Tennessee, fought with Cherokees, then moved west, looking for more fights.

By this time, Granddad could only whisper. The same year he retired from railroading, doctors in Kansas had cut out his voice box.

"Cancer of the larynx—too many cigarettes," was what they'd told him.

After that, he would startle fellow churchgoers by whistling hymns. He called his dog, Sandy, with a whistle I still keep on my desk.

My best teenage summers were spent on my grandparents' farm in Cassville—enjoying the fresh taste of raw milk and butter every day, scything grass beneath the boiling Missouri sun, and helping Granddad type the genealogical records of his Scotch-Irish ancestors all the way back to 1688 in County Derry.

Granddad's correspondence with relatives helped to found the annual Rankin Reunion at Mt. Horeb Presbyterian Church in Dumplin Valley. After a covered dish dinner on the grounds, we children would follow Granddad to the cemetery behind the church.

Granddad would then pause for silence, raise his cane, and point toward a row of gravestones.

"I am the fifth, your mother is the sixth, you are the seventh, and your children will be the eighth generation. No one except the Cherokee goes back further than that in East Tennessee," he would intone.

When Grandmother Rankin died in 1967, Granddad sold his farm and moved to Maryville.

"You can't take the mountains out of a mountain boy," he explained—another Rule of Life.

He bought the widow White's little house at "one-aught-five Ruth Street," where Mother could keep an eye on him and he could keep his independence.

"Well, what are you going to do, Lamar?" Granddad whispered in one of our last conversations.

He was rocking in a chair on his front porch.

"Maybe someday run for governor," I answered.

"I wouldn't," he said. "Politics is too hard. But if you do, aim for the top. There's more room there."

CHAPTER 6

Sleeping Through the Revolution

"We won't have to live in the same dorm with them, will we?"

—**A VANDERBILT UNIVERSITY COED, January 1962**

Nashville to New York City. 1958–1965.

IN THE SAME MONTH THAT I ENROLLED as a freshman at Vanderbilt University, September of 1958, James Lawson, an African American Methodist minister from Ohio, enrolled in Vanderbilt's Divinity School.

Although all my undergraduate classmates were White, a handful of graduate students were Black. The thirty-one-year-old Lawson soon began teaching workshops in downtown churches on how to use nonviolent tactics to challenge racial segregation.

Dr. Martin Luther King Jr. "had literally begged" him to move to Nashville, according to the *Tennessean.*

In his lectures, Dr. King sometimes would retell the story of Rip Van Winkle, the colonial villager who took a twenty-year nap in the Catskill Mountains. When the villager went to sleep, the sign on the town inn had a picture of King George III of England. When he woke up, the sign had a picture of George Washington. Rip Van Winkle had slept through the American Revolution.

"There is nothing more tragic than to sleep through a revolution," Dr. King had warned.[1]

That describes what was happening at Vanderbilt when Lawson and I arrived. Students were sleeping soundly through a civil rights revolution brewing downtown. The burning campus issue was whether coeds could wear Bermuda shorts at fraternity houses. One year later, in February 1960, 124 Black students walked into Nashville department stores and asked to be seated at lunch counters. When store employees refused, the students sat for two hours. Eighty-one were arrested for disorderly conduct and James Lawson himself was later arrested. The Vanderbilt Board of Trust unanimously asked Lawson to withdraw from school or be expelled for encouraging students to break the law—and for breaking it himself. Lawson chose expulsion. His expulsion created turmoil.

The next year, in September 1961, Chancellor Harvie Branscomb invited me to his office for the courtesy visit that accompanied my new position as editor of the campus newspaper. The *Hustler* was reporting the usual concerns—no majorettes in the marching band and the arrival of Charm Week. But what concerned Dr. Branscomb most was the damage to Vanderbilt caused by the Lawson expulsion, and the university's policy of excluding Black undergraduates from the school.

Branscomb was ready to retire, and he knew that the university's racial barrier would block attracting a successor who could continue Vanderbilt's climb toward national respect. Our meeting became the first of a series of visits, during which I became a behind-the-scenes ally in the chancellor's strategy to persuade the Board of Trust to change policy in its spring meeting.

On January 5, 1962, in my weekly column as *Hustler* editor, I criticized the university's "cowardly policy." On January 12, 1962, John Sergent, a pre-med student senator from Kentucky, introduced a resolution calling for "a committee to investigate the admittance of qualified negroes to all Vanderbilt Schools."[2] Sergent began touring fraternity and sorority houses, advocating his resolution to generally unfriendly audiences.

"We won't have to live in the same dorm with them, will we?" one Delta Delta Delta coed asked Sergent.

"Such an assimilation is both necessary and proper on the grounds of basic decency and human equality before the law," wrote the news editor,

Roy Blount Jr., a Decatur, Georgia student who later became a nationally known author.[3]

On the following Wednesday, the Senate voted 15–14 not to integrate, but also voted to turn the matter over to a campus-wide student referendum. "Students Veto Integration Proposal in Record Number," was the *Hustler* headline after the referendum.

* * *

On the morning of Friday, March 16, 1962, during my final semester, I was hustling out the door of my apartment when the telephone rang.

The chancellor's secretary was calling.

"Dr. Branscomb would like to see you in his office," she said.

"Now? I have on my blue jeans and a T-shirt. I'm on my way to hitchhike home for spring break," I replied.

"Come on, anyway," she insisted, and so I walked across campus to Kirkland Hall and into the chancellor's high-ceilinged office.

Branscomb was seated behind his desk. He looked the part of a university chancellor—sixty-five, stately, and conservatively dressed. He had been dean at Duke University Divinity School. In 1946, Vanderbilt had recruited him to help transform a regional university into one of national distinction.

The chancellor rose, gestured toward a tall man across the room, and, in his proper way, introduced us.

"Mr. Alexander, Mr. Vanderbilt."

"Mr. Vanderbilt, Mr. Alexander."

"Mr. Alexander, please be seated and give Mr. Vanderbilt your view of what the student reaction would be to the desegregation of the undergraduate college," the chancellor said.

Dressed for hitchhiking, I squirmed. I was seated across from the great-grandson of the tycoon Cornelius Vanderbilt, who, in 1873, had made the largest charitable gift at that time in American history—$1 million—to found a university that would help unite the country after the Civil War. Harold S. Vanderbilt was older than my grandfather and chairman of the university's Board of Trust. I told Mr. Vanderbilt what I had been writing since November in my editorials and columns.

"The student Senate and student body have voted against desegregation, but the uproar showed substantial student support for desegregation and an opportunity for the Board of Trust to act," I said.

Both men listened, said little, and after about half an hour, excused me. I walked back to my apartment, put on my track letter sweater with the big "V" on the front to make me a more appealing hitchhiker, walked to West End Avenue, and caught a ride to Knoxville where I took a White Star Line bus to Maryville.

At its spring meeting on May 4, the *Hustler* reported that the Board of Trust voted to "admit all qualified students to schools and colleges of the university without regard to race or creed."[4] The campus commotion surrounding desegregation had forced the issue. Later that year, the board chose University of North Carolina political scientist G. Alexander Heard as Vanderbilt's fifth chancellor. He surely would not have accepted the position had the university not desegregated.

After graduating, I often visited Dr. Branscomb, seeking career advice. He gradually lost his eyesight but remained alert, courteous, and always focused on the needs of others until his death at age 103 in 1998. He never complained about the Lawson affair, but I could tell that he felt misunderstood and hurt by it.

Branscomb and Lawson had a pleasant meeting on October 24, 1996, after the former chancellor had turned 102, according to Bill Carey's history of the university.

"It was a mistake," Branscomb said.

"I never thought you were anything less than a Christian man who was trying to do the right thing in a difficult situation," Lawson said.

* * *

On a brisk September morning in 1962, I flew from Knoxville to LaGuardia Airport for my first-ever visit to New York City.

I took a taxi to Hayden Hall at 33 Washington Square West in Greenwich Village. My purpose was to enroll in the New York University School of Law. I also was ready to see the world and test whether I wanted to spend my life in Tennessee, where six generations of my ancestors are buried.

I had won a Root Tilden Scholarship that paid for everything—tuition, books, room, board, one round-trip airline ticket, and $500 for living expenses. The goal of the scholarship was "to train highly talented young men for public service and to practice law in the grand manner." That fit my inclination toward public service and paid for law school. At the same time, going to NYU in bohemian Greenwich Village was an opportunity to turn my back on politics. NYU was no place for a Republican who planned on a political career in Tennessee.

On my first evening, I wandered down Bleecker Street looking for a meat-and-three supper. All I found were small diners serving exotic food. Later that night, I sat at my third-floor window studying the sights, marveling at so many buildings crammed together. I marveled even more at the swarm of characters milling about Washington Square. It reminded me of the first warm spring day when the sun entices every sort of creepy creature to crawl out of decaying wood. I stayed up late that night, watching and wondering how I had ever decided to spend three years in such a place. The swarm was still crawling the next morning.

My first order of business that morning was to join a line of students registering for classes. The tall student in front of me was upset.

"I left my money at home," he said.

"How much do you need?" I asked.

"Three hundred dollars," he answered.

"I'll loan it you," I said.

I had $500 in cash, the year's expense allowance that came with my scholarship.

The tall student gave me a look that said, *You must be some hillbilly who has never been to New York City.*

His name was Paul. He had grown up in a middle-class, street-wise New Jersey neighborhood, the son of Italian immigrants. Anyone schooled in that environment knew better than to loan money to a stranger. Yet, our backgrounds were more alike than might first appear. His mother was a seamstress. Later, when I spent the night at their home, she would "turn the collar" on my one white dress shirt while I slept. That is, she would take the collar off, turn it around so the frayed side did not show, and sew it back on. During my second and third years, we were roommates. That friendship led to attending fifteen Super Bowls. From 1989 to 2006, Paul Tagliabue was Commissioner of the National Football League.

During the preceding summer, the law school had asked about my preferences for a roommate during my first year.

"Someone with a background as different from mine as possible," I had replied.

That request produced Ed Lampert, a scholarly soul who lived on Long Island and had graduated from Colgate. Ed chose the desk by the only window in our third-floor room so he could open it to avoid the smoke of my Lucky Strikes.

Almost all our classmates were from New York City. Barney Haynes, from Shelbyville, Tennessee, and I seemed to be the only two from states between Manhattan and Miami. At first, Barney and I thought professors called on us so the class could hear *how* we talked. Then, we decided they called on us to determine whether we *could* talk.

* * *

Ed and I studied six hours a day. Instead of traveling home for Christmas, I stayed in Hayden Hall studying for January exams because I wanted to qualify for the law review. When grades for the first year came out, I was twenty-first in a class of 300—and only the top twenty were invited to join the law review.

During my second year, I wrangled permission to try to write my way onto the law review by composing a two-part tome entitled, "*En Banc* Hearings in the Federal Courts of Appeals."[5] That diligence made me a law review editor, but it also created one of the great regrets of my life. I had worked so hard that I did not take time to explore the many things one can experience for free in New York City.

In the summer of 1963, I found an opportunity to intern for US Attorney General Robert F. Kennedy. Working for Bobby Kennedy was a heady experience. The attorney general drove down Constitution Avenue alone in a blue convertible with the top down, his shock of hair blowing in the breeze. His shaggy dog, Brumus, wandered with him through the halls of the Justice Department. Everyone played touch football in the afternoons.

On Wednesday, August 28, during lunch break, I wandered onto the National Mall where I saw 250,000 people from the "March on Washington" stretched all the way to the Lincoln Memorial, where Martin Luther King Jr. was speaking. I could not see Dr. King, but over the speakers, I heard his rolling cadence: "I have a dream."

During the summer of 1964, Paul and I worked for the Los Angeles law firm of Gibson, Dunn and Crutcher. In August, on the way back to New York, we stopped in Shelbyville, where I was best man in Barney Haynes's wedding to Susan Archer. The law school friendships created with Barney, Paul, Ed Lampert, Bill Plunkett, and Ross Sandler, along with their wives, have lasted more than sixty years.

As my third year in law school began, I concluded that I would have a happier and more useful life back in Tennessee. Attorney General Kennedy had encouraged us summer interns to consider public service, and suggested that a good place to start would be with our local US attorney. I drove to Chattanooga to apply for a job.

"What is your political party?" asked the US attorney, a Kennedy appointee.

"Why, I'm a Republican. In Maryville, almost everybody is a Republican," I responded.

"Sorry. We only hire Democrats," he said.

"But I was told that in the Justice Department, political affiliation doesn't matter," I said.

"Who told you that?" the US attorney asked.

"The attorney general," I said.

"Well, that word hasn't made it to Chattanooga," the US attorney answered.

Infused with this dose of political reality, I landed a job with a Knoxville law firm starting in June 1965, when I was to graduate. Meanwhile, NYU Law Associate Dean Robert McKay suggested a detour. John Minor Wisdom, an admired federal judge, was looking for a law clerk. I drove to New Haven, where the judge was speaking at the *Yale Law Journal* banquet. Afterward, we visited.

"I have already hired a young man from Harvard, but I can pay you three hundred dollars a month in a messenger's position. I'll treat you like a second clerk," the judge said. The opportunity to live in New Orleans and learn from such a distinguished jurist was too tempting to turn down.

In the second week of September 1965, as hurricane season arrived, I flew to New Orleans to begin my job as messenger for Judge Wisdom, hoping that he would remember to treat me like his law clerk.

PART THREE

Three Wise Mentors

1965 to 1970

"We find that the Klansmen... are a fearful conspiracy against society."

—JUDGE JOHN MINOR WISDOM, 1965

"Always remember that the other fellow might be right."

—SENATOR HOWARD H. BAKER JR., 1967

"What would be the right thing to do?"

—BRYCE N. HARLOW, Counselor to the President, 1969

CHAPTER 7

Your Father's Mustache

"You're the worst trombone player in our organization, but you're just right for our kind of music."

—JOEL SCHIAVONE,
owner of Your Father's Mustache, 1966

New Orleans. 1965–1966.

I HAD NEVER HEARD JUDGE WISDOM SING.

But there he was, singing along with the banjo band, having more fun than anyone else at Your Father's Mustache, a Bourbon Street nightspot, on one special night in April, 1966. He was certainly having more fun than any of the other federal judges who were fidgeting in the front row.

I was the trombone player in the Mustache Stompers band when I was Judge John Minor Wisdom's law clerk. The truth was, I was the *substitute* trombone player when I was a *messenger* to Judge Wisdom. He had hired me as a messenger but said he would treat me like a second clerk. The judge proved true to his word—and the lessons I learned in the College of Wisdom have stuck with me all my life.

I arrived in New Orleans in mid-September, a few days after Hurricane Betsy had created storm surges reaching all the way to Lake Pontchartrain. I moved into an upstairs apartment on Felicity Street—not far from the Wisdoms' mansion at the corner of First and Coliseum streets in the

Garden District. From that day on, I was one of the family. The real law clerk had already arrived and unselfishly chosen the smaller of the two upstairs rooms. He was Gene Marans, a studious Montana native who helped found the Republican Ripon Society at Harvard.

Gene and I had offices next to the judge's chambers in the Wildlife and Fisheries building, just around the corner from Bourbon Street. Within a few weeks, I grew tired of earning only $300 a month, so, after work, I began touring French Quarter nightspots looking for a second job. In November, I found one playing in the Mustache Stompers banjo band on Tuesdays through Saturdays, substituting for whomever was off. One night it was for the trombone player, one night for the tuba, one for the piano, and two for the washboard.

Your Father's Mustache was conceived in 1962 by Joel Schiavone, a mustache-sporting, wisecracking, banjo-playing 1958 Yale graduate. His concoction of music, beer, and sawdust had spread to New York City, Cape Cod, Boston, St. Louis, and Detroit before arriving in New Orleans. These clubs featured a banjo band of young men wearing red-gartered shirts and straw hats in an atmosphere heavily influenced by beer, peanuts, and rambunctious singing.

Your Father's Mustache was billed as a place "where the time of your life is right under your nose" but it was not dangerous—except occasionally, such as when teams of women bowlers convened in New Orleans and, after a few beers, rushed the band members. This was somewhat in reverse of what was going on across Bourbon Street at the corner nightclub where Linda Some-Body was fending off male customers during her performance. I was the front line of defense against the charging women bowlers, thrusting my trombone slide as a bayonet, urging them back toward their tables in between choruses of "Mississippi Mud" and "You're a Grand Old Flag."

I preferred the trombone because it drowned out everything else. But it was the washboard—strummed with an old spoon—that Judge Wisdom liked best. And it was the washboard that I was playing the night he prodded the other six Fifth Circuit judges to occupy the front row, wedged between disorderly college students and the blaring band, perfectly positioned en banc in the midst of roaring cross currents of noise. While the other judges squirmed, Judge Wisdom had fun.

Judge Wisdom generally had lots of fun. Gene and I often drove him to lunch at Commander's Palace, a Garden District restaurant noted for Creole food, where his favorite waiter would escort him to *his* corner table. The judge would order turtle soup and Dewar's scotch with "two rocks" (that is, cubes of ice). After a sufficient interval, he would order a second turtle soup and another Dewar's. Then, we would not see him for the rest of the afternoon.

After a few months, I discovered that, during these afternoon absences, the judge would visit the Louisiana Club to play money bridge, a skill he acquired to supplement his income during the Depression days when he was starting his law practice. He made up for these double Dewar's lunches and afternoons of bridge by hauling home bulging briefcases when we drove him to First Street for dinner—after which he would work late into the night on his "big cases."

The judge also enjoyed putting a self-important lawyer in his place.

"Judge, will you hold for Lawyer Brown?" a lawyer's secretary once asked on the telephone.

"Of course not," the judge said before slamming the phone down.

Ever since, including while I was governor and senator, I have dialed the numbers and placed my own calls.

* * *

Judge Wisdom was a man of medium build. His face had arching eyebrows, piercing eyes, a hawk nose, and usually a broad smile. When those features settled into repose, they could terrify unprepared lawyers. He exuded energy even when he assumed his favorite position, leaning back into his chair with his collar open and his tie askew.

His wife, Bonnie, was proper, pert, bright, and opinionated. Both she and the judge had a long Louisiana lineage. Ironically, the judge's time on the court was spent overturning the segregationist policies of both their ancestors. Bonnie's great-grandfather was chief judge of the first Louisiana Supreme Court. John Wisdom's grandfather was the Louisiana lieutenant governor during the Civil War, and the judge's stepfather was a delegate to the state's secessionist convention.

Each day, Gene and I drove the judge to and from work in Gene's Volkswagen Beetle—not only because the judge's driving was erratic, but also because he wanted to know his clerks. He often invited us to stay for dinner. These daily visits provided opportunities for the judge and Bonnie to offer advice. The judge offered advice about my Mardi Gras date. Bonnie improved my manners. She instructed me that dinner was always at 6:00 p.m. and that it was mu*stache,* not *mus*tache. She made sure I learned what to do with an artichoke. (I had never seen one before, at least one presented on a nice table with dinner.)

Dinner at the Wisdoms' was correct, but not as formal as it was at other stately First Street mansions, where the dining table might be so long that a husband and wife, seated at either end in formal attire, would rarely have to deal with one another. The Wisdoms relished practicing New Orleans traditions—he never quit his men's club, and she entertained ladies in her parlor once a week when only French was spoken. After dinner, ladies would retire to one room, men to another. In their conversations, they competed to obliterate any threat of silence.

"How long have you been married?" I once asked the judge.

"Forty years of bliss, but never a peaceful moment," he said, smiling at Bonnie.

Judge Wisdom delighted in being a Republican. When he was in law school, Louisiana Republicans were few. The weakness of the Republican Party helped to produce the "Kingfish," populist Governor Huey P. Long. Wisdom joined a coterie of men who formed a secret pact to "go armed if summoned" against Long if it became necessary to resist his tyranny, the judge told me. During weekends, these "square dealers" would muster in Baton Rouge with their guns.

"John Wisdom never shot a gun in his life," Bonnie said, worrying that the judge with a gun was a greater threat than Huey P. Long.

What galled Wisdom most was not, in fact, dictatorial Democrats, but spineless Republicans. Southern Republican parties had degenerated into patronage parties existing mainly to hand out federal jobs whenever a Republican president took office. Since these weak organizations had no chance of winning state and local elections, Democrats felt free to govern in corrupt and dictatorial ways.

"I chose the Republican Party because I felt the lack of a two-party system was a main reason for the development of our demagogues. The rise of demagogues in Deep South states, such as Louisiana, was directly attributable to the absence of a party out of power as a check on the abuses of the party in power," Judge Wisdom told me in 1993.

The judge's anger at the lack of a two-party system struck a chord with me. It made me eager to return home and join Bill Brock and Howard Baker, who were challenging one-party rule. Middle Tennessee Democrats had dominated Tennessee politics since the Civil War, disenfranchising Republicans and Blacks in the eastern and western parts of the state. Republican leaders had tolerated that system in exchange for control of patronage when a Republican president was in office.

During the 1930s, both Bonnie and John Wisdom fought the Long machine and set out to build a statewide Republican party. Still, in 1952, in a state with a population of 2.8 million, there were fewer than 1,500 registered Republicans. In February of that year, fifteen Eisenhower leaders from eleven Southern states elected Wisdom as chairman and Atlanta attorney Elbert Tuttle as vice chairman of "The Southern Conference for Eisenhower," part of a national draft movement. Wisdom used his legal skills at the 1952 Republican National Convention to seat a Louisiana delegation loyal to Dwight Eisenhower instead of Ohio Senator Robert A. Taft. In Texas, Houston attorney John R. Brown did the same, helping to throw the nomination to Eisenhower.

* * *

In 1957, John Wisdom's Republican credentials and legal prowess earned him Eisenhower's nomination to the United States Court of Appeals for the Fifth Circuit. At that time, the court had seven appellate judges and, until 1981, included all the states in the Deep South. Earlier, Eisenhower had nominated Tuttle and Brown to the same court. These three appointments came to a crucial court at a pivotal moment in American history.

When Wisdom became judge, few Southern public schools were desegregated, few Blacks were registered to vote, and Black officeholders were unheard of. During the late 1950s and 1960s, these three Eisenhower Republican Judges—Brown, Tuttle, and Wisdom—together with

Truman appointee Richard Rives, formed a majority on the seven-judge Fifth Circuit to implement the desegregation of schools required by the May 17, 1954, Supreme Court decision in *Brown v. Board of Education* of Topeka, Kansas.

To accomplish this, "The Four"—as an outraged fellow judge called them—regularly overturned rulings of segregationist lower court federal judges in six Deep South states—Louisiana, Mississippi, Texas, Alabama, Georgia, and Florida. These federal district court judges reflected the views of the Southern Democrat segregationist United States senators who had handpicked them. But those segregationist senators had not been able to block the three Eisenhower appellate judges. Senate practice did not permit a senator to veto the nomination of an *appellate* judge from the senator's state, but it did permit a senator to veto the nomination of a *lower court* federal district judge from his state.

Judge Wisdom was the most eloquent spokesman for the court majority in these civil rights controversies. On September 28, 1962, the Fifth Circuit held Governor Ross Barnett of Mississippi in civil contempt, ordered him arrested, and to pay a fine of $10,000 a day unless, within a week, he admitted James Meredith to the University of Mississippi. Judge Wisdom wrote the opinion. On October 1, 1962, Meredith became the first Black student to enroll at Ole Miss.

"[He was] the penman, architect and genius who wrote the seminal decisions that integrated the public schools of the Deep South," said the dean of the University of Florida law school, Frank T. Read.[1]

Judge Wisdom chose his words with care. After dinner, he and Bonnie would dash to the proper edition of *Webster's* to settle spelling disagreements. To encourage his clerks to use plain English, the judge compiled "Wisdom's Idiosyncrasies," seventy-five "suggestions. some of which you learned in elementary school from Miss Thistlebottom before you ever heard of Strunk." These included:

- There should be one idea to a sentence.
- Use one word instead of two; two instead of three, five, and so on.
- Use no weasel words—"very," "quite," "rather," "somewhat."
- The adjective is the enemy of the noun; the adverb is the enemy of the verb. Think of the right word.

- No need for elegant variation. Do not be afraid to repeat.
- Avoid "which," an ugly word.
- Avoid vogue words.
- Beware of metaphors.
- Simple is better.

"[Wisdom's] style exhibits eloquence, energy, intellect, classical learning, pith, and vigor. [His] opinions are works of art," Judge Tuttle said.[2]

But those opinions repelled many friends at his club, in his neighborhood, and in his Mardi Gras krewe, and made the Wisdoms' First Street home the target of a cross-burning.

* * *

On Saturday, April 16, 1966, Richard M. Nixon arrived in New Orleans on a national tour seeking support for a 1968 presidential campaign. Nixon came to First Street to visit the judge. The two men had known one another as far back as the 1952 Republican convention, when Wisdom and Tuttle had helped Eisenhower defeat Taft. The judge believed he and Nixon shared similar attitudes on civil rights.

Judge Wisdom invited Gene and me to join a small reception at First Street to meet Nixon. After a few minutes, Nixon and the judge disappeared into the study for half an hour. No one knows what secrets they swapped. To me, it seemed unusual that Nixon would spend so much of his New Orleans visit with a judge who could not participate in politics. Perhaps their friendship was stronger than we knew. Gene and I hoped the visit was to talk about the possibility of a Wisdom nomination to the US Supreme Court if Nixon were elected.

Nixon wrote Wisdom a letter four days after his New Orleans visit, in which he reaffirmed that he and the judge had similar views on matters of race.

A Supreme Court nomination never came Wisdom's way, even after the embarrassing failures of President Nixon's nominations in 1969 of Clement Haynsworth and G. Harrold Carswell. Nixon's view apparently had changed between his 1966 letter and his 1969 nominations, probably

RICHARD M. NIXON
20 BROAD STREET
NEW YORK, NEW YORK

April 20, 1966

Dear John:

It was a real treat to see you again if only briefly during my visit to New Orleans and I particularly appreciated the opportunity of seeing your beautiful home.

The Federal Bench is indeed fortunate to have a man of your caliber serving on it. My only regret is that the Republican Party in Louisiana is thereby denied the leadership which you could undoubtedly give it. At least we get a break in the fact that your lovely wife and daughter do not have to operate under the same inhibitions!

I hope you can continue to give some helpful advice on an off-the-record basis to Republicans who are interested in building on a solid basis for the future in the South. It is vitally important that we adopt as our objective not just building a party which can win the next election but one which can win over the next generation. There is no future in the race issue for either party. I have been encouraged that an increasing number of Republicans recognize this basic truth.

Pat joins me in sending our very best wishes,

Sincerely,

Dick

The Honorable John Minor Wisdom
400 Royal Street
New Orleans, Louisiana

because John Wisdom did not fit Attorney General John Mitchell's Southern strategy.

"[He's] a damn left winger. He'd be as bad as Earl Warren," Mitchell told a Republican governor, according to the *Baltimore Sun*.[3]

At the end of July, on my last night at Your Father's Mustache, the clarinet player was trying to say something nice about my leaving.

"We'll miss our trombone player even though he is not a real trombone player. He is going back to Tennessee to work in a political campaign," he told the crowd of beer drinkers.

I had not been a real law clerk either, but I had been treated like one by a wise and moral man who was a skilled litigator, gifted scholar, and writer of powerful opinions securing equal rights for Black Americans—a man who had fought political wars, won big legal cases, ridden carnival floats, played money bridge at clubs, and found his way deep into the lives of his friends, many of whom were his former law clerks.

The judge died on Saturday, May 15, 1999, two days before his ninety-fourth birthday and after forty-two years as an active or senior judge. From the privacy of his judicial chambers, he had watched me in public life use the lessons I had learned in the College of Wisdom. He had attended my inauguration as governor, sworn me in as US education secretary, and cheered behind the scenes when I ran for president. The judge's broad-gauged life had become my model for the practice of law in the grand manner.

It has always seemed to me that a judge who would convene the United States Court of Appeals *en banc* to hear his favorite washboard player at Your Father's Mustache also was likely to be the kind of man who would order Governor Barnett to admit James Meredith to Ole Miss.

CHAPTER 8

Lincolnites

"I'm a Republican and a Presbyterian.
I fought to save the Union, and I vote like I shot."

—JOHN ALEXANDER, my great-grandfather

Knoxville, Tennessee. The 1960s.

IT WAS A SWELTERING AUGUST AFTERNOON on Republican Day at the 1960 Illinois State Fair in Springfield.

In between cattle and sheep shows and harness racing, the state's senior Republican, Senator Everett McKinley Dirksen, was stirring the crowd of thousands with his oratory. Dirksen was explaining why Richard Nixon, the Republican nominee for president, was a better choice than the Democrat, Senator John F. Kennedy.

Seated on the podium behind Dirksen were his daughter, Joy, and her husband, Howard H. Baker Jr., then thirty-five years old, but whose five-foot-seven-inch height, windblown brown hair, and boyish face made him seem even younger.

"Jack Kennedy is a nice young man but all they can say on his behalf is that he was a PT boat commander in World War II," Dirksen thundered.

Then, Dirksen paused, and with a theatrical sweep of his arm, the white-haired Republican leader pointed toward Baker.

"Why, my own son-in-law, Howard Baker Jr., sitting right here, was a PT boat commander in World War II, and I've never heard anyone suggest that he was qualified to serve in any public office," he said.

Whatever Baker's qualifications, Dirksen's prediction about his son-in-law's bleak political future seemed grounded in reality. There had never been a Republican United States senator popularly elected from Tennessee, and there had been no Republican governor elected since Alf Taylor was elected in 1920.

Yet, there were stirrings of Republican ascendancy in Tennessee encouraged by those like my father, who practiced his politics the way I practiced the piano—systematically. He practiced it on weekends over coffee at Byrne Drug store. He practiced it in the county courthouse on Saturday mornings and at City Hall on election nights, helping to count paper ballots. He was a faithful member of the Republican Executive Committee.

I grew up in a bastion of Republican insurrection that had existed since the Civil War, when Tennessee seceded from the Union, and our part of the state decided not to go along. Scott County, where Howard Baker grew up, even voted to secede from Tennessee after the state left the Union. My father's grandfather, John Alexander, was a Union soldier.

My mother's ancestors were Lincolnites too. During the Civil War, the Reverend Nathan Hood, a preacher with Confederate sympathies, mounted the pulpit at Mt. Horeb Presbyterian Church in Jefferson County.

"May East Tennesseans who join Union forces die, and their bones decorate and grow white on the top of Cumberland Mountain," he prayed.

With that, Mother's great-grandfather, Christopher Rankin, and his seven sons rose from their pews, walked out, and, with other Union sympathizers, formed Hebron Church a few miles down the Valley.

Since the end of the Civil War the descendants of these Union soldiers had made certain that no Democrat was elected to Congress from our Second Congressional District. To maintain that tradition, Republicans in Scott County would haul a conspicuous drunk to the town square, round up the children, and tell them the drunk was a Democrat "just to get them off on the right foot."

"There are plenty of people around here who have never spotted their vote for any Democrat," my grandfather told me.

In a state where no Republican had won a statewide election for nearly fifty years, Howard Baker Jr. was the best prepared to try to change things. He had absorbed political skills by osmosis. His pistol-wielding grandmother, Lillie "Mother Ladd" Mauser, was the first woman sheriff of Roane County, distinguishing her three-month appointive position by single-handedly capturing four escaped prisoners who had shot the sheriff—her husband—in a jailbreak.

In 1938, Howard H. Baker Sr. was the Republican nominee for governor, and, in 1950, he was elected congressman from the second congressional district. Meanwhile, Howard Jr. had married the daughter of Senator Dirksen in 1951 and worked for a while in Washington, DC, on a Senate committee staff.

When I was ten years old, the senior Baker was elected to Congress, and my father took me to the courthouse to meet him. Mr. Baker gave me a dime, and I was certain that I had just met the most respected man I was ever likely to meet, other than my father and the pastor of our church.

* * *

Congressman Baker died on January 7, 1964, and the editor of the *Knoxville Journal,* Guy Lincoln Smith Jr., along with other leading Republicans, encouraged Baker Jr. to run to succeed his father. Junior declined, and his stepmother, Irene, the widow of Congressman Baker, was elected to succeed her husband.

"There ought to be a rule that when congressmen die, their widows should be buried with them," Smith grumbled.

Instead of running for his father's safe House seat, Baker announced his candidacy for the US Senate seat held by Democrat Ross Bass. Baker lost the 1964 race but surprised almost everyone by winning 47.4 percent of the vote.

In 1966, Baker decided to try again. His opponent was Governor Clement, who had defeated Bass in the Democrat primary. It was a great help for Baker to have Guy Smith in his corner, who was Tennessee's most powerful Republican of that era. Smith had once served as chairman of the state Republican Executive Committee, but the real source of his power was that since 1937, he had been the editor of Knoxville's morning newspaper, the *Knoxville Journal.*

The *Knoxville Journal* had descended from William "Parson" Brownlow's *Knoxville Whig and Rebel Ventilator,* a Civil War-era newspaper. In the *Whig,* the irascible Brownlow, who later became governor and US senator during Reconstruction, hurled insults in every direction—at preachers, bootleggers, Democrats, Methodists, and Confederates, among others.

Smith's *Journal* was the source of truth for East Tennessee Republicans, who constituted most of the Republicans living in the state at that time. Like Brownlow, Smith used his front page to reward candidates he favored and punish those he opposed. Holding court in his office on Gay Street, Smith was an imposing figure. Crusty, unsmiling, and unkempt in dress, he would lean back in his chair behind a long desk cluttered with boxes, newspapers, and assorted artifacts.

Usually, he had two Camel cigarettes lit at once. One would be burning in the ashtray on his desk. The other he would hold out to his side, extend his index finger, and deliberately flick its burning ashes into a trash can filled with wastepaper. When I visited Mr. Smith's office during the 1966 campaign, I found it difficult to focus on what he was saying because I was watching so closely to see if the ashes he was flicking would light a fire in the wastebasket—which had happened more than once.

In those days, Smith's office was, in fact, the headquarters for the Tennessee Republican party, in much the same way editor John Seigenthaler's Nashville *Tennessean* office was the headquarters for the state Democrat party. From this throne, Guy Lincoln Smith Jr. called the shots.

"When is one of you young SOBs going to get old enough to run against Brown Ayres?" he growled when Victor Ashe, later mayor of Knoxville, and I were visiting in his office during the Baker campaign.

Despite his sentiments about Congresswoman Baker, Guy Smith liked the Bakers. And so, for years, my daily breakfast reading of the *Journal* offered a steady diet of stories describing the importance of the Baker family. Insofar as I could tell, they were the First Family of Tennessee Republican politics and, therefore, I assumed, must preside over an impressive political machine.

* * *

Howard Baker Jr. agreed to meet with me when I flew home from New Orleans for Easter weekend in 1966.

In Baker's Knoxville law office, I found a handsome young man smoking cigarettes—that was Baker—and a rumpled fellow sitting beside him who had the deep and practiced voice of a television announcer. That was J. Hugh Branson, who actually had been a television announcer and now served as a strategist for Baker.

Branson occasionally would offer strategic wisdom.

"Sometimes you're up and sometimes you're down, but you're not always up," was one Branson maxim that did have a certain profundity.

Baker invited me to join his campaign when I was to leave Judge Wisdom in late July, but, because of a shortage of funds, I would have to be a volunteer. Remembering how I had started as a messenger with the judge and then found another job on Bourbon Street to make ends meet, I agreed.

Baker directed me across Gay Street to the first floor of an office building where I expected to find the impressive Baker political machine. Instead, I was greeted by Ruthie Edmondson, a pleasant widow I knew from Maryville. In a back room, Billy "Squire" Hamby, a justice of the peace from Anderson County, was smoking cigarettes and whispering confidential information into a telephone. Hamby was deeply engaged in conversations with those he described as "rats in the barn," the cagiest and most powerful election day operatives in mountain counties. From another room came an awful clacking noise. When I opened that door, there sat Victor Ashe, a Yale student home on vacation, who was pounding on a typewriter, writing press releases.

That was it. That was the Baker machine. I returned to New Orleans surprised, but thinking that, while I had no experience in politics other than what I had learned at Boys State and from my father and Judge Wisdom, apparently no one else in the Tennessee Republican Party had much more than I did.

I might be able to help the Baker campaign when I returned in July.

CHAPTER 9

Rats in the Barn

"Chapter II: There is no school for practical politics. Most people learn by jumping in feet first."

—LAMAR ALEXANDER'S LITTLE PLAID BOOK

Campaigning in East Tennessee. 1966.

ONE REASON HOWARD BAKER WON the Senate Republican primary on Thursday, August 4, 1966, was that he knew how to work with "rats in the barn," and his opponent did not.

The opponent was no pushover. Ken Roberts, a six-foot-five-inch lawyer, grew up in Kingsport in an Appalachian region rich with Republican voters. The Nashville-based Roberts effort was so well-funded and efficient that it could have been a model for a campaign for president of the state Junior Chamber of Commerce.

The Baker campaign, on the other hand, was inefficient and always short of funds, but it knew what to do in mountain counties where Republican "rats in the barn" reigned supreme. After work each afternoon, a small contingent of Knoxville lawyers would drive to rural counties to commune with these political savants to make arrangements for Baker's election.[1]

For these "rats in the barn," no joy exceeded the sport of politics. In general stores, in Republican Executive Committee meetings, and at

Lincoln Day dinners, they debated, polished, and practiced their craft. They anticipated the coming of election season as avidly as Volunteers looked forward to Football Time in Tennessee. They honed skills that had descended through generations ever since their ancestors had abandoned Tennessee when Tennessee abandoned the Union.

These were Lincoln Republicans and, since there were so few Rebels or Democrats to vanquish in eastern counties (Republican nominees often received 80 or even 90 percent of the vote), they concentrated their attention on one another. Factions formed and reformed based on grudges no one could remember. Someone was always out and someone was always in—and usually, it was not the same someone. Navigating these alliances was essential to winning elections. Baker's 1964 Senate race and his political lineage gave him a head start, but knowing how to work with "rats in the barn" made the difference.

One such "rat in the barn" was Riley Washington King, the manager of the Sevier County garbage dump. Riley not only had "passion for the downtrodden," as was said at his funeral, he knew where the downtrodden lived, how many family members they had, and how they voted. He understood that the vote of the downtrodden counted as much as the vote of the upscale, and that there were many more downtrodden.

After defeating an upscale lawyer to become Republican county chairman, Riley told his friends, "He said I didn't have this, and I didn't have that, and I didn't have the next thing, but I had the votes." Because he could get the votes, I was in the parade of office seekers who paid a courtesy call at the Solid Waste and Recycling Center. Riley had been elected county commissioner and had secured a job with the county, as did many of the other twenty-four commissioners. Together, they constituted a formidable congregation of "rats in the barn" who usually determined the results on election day.

Foremost among these "rats in the barn" was the congressman from the First Congressional District, James H. "Jimmy" Quillen. He was one of them, and he knew the rest of them. Together, these practitioners of the political arts formed alliances that monitored factions, nursed grudges, uplifted some candidates, and submerged others, until county by county, they became the most powerful force in the most Republican congressional district in the state.

Quillen, who eventually served thirty-four years, was an unctuous man and a suspicious and eccentric ally. Politicians wisecracked that Republican candidates needed a passport from him to enter his district. We cautioned our girlfriends and female staff members not to ride in elevators with Quillen or sit next to him because the congressman enjoyed pinching their bottoms and rubbing their legs. This was in an era when there was little retribution for such behavior.

The advent of strong Republican candidates for statewide races during the 1960s provided new opportunities for Quillen and his allies to wield influence. The candidates came calling, first for support in the primary, and then in the general election when it was necessary to run up a 75 percent margin of victory in the First Congressional District. A Republican nominee needed such a lopsided result to offset Democrat margins in Middle and West Tennessee.

Statewide Republican nominees who crossed Quillen paid a price, as former governor Winfield Dunn found out. Dunn, who, in 1986, had secured the Republican nomination once again, visited Quillen to make amends for Dunn's veto of a medical school in Quillen's district that was eventually built and named for the congressman.

When Dunn arrived to pay homage, Sevier County executive Larry Waters was also in the room.

"Jimmy, we have had differences, but I am the Republican nominee. I need your support and I am here to ask for it," Dunn said.

"Oh Winfield, let bygones be bygones. You know I *always* support Republicans from the courthouse to the statehouse to the White House," Quillen said.

Dunn left happy. Quillen turned to Waters.

"Can you believe that SOB thinks I'm going to support him?" Quillen said.

Dunn lost the First Congressional District and the governor's race.

* * *

The most important campaign day was the Saturday before the November general election. On that day, it was necessary for any statewide

Republican nominee to show off Congressman Quillen's support so they could roll up a big margin in the First Congressional District.

At 7:30 a.m. on Saturday, November 5, 1966, a large bus decorated with a banner proclaiming "Quillen–Baker Bandwagon" rolled up to the front of the Sevier County courthouse. Quillen's name, not Baker's, always came first. Hillbilly entertainers "Red 'n Fred" from Cas Walker's *Farm and Home Hour* television show in Knoxville had already been picking, fiddling, and singing long enough to draw a crowd.

The county Republican chairman introduced Quillen while "Red 'n Fred" packed their instruments and rushed ahead to the Dandridge courthouse to draw the next crowd. Gesturing extravagantly, the congressman stirred the electorate with colorful stories and improbable claims, even taking credit when the sun broke through the mountain mist.

After what seemed like too long, Quillen introduced Baker. The voters, surging forward to listen, were surprised to hear Baker's big voice issuing from such a small man. Baker obliged the crowd by offering even more colorful stories and more improbable claims. Long after the bandwagon drove away, the satisfied Republican faithful remained at the courthouse, arguing about whether Democrats would get as many as a thousand votes on Locust Ridge—if any at all.

The first year in which I was involved in a real political campaign was 1966. Saturday morning courthouse crowds were large back then. People wanted to touch their politicians when hearing their politics. The politicians responded by improving their stories as the bandwagon meandered among the hills and valleys to county seats.

At the first stop in Sevier County, Quillen had said, "I telephoned Defense Secretary Robert McNamara and he told me, 'Oh, Congressman Quillen, we don't have enough caskets to send home all of our boys who are being killed over there.'"

By late afternoon, the bandwagon had stopped at White Pine, Newport, Morristown, and Rutledge. At the Hawkins County courthouse in the upper end of the district, Quillen was moved to tears recounting his conversations with McNamara.

"I said, 'Bob, oh, tell me, Bob. Tell me when our boys will be coming home. And then Bob said, 'Oh, Jimmy, I don't have enough caskets,'" Quillen wailed.

As darkness descended, despite falling snow, hundreds gathered for a covered dish supper in the high school gymnasium in Mountain City. The speakers did not wind down until 10:00 p.m. Their stories had become as outrageous as campaign speeches a century earlier, when opposing candidates came only once to a town, spoke for three hours each, and then rode away together on horses to the next county, confident that there would be no one there who could contradict any of the tall tales they told in the last county.

Baker's general election opponent in November 1966 was Governor Clement. Baker's cool personality was better suited to the new campaign medium of television than Clement's fiery oratory. But Baker had a challenge. The August Democrat primary had attracted three times as many voters as the Republican primary did. This meant that, in November, Baker would have to persuade hundreds of thousands of Democrats to vote Republican.

This required an intricate political balancing act. Baker was courting White Democrat descendants of Civil War rebels in Middle and West Tennessee who couldn't stomach LBJ's Great Society and civil rights laws. At the same time, he had to develop a relationship with John Seigenthaler, the liberal editor of the Nashville *Tennessean*.

The courtship of Seigenthaler was so successful that, for the first time, the *Tennessean* assigned a staff member to report on a Republican statewide campaign. For this assignment, Seigenthaler chose Tom Ingram, a nineteen-year-old David Lipscomb College student who had written stories about the John Birch Society—an organization dedicated to finding a communist under every rock—and its unsuccessful efforts to take over Nashville's Republican party. Ingram's daily dispatches from the Baker bandwagon—usually displayed on the *Tennessean* front page next to a story about Clement—sent Democrat readers the surprising suggestion that this Republican candidate named Baker might not be all bad. Riding with Ingram on the bandwagon was the beginning of a crucial friendship in my political life.

To reassure Seigenthaler, Baker courted Black voters more than most Republican candidates had.[2] This taught me that that appealing to Black voters was not only the right thing to do, but also important to many White voters who thought Republicans should be appealing to Black voters. Baker's lesson fit my upbringing and beliefs, and influenced my actions later.

* * *

There was no money for weekly tracking polls, but Sam Newman, Baker's television producer, invented a solution. Newman organized volunteers to conduct Saturday surveys in metropolitan area shopping centers. The first shopping center surveys showed Baker with more strength than expected.

Those encouraging results brought to the forefront Dr. E. Carleton Bellows, president of the Tennessee Voter Institute, a pseudonym Newman had invented to sponsor his unscientific polling enterprise.

Each weekend, Newman, on behalf of the fictitious Dr. Bellows, would issue a press release announcing favorable results from the shopping center polls. This produced media coverage that helped get the talk right and added to the campaign's momentum.

About three weeks before election day, I sat down in the Andrew Johnson Hotel lobby after work for a cup of coffee with "Squire" Hamby, Baker's political organizer.

"Have you figured out what job you want?" Hamby asked.

Even though no one else was within forty feet, Hamby was whispering in a voice he usually reserved for strategic conversations with "rats in the barn."

"The senator has a good chance of winning," he said.

Hamby had begun calling Baker "senator" about two weeks earlier, I believe—the first person to do so.

"Is there a job that goes with this?" I asked with surprise.

I had not even thought about what came after the election. I expected to go back to practicing law in Knoxville.

"There are plenty of jobs, good ones. You might want one in Washington. I'm going to stay in Tennessee," Hamby said softly.

On the weekend before the election, I stood in the background as Baker presided over a press conference at the Knoxville airport.

"Will it be close?" a reporter asked.

"I will win by 100,000 votes," Baker said.

I was astonished by this extravagant prediction, which exceeded even the optimism of Dr. E. Carleton Bellows's shopping center polls. On the next Tuesday, November 7, when Baker did win by that margin, it taught me to show more respect for his political instincts. Two weeks later, he asked me to join his Washington, DC, Senate staff.

I reported Baker's offer to Harley Fowler, the elderly Knoxville Republican in whose law firm I had worked during the summer of 1965. He was not encouraging.

"If you go to Washington with Howard, you'll never come home," Fowler said.

CHAPTER 10

"The Luxury of an Unexpressed Thought."

*"Rule 33. Know when to stand up.
Know when to speak up. Know when to shut up."*

—**BENJAMIN DISRAELI,**
in *LAMAR ALEXANDER'S LITTLE PLAID BOOK*

Washington, DC. 1967–1969.

On Wednesday, January 4, 1967, I experienced the first indignity accorded new senators and their staff, namely being crammed into basement rooms while we waited months for permanent offices.

It was the second day of the 90th Congress. I had driven from my rented home in northwest Washington, DC, to the Old Senate Office Building, across from the Capitol. I parked in a temporary space, and walked into the basement where I took my temporary seat at a temporary table next to Senator Baker's temporary desk. Baker and his staff of fifteen were stuffed into a single room, along with Massachusetts Senator Edward Brooke and his staff. The two offices were separated only by partitions.

Another new senator was Oregon's Mark Hatfield. As a former governor, he was accustomed to more respect. So over the next few weeks, Senator Hatfield wandered the halls of the Senate office building and the

Capitol with a notebook, counting the rooms that had been assigned to Senator James O. Eastland of Mississippi, chairman of the Judiciary Committee. That number was thirty-four.

Hatfield indignantly reported this number to the Republican caucus and added that he believed that some person was actually living in one of Eastland's rooms. Hatfield had seen a tray of food placed on the floor outside the door of the room, then watched. As the door opened, two arms reached out and brought the food inside. Years later, when Hatfield was the Committee on Appropriations chairman, I asked him how many rooms were assigned to him. He smiled.

For a while, I was Baker's only legislative assistant. I was also his speechwriter, or at least I thought I was. There was one problem—Baker never said what I had written. I asked for a meeting.

"Senator, we have a problem. You never deliver the speeches I write. What am I doing wrong?" I asked.

"We have a perfect relationship. You write what you want to write and I'll say what I want to say," Baker responded.

Baker enjoyed that conversation so much that he must have told the story 200 times.

One of my assignments was writing Baker's maiden address. A senator's first floor speech is a valued tradition, and a large number of senators had come to listen. Baker took the floor on Thursday, March 9, 1967. I was seated by his side at a staff desk. He spoke earnestly, and for too long. After his remarks, Senator Dirksen, his father-in-law, walked over to congratulate him, and to teach him—and me—an important lesson.

"Well, Senator Dirksen what did you think of the speech?" Baker asked.

"Howard, occasionally you might enjoy the luxury of an unexpressed thought," Dirksen said.[1]

* * *

In those days, staffs were smaller and Senate life was slower and friendlier. Delaware Senator J. Caleb Boggs would arrive at his office at 8:00 a.m., open and answer mail, and by 8:30 a.m., be downstairs in the cafeteria having coffee with any staffer who wished to join him. Reporters of the stature of David Broder of the *Washington Post* and Bob Novak of the

Chicago Sun-Times would drop by the office and visit with staffers, even those as junior as I was.

While there were sixty-four Democrats and only thirty-six Republicans then the Senate was not as partisan as those numbers would suggest. Conservative Southern Democrats often voted with Republicans, and liberal Northern Republicans often voted with Democrats. Senators Ted Stevens, an Alaska Republican, and Edmund Muskie, a Maine Democrat, even carpooled together to and from the Capitol each day.

There were fewer weekend trips to home states. Many Senate families lived year-round in Washington, DC. Their children attended school there and they got to know one another during evening and weekend social events. Televised campaigning was in its infancy, so round-the-clock fund-raising to pay for TV ads was not necessary, leaving time for such family get-togethers.

In April of 1967, the *Washingtonian* magazine published an article about Democrat senators excelling at tennis. I suggested that Republican senators should show that they, too, could play tennis. I drafted a speech, and Baker issued a challenge to Democrats. We recruited the humorist Art Buchwald to serve as referee, and the match was set for Thursday, July 6.

The Republican tennis team included three new senators—Chuck Percy of Illinois, Brooke, and Baker—and one veteran, sixty-five-year-old Strom Thurmond of South Carolina. Thurmond may have been older, but he regularly demonstrated his vigor, first, by wrestling and pinning to a hearing room floor sixty-four-year-old Texas Senator Ralph Yarborough, and, second, by marrying Nancy Moore, a former Miss South Carolina who was twenty-two at that time.

"Strom, we all certainly hope that we can be here for your one-hundredth birthday party," Senator Robert Byrd of West Virginia said years later at Thurmond's ninetieth birthday celebration.

"Now, if you'll eat right, exercise, and take care of yourself, maybe you *can* be here," Thurmond retorted.

Thurmond remained in the Senate until he was one-hundred.

Despite Thurmond's fitness, there was a complication. Baker had assigned Thurmond to play doubles with Brooke. In 1948, Thurmond had been the segregationist Dixiecrat candidate for president, and Brooke was African American. When Thurmond found out he was to be teamed with a Black senator, his office called to say that Thurmond would not participate.

"I've gotta think of the folks back home. It's nothing against Senator Brooke, you understand," Thurmond told Baker.

Baker played with Brooke, and Thurmond teamed with Percy. The Democrats won the match.

* * *

In every era, one member of the Senate seems to rise above the rest.

In the 1960s, that senator was Dirksen, the Republican leader since 1959.

"In the Senate, the entire apparatus can be summed up in one word—Dirksen," Bryce Harlow wrote in a March 1966 letter to former President Eisenhower.[2]

Dirksen had arrived in the Senate in 1951 after unseating the Democrat Majority Leader Scott Lucas. His home was in Pekin, then a town of about 20,000 on the Illinois River, named because it was thought to be exactly on the opposite side of the world from Peking, China.

"There are a lot of senators who are worse than they look. Dirksen is the only one who is better than he looks," one colleague said, according to Dirksen's memoir.

Dirksen had a rumpled appearance and flowing white hair. Although he didn't need glasses to see, he wore large black-rimmed spectacles without lenses because he believed they made him look better on television. His gravelly voice sounded like a growl rumbling around in a basement, looking for a way to escape. And when that growl did escape, it commanded attention, whether recording Christmas stories, urging that the marigold become the national flower, or appearing in the "Ev and Charlie Show" press conferences with House Republican leader Charles Halleck.

Dirksen's sense of theater was unerring. When introduced to speak, he would pause strategically at the back of the room until the applause died down, and then amble toward the front, enjoying the need for the audience to continue to applaud. When he finally delivered his speech in that deep growl, it was a succulent work of art.

"I don't choose my words for what they mean, I choose them for how they taste," he would say.

I observed Dirksen carefully as I tagged along with Baker. On Saturday afternoons, I would sit next to Dirksen on the lawn outside his Virginia home as he tended gladiolas while taking calls from the White House. He never took a note from those telephone conversations, and would later repeat them with specificity on the Senate floor.

His skill at compromising to enact legislation was legendary.

"I consider myself a conservative—probably not as conservative as some, not as moderately liberal or liberally moderate as others," he said.

Democrat presidents relied on him. In October 1962, during the heat of Dirksen's reelection campaign, President Kennedy ostentatiously flew the Republican leader back to Washington, DC, in Air Force Two for advice about the Cuban Missile Crisis. Dirksen's relationship with President Johnson was even more intimate. Some mornings, Dirksen would arrive unannounced at the Johnson White House for breakfast. Sometimes, it was in the evening for a glass of whiskey. The Navy mess steward knew exactly how the senator's eggs were to be prepared and which bourbon he favored.

Senate observers eagerly anticipated the first public disagreement between Dirksen, the leader, and his son-in-law, the new senator. Baker selected an opportunity that would establish his independence in a way that showed respect for Dirksen. Baker, forty-one, teamed up with Senator Ted Kennedy, thirty-five, against two seventy-one-year-old grizzled lions—Dirksen, and Judiciary Committee Chairman Sam Ervin—whose Southern drawl, folksy ways, and bushy eyebrows disguised his Harvard degree.

The issue was whether or not state legislatures could gerrymander voters into oversized legislative districts. I wrote speeches helping Baker and Kennedy argue for "one man, one vote," in accordance with a recent Supreme Court decision. Dirksen and Ervin argued for the traditional states' rights position: that the federal government has no business interfering in state election laws. The rookies won, persuading seventy-one of their colleagues to join with them to defeat the veteran senators.

* * *

Dirksen was also the key player in the legislative saga that culminated in the "Civil Rights Act" of 1968. LBJ's tight relationship with the Republican leader provided the impetus for its passage.

Late one afternoon in early 1968, Baker was in his father-in-law's Capitol office when he heard one end of a telephone conversation.

"No, Mr. President, I cannot come down and have a drink with you tonight. I did that last night. And Louella is very unhappy with me," Dirksen was saying.

"About a half hour later, I heard a commotion in the hall outside Dirksen's office, and the president of the United States walked through the door, followed by a pair of beagles," Baker told me.

"Everett, if you won't come down and have a drink with me, I'm here to have one with you," President Johnson said.

The two disappeared into Dirksen's back office to discuss the "Fair Housing" civil rights bill that was then being crafted around a long table in his outer office.

For several weeks, the scene around that long table had resembled a legislative potluck supper, with everyone welcome to bring something for the feast. Senators from both parties brought stacks of amendments. How broad would the bill's ban be on racial discrimination in housing? Would the new law expand the 1964 "Civil Rights Act" that prohibited discrimination in employment? Would it speed up the Supreme Court's decision to desegregate schools? Senators and staffers were constantly coming and going, reviewing amendments, and searching for a formula that could achieve the sixty-seven votes that were needed to cut off debate and end the Southern Democrats' filibuster.

Years later, Baker's press secretary, Ed Miller, described the scene.

"Baker and Lamar worked long hours drafting and redrafting the language of the bill, submitting sections of it to the various interested parties. It all came down to a final meeting in Dirksen's office, in which a number of last-minute changes and insertions were agreed to by several GOP senators. As a secretary finished typing these new paragraphs, Lamar and I and some of Dirksen's staffers literally cut and pasted them into the bill. The 'Civil Rights Act' of 1968 was passed. Baker got very little credit for it, but it was well known among Senate insiders that his role had been crucial, and it established him as a major player among the leaders of both parties after only about a year and a half in the Senate," Miller said.

Twenty-nine Republican senators, including Baker, voted for the "Civil Rights Act" because of Dirksen's leadership. Only three voted "no."

On Thursday, April 11, 1968, President Johnson signed the Fair Housing legislation. Baker was in Tennessee, but New York Senator Jacob Javits's assistant invited me to attend the 1:45 p.m. White House ceremony.

I was more amused than impressed by what I saw there.

I wrote in my notes: "Speaker McCormack arrived before the president. He was stately but resembled a walking automaton. Senator Javits commandeered the middle seat in the front row. Senator Hart, who did much of the patient work on the bill, was crowded behind several legislative assistants to one side. The band played 'Hail to the Chief.' In came the president and Lady Bird, who looked beautiful. Following the president's remarks, all gathered and shoved and pushed to stand and watch him sign. It looked like a bunch of milling school children."

Dirksen died on September 7, 1969. I wrangled a seat on Air Force Two, which was carrying a planeload of senators to Illinois for the funeral. After landing in Peoria, we drove to Pekin. As we approached the small river town, children lined the streets, tossing yellow marigolds toward the cavalcade escorting the senator who had once told them Christmas stories.

* * *

Three years after the funeral, the senator who would have benefited most from Dirksen's admonition to "enjoy the luxury of an unexpressed thought" arrived in Washington, DC.

That senator was Joseph R. Biden Jr. He was friendly, garrulous, thirty years old, and newly elected from Delaware. In a body known for its long-winded orators, Biden soon became the champion. As chairman of the Foreign Relations Committee, he would often open a hearing with forty-five minutes of remarks, although the customary time was five minutes.

Senator Lindsey Graham, in a story that must be exaggerated, told me of how he and Biden once were seated across from each other on a six-hour military flight from Washington, DC, to London. It was early evening when the plane took off.

"I asked Joe a question just after we took off. He began answering. I leaned back in my seat and went to sleep. I woke up about the time we were landing in London, and Joe was still talking," is how Graham told the story.

On Friday, July 2, 2010, thirty-seven senators on a plane to West Virginia for Senator Robert C. Byrd's funeral organized a pool to guess which of twelve speakers would go on the longest. Twenty-one minutes was the lengthiest time predicted. Vice President Biden spoke for twenty-two.

The crowd at the three-hour outdoor ceremony applauded whenever Biden would wind down—which only encouraged him to tell another story. Senators in their seventies (at least three were eighty-six) looked as uncomfortable as nursing home residents wheeled out into the sun during the hottest part of the day. It seemed like an excellent way to make sure that at least one more senator departed life along with Byrd.

Obama, whose face showed impatience with Biden's remarks, spoke for eleven minutes. Even President Clinton limited himself to sixteen. The next day, when I read that the vice president was making an unexpected visit to Iraq, I wondered if Obama had sent him there as punishment for his long speech.

In December of 2012, after hearing Biden often refer to himself during remarks at Senator Daniel Inouye's memorial service, I added a new rule to my *Little Plaid Book*: "When asked to speak at a funeral, remember to mention the deceased as often as yourself."

CHAPTER 11

Sliding Into First

"We knew we were going to be married two months after we met."

—**HONEY, November 1968**

Washington, DC. 1967–1968.

SUMMERTIME SOFTBALL GAMES BETWEEN SENATORS' staffs are among the best ways for young people working in Washington, DC, to get to know one another.

Everyone plays—staffers, senators, executive branch workers, off-duty police, lobbyists, and other "ringers" recruited for their physical attributes, not all of which have to do with pitching, catching, and fielding.

These merry contests occur on weekdays after work on the National Mall, a greenway bordered by museums, art galleries, and monuments that extends between Independence and Constitution Avenues from the Capitol to the Washington Monument.

In the summer of 1967, Baker's staff was playing softball against Senator John Tower's staff when a stunning girl in red shorts on the Tower team slid into first base. Her name, I quickly found out, was Honey Buhler.

"Lamar says I slid into first base—which I say is crazy, because I never got a hit and I had no reason to be sliding into any base," Honey later said.

Of course, no one slides into first base, but I was so dazzled that I remember it that way. I was smitten. And—we won the game.

I am an average softball player, but after seeing Honey, I began to play softball in the way a peacock struts through a barnyard. My first at-bat resulted in a line drive over the left fielder's head, and, with blazing speed around the bases, I turned it into a home run. (*She must have noticed that,* I thought.) My second hit was a flat-out home run. (*There!*) Then I hit a triple. Then, another home run. Baker's team tromped Tower's, and we proceeded to the event for which the softball game was the excuse—the postgame party, where I pursued Honey, performing my best version of a desirable suitor.

Honey was lovely, bright, and always cheerful. She had grown up in the south Texas town of Victoria.

"I grew up outside of town, and we raised sheep and chickens. We had several small ranches, so I grew up riding horses," she said in an interview. "I was a very rambunctious little girl, willing to try just about anything. I remember one of my father's favorite stories was about when I kicked him in the shin. Once, I climbed up on the roof. My father gave me a BB gun for Christmas one year, and I did some shooting with him when I was younger. I've always been an early riser, and I used to spend weekend mornings with my father rounding up cattle because it got me out of the house at 5:00 a.m. And everyone else could sleep," she said.

Honey was captain of the cheerleading squad at St. Stephen's Episcopal School in Austin. "[She was] the prettiest girl in the school," according to a male classmate.

Her mother's preference led Honey to Smith College in Northampton, Massachusetts, whose graduates included Nancy Reagan and Barbara Bush—but no men.

"I really wanted to go to Stanford, but they weren't taking Texas girls then, or at least not many," Honey told me. Honey made lifetime friends at Smith, but never really liked the school.

Smith was all girls—a new and unwelcome experience for Honey. And it was culturally unlike south Texas—too liberal for her taste. She helped found a Republican Club, and campaigned vigorously for Barry Goldwater. Classmates nicknamed her "Honey the Hawk."

"I felt that once we had made a commitment in Vietnam that we should follow through and get it over with, rather than do a halfway job. I felt the protests were hampering those efforts," she said.

Two years later, she campaigned for liberal Republican Senator Ed Brooke's reelection in Massachusetts.

Honey majored in American Studies and graduated in May, 1967.

"I had two job offers. One was to go to Europe and work for ITT, and one was to go to Washington to work for Senator Tower. I went to Washington. I just felt that was more my calling," she said.

From the night of the Baker–Tower softball game, for me, it was love at first sight. On Sunday, October 1, 1967, I typed and mailed a letter to my parents.

"As far as I know, I will be home on October 13 and go to the UT-Ga-Tech game on October 14, then hike up [Mt.] LeConte on the 15th. I will probably bring a date from here for the weekend, and I wonder if we could put her up at the house. I should hope you wouldn't go to a lot of trouble for it all. My date will be a girl named Honey Buhler, from Victoria, Texas, who works for Senator Tower. I hope she can hike," I wrote.

Not only could Honey hike, she scampered up 6,593-foot Mt. Le Conte well ahead of me and four friends who went along with us. When she and I returned to Maryville, my mother made sure that we stayed in separate bedrooms.

With our different backgrounds, I had wondered how comfortable Honey would feel in East Tennessee because she knew that it was where I intended to spend my life. But she loved the Great Smoky Mountains, especially when the fall colors were at their peak. She charmed my parents.

"The whole experience was beautiful," she wrote in a thank-you note to my mother.

Later, she said, "I thought Lamar was very bright and sincere, interesting. But Tennessee? What a funny place to live. Did he have a washing machine on his front porch? A few months later, I visited his family and climbed Mt. Le Conte. I fell in love with the entire state."

At dinner back in Washington on October 26 (the day John McCain was shot down in Vietnam), Honey gave me John Steinbeck's book, *America and Americans,* with a note.

"To Lamar, because you too appreciate what America and Americans are, and because you, like John Steinbeck's America, will always go forward. With love, Honey."

When spring arrived in Washington, Honey and I would carry our lunches outside the Old Senate office building and sit and talk on the grass amidst the daffodils and cherry blossoms. When we were apart, we would have long telephone conversations the way high school sweethearts do, even when we had nothing to say.

* * *

Howard Baker was not happy when I told him told him in May of 1968 that I was leaving his staff to go to work for Citizens for Nixon–Agnew.

"I could have called John Mitchell. I could have gotten you a better job," Baker said.

I instantly realized that I had made the kind of amateurish mistake a twenty-seven-year-old thrust into high-level politics can make. I was embarrassed, not because the senator might have gotten me a better job, but because I knew he wanted the best for me and was hurt. I apologized for being so clumsy.

John Mitchell, Richard Nixon's dour, pipe-smoking law partner, ran the *real* Nixon campaign in New York City. That is where the better jobs were. The Citizens group was housed in Washington's historic, newly refurbished Willard Hotel, so near the White House that the word "lobbyist" was coined to describe the favor seekers who would congregate in its lobby.

The Citizens campaign had a double purpose. The first was to attract support from voters, especially Southerners, who weren't yet comfortable labeling themselves Republicans. Second, the Citizens campaign was a convenient repository for anyone John Mitchell didn't want around the real campaign.

But the Willard Hotel operation also included a number of Nixon loyalists whom Mitchell did trust. One of those was John W. Warner, a debonair Marine captain who first married Elizabeth Taylor before becoming a senator from Virginia. Another was Tom Evans, a Nixon law partner who, in May 1968, gave me a job. That job had the high-sounding title of National Director of Planning for United Citizens for Nixon–Agnew. My assignment was to create hundreds of Nixon Clubs that would attract Democrats and Independents, especially in the South.

At the time, my roommates and I were living in a large three-story mansion at the corner of Foxhall and Klingle Streets in Northwest Washington. We called it "Klub Klingle." There always were at least five roommates—not counting women who would occasionally spend the night—and plenty of late-night activities. One roommate was Glover Roberts, from Gulfport, Mississippi, who was a minor Klub Klingle celebrity himself because his first cousin was Jimmy Buffett.

Glover told me there were two young men in Mississippi, both former cheerleaders at Ole Miss (there, that's considered a high honor), about whom everybody said, "he will one day grow up to be the governor of Mississippi." That prediction was the highest possible compliment for a promising young man, since, at that time, Mississippi had a limited number of avenues that could lead to success.

One of the young men everyone was sure would grow up to be governor was another of our roommates, Trent Lott of Pascagoula. After a few months, Lott moved out of Klub Klingle, alleging it was "too rowdy." The other promising young man from Mississippi was Thad Cochran of Jackson, a genial, baseball- and piano-playing lawyer. I persuaded Thad to become Mississippi cochairman of Citizens for Nixon–Agnew, and my job for that state was done. The predictions about these two didn't miss the mark by much. Cochran, in 1978, and Lott, in 1988, became the first two Mississippi Republicans elected to the United States Senate since Reconstruction.

Washington was always filled with talented young men and women with political aspirations, and many found their way into the Citizens campaign. One I hired was Brian Lamb, who later created C-SPAN. There were also more prominent citizens. To me, the most impressive of these was Bud Wilkinson of Oklahoma, then the country's most celebrated college football coach. Wilkinson was smiling, approachable, and inspiring. I could see why any young athlete would want to play for him.

The year 1968 was a blur of excitement, tragedy, and turmoil. On Sunday evening, March 31, Honey and I were in Baltimore watching President Johnson on television with our friends Carole and John Sergent.

"There is a division in the American house," the president said, and declared that he would not run for reelection.

That threw presidential politics into chaos. A few days later, on Thursday, April 4, in Memphis, Martin Luther King Jr. was shot dead while standing on the second-floor balcony outside his room at the Lorraine Motel. Riots erupted in major cities, including Washington. At about 5:00 a.m. on Wednesday, June 5, I telephoned Senator Baker to tell him that I had just heard that Robert Kennedy had been shot at the Ambassador Hotel in Los Angeles. Kennedy died the next day.

Honey and I did not see each other much that summer and fall. She was campaigning with Tower. I was busy planning the Citizens for Nixon–Agnew national meeting in Indianapolis. The Democratic National Convention in late August in Chicago turned into a street riot, with Mayor Richard Daley's police fighting protesters while Hubert Humphrey emerged as the challenger to Nixon. The country was in flames. Alabama Governor George Wallace ran as an independent candidate winning 13.5 percent of the vote, but not enough to deny Nixon a victory on Tuesday, November 5.

* * *

After the election, Senator Baker invited me to return to his staff while I decided what to do next. One evening in late November, Honey and I drove to a restaurant on M Street in Georgetown. Over a dinner of manicotti, I made one of the clumsiest romantic proposals of all time.

"I'm out of a job. We have some time. Would you like to get married?" I asked.

"Yes," Honey answered.

Bette Jo Buhler was both delighted and horrified when she learned that she had just six weeks to plan for the first marriage among her five children.

In December, Honey and I were about to have dinner in a northwest Washington hotel when we saw Bud Wilkinson and his wife, Mary. They invited us to join them. Over dinner, Wilkinson discovered that I was without a job.

"I'll call Bryce Harlow," he said.

That seemed to me to be a generous offer, but one that had little chance of success. Nixon had appointed Harlow as the first staff member of his new administration. While I had never met Bryce Harlow, it seemed like everyone else in Washington had, and, on both sides of the aisle, they respected him. The newspapers said he was receiving two hundred telephone calls a day.

Harlow took Wilkinson's call, agreed to give me an interview, and, to my surprise, hired me to be his executive assistant in the White House beginning Monday, January 20, 1969. My salary was to be $20,000 a year. Based on the promise of this new largesse, I persuaded Commerce Union Bank in Nashville to loan Honey and me enough money to buy our first home—a three-bedroom white frame structure near American University in northwest Washington.

This has to be the luckiest month of my life, I thought. Here I was, landing a job that every young Republican in Washington would want, buying our first home, and, best of all, marrying the spectacular girl in red shorts who slid into first base at the Senate softball game in the summer of 1967.

CHAPTER 12

Cultural Collision on Texas Roads

*"I think he's very interested in politics.
Don't you think you'll get tired of that?"*

—**BETTE JO BUHLER, Honey's mother, November 1968**

Victoria, Texas. January 4, 1969.

Our wedding in Victoria, Texas at 5:00 p.m. on Saturday, January 4, 1969, was a collision of cultures.

Following the discovery of oil in Victoria during the 1930s, this small town became one of the richest per capita in America. An example of its wealth occurred when members of the O'Connor family tried to build a swimming pool in their backyard twice, but, to their dismay, struck oil each time. The family invited a Catholic priest to bless a third try. This time, they were lucky. They did not strike oil and were able to build their swimming pool.

Honey's father, Frank Buhler Jr., had inherited large ranches with no oil or gas, but he did have banking interests and real estate developments that provided a substantial income. And Frank liked to have a good time. For several mornings before breakfast, during a week of wedding festivities, Frank served gin fizzes to my roommates at the Christopher Inn. The motel sign accurately proclaimed, "Welcome Frank Buhler Party." At lunches at the Victoria Country Club and at receptions and dinners at nice homes, Honey's mother, Bette Jo, entertained with Texas beef, caviar, and fine wine. This was my first experience with caviar.

My parents lived a different life. They had been teachers, owned no ranches, had no business interests, received no inheritance, and earned modest incomes. They were hardworking, straitlaced Presbyterian teetotalers who were wary even of Maryville's St. Andrew's Episcopal Church because it served real wine with communion. They had never even considered joining a country club. Being sensitive to such a difference in family incomes, when Frank Buhler sent Andy Alexander the bill for the rehearsal dinner at Victoria Country Club, an event traditionally hosted by the groom's parents, he privately discounted the amount to $127.

Our families had other cultural differences. In October 1967, during my first visit to Victoria, Frank woke Honey and me at 4:00 a.m., and drove us in his Jeep along muddy roads on his Redbud Ranch. (Redbud once was Red*bug* but the Texas Redbug has a disagreeable habit of crawling up your leg and biting you on the crotch, and no one wanted to be reminded of that. So the ranch name was changed, even though the redbud tree does not prosper in South Texas soil as well as the mesquite and prickly pear do.) We arrived at a deer stand twenty feet high in a live oak tree. Honey and I climbed in. Frank sped away. I marveled at a father who would offer a young man he had just met such an opportunity to be alone under the stars with his alluring daughter.

On other days, Frank would load a half dozen yelping bird dogs into cages on a trailer hitched to his Jeep, and we would go quail shooting or, more accurately, dog hollering. This escapade consisted mostly of Frank shouting at impatient dogs who would be set free, and then misbehave by stumbling over the quail they were supposed to be pointing toward, or by running so far away that it took the rest of the hunt to find them.

My most vivid memory of those hunting and shooting expeditions is of careening with Frank down muddy, rutted ranch roads in his heavy-treaded, big-wheeled Jeep that was hitched to a bumping trailer full of howling dogs. Our caravan frequently ground to a halt, stuck in the mud. Correcting this predicament required hooking a chain from the winch mount on another Jeep to the stuck Jeep and yanking it out of the mud, which splattered in all directions. Then, Frank would resume careening until we were stuck again, and the extraction procession would begin anew. Frank was skilled at these activities, having practiced them almost daily for years.

"What does your daddy do?" a third-grade teacher once asked Honey's sister, Jessica.

"Daddy is a hunter," Jessica replied.

During the season, quail shooting was an every morning pursuit for Frank and his buddies. They recorded in a notebook the precise number of birds each had shot. Since I had rarely shot a gun except in Boy Scout camp, I performed poorly in all these Texas tests of manhood, but found that I enjoyed shooting quail, which is something I have continued to do.

Over the years, I have learned that in Washington, DC, people at lunch talk about politics. In New York City, they talk about money; in Silicon Valley, it's startups; in Nashville, it's songwriting—and in Texas, they talk about what they have shot.

* * *

One area of consensus between the Buhlers and the Alexanders was Republican politics.

My parents were congenital Republicans, descended from Lincolnites. The Buhlers' Republicanism was of a more recent vintage. Upon moving to South Texas after World War II, Bette Jo was aghast, first, at the 100-degree summer heat, which caused her to drive her station wagon full of children every June to her father's home in Hayden Lake, Idaho, where the temperature was cool and the air was dry.

Her second shock was experiencing Lyndon Johnson's politics. She considered his ascent to power and the exercise of it to be corrupt. Frank approached politics with a businessman's practicality. Bette Jo was a reformer. Like the Wisdoms in Louisiana, she saw how a century of one-party rule had bred backscratching, skullduggery, and mediocre government.

She set out to change things. Employing her considerable social and organizational skills, she helped build the Republican Party of Texas, serving on its state executive committee with John G. Tower of Wichita Falls, a five-foot-four-inch, self-assured Navy veteran, professor, and country music radio announcer who was the son of a Methodist minister.

Tower had returned to Texas from a year of study at the London School of Economics, with affectations in manner and speech that included tailored suits and carrying cigarettes in a silver case tucked in his jacket pocket. Other than his boots and his imposing name, John G. Tower did not present the image one might envision of a Texas United States senator. But on Thursday, June 15, 1961, after LBJ was elected vice president, Tower became the first Republican US senator from the South since Reconstruction.

Bette Jo cochaired the Texas Republican Party, and, in 2001, the National Republican Congressional Committee named her Republican of the Year. She also organized a multi-county health clinic based in Victoria and hosted parties. On a bus traveling to a party she was organizing, she fell ill, and died at home soon thereafter, on Monday, January 9, 2017. She was ninety-five.

Our two families were also bound together by the affinity that naturally exists between Texans and mountain Tennesseans. Tennesseans believe that we founded Texas. As governor in 1986, I planted a redbud tree at the Alamo in honor of the thirty-two Tennesseans who died there—more than from any other state. The most famous of them was Davy Crockett, who, after losing a West Tennessee congressional election, mounted the courthouse steps and said what every losing candidate has always wanted to say to voters who reject him.

"I'm going to Texas, and you can go to hell," he said.

A former Tennessee governor, Sam Houston, proved that a judicious retreat can sometimes cause more cities, streets, and airports to be named after you than making a brave stand that leads to your death. Houston pulled back his army of Texas revolutionaries after its loss at the Alamo, lured Mexican General Santa Anna to San Jacinto, defeated the Mexican army, and captured Santa Anna.

Language is culture, and there is great similarity between patterns of speech in the East Tennessee mountains and Texas. I have taught our children and grandchildren that, if you want to be a bona fide East Tennessean—or Texan—you must learn how to say the following sentence properly.

"It's a right bright night for a nice knife fight."

Properly saying those ten words requires pronouncing the "i" in a flat way, as if you were saying "dye," that is. "It's a ryte bryte nyte for a nyce knyfe fyght." (If you are not from either East Tennessee or Texas, it is unlikely that you will have any idea of what I am talking about.)

At first impression, it would seem that Texans with their bravado, and East Tennesseans with our reticence are different species, but our personalities are mainly products of the physical environments in which we live. East Tennesseans reside in valleys and coves shadowed by ridges as high as 6,600 feet; most Texans live on wide-open plains. An East Tennessean will prefer a sheltered cabin by a creek in the woods; a Texan will prefer the longest view possible from his front porch. When he first meets you, an East Tennessean will give you some space; a Texan will tell you more than you want to know.

Summing it up, a Texan is no more than an East Tennessean with broader horizons, and, after a while, both usually find one another congenial—as did the Buhlers and the Alexanders.

* * *

The rector who performed our marriage at Victoria's Trinity Episcopal Church later ran off with a parishioner who was not his wife.

Honey was laughing, happy, and prettier than ever. After the wedding reception at Victoria County Club, she and I escaped my roommates, boarded a plane supplied by her father, spent the night in Austin, and flew to Cozumel for a honeymoon.

One day, we hired a battered, single-engine plane with a pilot who flew us to the ruins of Tulum, landed in a grass field, and flew away, promising to return. He did return, but on our flight back over the Gulf of Mexico, the door on my side of the plane flew open.

"*Cerrada, cerrada!*" the pilot shouted, and I suddenly had the job of holding the door closed until we landed in Cozumel.

We arrived back in Washington on Saturday, January 11, and took a taxi to our new home. As we stepped onto the front porch, we heard noises. When I opened the door, the house appeared to have been ransacked. Thinking a burglary was underway, I called the police, who arrived quickly, pulled out pistols, stormed the house, and discovered a squirrel that had been locked inside for the ten days of our absence, chewing windows and furniture. The police chased the squirrel out of the house and left. Honey and I settled down amidst the damage for our first married night in our new home.

It would be ten days until President Nixon's inauguration and eleven days before I would move into the West Wing of the White House for my new job with Bryce Harlow.

"Andy was the most beautiful boy on campus," one of Dad's classmates told me. Flo Rankin met Andrew Alexander in 1931 during her one semester at Maryville College. Both were from families that had lived for six generations in the Tennessee foothills of the Great Smoky Mountains. They saw each other only three more times before their marriage in 1939. I was born the next year. Both Andy and Flo became teachers.

"God gave us this beautiful day to rake leaves," Mother would rule on sunny October afternoons when the maples, oaks, sweet gums, and poplars along Ruth and Oak Park were red and golden and burning leaf piles scented the air. Such rulings led me also to see God as responsible for making the hedge grow high, so I could cut it, and making the white paint peel off our frame house, so I could paint it. In pronouncing rules, mother had a habit of improvising on God's intentions.

"Stop the monkey business. Your left hand is jumping all around. You've been playing that Jerry Lee Lewis again!" Miss Lennis Tedford, my piano teacher, said. I began lessons at age three. When I was five, I performed on a nine-foot Steinway in my first recital. After learning that Mozart had composed his first minuet at age five and his first opera at eleven, I reasoned that if he could do those things at those ages, perhaps I could amount to something, too.

At age fourteen, with these intrepid explorers, I had tasted for the first time the pleasures of Red Man chewing tobacco. When I crawled from the fifty-six-degree cave into the hot July sun, the change in temperature made me so pukey sick that I never chewed again. I'm second from the left in the back row.

Photo courtesy of Vanderbilt University

"I have never had three boys as fast as they are. Run one hundred yards," the Vanderbilt track coach said to me one day in 1960 as I was exercising on the university track. I did. "10.1 seconds. Remarkable," he said, looking at a big stopwatch. "Why don't you be the fourth?" The next year our 440-yard relay team set a school record. (I have always thought that Coach Herc Alley fudged my time to recruit his fourth runner.) Running track taught me this lesson: join a team with people better than you are. I'm in the center, back row.[1] *Courtesy of Vanderbilt University.*

"Our trombone player's going back to Tennessee, but he's not a real trombone player," the clarinet player told beer drinkers at Your Father's Mustache in New Orleans on a hot August night in 1966. I was leaving my clerkship with Judge John Minor Wisdom to work in Howard Baker's senate campaign. I was not a real law clerk either. The judge was paying me a $300 a month messenger's salary which is why I needed a second job on Bourbon Street.

Saturday morning courthouse crowds were big in November, 1966, when Congressman Jimmy Quillen (speaking) and Howard Baker (behind Quillen) campaigned in mountain counties, competing to tell the most outrageous tales. Country comedian Archie "Grandpappy" Campbell stands between them. Pickin' and singin' by hillbilly musicians Red 'n' Fred had attracted the crowd. In those days, people wanted to touch their politicians when hearing their politics. It was high entertainment and my first exposure to a real political campaign.

Eighteen months after Honey and I met during a senate softball game in the summer of 1967, we were married on Saturday, January 4, 1969, in Victoria, Texas. Two weeks later, on January 21, the day after President Nixon's inauguration, I went to work for Bryce Harlow in the White House fifty feet from the Oval Office. Joy and Howard Baker hosted a reception for us at their Washington, DC home, where Sen. Baker took this photograph.

Nashville Banner Archives, Special Collections Division, Nashville Public Library

"Nixon's resignation puts Watergate behind us," I told Honey in August 1974, after winning the Republican nomination for governor. I was wrong. A Democrat congressman already was offering himself as a "Ray of Blanton Sunshine" to the tune of a Coca-Cola commercial. Although Ray Blanton had an unsavory reputation, he was a Democrat. In November, I lost badly. "They come out of the hills, people we hadn't seen voting in fifteen years. It was too many Democrats, mad about Watergate," one supporter told me.

"What is he thinking? He'll be hit by a truck," my mother said—and on the twelfth day of my walk across Tennessee, a white pickup truck did hit me. I picked myself up and resumed my 1,022-mile, six-month journey. Every day I wore my red and black plaid shirt and tried to shake a thousand hands. I spent the night with seventy-three families, eating their meals and attending their ball games and church services. The walk made me a better candidate and a better governor.

Photo courtesy of Robin Hood

"People laugh about the red and black shirt," Honey said. "Lamar and I picked out the shirt at a local army surplus store and we made that decision together. Everybody wears one of those shirts and if you are going hiking, you are likely to wear a plaid shirt, not a blue suit, so this was just a logical thing."

Along my six-month walk, I auctioned my plaid shirts to raise campaign funds. At first, $25 was a good price. In Columbia, after television ads of my walk had started, a supporter paid $500. Then, guitar-playing Jerry Reed of Smokey and the Bandit *fame began showing up at campaign events wearing his plaid shirt. Sales and prices soared. In this October 1982 photo, Jerry and I are performing during my reelection campaign.*

"Mama don't 'low no washboard playin' 'round here," sang the four students who had dropped out of the University of Tennessee to form Alexander's Washboard Band. From the back of a flatbed truck, at high school assemblies and at rallies, I sang along while playing the washboard—and sometimes the trombone. Then I would deliver a speech and walk on to the next campaign stop. Three of the boys walked with me while the fourth drove the truck.

Photo by Nancy Warnecke for USA Today Network via Imagn Images.

"This is the kind of thing where 100 things could go wrong and 99 of them probably will," I told my chief of staff. No American had ever done what we were about to do—but I knew that I had to do it. On Wednesday, January 17, 1979, Democrat leaders swore me, a Republican, into office three days early to stop Gov. Ray Blanton from pardoning prisoners who had paid cash for their release. As I talk to reporters after taking the oath, Honey holds the family Bible while Leslee, seven, Drew, nine, and Kathryn, five, stand in front and Lt. Gov. John Wilder, Speaker Ned McWherter, and Chief Justice Joe Henry watch.

"Walk in Parades. If it's the Mule Day parade, walk at the front," Lamar Alexander's Little Plaid Book *advises. For many years, our family walked at the front of the parade when one hundred thousand mule lovers celebrated in* Columbia, Tennessee. *Usually, I invited local cub scouts to walk with us, making it less likely that some unhappy citizen along the route would shout something unpleasant at me.*

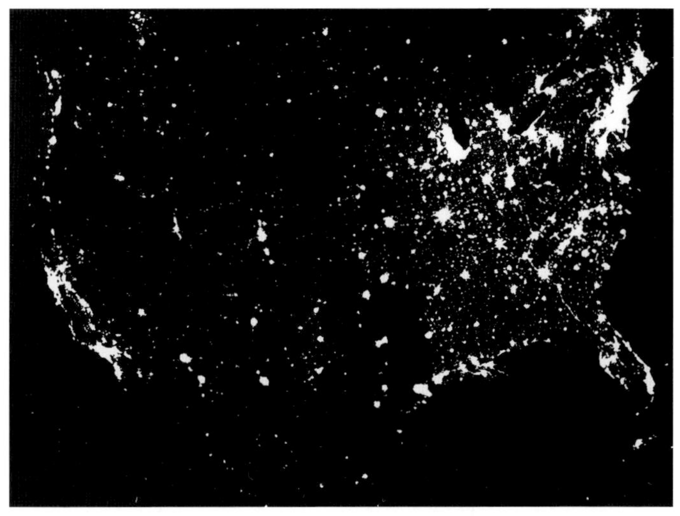

Photo courtesy of NASA

"Where is Tennessee?" the Nissan chairman asked at dinner in Tokyo in November 1979, as he studied this satellite photograph of the US with all its lights on at night. "Right in the middle of the lights," I said, pointing to the center of a brightly lit nation. This became the most important map in Tennessee's future helping to persuade Nissan and other auto companies to locate plants in a centrally located state with a right to work law, thus reducing shipping costs of millions of cars and trucks and avoiding problems with organized labor.

"The other fella might be right," Howard Baker would say. Sen. Baker inspired me to help him build a two-party political system in Tennessee. His governing style made him a popular and effective senate leader and taught me lessons about how to make every day count in a public life. His pragmatic ways were also a big part of what the Tea Party didn't like about me. Howard Baker had more influence on my life than anyone outside my own family.

"The governor can only play in the key of C," guitarist Chet Atkins joked when I played a piano duet with Floyd Cramer during a benefit concert in November 1981, at East Tennessee State University which also included saxophonist Boots Randolph. I asked the legislature to appropriate funds to support Tennessee's symphonies and community orchestras and then I performed with them in twenty-seven concerts to raise more money. I played the piano at the Grand Ole Opry, too, usually accompanying Roy Acuff, who sometimes introduced me as "Larry."

Photo courtesy of Bill Welch

It was the closest I ever came to feeling like a Beatle. On a warm Memphis evening in June 1982, two hundred and fifty thousand people lined the banks of the Mississippi River for the annual "Sunset Symphony." Wearing a white tuxedo over my red and black plaid shirt, I banged out Jerry Lee Lewis's "Great Balls of Fire" while standing up, tore off my jacket, and kicked the piano bench off the stage.

"Governor, would you please get out of the way so we can see her?" a woman shouted at me at the opening of Dollywood in 1986. Dolly Parton used her celebrity to provide books to millions of children, to help victims of fire in her home county, and to provide funding to speed up a COVID vaccine. The Little Plaid Book *suggests: "If you want to be noticed, don't ride in a convertible with Dolly Parton."*

"Rooster today, Featherduster tomorrow." On the first floor of the Tennessee State Capitol, there is space for only eight portraits of former governors. That means that when a retiring governor's portrait is hung, an earlier governor must be moved to the basement. This is my portrait, painted by Ann Street in 1986, on its way to the basement.

"It helps to talk a story," Alex Haley told me three weeks before Christmas 1987, on a cargo freighter far out in the Pacific. After dinner, we would climb to the second deck, admire the stars, and talk about books we were writing. Alex would practice a phrase and then polish it, judging my reaction to each serving just as musical performers and politicians listen to audiences to determine what resonates. Ten years earlier, almost nine of ten Blacks and more than seven of ten Whites had watched at least one episode of Alex Haley's Roots *on the ABC network.*

"We've got to get out of here," Honey said one night at the dinner table after seven years in the governor's residence. "I mean really out of here, a long way away. We need some space, to see ourselves from another perspective. We need to get to know each other again." So on the day I left office in January 1987, our family with three teenagers and a seven-year-old flew to Australia for six months off. "The others are running for president and you're running for the other side of the world," one reporter protested.

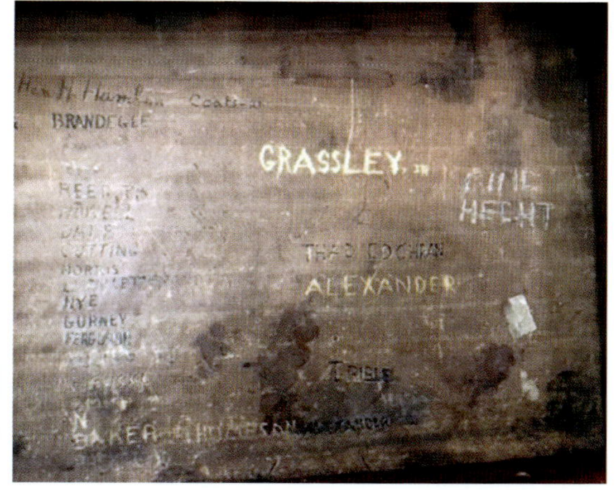

I chose a desk on the senate floor once used by Howard Baker and then Fred Thompson. During a late-night session in 2018, I followed the tradition of scratching my last name in the drawer of the desk next to their names (lower left of photograph). I actually scratched my name twice since the first time it was nearly invisible.

"It's my positive addiction," Honey said about her love of running. She usually ran two to three miles a day, up to twenty-five miles a week—by the governor's residence, around the Emperor's palace in Tokyo, along the sidewalks of Sydney, up and down mountain roads, between rows in soybean fields during a campaign stop. In 2005, we did something she had always wanted to do: climb Mount Kilimanjaro. She and I camped at fourteen thousand feet while Kathryn and Will climbed to the top.

"Go Tell It on the Mountain" was the tune that Virginia Democrat Sen. Tim Kaine played on his harmonica as I played the piano in the atrium of the Hart Office Building on Saturday afternoon, December 16, 2020. The senate had passed a resolution asking me to play Christmas carols. A piano had been moved in. It was the last workday of a contentious session. Trump would not concede the election. Tempers were hot. Word spread. Soon, singing senators and staff filled seven floors of balconies. There was a good feeling all around.

CHAPTER 13

Fifty Feet from the Oval Office

"Rule 296. If someone on behalf of the president asks you to do something for the president, ask to speak with the president."

—*LAMAR ALEXANDER'S LITTLE PLAID BOOK*

Washington, DC. 1969–1970.

On Tuesday, January 21, 1969, the day after President Nixon's inauguration, I drove my Mustang to the back entrance between the White House and the Executive Office Building and showed my pass to the guard.

I parked outside the West Wing and walked through its basement entrance. In an office on my right, leaning over a desk, studying documents and smoking cigarettes, sat General Alexander Haig, executive assistant to National Security Advisor Henry Kissinger. I showed my pass to a second guard, turned left, walked along walls already adorned with large photographs of President Nixon and his family, walked upstairs, turned right, and entered Bryce Harlow's spacious office.

This was where I would be working.

In the Tennessee mountains, your status is measured by the size of your smokehouse. In the White House, status is measured by the distance of your office from the Oval Office. Harlow had chosen a large room in the West Wing about fifty feet from the Oval Office. Over the years, it has become the vice president's office.

Harlow had his choice of offices because he was Nixon's first staff appointment—Assistant to the President for Legislative Affairs, the same job Harlow had for Eisenhower. The obsession with proximity to the Oval Office explains a lot of White House behavior. For example, why Chief of Staff H.R. "Bob" Haldeman offended Nixon's longtime secretary, Rosemary Woods, by taking the office just outside the Oval Office for himself, and relegating Woods to the basement. And why, after four months, Haldeman drove Vice President Agnew out of his office in the southwest corner of the West Wing so Haldeman could have that office for himself.

Lust for proximity explains why Henry Kissinger found a way to maneuver his office from the basement to the first floor next to Harlow's office. More than that, while Harlow was on vacation, Kissinger commandeered an even more prized status symbol—Harlow's private bathroom. Working with Haldeman, Kissinger sealed off the bathroom in Harlow's office and created a door to the hall that led to Kissinger's new first-floor office.

Harlow's new job had begun with a presidential eruption. Just a week after Nixon announced Harlow's appointment, a telephone call came from President Lyndon B. Johnson.

"Doesn't the SOB know that we have one president at a time?" Johnson shouted to Harlow.

President-elect Nixon had been making public statements on foreign affairs and Johnson was furious. So LBJ had called to complain to the person he knew best at Nixon headquarters.

While President Johnson continued his telephone tirade, Harlow's secretary interrupted.

"Mr. Harlow, President Eisenhower is on the phone and wants to speak with you *now*," she said.

With the current president shouting on one line and the former president holding on another, President-elect Nixon's aide, Larry Higby, rushed in.

"Mr. Harlow, Mr. Harlow! Mr. Nixon wants to see you in his office... immediately!" Higby exclaimed.

It seemed that everyone in Washington, DC, including presidents, wanted a piece of Bryce Harlow.

Harlow had first arrived in Washington in September 1938, to take a job on the House of Representatives library staff so he could finish his thesis on the Ways and Means Committee. He intended to return home to teach, but in 1941, five months before the bombing of Pearl Harbor, he joined the congressional relations staff of Army Chief of Staff General George C. Marshall.

One of Harlow's skills was flawless stenography.

"I was a popular fellow in a roomful of generals giving orders, because I was the only one who could write the orders down as fast as the generals were giving them," he told me.

In 1946, after the war, he moved back to Oklahoma to the family publishing company. But only a year later, the Republican chairman of the House Armed Services Committee lured him back to Washington for a second time. That was when he first met California Congressman Richard Nixon.

"Harlow was one of a kind. There will never be another one like him," Nixon wrote in a 1987 letter to me. "I vividly remember seeing him in 1947 on the handball court in the old House office building. He was a fierce competitor, but a completely gracious gentleman at the same time."

In 1951, Harlow again returned to Oklahoma. The following year, newly elected President Eisenhower called to ask him to join his congressional relations staff. He came back to Washington, DC, for the third time.

"When the president of the United States himself asks you to do something, you must do it, unless you have an overwhelming personal reason not to do it," he told me.

Harlow revered Eisenhower and, in turn, most said he was Eisenhower's favorite staff member. He began spending more time as a speechwriter. White House speechwriters have an outsize influence, since presidential policy utterances must first find their way into a speech, and the speechwriter is the one who composes the speech. In that role, and because Eisenhower trusted him, many believed Harlow had more influence on major decisions than anyone else.

When Eisenhower left office in 1961, Harlow moved to Proctor & Gamble's Washington, DC, office to handle government relations. For eight years, while the Democrats held the presidency, he was the conduit to both Eisenhower and Nixon, reporting goings on in the nation's Capital.

* * *

When I arrived for work at 7:00 a.m. on Tuesday, January 21, Harlow was already on the telephone, and his secretary, Sally Studebaker, was writing down names of other early morning callers. In between calls, Sally and I unpacked boxes.

The spacious West Wing office seemed too large at first for Harlow, who was five feet, three inches tall, slightly built, and balding. While his physical stature did not fill the room, his personality did. Even though he was the busiest man in the White House, he gave his full attention to anyone who engaged him—unlike most in public life, who focus on the next person before they have finished a conversation. Harlow's capacity for genuine interest in each person with whom he was speaking made him late for appointments, and caused unanswered telephone messages to stack up, but it also made him sought-after and beloved. I soon began calling him Bryce because every other White House staffer did.

His desk faced south in the middle of the big office. Mine faced east and was pushed next to his. Our days were spent with Bryce talking on his phone, while I returned calls that he did not have time to answer. Oklahoma Governor Dewey Bartlett had his own strategy for breaking into the line of callers. Bartlett would place the call himself, then stay on the line for as long as it took for Bryce to eventually answer. I have used that tactic often myself.

Smoke enveloped the office as Bryce consumed one Dual Filter Tareyton cigarette after another. I was then smoking Luckies. Members of Congress were the most frequent callers. One such caller was a Democrat committee chairman who complained that a Republican congressman had announced a project in the chairman's district instead of allowing the Democrat to make the announcement, as had been done under the Johnson administration.

"Mr. Chairman, we want to be exactly fair on this. Give me a few minutes to check on it, and I'll call you back," Bryce said.

He then called Larry O'Brien, who had been in charge of Congressional relations for Johnson.

"Larry, how did you handle grant announcements?" he asked.

"Why, we let the Democrats do it because they were members of the president's party," O'Brien answered.

Harlow then called the complaining chairman.

"I just checked. I talked with Larry and we're going to be fair. We're going to do it exactly the way LBJ did it. We're going to let members of Congress of the president's party make the grant announcements," he said.

The Democrat chairman didn't like the answer, but he chuckled at how gracefully Harlow had handled it.

At fifty-two, Harlow, by himself, had about as much Washington, DC, experience as the rest of the White House staff combined. The amateurism of some eager Nixon staff members soon offended the lions on Capitol Hill. Relations between the White House and the Senate ground to an impasse.

Nixon dispatched Bryce to break the stalemate. Late one afternoon, I rode with him to the Capitol, where we found a gaggle of Democrat committee chairmen enjoying bourbon in Senator Eastland's hideaway office.

Harlow bent down on one knee before the assemblage.

"Gentlemen, I see before me, if I am counting correctly, one hundred and fifty-five years of accumulated experience and wisdom. I understand there have been some issues with the White House. I hope we can resolve them," he said.

The chairman guffawed. They all knew Bryce and were so amused and flattered by his exaggerated gesture of respect that the impasse melted.

Harlow's lesson still resonated with me forty-five years later, when I became chairman of a Senate committee. At the beginning of a congressional session, I always telephoned both the senior Democrat and the senior Republican of the House committees with whom I would be working, and asked if I could walk across the Capitol and visit their offices. It was so rare for a senator to volunteer to come and see a House member that the gesture always started our relationship off on a good footing, and often led to legislative results.

After six months, Bryce created a small cubbyhole office for me, carved out of Sally's suite, and I moved my desk out of his office. That cubbyhole office is still there and still small—but highly prized because it is only fifty feet from the Oval Office. At the time of this writing, it is occupied by the vice president's chief of staff.

For those first six months, Bryce rarely asked me to leave the office during his telephone conversations or meetings. For twelve hours a day, I sat at my desk next to his, marveling at his skills and absorbing wisdom as he dealt with the complex issues that found their way to the highest levels of government. I had earned my bachelor's degree in politics and government at the college of Judge Wisdom and from Senator Baker, but I was earning a PhD in government and politics from Bryce Harlow.

* * *

A former campaign aide can be efficient. A businessman may have become rich because he did one or two things well. But I learned quickly that navigating the nooks, crannies, nuances, and pitfalls that accompany almost every matter that comes to the White House requires different skills. Many of those who worked in the White House were so narrow-gauged that they couldn't discern a human frailty if it were to smash them in the face. They may have been trained at the best schools and edited the finest law reviews; they may have been able to perform mental gymnastics of Olympic quality; and their efficiency might be unsurpassed. But when faced with a complicated decision, they couldn't make one worth two cents.

Asking White House aides who have never been to Washington, DC, to handle complex matters for the president is like sending a Wall Street lawyer into a rural Tennessee courthouse to try a case. The Wall Streeter is likely to be skinned alive without knowing what happened to him.

Occasionally, a prudent Nixon staffer would seek Bryce's advice before plowing ahead and creating a problem. Peter Flanigan, a buttoned-up New York investment banker who had been an advance man in the 1960 presidential campaign, had been assigned the role of White House liaison to federal independent regulatory agencies.

One morning, Peter walked into Bryce's office.

"Bryce, I need your advice. I am going to call the Federal Communications Commission about a television license that has been held up for a year and a half. One of the president's best supporters is an applicant for that license. We are a pro-business administration. Such a delay is outrageous. This is my portfolio. All I intend to do is to ask about the delay, about the status of the case," Peter said.

"Peter, do you remember Sherman Adams?" Bryce asked.

"Of course. He was Eisenhower's chief of staff who had to resign in disgrace," Peter answered.

"Do you remember why he had to resign?" asked Bryce.

"Not precisely," said Peter.

"He had to resign because he telephoned an independent regulatory agency about the status of a case on behalf of a supporter who had given him a coat for Christmas," Bryce said.

"Is that all?" Peter asked.

"That is all," Bryce replied.

Flanigan decided not to make the call.

Bryce's ethics set an example. At the invitation of a friend, he had planned a short vacation in Mexico with his wife, Betty. He had first determined that the friend had nothing to do with the government, so the trip would present no conflict of interest. A couple of weeks before the trip, the friend called and asked for a small favor. The next day, I heard Bryce call the friend.

"I'm deeply sorry, but we'll not be able to make the trip because something has come up," he said.

Some of his best advice was offered to those of us who were young and impatient. I once complained that the president was not taking stronger action on civil rights.

"Remember, just a little tilt here can create an earthquake out there," he said.

* * *

Other times, he cautioned aides who were eager to drag an issue into the White House so they could help decide it.

"Remember that our job as staffers is to push the merely important matters out of here and back to the Cabinet so that we can reserve the truly presidential issues for the president himself to decide," he would say.

Years later, as a senator, I attended meetings during which senior Obama aides described decisions they were making concerning the war in Afghanistan. Remembering Bryce's counsel, I was sure these decisions should instead have been made at the Pentagon by generals and the Secretary of Defense.

When any issue was especially complex, Bryce would tell an Eisenhower story.

"The Eisenhower Cabinet had been in a swivel over a difficult decision. Ike went around the room. Each Cabinet officer offered a different opinion," Bryce said.

"Unless we do it this way, it will damage national security," said the secretary of defense.

"That will create grave foreign policy implications," said the secretary of state.

"Because of financial considerations, I must insist on a different path," said the secretary of the treasury.

And on it went.

Becoming impatient, the president asked, "Well, what would be the *right* thing to do?"

The secretary of state, sitting next to the president, answered first.

"Oh, well, the right thing to do would be..." And around the table it continued, with each secretary setting aside the narrow interests of his department and agreeing that *that* would be the right thing to do.

"Well, then, that is what we will do," the president said, and he sent Press Secretary Jim Hagerty to tell the media.

I often repeat this story to skeptical students who believe it is naïve to base decisions upon the answer to the question, "What would be the *right* thing to do?"

"If the supreme allied commander who won World War II, who was head of NATO, president of Columbia University, and president of the United States can make decisions that way, perhaps you could too," I suggest.

CHAPTER 14

If Nixon Had Listened to Harlow

"Rule 14. Tell the Truth. It's the right thing to do, and it will confuse your opponent."

"Rule 58. If something embarrassing happens, announce it yourself before someone else does."

—LAMAR ALEXANDER'S LITTLE PLAID BOOK

Washington, DC. 1969–1970.

WHEN HE WAS REELECTED PRESIDENT in 1972, carrying all but one state, Richard Nixon was on his way to becoming the most consequential of the ten presidents with whom I have worked—and one of the most consequential in American history.

Historian Jon Meacham suggests this "portrait test" for presidents. "When you leave office and White House visitors see your official portrait, what will be the first thing that comes to their minds?"

Nixon's first term provided an impressive list of possible answers for his portrait test: beginning direct relations with China; ending the Vietnam War; creating the volunteer army; signing the "Clean Air" and "Clean Water Acts;" creating the Environmental Protection Agency; establishing the Philadelphia Plan that set aside jobs for racial minorities;

Senate confirmation four Supreme Court Justices; and a revenue sharing program that provided billions for state and local government.

Nixon temporarily established wage and price controls to try to tame inflation. He ended the money supply's reliance on the gold standard, reorganized the post office, eased the Cold War with the antiballistic missile and Strategic Arms Limitation Treaties, and brokered agreements with Egypt, Syria, and Israel. To avoid sending American troops overseas, he promulgated the Nixon doctrine: give them weapons and let them fight.

He accomplished all of this while working with a Democrat Congress that did not approve some of his most innovative proposals, such as a "negative income tax" that provided federal dollars to the working poor. A version of this concept, first advocated by Milton Friedman, later became the basis for the Earned Income Tax Credit.

Nixon did much of his own thinking. I often saw him escape the Oval Office—where he didn't like to be—by walking out of the West Wing to his second-floor office in the Executive Office Building. For hours, he would work there alone, mapping out plans on a yellow pad. His sense of strategy and broad experience as congressman, senator, vice president, and presidential candidate were the source of much of his innovative presidency.

Nixon also deserves credit for assembling the other source of his innovative accomplishments—a diverse and talented staff. Henry Kissinger, a Harvard professor who had advised Nelson Rockefeller, was the architect of the China initiative. Daniel Patrick Moynihan, another Harvard professor and a Democrat, pushed the negative income tax. George Shultz, who eventually held four Cabinet positions, created the Philadelphia Plan. Former Texas Democrat Governor John Connally oversaw the elimination of the gold standard. John Mitchell implemented the Southern strategy that helped produce Nixon's overwhelming reelection in 1972. The distinguished economist Arthur Burns provided advice on domestic issues.

One morning in 1969, Harlow slipped out of the White House and drove to Capitol Hill, where he persuaded future Defense Secretary Donald Rumsfeld to leave Congress to head the Office of Economic Opportunity. Rumsfeld brought with him his assistant, future Vice President Dick Cheney.

Many of the younger members of the White House staff were talented too. Accompanying Professor Moynihan from Harvard were his "whiz kids," who later made names for themselves. They included Chris DeMuth, president of the American Enterprise Institute, and Chester Finn Jr., the leading conservative education thinker and writer. Three young White House staff assistants would become United States senators—Richard Blumenthal, Elizabeth Dole, and myself. So did Moynihan.

Nixon recruited *Time* magazine editor Jim Keogh to manage a stable of White House speechwriters who later went on to remarkable careers—the Pulitzer prize-winning William Safire at the *New York Times*; Pat Buchanan as a pundit and presidential candidate; Lee Huebner as publisher of the *International Herald Tribune;* and Raymond Price, Nixon's chief speechwriter.

The White House continued to attract talented young people during Nixon's first term. One morning in 1970, a Kentucky friend telephoned to recommend a young Wellesley graduate from Louisville for a White House job.

"Those jobs are hard to get," I said, but agreed to see her anyway.

The young graduate was Diane Sawyer. When I met her, I immediately called Press Secretary Ron Ziegler.

"I don't have time to see her," he said.

"You'll be sorry if you don't," I countered.

Ziegler met Sawyer and hired her on the spot. She later became the first woman correspondent on *60 Minutes* as well as an ABC network news anchor.

Nixon took pride in the breadth and quality of his advisers.

"They often disagreed on issues, but this gave me the benefit of well-thought-out options when I had to make tough decisions... they shared one characteristic in common: they were heavyweights. Too often today, advisers to public officials are sycophants who are very good at buttering up the boss, but who aren't effective in giving him the advice he needs to hear," he wrote to me in 1987.

Eventually, the "heavyweights" were not the advisers to whom Nixon was listening.

On Tuesday, November 4, 1969, the White House announced that Harlow and Moynihan would become counselors to the president, with higher pay and Cabinet rank. In truth, they were being kicked upstairs. Harlow became less involved in day-to-day White House operations, and Moynihan lost control of domestic policy to John Ehrlichman. Meanwhile, Chief of Staff Bob Haldeman aggregated power by controlling the president's schedule.

Crew-cut Haldeman was a model of efficiency. Ehrlichman, as manager of the Nixon campaign plane, was celebrated for his punctuality, once leaving a reporter on the tarmac who was one minute late for the scheduled takeoff. Haldeman and Ehrlichman were building a wall around the Oval Office. Efficiency was trumping deliberation and consideration of differing opinions.[1]

The new White House atmosphere was squeezing out Harlow. In the spring of 1970, he told Nixon that he would leave at the end of the year, although he effectively left even earlier.

* * *

Nearly two years later, a bizarre incident destroyed the promise of the Nixon presidency.

On June 17, 1972, District of Columbia police arrested five employees of the Nixon reelection campaign for breaking into Democrat headquarters at the Watergate Hotel. More accurately, Nixon himself destroyed his presidency with the way he responded to that incident. He lied about it and tried to cover it up. On Friday, August 9, 1974, Nixon resigned the presidency.

One cannot overlook the paranoia that was the cause of his mistakes. Harlow speculated on the source of Nixon's dark personality.

"I suspect that my gifted friend, somewhere in his youth, maybe when he was very young, or in his teens, got badly hurt by someone he cared for very deeply or trusted totally—a parent, a relative, a dear friend, a lover, a confidante. Somewhere, I figure somebody hurt him badly. From that experience and from then on, he could not trust people ... and if you don't trust people ... you're in a bad fix."

But just as Chief of Staff Howard Baker's mature presence in 1987 and 1988 helped the Reagan presidency survive the Iran–Contra scandal, I am convinced that the Nixon presidency would have survived if Nixon had listened to Harlow instead of Haldeman and Ehrlichman. For eighteen months, I knew, watched, and worked with Haldeman and Ehrlichman in the West Wing. I do not believe that they were evil. I believe they were in over their heads. Their experiences as advertising executive and land use lawyer, respectively, then as campaign advance men, did not prepare them for dealing with a complex White House crisis. They had never before been in such deep water and had no idea how to surface.

In a letter to me on April 16, 1985, Bryce told me what advice he had given Nixon in 1972. I had asked him to repeat a story he'd told me earlier about how President Eisenhower had handled a difficult incident. The letter is worth reprinting:

> Dear Lamar:
>
> ...we're talking of 31 years ago—1954. The DixonYates matter was in full flower—a festering scandal involving, among others, the Director of the Budget. Allegations of conflict of interest intensified, and the fangs of the media vampires were full out and adrip with venom as the search escalated for victims. In time it became necessary for the President to put out a public statement because the integrity of his whole Administration was coming into question.
>
> We staff functionaries...laboriously contrived an apologia—a mealy-mouthed, evasive, convoluted, turgid bureaucratic squid squirt—intended to blot out all possibility of further suspicion.
>
> Then we gathered in the President's office. With a flourish, Jim Hagerty handed Ike our handiwork. We all sat silently as he intently read every word.
>
> Suddenly, he threw the statement over Hagerty's head and out into the middle of the Oval Office. Plainly, he was M-A-D, and he showed his famed temper. His blue eyes flashing, his 5-Star look on, his face brick red, he had at us with his best guttural ultimation: "You listen here boys," he said, "I'll never put out any drivel like that as long as I'm around this place. You've got to understand that the right thing to do in cases like this is always to tell the truth. Put out the facts very fast, don't get cute about it, just say exactly what the facts are, and make it as simple as you can and as short as you can. That way the whole damn mess will blow over and be gone in a week or 10 days, and the public will back you for being honest about it. Do it this way like you

> boys have it here—and we'll all be up to our necks in trouble and will deserve it."
>
> We filed out of the office chastened and embarrassed but with a lesson in responsible leadership that I, for one, will never forget.
>
> He was right, by the way. As soon as we got the facts out, the whole thing died away.
>
> That, incidentally, was what I urged that Nixon and Stans do with Watergate in 1972. It would have hurt a few people but saved the Presidency....
>
> Keep going with your marvelous service to Tennessee. Somewhere down the road, some other lightning will strike—it has to—and off you'll go to exciting new services to the American people of vast importance. I can hardly wait!
>
> Bryce N. Harlow

In 1970, as Bryce was leaving the White House, he encouraged me to think about leaving too. Looking back, I believe he sensed that things were headed in the wrong direction, and he did not want me to be tarred with it.

There was another reason that he believed I should consider leaving. Three times he had tried unsuccessfully to go home to Oklahoma from Washington, DC.

"Washington, DC, is a sticky place," Bryce told me. "If you stay much longer, you will never go home. You can stay and leave, but you will keep bouncing back, as I did three times. I've had a wonderful life here, but I often wish that I could have lived two lives, one in Oklahoma and one here."

So, as my first year in the White House came to a conclusion, I began thinking about moving back to Tennessee. Working in the West Wing was intoxicating for someone twenty-nine years of age. I ate breakfast and lunch in the White House mess, attended meetings with the president and congressional leaders, and participated in conversations on weighty issues.

Howard and Joy Baker introduced Honey and me to veal piccata, pommes soufflées, and Pouilly-Fuissé wine at the Rive Gauche restaurant. We ate meals at Sans Souci with Robert Novak and other reporters plumbing for inside information. But I realized that whatever influence I had in Washington was derivative—first from a United States senator and now from the president.

In truth, there were only 537 people in Washington who had earned positions of influence by being elected—the president and vice president, one hundred senators, and 435 congressmen. All the rest of us—staff, lobbyists, government contractors, even the media—depended on these 537 for whatever power that we had.

I wanted to stand on my own, and the only way to do that was to go home and earn that right. I had been away from Tennessee for nearly eight years, since departing Maryville for New York University in 1962. Since then, I had lived in New Orleans, Los Angeles, New York, and Washington, DC. I was becoming dangerously close to being *from* Tennessee, not *of* Tennessee.

There was still another reason to think about going home. Our family was growing. I had not anticipated how radiant Honey would become during her pregnancy.

"You are prettier than ever," I told her.

On Saturday afternoon, September 20, I was in Providence, Rhode Island, serving as groomsman in the wedding of a Klub Klingle roommate. Honey had not attended, which turned out to be fortunate, since, during the wedding reception, I received an urgent message that she was on her way to George Washington University Hospital. I caught the next flight to Washington National Airport, rushed to the hospital, and took an elevator up to the waiting room.

This was before fathers were allowed to attend their birthing wives, so I sat waiting with a young African American man whose wife was about to have their first child. Both babies would be boys.

"What will you name your son?" he asked me.

"Andrew Franklin Alexander, after both his grandfathers. What about yours?" I asked.

"Richard Nixon Jones," he said proudly.

Our son, Drew, was born just after midnight on Sunday morning, the 21st. He was a stocky, cheerful baby with big brown eyes and blond hair. Honey's parents paid for a night nurse to stay with us for three weeks at home, which was a great help.

I, on the other hand, was not much help, leaving for the White House at 6:30 a.m. every morning and returning most evenings after 8:00 p.m. Honey and I took Drew everywhere we went—to dinner, to parties, to the park, to the beach. He was the first baby among the couples in our rambunctious crowd. Our friends doted on him.

* * *

In January 1970, I came up with a bright idea that would take me home and let me stand on my own two feet. I would run for the United States Senate.

I would be thirty on July 3—old enough to serve, if elected. The statewide Republican Party in Tennessee was new. I had been around for most of its life. The only Republican contenders for Albert Gore Sr.'s Senate seat were two new congressmen from Tennessee—Bill Brock of Chattanooga and Dan Kuykendall of Memphis, as well as country and western singer Tex Ritter.

In 1970, Baker, then forty-four, and Brock, thirty-nine, were the leaders of the Tennessee Republican revival. Both were East Tennesseans with conservative policies who went on to have distinguished careers in public service. But the Tennessee Republican party was still young and small. In this adolescent setting, Baker and Brock competed like two roosters in one barnyard.

I stayed late at the White House, phoning key Tennessee Republicans to inquire about their general well-being, just to impress them when they heard, "This is the White House operator." My Klub Klingle roommates thought my scheme was over the top. They persuaded me to make a three-day trip in January to consult with Tennessee GOP leaders.

They designated one roommate, M. Lee Smith, to travel with me. We began our tour with a visit to May Ross McDowell, seventy-one, the former mayor of Johnson City.

"Mrs. McDowell, I am considering running for the Senate," I said.

"The *US* Senate?" she asked incredulously.

Hers was one of the more favorable reactions I received as we made our way westward. Our last visit was in Memphis with a dentist and former Republican county chairman who was thinking about running for governor, a political idea that seemed to me even more outlandish than my running for the Senate. The dentist, a kind and engaging man by the name of Dr. Winfield Dunn, joined the chorus of those advising me that I should leave the race to Brock. I returned to Washington, having learned a lesson about why a staff position in Washington is not comparable to building your own base.

On Saturday morning, August 15, 1970, Bryce wrangled five minutes from President Nixon's schedule so that the president could tell me goodbye. It was a "stand up" visit. Oval Office visitors who sit down tend to stay a while. This usually meant the difference between five and fifteen minutes of the president's time.

I had stepped foot in the Oval Office no more than a half dozen times during my eighteen months in the White House. I had never had a one-on-one meeting with the president until now.

Bryce, standing respectfully to one side, began the conversation.

"Lamar is going home after eighteen months here," he said.

"What are you going to do?" Nixon asked.

"I'm going back to Tennessee to manage the campaign of Winfield Dunn, who won the Republican nomination for governor," I replied.

"Tennessee, eh? Tennessee and Indiana are the two states with the nut-cuttingest politics I know. You might want to be careful," the president said.

That was the entire conversation.

White House photographers later provided a photograph of the meeting, which showed me pointing a finger at the president's chest as if I were warning him that something bad was about to happen.

It was, but none of us knew that at the time.

PART FOUR

A Walk Across the State

1970 to 1978

"Wait a minute. I want to know why you want to be governor. You're going to have to convince me first. I have to be convinced that this is the very best thing for the state, and for you and for us."

—HONEY ALEXANDER, Nashville, May 1978

CHAPTER 15

Coming Home

"My dear, who WERE you?"

—A BELLE MEADE MATRON TO HONEY,
Centennial Club luncheon, 1970

Nashville. 1970–1973.

"Will you come manage Winfield's campaign?"

I said, "Yes," almost before Memphis attorney Harry Wellford finished his question. I was ready to go home and here was just the right opportunity. In a stunning upset on Thursday, August 6, 1970, Memphis dentist Winfield Dunn, won the Republican primary for governor.

Wellford had been the volunteer manager of Dunn's shoestring campaign. But Wellford's law firm said that was enough time off, and to come back to work. So the next day, Wellford, whom I knew from Howard Baker's 1966 campaign, telephoned me at the White House.

I recruited two of Baker's top aides, Lee Smith and Ralph Griffith. I called friends in Knoxville—Sandy Beall, David White, and Sam Furrow, all in their twenties and with zero political experience—and asked them to meet me in Nashville on Labor Day to put together a campaign. Honey and I sold our Washington, DC, home and rented a Nashville apartment.

I had been summoned to save the state from John Jay Hooker Jr. A forty-year-old Nashville lawyer, Hooker believed that he was destined to be president of the United States, but that he must first prove himself worthy by being elected governor. Six-foot-three, slyly handsome, and irrepressible, Hooker created a spectacle wherever he appeared.

Sometimes he wore a three-piece suit and a Homburg hat, always a red-and-blue-striped tie. Tie knot lowered, coat thrown over his shoulder, red suspenders snapping, Hooker had no trouble filling the Hohenwald town square. Young women and farmers paid rapt attention as he proclaimed that "the rising tide must lift all boats," a vision borrowed from his idol, John F. Kennedy.

"He was the greatest political orator I ever heard," *Tennessean* editor John Seigenthaler told friends.

"It was as if The Beatles had arrived," his twenty-two-year-old driver, Hal Hardin, said.

The immediate obstacle to Hooker's presidential trajectory was Dr. Dunn. Also six-three and handsome, with black hair and an earnest smile, Dunn was determinedly cordial. There are pure hitters in baseball and pure shooters in basketball, but Dunn was as pure a talent on the campaign trail as the Tennessee Republican party ever produced.

Dunn won the primary by attracting more than 90 percent of the votes cast by his fellow Shelby Countians. These West Tennesseans had grown tired of fifty years of Middle Tennessee Democrats monopolizing the Capitol. East Tennesseans were also fed up. There had not been a Republican governor—and the patronage and power that goes with the office—since 1920. Most Tennesseans could not imagine a Republican winning the governor's race, but polls showed Dunn gaining. Perception catching up with polling reality made it appear that the Dunn campaign was surging.

Meanwhile, we followed rules about how to run for governor, which now are recorded in the *Little Plaid Book:* "Hold at least one $100-a-plate, fund-raising dinner, where, for $200, the donor can stay home. Be well organized, but be surprised if your campaign is. Never organize a campaign so well that it can't burst out of control to win. Never have more chairs than people at a political event. Never hold a political event in a room large enough to hold everyone who shows up."

Ignoring Hubert H. Humphrey's warning, "If you sling a pail of mud, expect a load of garbage back in the face," we began October with TV ads showing the Capitol crumbling in the event of Hooker's election. Then came ads with lovely outdoor scenes and a jingle proclaiming, "From Mountain City to the Memphis delta, Winfield Dunn's the man for you and me."

This one-two, non-substantive advertising punch, plus the forces of regional jealousy, resentment of the Great Society, hunger for patronage, weariness of one-party rule, and the imperative to save the state from Hooker, made Dr. Dunn the first Tennessee Republican governor in fifty years. On the same Tuesday, November 3, 1970, Bill Brock defeated Albert Gore Sr. to become the state's second popularly elected Republican US senator.

Dunn asked me to direct his transition with the retiring Governor Ellington. I knew little about such a process, but as much as any other Republican, since, for half a century, there had not been a transition between a Republican and a Democrat governor. This novelty made for awkward moments, many produced by patronage-hungry mountain Republicans.

Coolidge Whitaker drove two hundred and twelve miles from Rutledge to Nashville, stormed into my office, laid his pistol on my desk, and said that he intended to be Grainger County patronage chairman. I did not disagree. A carload of Unicoi County Republicans drove two hundred and eighty-seven miles to say they wanted every state employee in the country fired—*right now.*

"How many are there?" I asked.

"Seventy-six."

"Wouldn't it be hard to find seventy-six Republicans for those jobs?" I said, stalling for time.

"Here are the names of seventy-six Republicans," their leader said, producing a list.

* * *

After helping Dunn with the transition, I concluded that it was time to stand on my own.

I became the junior attorney at Dearborn, Warner, and Alexander, practicing law downtown alongside two established lawyers, one from

Harvard and one from Yale. David K. "Pat" Wilson, Tennessee's chief Republican fundraiser, was my first client. He gave me a retainer of $300 a month, equal to my monthly salary as a messenger for Judge Wisdom.

Honey and I plunged into Nashville life, building our family and doing what we could to help the community. She cofounded Leadership Nashville and helped Family & Children's Service so much that today, its headquarters is the "Honey Alexander Center." At Bud Wilkinson's invitation, I teamed up with Bill Willis, Hooker's former campaign manager, to chair the Tennessee Council on Crime and Delinquency.

In 1971, Nashville was vibrant and appealing with a small-town feel that its leading citizens were determined to preserve. But Nashville was also uncertain of itself. Many wealthy citizens who lived in splendid houses with large lawns in Belle Meade on the western end of town worried about the arrival of unkempt country musicians. Nashville was becoming "Music City." Belle Meade citizens preferred "Athens of the South." Belle Meade families still maintained social influence, but by then, there were enough newcomers to make one's way without having six local generations on one's resume.

For Honey and me, the years 1971 to 1973 were the most peaceful of our marriage. With three Republicans—Dunn, Baker, and Brock—having been recently elected, there were no tempting political vacancies. In 1972, our law firm merged with another. I kept my distance from Baker's 1972 reelection campaign, serving only as its counsel. We bought and moved into a home in Green Hills. On St. Patrick's Day, Friday, March 17, 1972, Honey gave birth to our first daughter. Since Honey did not use her given names, her first name went to Leslee.

On Wednesday, February 7, 1973, the United States Senate created a select committee to investigate the Watergate break-in. The Republican minority leader, Hugh Scott of Pennsylvania, named Senator Baker as vice chairman.

"I suspect Scott thought it was a way to get rid of me," Baker told me, only half joking.

Baker had competed with Scott for Republican leader twice.

Baker asked me to serve as Republican counsel to the committee. Remembering Bryce Harlow's advice about how sticky Washington is, I said, "No."

"Drew is three, Leslee is eight months old, I am just starting law practice, and we are settling into our new home. I have no experience as a criminal lawyer. And, the truth is, I have no appetite for investigating the people I used to work with. Why don't you ask Fred Thompson to do it? He has had more law practice than I have and has been an assistant United States attorney," I said.

The Watergate hearings were shown on all three television networks five days a week for several months

"What did the president know and when did he know it?" Baker asked.

"Mr. Butterfield, are you are aware of the installation of any listening devices in the Oval Office?" Thompson asked.

The two became instant TV celebrities.

So did other committee members. One of them, Senator Daniel Inouye of Hawaii, who lost one arm during World War II, told me that pollster George Gallup had visited him during the hearings.

"Do you know who the best-known American is?" Gallup asked Inouye.

"I assume President Nixon," the senator said.

"Do you know who is second?" Gallup asked.

"I have no idea," Inouye said.

"It is you," Gallup said.

"How could that be?" asked Inouye.

"Americans have never seen a Japanese American with one arm and a strong voice perform so well for so long on television. You're hard to forget," Gallup said.

As the hearings wore on and 1974 approached, my political juices began to stir.

"Have you ever thought about running for governor?" asked Jere Griggs when I spent the night in his Humboldt home after speaking at a Republican event.

"I think I might," I replied.

During the 1960s, all the action had been in Washington, DC. I had even explored running for the Senate myself. Now, having tasted state government, I saw that a governor could do more than a senator to help people directly on the issues I cared most about. Tennessee was third from the bottom in family incomes. There were almost no auto jobs. Textile jobs were headed overseas. There was more interest in NASCAR and football than in better schools and universities. Blacks lived in separate neighborhoods and seemed excluded from economic success. The "anything is possible" spirit I had grown up with in Maryville had not pervaded most Tennessee communities.

By law, Dunn could not seek reelection. No one who had competed against him in 1970 was running again. I had been the student of Judge Wisdom, Howard Baker, and Bryce Harlow in all three branches of government. I had managed a statewide campaign and a transition between governors.

At age thirty-three, I brazenly figured that I might be as good a candidate for governor in 1974 as anyone else in our young state party.

CHAPTER 16

Losing and Wallowing

"Rule 112. Keep a graceful concession speech handy."

"Rule 116. When you lose, the best thing to do is go to bed as early as possible."

—LAMAR ALEXANDER'S LITTLE PLAID BOOK

Nashville. 1973–1974.

I EASED INTO RUNNING FOR GOVERNOR.

I commandeered Honey's 1966 Plymouth Valiant and began traveling the back roads of East Tennessee, where 60 percent of Republican primary voters then lived. County by county, I searched out "rats in the barn." I had learned that navigating among the accumulated grudges of these Lincolnite politicians was the main skill required to win a Tennessee Republican primary.[1]

In one faction-ridden county, I appointed a committee without a chairman because any chairman's enemies would have outnumbered the votes he brought with him.

In Hawkins County, where I had no organization, I asked the large and jovial county judge to gather the appropriate rats. We convened in the courthouse.

"Who will be your county manager?" asked the judge.

With nothing to lose, I threw out a subversive assumption.

"I don't know, but I do hear that Bruce Hurley will be Nat Winston's manager," I said.

With that, Roy Morgan, Joe Simmons, and Colby Reeves rose from their chairs, stomped out of the room, and began organizing my campaign. They were three of State Representative Hurley's political enemies. Hurley had so many that it was hard to see how he could have ever been elected. On primary election day, I carried Hawkins County.

Nathaniel Taylor "Nat" Winston was the leading candidate in the primary. At age forty-seven, he was a friendly, storytelling, banjo-picking psychiatrist from Nashville. Although he was descended from a storied East Tennessee family, Winston did not understand much about "rats in the barn." Neither did the third candidate, Dortch Oldham, a fifty-five-year-old earnest and wealthy retired CEO whose company dropped off college students in remote regions to sell Bibles and other books. Since all three of us candidates now lived in Nashville, I bought dozens of billboards along East Tennessee highways proclaiming "Lamar Alexander: East Tennessee's Own," appealing to the hunger of mountain Republicans for more say in state government.

Late on a hot Sunday night in Nashville, June 2, 1974, Kathryn's kicking in Honey's stomach announced an imminent arrival. I was in the living room leading a campaign meeting when Honey appeared in her robe at the bottom of the stairs.

"It's time," she said.

There was a firehouse scramble. Political savants disappeared into the night. I ran to bring the car to the end of the sidewalk. Two hours later, Kathryn Rankin Alexander, wet and wiggling, was bawling in her mother's arms at Vanderbilt Hospital. We gave her Honey's second unused name.

Good news followed good news. Six weeks later, on Thursday, August 1, I won the Republican nomination for governor, and Democrats picked West Tennessee Congressman Ray Blanton. I could not believe my good luck.

"Are you serious?" one Capitol Hill reporter asked when Blanton announced his candidacy.

Howard Baker had trounced Blanton in the 1972 Senate race. The congressman had an unsavory reputation. There were rumors that he had greased the railroad tracks ahead of Baker's 1972 campaign train. There was muttering of bid rigging involving his family's paving companies. He had a reputation for entertaining women who were not his wife.

On Thursday, August 8, I watched on television as President Nixon announced his resignation. I was disgusted by the Watergate affair. I wondered what would happen to friends I had worked with whose names now appeared in the news. *Well, at least the president has done Republicans a favor,* I thought.

"The resignation puts Watergate behind us. The voters and the press have their pound of flesh," I told Honey.

I was wrong.

Blanton was already offering himself as a "Ray of Blanton Sunshine" to a Dottie West tune that had become a Coca-Cola commercial. Although every newspaper editorial was in my favor, Blanton had advantages. He was dark-haired, handsome, and self-assured. His rural childhood gave him the aura of a common man. And, in the year of Watergate, he was a Democrat.

Nothing I did or said knocked him off track. At a debate in Knoxville on Tuesday, September 15, I turned to Blanton, extended my arm, and pointed at him.

"You are a bad person," I said, and began to offer evidence.

Blanton, who was smoking a cigarette, appeared unfazed at first. But as I went on, his face turned red. Then, his body grew tense. Finally, he took the lit cigarette in his right hand and snuffed out the burning end in the palm of his left hand. He showed no evidence of pain.

On the second Sunday in September, when I came home from morning services at Nashville's Westminster Presbyterian Church, Howard Baker called.

"What do you think about what Ford has done?" he asked.

"What has he done?" I asked.

"Pardoned Nixon," Baker said.

"What does that do?" I asked.

"I'm afraid he's bought the whole problem for himself and for the rest of us," he said.

I knew that "the rest of us" meant me.

As I traveled from town to town, voters were not saying much. Their faces wore that blank look that candidates learn to read.

We are listening to be polite, but we have made up our minds. You have embarrassed us, and we are going to throw you out of office to let you know what we think of that, was the message they had decided to send to Republicans.

Honey felt the campaign sinking. Others felt it, too. At first, I was angry. Then, I lost the incandescence that everyone recognizes in the face of a candidate who knows he is winning. I looked and felt like a loser, tired and unconvincing, hollow and empty. As a last-minute maneuver, the campaign borrowed $50,000 to buy a full-page ad in twenty-five newspapers that had endorsed me.

On election night, bad news arrived as hard and fast as a gunshot. I was flipping the car radio dial on the way to our victory party when the announcer reported that voting was close in the mountain counties where I should have been winning big. When we reached the Rodeway Inn at 7:30 p.m., TV stations all agreed—Blanton had won.

Most supporters driving from East Tennessee to the victory party turned around and went home when they heard the news on the radio. Those who did come gossiped solemnly. Being the losing candidate at your victory party is the closest you ever come to experiencing your own funeral.

"You could smell it coming. Them mountain Republicans wasn't talking. They was getting ready to vote wrong," one said.

"They came out of the hills, people we hadn't seen voting in fifteen years. It was too many Democrats, mad about Watergate," another agreed.

"There'll come a day," one woman reassured me.

"Don't kid yourself. It'll be fifty years before we elect another Republican governor," another said.

A woman put her worn face close to Honey's.

"God didn't want you to win. Things work out for the best, don't they? That political life would have been no good for that family of yours. Those sweet children would have grown up without a daddy. It's a mean business. I know what I'm talking about," the woman said.

Honey and I were home by 9:00 p.m., trying to think of something upbeat to say. But we were drained, our eyes hurt, and our arms and legs were heavy. I had let everyone down. And what was there to show for it?

"We'll just have to pull ourselves together and go on, pick up where we were, or start something new. It may take a while," Honey said.

We walked upstairs and went to bed—but not to sleep—until long after midnight had ended the day.

* * *

Campaigns end, win or lose.

Either way, it's sudden death. The difference is that when you win, a new life is sitting up there, like a polished apple waiting for you to take a bite. When you lose, you don't know where to go from where you are, and the hardest thing is that there seems to be nothing but the end. The loser must discover a new life, and that usually involves wallowing. Wallowing is precisely the word for the process, which becomes uncomfortably long for the wallower—and uncomfortably messy for those watching.

I began by rebuilding my law practice, which took months and was not much fun.I bought and sold houses to make extra money to reduce the $50,000 campaign debt. To discuss how to pay it off, I would arrange a small dinner at Jimmy Kelly's restaurant every few months with my remaining supporters—most of whom had cosigned the note.

Losing was hard on Honey.

"I took the loss very personally. I couldn't understand why Lamar wasn't elected. I was depressed and very unhappy with myself. Kathryn was born in June and was my appendage for four years. After Lamar lost that first race, I cocooned for a while," she said.

On Honey's thirtieth birthday, Sunday, October 12, 1975, Bryce Harlow, now counselor to President Ford, called me at home.

"The president has something he'd like for you to do," Harlow said.

I had worked with Gerald Ford during White House congressional leadership meetings. I saw him as an affable and honest man with a legislative temperament in an executive position. He had put the country first when he pardoned Nixon, gave amnesty to Vietnam draft dodgers, and fought inflation. He was the right balm during a time of turmoil, and the only Republican Democrat leaders would approve as vice president after Spiro Agnew resigned in disgrace.

Two days later, at 1:45 p.m., Harlow escorted me into the Oval Office, where the president was meeting with Chief of Staff Donald Rumsfeld, Deputy Chief Dick Cheney, and Howard "Bo" Callaway, the chairman of the President Ford Committee.

"We'd like for you to be executive director of our presidential campaign—the campaign manager. We need someone else to, sort of, run it, on a day-to-day basis," Ford said.

After a thirty-minute meeting, I left without saying yes or no.

The next day, I telephoned Harlow.

"I can't do it. I did not want to admit it to the president, but my personal life is a wreck. My job, family, and budget would not survive a year in politics running a presidential campaign," I said, and went back to my wallowing.

Early the next year, Honey had a miscarriage while I was away in Maryville. It was so early in her pregnancy that we never knew whether it was a boy or a girl. I kept wallowing. I attended the 1976 Republican National Convention in Kansas City as a reporter for WSM-TV, instead of as a delegate. In November, Watergate devastated Republican candidacies for the second straight election. Ford lost to Jimmy Carter, and Democrat Jim Sasser defeated Senator Brock.

There seemed to be little future for the Tennessee Republican party, and certainly no political future for me. I continued to head in other directions. I practiced law and dabbled in business. For $30,000, I bought 10 percent of Sandy Beall's startup restaurant company, Ruby Tuesday, Inc., and became its counsel.

In November 1976, Beall and his wife, Kreis, and Honey and I bought Blackberry Farm, a rundown nine-bedroom bed-and-breakfast with vines growing through the windows in West Millers Cove outside Maryville. We borrowed $100,000 of the $128,000 that we paid for it, and for options to buy several thousand adjacent acres. The Bealls wanted to one day turn the farm into "a nice inn." We enjoyed working together toward that goal, although in 1993, Honey and I traded our interest in the inn for adjacent land and lots.

Our second goal was to protect the land along sixteen miles of the Chilhowee Mountain ridge at the entrance to the Great Smoky Mountains National Park. Over four decades, working with a few other families, we exercised land options to place conservation easements on nearly nine thousand acres, protecting the view and wildlife between Chilhowee Mountain and the most visited national park in the US.

Our third goal was to build a family cabin. Honey and I knew exactly where we wanted ours. Blackberry Farm is adjacent to Mountain Homes, a 1,000-acre property on which thirty Maryville families, including my parents, had built modest cabins.

In the late afternoons during the 1970s, Honey and I loved to drive our 1974 Volkswagen Thing with its canvas top down to a field overlooking the Mountain Homes meadow below Chilhowee Mountain. We would drink martinis and imagine that one day, we would build our own cabin on that very spot.

In 1983, Honey found a 200-year-old log barn in Washington County. The Caylor Brothers of Townsend numbered the logs, moved them to our special spot above the meadow, and built a cabin that, over the years, became our home.

CHAPTER 17

My Red-and-Black Plaid Shirt

"Rule 114. If you lose, don't be afraid to try again."
"From a lot of at-bats eventually come some hits."

—TOM PETERS,
in *Lamar Alexander's Little Plaid Book*

Washington, DC, and Nashville. 1977.

After the scoundrel Ray Blanton drubbed me in 1974, neither Honey nor I expected there would be a second campaign for governor.

"I thought that was the end of politics," Honey said.

"Tennesseans will not elect another Republican governor for fifty years," wrote the political columnist for Nashville's *Tennessean*.

My attitude toward running a second time began to change during the celebration of our eighth wedding anniversary on Tuesday, January 4, 1977. Honey was happy, surprised that I was making such a fuss over dinner. We had waited until Drew, seven, and Leslee, three, were asleep. Honey had sautéed thin slices of veal, my favorite dish. I put candles on the old country table in the dining room that we had bought with our savings on a Christmas trip to Texas. We both liked the feel of old furniture and hoped someday to afford more. There was snow outside.

"Snow always makes me feel safer and cleaner and happier," Honey said.

Senator Baker's telephone call interrupted our meal. Earlier that day, Republican senators had elected him their leader.

"I need your help. I want you to organize my leader's office, help me get off to a good start, and stay with me for a while," Baker said.

To my surprise, Honey said, "Why don't you do it? It'll be good for you."

I knew she was right. I had become purposeless and was wallowing in my defeat, the $50,000 campaign debt, and the difficulty of restarting a law practice.

I arrived in Washington, DC, in time for Jimmy Carter's inauguration on Thursday, January 20, 1977. With Senate credentials, I was able to watch his inaugural address. I liked it when Carter walked to his inauguration. I liked his promise, "I'll never lie to you," and his other small-town virtues. But even as he was being sworn in, Washington insiders were making fun of him.

They said he was too Southern, too stiff, and too inexperienced—or, even worse, that he was not up to the job. He was a humorless engineer with a big smile, a peanut farmer unprepared for the presidency. They scoffed when he brought with him a crew from Georgia who knew even less about Washington, DC, than he did.

His single-minded focus that won the presidency eventually produced the Panama Canal Treaty and a Middle East peace agreement, but otherwise, his timing seemed off. In his book *Crackers,* Roy Blount Jr. wrote about the Carter presidency:

> I got the redneck White House blues.
> The man just makes me more and more confused.
> He's in all the right churches,
> And all the wrong pews.
> I got the redneck White House blues.[1]

At their Tuesday policy lunches, I was surprised to see thirty-eight living and breathing Republican United States senators ready to fight. Many had survived elections during the Watergate hangover in 1974 and 1976. They were optimistic, especially since Carter already was having problems.

A friend, Wyatt Stewart, suggested that I should meet Republican campaign consultant Doug Bailey. So, one April morning, I took a taxi to Bailey's Washington, DC, office, where I spent an hour getting to know this scholarly, bespectacled, cheerful man. Bailey and his partner, John Deardorff, had become the preeminent Republican consultants. In the late 1970s, their firm had eleven of the country's nineteen Republican governors as clients. Most interesting to me was that, after the 1974 Watergate debacle, Bailey–Deardorff had represented seven of the twelve Republican governors still holding office.

In 1976, they helped President Ford cut Jimmy Carter's twenty-point lead in the polls to two points on Election Day. To the tune of a campaign song, "I'm Feeling Good About America," the firm made television commercials focusing on Ford's likability.

"We said to ourselves, what the country knows about Gerald Ford is that he pardoned Nixon. Let's tell them more. Let's give them a view of Jerry Ford, the man, that's upbeat," Bailey told the *New York Times*.[2]

Bailey showed me one Ford television commercial that was not cheerful, however. It began with gunshots recalling the September 1975 assassination attempts against the president. The black-and-white commercial was so unsettling that Ford refused to use it, although Bailey told me he believed it would have reelected the president.

Bailey's upbeat approach appealed to me. My 1974 campaign consultant had been F. Clifton White, Barry Goldwater's chief strategist in the 1964 presidential run. White was gregarious, respected, and loyal, but not exactly cheerful. He delivered his strategic advice mostly by telephone. Bailey was different. Bailey did it all. He not only suggested strategy, but also wrote detailed campaign plans hundreds of pages long. He produced television commercials. He would fly to his candidate's state once a week.

When I returned to Nashville in April, I told Honey that 1978 would be a Republican year and that I was thinking about running for governor again.

"I was against it. I couldn't bear the thought of another campaign, possibly another loss," she later recalled.

She did agree that we could invite Bailey and Tom Ingram, my 1974 press secretary, to meet at our home one May evening.

Needlepointing furiously, Honey minced no words.

"You really need to decide for yourself why you want to be governor. And the second thing is, you ran a lousy campaign in 1974. Could we change the campaign mode? There is no need for you to run again if you run like you did in 1974," she said.

Turning to Bailey and Ingram, Honey went on.

"Lamar has to be more natural, be himself. He can't spend all his time with the same Republican politicians the way he did before. He spent too much time flying from one little airport to another little airport. He has to get out and meet the people, walk down the street where they live. Campaigning the way people campaign today is really dumb."

So, the four of us started talking about how this campaign could be different.

"What do you enjoy doing? You love to be outdoors. You love to take a hike. You love music," Honey said to me, answering her own question.

Ingram remembers how we settled on walking across the state in a red-and-black plaid shirt.

"Someone asked Lamar what he liked to do most when he wasn't working. He said, 'I like to put on my plaid shirt and go hiking in the Smokies.' Then Honey said, 'Why don't you just walk across the state? Walk and meet the people, play the trombone and the washboard like you did in New Orleans,'" Ingram recalled.

Bailey chimed in.

"Shake a thousand hands a day. Wear some clothes that everybody will recognize. Do what you like to do. That should be your campaign."

I knew instantly that they were right.

The next week, Honey and I bought every size large red-and-black plaid shirt at Friedman's Army Navy surplus store on Hillsboro Road—maybe fifteen shirts—fifty pairs of wool socks, and ten pairs of long underwear. I already had in my closet two well-worn plaid shirts; I hung the new shirts on our backyard fence so they would weather and not look so new. Doug Bailey returned to Washington, DC, to write a campaign plan. Ingram agreed to be the campaign manager for a walk across the state beginning in January.

That gave us six months to get ready, and we needed every day of it.

* * *

A walk across the state, like a watch, appeared simple enough on its face, but underneath, it required complex parts to work.

A few weeks after the May meeting, Bailey returned to Nashville with a 400-page plan, for which I paid $20,000. Ingram interviewed twenty members of the University of Tennessee marching band and hired four.[3] They took a break from school and formed Alexander's Washboard Band.

"These are not the four best musicians," Jay Julian, the band director, protested.

"I'm not hiring them for their musical ability. I'm hiring personalities," Ingram said.

One would drive a flatbed truck. The other three would walk with me. At stops along the way, I would climb up onto the truck with my trombone or washboard, join their drums, electric piano, and tuba performing various versions of "Momma Don't 'Low No Music Playin' Round Here" and "Alexander's Ragtime Band." After the music drew a crowd, I would deliver rousing remarks. Then, off we would go to the next stop. When we performed at high school assemblies, the college boys were a big hit with teenage girls—who we'd hoped would go home and tell their parents about the boys in the band and the candidate in the red-and-black shirt.

In the fall, Ingram and I recruited Keel Hunt, a *Tennessean* reporter, and Lewis Lavine, a Vanderbilt economist, to plan the walk. Lavine became the scheduler, but first he had to design the route. It took two months. My 1,022-mile journey would begin in Maryville and travel east to Mountain City. This meant traversing East Tennessee twice, but that was where 40 percent of Republican voters lived at that time. Then, the route would head west across Middle Tennessee to Memphis.

I would walk an average of 8.23 miles a day, put an "X" down with white railroad chalk on the highway to indicate where I'd stopped each afternoon, and return to that "X" the next morning to resume walking. By the time I ended each day, campaigning at stores, schools, restaurants, banks, retirement centers, churches, and farms—wherever I could find a hand to shake—I would have walked sometimes as many as fifteen to twenty miles.

On December 9, Hunt produced a fifteen-page memo describing the first fourteen days of the walk in detail. For example, Day XIII was to look like this:

> Day XIII: This is the first full day in Cocke County. Arrival in Newport will not come until tomorrow. Lamar continues south on Highway 160 to Bybee. About 4.4 miles into today's walk (3.5 miles past Centerview School, on the left) is the Bybee Market. The market has a good-sized parking lot on Highway 160, and the store manager (Ronnie Ellison 1 623-9817) told me he would get a lot of folks together for a rally whenever Lamar is in the area. Issues are roads and bad bridges.

There was a chairman for each day, a chairman of the day's walk, a route-planning map, and a volunteer who knew the route thoroughly and would decide who walked at the front. There were prizes for those who recruited walkers, and for the walkers themselves.

The goal was to have things so well-organized that I wouldn't have to worry about surprises and could be spontaneous when meeting people. We kept the planning secret, although we joked that the idea was so outlandish that no one would believe it if word slipped out.

"It was revolutionary. It put Lamar in places where Tennesseans do what they do every day. He stayed in homes at night instead of hotels, and he rode in trucks instead of flying. He stopped at almost every school," Ingram said.

Honey created her own plan. On campaign visits, she would stop by the community daycare center before meeting with the Republican women's club.

"I acquiesced to running for governor only because I was persuaded that I could do more to help children and families. That won me over," she said.

The weather forecast was horrible for Thursday, January 26, 1978—the day the walk was to start—but I was ready to go.

CHAPTER 18

Hit by a Truck

"Rule 55. Watch your step."

"Politics is more dangerous than war, for in war, you are only killed once."

—WINSTON CHURCHILL,
in *Lamar Alexander's Little Plaid Book*

Maryville to Newport. January 26–February 4, 1978.

MOST PEOPLE THOUGHT I HAD LOST MY MIND.

I was standing on the front porch of my parents' home in Maryville. The temperature and wind had combined for a chill factor of twenty-seven degrees below zero, "one of the worst bundles of bad weather demons have thrown at East Tennessee in years," the *Knoxville News Sentinel* said.

"I will campaign for governor by walking for six months across the state," I announced to a handful of skeptical supporters and reporters.

It was Thursday, January 26, 1978, and the end of my walk route in Memphis was 1,022 miles away. It was so cold that the trombone player's slide froze. Doug Bailey's camera motors froze too, temporarily derailing his plan to send film of the announcement to television stations. A volunteer swapped cookies with a TV reporter in exchange for a copy of his station's film, and then cajoled a pilot to fly the film to Nashville, Chattanooga, and Memphis in time for the evening news.

Capitol Hill reporters grumped and huddled in warm cars, except when they tried to entice local residents to make fun of the walk.

Tom Ingram told them, "We're not going to explain it to you, but I dare you to come and walk ten days. See for yourself and then we'll see what you think."

My father was embarrassed. Mother was worried.

"What is he thinking about? He'll be hit by a truck walking up and down those highways," she told Keel Hunt.

On that first freezing day of the walk, I wore what became my uniform—khaki trousers, a red-and-black plaid shirt, a red windbreaker, gloves, and a blue stocking cap. I also wore three pairs of wool socks, thermal underwear, and L.L. Bean hiking boots, size 9.5.

"This campaign is going to the people," I said, and stepped off the porch, followed by a few supporters.

The first representative of the people that I met was sitting in a pickup truck parked at Broadway Food Market with the driver's side window open. I stuck out my hand.

"I'm Lamar Alexander. I'd like to be your next governor," I said.

Without a word, the driver rolled up the window.

I received friendlier receptions at Maryville High School and Fort Craig Elementary School, where I saw my former football coach. At Asbury Acres Retirement Center, I played the piano for my former piano teacher, wondering if she would remind me that "[my] left hand is jumpy." As darkness descended, I walked carefully along the left shoulder of Highway 411, waving at surprised drivers speeding home after work.

I stopped for the night at the farm of Garland and Tommie DeLozier, where I sat close to a hot fire, ate a big supper, swapped stories with twenty or thirty neighbors, and piled into bed at 9:30 p.m. The dog barked at 3:00 a.m. After only one day on the road, I was so tired I didn't care.

The DeLoziers were an example of the seventy-three families the staff had selected to host me for a night. Garland was a leader in the county Farm Bureau, offering a rural contrast to my growing up in the city of Maryville. The idea was that when Blount Countians heard that the DeLoziers had invited me to stay with them, they would have to conclude that I couldn't be all bad.

The walk, in a way, became my penance.

"I don't blame myself for Ray Blanton, but I do blame myself for letting him win," I told the people.

And it was an opportunity for penance by the voters too, who had become disgusted with Blanton's performance. On the same cold day that I began my walk, the governor had flown the state Learjet to the warmth of Jamaica with a girlfriend and a physician. His press secretary explained to disbelieving reporters that the governor was going there to arrange for a sale of soybeans to China.

Lewis Lavine calculated that, of the families with whom I would spend the night, sixteen were farmers, sixteen worked in retail, four were physicians or dentists, four were public employees, and twenty-one were small businessmen. There were three attorneys, two ministers, and two newspapermen; three were retired, and one was unemployed. Each night, the four band members and other staff would also stay with local families, adding 129 families to the seventy-three families with whom I stayed.

The walk created unexpected conversations. In Sevierville, I shook hands with a missionary doctor, Robert F. Thomas, who had delivered Dolly Parton in a one-room cabin on the Little Pigeon River. And I developed a new skill. I could remember the names of factory workers I'd met at 5:30 a.m. when I saw them again in the afternoon at a school softball game or at the volunteer fire department. Still today, I remember the families I stayed with and the Tennesseans I met along the walk. I was concentrating on each person I met. I was on a mission, not thinking about who or what would come next.

There was no social media to distract. If I wanted to make a telephone call to interfere with campaign management, I had to find a pay phone along the highway. Eventually, I gave up trying. This departure from my normal micromanaging made me stop planning and start paying attention to each person I met.

* * *

On the ninth day of the walk, as I crossed Main Street in Newport, a white pickup truck coming from my left slammed into me and flipped me over its hood. The driver leaped from the truck, saw a man in a red-and-black plaid shirt sprawled on the pavement with campaign brochures scattered far and wide, and realized who she'd hit.

"Oh my God! Why did it have to happen in Newport?" she said with horror.

Merchants who'd heard brakes squeal pressed their noses against storefront windows, watching wide-eyed. My left foot stung, but mainly, I was embarrassed to find myself lying on Main Street in the midst of startled onlookers on a busy Saturday morning.

Well, after one week, this puts an end to my big idea of walking across the state, I thought.

I got up quickly, scooped up as many brochures as I could, and limped across the street into Overholt's Hardware—and, as if nothing had happened, began offering brochures to startled shoppers.

I hobbled to the town infirmary, which fortunately was also on Main Street. A doctor examined my left ankle. It was already beginning to swell.

"Without your heavy boot, it surely would have been broken," he said.

Meanwhile, a block away at the Cocke County courthouse, Honey was shaking hands while the washboard band entertained a noontime audience. No one had missed me. Favoring my tender left foot, which was now tightly wrapped inside a loosely tied boot, I shuffled over to join them, while keeping an eye out for more pickup trucks.

As the band played, Tom Ingram—who was traveling with me that day—called Keel Hunt at the Nashville campaign headquarters.

"He's been hit by a truck in Newport. He's okay, but he won't be able to walk for a few days," Ingram told Hunt.

The two discussed the problem—I still had five and a half months to walk before I would reach Memphis. They talked about how to explain my encounter with the truck to supporters—including my parents—who had been warning that walking along a highway waving at pickup trucks was a dangerous and dumb way to run for governor.

After the washboard band stopped playing and onlookers had drifted away, I ate lunch with county political leaders. Then, I returned to Main Street, where I used white chalk to write an "X" on the street where the accident had happened. That was where I would resume the walk as soon as I was able. Staff drove me fifty-two miles to our family cabin in West

Millers Cove. When I arrived, I noticed for the first time the white paint smeared on the left shoulder of my red windbreaker where the truck had hit me.

I stayed off my feet for three days.

CHAPTER 19

Shaking 1,000 Hands a Day

"Rule 73. Walk in parades."

"Rule 74. If it's the Mule Day parade, walk at the front."

—*LAMAR ALEXANDER'S LITTLE PLAID BOOK*

Morristown to Memphis. February 8–July 6, 1978.

My foot healed quickly so I resumed the walk in Morristown on Wednesday, February 8, as scheduled.[1]

The next day, I reached Greene County, where I spent four days walking from Mohawk to Chuckey, staying with families and attending their basketball games, church services, and civic club meetings. Early each morning, I shook hands at factory gates. My campaigning dominated the front pages of the daily *Greeneville Sun.* I must have met most of the voters in the county.

On Roan Mountain, I stayed with John I. Morgan, who was such a Lincolnite that he still called Democrats "Rebels." Five months later, at the western end of the state, where descendants of Confederates lived, I would spend the night in Grand Junction with ninety-year-old N.T. Richardson and his wife, Mary Ellen.

N.T. showed me a painting in his front hall of a girl riding a horse.

"That's my mother. She's riding to Corinth to warn that the Yankees are coming," he said.

On Wednesday, February 23, trudging up Doe Valley toward Mountain City in three feet of snow, I was closer to Canada than to Memphis. Each day, the grass grew greener. Now, the weather was not cold enough for long underwear. A few fishermen recognized my red-and-black shirt and waved as they drove by.

As the washboard band members and I made our way through Hawkins County, a woman working outdoors shouted at us.

"Hey, you boys stop shooting my rabbits!" she said.

When she found out what I was doing, she gave me the formula for being elected.

"Don't make any promises. We've heard them all before. Just do the best you can. Second, keep the taxes down. We can't afford more. Third, for heaven's sake, behave yourself when you get in. We're sick and tired of being embarrassed by all these politicians we hear on the radio. And one more thing—don't get too big for your britches," she said.

As temperatures rose, Honey went shopping in Loudon for lightweight red-and-black plaid fabric.

"In this weather, a flannel shirt won't do," she said.

As we walked east on State Route 127 approaching Cumberland County, my county chairman telephoned Tom Ingram.

"We've got trouble. Someone has tacked a poster on the county line sign saying, "N*** don't show your face after dark," Hill said.

I talked this over with the band members including Terry Tabors, the African American trombone player, and we decided they would spend the night at Cumberland Mountain State Park, as planned, while I stayed with a Crossville family. That was the only racial incident during the walk. On other nights, Tabors and I stayed with both White and Black families.

In DeKalb County, a Channel 2 television cameraman from Nashville was on hand to film a random conversation along the walk.

"I'm Lamar Alexander. I'd like to be your next governor," I said to a man named Luke.

"I think we can work something out. For two dollars, I'll vote for you and get all the people around here to vote for you just like I do it for Frank [the local state representative]," Luke said on camera.

On a Saturday afternoon in May, I stopped at a farm equipment store on Highway 96 near Columbia. With a few farmers, I watched Governor Blanton announce on television that he would not seek reelection. The newspapers that day carried stories about FBI investigations into the possibility that the governor's counsel had sold clemencies for cash.

My campaign was still an uphill climb. Bob Clement was far ahead in the polls, and the other Democrat candidate, Knoxville banker Jake Butcher, seemed to have unlimited money. Democrats had won the last two statewide elections and dominated the state government.

When I spent the night with families, I ate like a horse at their dinner tables—chicken, roast beef, meatloaf, boiled potatoes, salad, hot biscuits, more vegetables, two or three desserts, and iced tea in extra-big glasses.

"Have some more. Don't you like the beans?" my hostesses would urge.

Despite my appetite, I was in my best physical condition ever because of my walking. Each week, Honey stuffed a feather pillow into my traveling bag. I forgot to pack it so many mornings that I left a trail of feather pillows in homes from Mountain City to Memphis.

At 5:30 a.m. on Thursday, June 15, after spending the night with the Blakely family, I shook hands at the Levi Strauss factory in Ramer. The women coming to work complimented my plaid shirt. When I went inside, I learned why. Most of Levi's red-and-black shirts of the kind I wore were being made at *that* factory.

The red-and-black paid shirt had become my trademark, but it was not always well-received, especially by some supporters.

"He's making a fool of himself," one said.

When I wore the shirt in the first televised debate with other candidates, fundraisers complained.

But the standard I followed was, *Am I comfortable wearing it?*

If I was, I wore it, and if I wasn't, I didn't.

In late June, walking along Highway 69 nearing Memphis, word came that my primary opponent, Representative Harold Sterling, planned to "ambush" me at the Shelby County line as a way of making news. I sped up, walking twenty miles instead of ten on the day before the planned ambush, and strolled across the county line two hours before the ambushers arrived.

* * *

I can't blame my loss in 1974 entirely on Watergate. The truth was, I had been a purposeless, dull, and uninspiring campaigner. Years at Vanderbilt and New York Universities, living in Los Angeles, New Orleans, and Washington, DC, had diminished my familiarity with the people and their lives that a seventh-generation Tennessean ought to have. Friends said that I was even losing my East Tennessee accent.

"When you stop sounding like where you grew up is when you start getting into trouble," Roy Blount Jr. had warned.

"The 1974 campaign actually was a textbook campaign in many ways," Tom Ingram said, "but it was devoid of heart, soul, and authenticity."

The walk made me a more appealing candidate. Putting on the red-and-black plaid shirt and staying with families transformed me from what I had become into myself again. Pretty soon, it felt natural to get out of bed at 5:00 a.m., the way I once did delivering the *Knoxville Journal.* I felt at home shaking hands at factories, eating breakfast with farmers, walking ten miles, and watching eighth-grade basketball games. I even got used to walking along the left shoulder of a highway, waving at honking pickup trucks and cars.

In October, Jake Butcher ran television ads accusing me of "selling whiskey out of the basement of a church." As a lawyer for Ruby Tuesday, my job had been to find a defunct nonprofit charter so diners at its Gatlinburg restaurant could join a private club and order a drink, at a time when liquor by the drink was illegal. The charter I had found was for the "Good Shepard Episcopal Church." To get rid of the issue, I sold my 10 percent interest in Ruby Tuesday for the set price of $60,000. The next year, someone else bought that same interest for $1 million. After that, it was hard to eat at Ruby Tuesday.

As the campaign wound to a close, Honey canceled her campaign events, which was very much unlike her.

"I'm sick. I need to get to the cabin for a couple of days. I'm pregnant," she told Cathy Garner, who was traveling with her. "You're sworn to secrecy. If you tell the campaign they will make something out of it, and I don't want that."

Honey was campaigning again before the end of the week, but she didn't tell me until after election day that she was expecting our fourth child.

Ten days before the November election, a survey by Senator Baker's pollster showed that I could not win. That shook me. But an hour later, at the Bijou Theatre in Knoxville, I made the best speech of my life.

"This friendly tortoise in the red-and-black shirt is going to defeat that fast rabbit with a lot of lettuce," I promised cheering supporters, with a swipe at Butcher and his wealth.

Five days later, I felt the tide shifting. I sensed that I was winning, just as I knew in 1974 that I was losing. Butcher, who had defeated Clement in the Democratic primary by making fun of "Little Bob," was now having trouble appealing to Clement Democrats.

Still, one thing eluded me. When the walk had ended four months earlier, I couldn't do what Honey had insisted that I be able to do—say precisely why I wanted to be governor and what I hoped to accomplish. But I had come a long way. I had learned that the need for better roads, jobs, schools, and higher family incomes was more than a slogan. I was troubled that I had met so few Black business owners. I wanted to do something about towns that were trying to be like some other place instead of celebrating what made them special. I was even more convinced that holding public office was the best way I could change things to help the most Tennesseans. I believed that much to my core.

When I began my walk in the snow and ice on January 26, the Nashville *Banner* had written, "It is alternately shrewd and downright risky—a cunning political maneuver and transparent political hype...however, it could be just what Alexander needs to propel himself into the state house."

Five months later, the First National Bank thermometer in Memphis said 106 degrees when Honey, Drew, Leslee, Kathryn, and I stuck our feet in the Mississippi River. It had become clear to me that the walk and the red-and-black plaid shirt were real.

Again, Honey had been right.

"It's the *other* kind of campaigning—photo ops, soundbites, and robocalls—that is gimmicky," she had said.

A real campaign was meeting 1,000 people a day, staying in their homes, saying grace at supper, asking for their help, and trying to understand how to help them. In that kind of campaign, I had not only sharpened my purpose, but I must have radiated it because voters elected me.

On Tuesday, November 7, 1978, I won by 661,959 to 523,495, even carrying Nashville, where only 10 percent of voters identified as Republicans. But winning was a lot like turning thirteen. Much of the joy of the moment had been used up in anticipation of the event.

One thing I know today for sure—the walk and the red-and-black plaid shirt made me a better candidate and a better governor, and provided me with a deep connection to the people of Tennessee that has survived through many campaigns and many opportunities for public service over many years.

PART FIVE

A'swiveling in the Governor's Chair

1979 to 1987

"I'm going to help him, because if he succeeds, the state succeeds."

—SPEAKER NED RAY McWHERTER,
Democrat, November 1978

CHAPTER 20

"Amazing Grace" for Billy Graham

"I play the piano, too."

—A SECOND-GRADER
visiting the governor's office, 1980

Nashville. June 1979.

"WILL YOU PLAY THE PIANO at Reverend Graham's Nashville crusade?"

The invitation arrived in June 1979. I was thirty-eight, had been governor for all of six months, and Billy Graham was asking me to perform in front of 35,000 people at Vanderbilt's football stadium. I should have been intimidated but I wasn't. I'd been playing the piano in public since my first recital at age five.

This was Graham's second Nashville crusade, so Tennesseans had become familiar with the precision and complexity of these events. The strong singing of song leader Cliff Barrows, the 500-member choir, and thousands in the stadium would drive temperatures even higher in the steamy summer nights. After a while, George Beverly Shea would quiet the crowd as he sang "How Great Thou Art." Then, Billy Graham would stride to the podium, Bible in hand, to deliver the message and call down to the football field those who wished to be saved.

The night I played at the crusade, I pounded out "Amazing Grace" on a nine-foot Steinway. The first time I had performed this arrangement was a few weeks earlier with the Nashville Symphony in Centennial Park. On that night, while the symphony and I were in the midst of Paderewski's "Minuet In G," two people began running through the crowd, unfurling a banner. I was not surprised. I had been wondering if it would be possible for a governor to perform without an interruption at an open-air concert before two thousand people.

The crowd had surged forward, pushing the front row nearly onto the stage. In the second row, someone suffered a seizure, and paramedics fought their way to the patient, who was just below me.

I kept playing.

The television cameramen, eager to record my wrong notes, tried every angle, including one just above the piano strings, with the camera shoved six inches from my face.

I kept playing.

At one point, I lost my place in the music and the orchestra raced about four measures ahead. I kept my eye on the maestro's baton and made sure I finished playing at the same time the orchestra finished. No one seemed to notice.

The Sunday afternoon concert brought a lot of joy to a lot of people, as music has always brought to me. Since my first piano lesson at age three, music had become an essential part of my life. The metronome was my steady friend, its beat my closest companion. Its tick-tock, tick-tock, tick-tock became a part of me, measuring my struggle with Bach's counterpoints, Rachmaninoff's hard left hand, Mozart's runs, and Czerny's arpeggios. Mastering Czerny exercises made me feel better prepared for almost anything. Amid the busyness of life on Ruth Street, music resonated within me and gave me peace, especially Mozart's sonatas and the gospel songs of Albert E. Brumley.

And music was fun—whether I was playing Elvis tunes for friends, hymns at school assemblies or church, singing in choir practice, playing melodies for girls who hung around the piano in our law school dormitory, or sliding my trombone with the Mustache Stompers on Bourbon Street or on the back of a flatbed truck with Alexander's Washboard Band.

On Saturday mornings, I would drive from the governor's residence to the Steinway store and play various pianos, comparing their tone and personality. I bought a seven-foot Steinway Model "B" for our mountain cabin, causing Honey to build a separate office for me "to get the noise of your piano and typing on your computer out of the house."

Because music seemed to be the one thing that united the three grand divisions of our long state, I asked—and the legislature agreed—to appropriate funds to endow local orchestras. My appearance with the Nashville Symphony was the first of twenty-seven concerts in which I performed on the piano with community orchestras to raise additional funds. At the invitation of Governor Pete du Pont, I performed with the Delaware Symphony Orchestra.[1]

Being invited to play the piano at the Billy Graham crusade resurrected boyhood memories of when Dad would lead singing at church, and I would play hymns on the piano. We were Presbyterians, not Evangelicals, but I knew many of Brumley's gospel tunes by heart—such as "Turn Your Radio On," "I'll Fly Away," and "There's a Little Pine Log Cabin"—and I liked to jazz them up the way I had heard them on Sunday morning radio. I would tell Dad that if we only had a tent and a collection plate, we could go on the road.

Dad had a pure tenor voice and his love for singing went back to *his* boyhood. His father's farm was next to the National Campground on the edge of the Little Tennessee River where the Cherokee civilization had once flourished. Neighbors created the campground after the Civil War with the hope that good singing and strong preaching in weeklong meetings would unite the Confederate and Union families who had been bushwhacking each other. Families would bring food and bedding on wagons and camp outdoors.

"Let everybody sing like we're getting the clothes off the line in a hard shower," was how Dad described the way they went at it. On hot August nights, he could hear the singing from the family's nearby white frame farmhouse.

"Are you any relation to Charles M. Alexander?" Cliff Barrows had asked me the night before I played the piano at the Graham crusade.

"Yes," I told Barrows. "We're cousins who grew up in the same county. His grandfather and my great-great grandfather were brothers." His face brightened.

"Charles M. Alexander was the world's greatest song leader at the turn of the century," Barrows said. "He studied under Dwight Moody, traveled with Billy Sunday, and went around the world to England, Australia, and even Japan with Wilbur Chapman and R.A Torrey. Those meetings drew thousands. And he was the one who brought them to their feet, singing their hearts out. He inspired me to do what I do today."[2]

A month after the Nashville crusade, Barrows sent me a book about Charles M. Alexander's life. I turned the pages at random, starting on the last page. When I reached the front page, I stared at it. There was this signature:

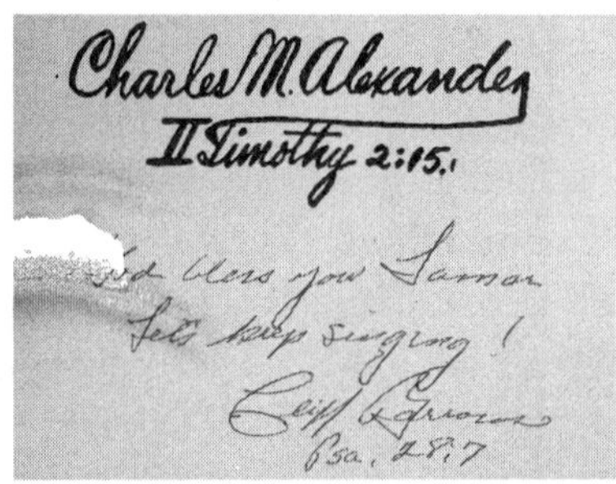

In 1895, that verse had been his "year-text," used around the world wherever he led singing. My mind flashed back six months to my early swearing-in. Honey had found and remembered to bring to the ceremony the Bible first used by my great-grandparents at their marriage in 1868. I had opened the Bible to II Timothy 2:15 and placed my left hand on it before I raised my right hand to take the oath of office. I chose the verse that had been my father's favorite: "Study to shew thyself approved unto God, a workman that needeth not to be ashamed, rightfully dividing the word of truth."

Dad never told me why this verse meant so much to him. If I had not been invited to play the piano for Billy Graham and to meet Cliff Barrows, I might never have known that the verse was important to Dad because it was important to Charles M. Alexander.

II Timothy 2:15, as my parents taught it, had become my primary Rule of Life—"Work: Figure out what God has put you on this earth to do and get busy doing it." A Sunday school lesson from Psalm 90:12 added urgency: "So teach us to number our days, that we may apply our hearts unto wisdom." In other words, make every day count.

Together, the two verses produced a recipe for a purposeful life.

CHAPTER 21

The Japanese Are Coming

"Rule 178. Don't be afraid to put most of your eggs in one basket—
as long as it's the right basket."

—LAMAR ALEXANDER'S LITTLE PLAID BOOK

Nashville to Tokyo. 1979.

On a snowy evening in late February 1979, Honey and I stepped out of a Yellow Cab to attend our first White House dinner.

The occasion was the president's annual tribute to the National Governors' Association, of which I had become a member just five weeks earlier. Honey, who was six months pregnant, had flown from Nashville to Washington, DC, that morning.

Our taxi had driven along the winding drive through the south lawn to the ground-floor entrance. There, it joined a procession of black SUVS driven by state troopers who were depositing other governors and their spouses. It had not occurred to me that it was necessary or even appropriate to use state airplanes and troopers to travel to Washington, DC.

As photographers' flashbulbs popped, Honey, lovely in a long light blue gown, and I, in a dark blue suit, walked into the Diplomatic Reception Room. We climbed wide stairs to the first floor, where we mingled with other governors, Cabinet members, White House staffers, and their spouses. Some guests wandered among the pillars and along the walls examining presidential portraits. The gathering was not large. Capacity for the State Dining Room is 140.

Trumpets played "Hail to the Chief," announcing the arrival of the president and first lady. After "doing away with the ruffles and flourishes of that sort of thing for a little while," Jimmy Carter had recently reinstated the trumpets.[1] His detractors gossiped that the real reason for changing his mind was that without the trumpets, nobody noticed when Carter entered the room.

The dinner was an elegant affair. Honey loved the bowls of white camellias and red roses on the mantle above the fireplace. Guests sat at round tables of ten. At the center of each table were lilies of the valley.

"Rosalynn helped to pot these lilies of the valley and they're for you to take home with you as a memento of tonight," the president said.

Following dinner, the president made remarks before toasting the governors. His message boiled down to this: "Governors, go to Japan. Persuade them to make in the United States what they sell in the United States. Bring their plants and those jobs to your states. And while you're there, persuade those Japanese to buy more of what we sell."

Carter's goal was to turn governors into fifty trade ambassadors. The size of the US trade deficit with Japan—then the world's two largest economies—was embarrassing to both countries. Considering how many Americans were buying, driving, sitting on, playing with, and watching the screens of Japanese products, some worried that the Japanese economy would become number one. The president meant for us governors to help him do something about that.

While the president spoke, I was thinking that I had walked 1,022 miles across Tennessee, spent the night with seventy-three families, tried to shake 1,000 hands a day, and not one Tennessean had said to me, "I sure hope one of the first things you do as governor is go to Japan."

But I was also thinking about what Lillian Knight had said when I spent one of those nights with her family in Rutherford County. Lillian was the Lascassas Elementary School secretary, and her husband, Billy, the local postmaster.

"I am sad tonight. My twin boys are smart, but they'll never find a good job around here, and I'll never see my grandchildren," she said after her children had gone to bed and the living room was quiet.

My walk reminded me that the Knights were not the only Tennessee family worried about finding good jobs. Back then, our state was the third lowest in family incomes. The national economy was in shambles. In a turbulent world, the most important trends were headed in one direction and Tennessee was headed in another. Add recent scandals in state government to that gloomy scenario, and Tennesseans' confidence was at a low ebb.

"My goal is to raise family incomes," I had pledged in my inaugural address.

One way to do that was to take Carter's advice. He encouraged governors to travel to many countries. He had traveled to ten himself as governor, he said. But I figured that the world is big and I am only one governor, and that if I pick one objective and focus on it with everything I've got for as long as I am in office, I could wear everybody else out.

The next week, I invited Dean Rusk, who had been secretary of state to Presidents Kennedy and Johnson, to Tennessee to teach me how to build relationships with Japan. Soon thereafter, Economic and Community Development Commissioner Jim Cotham took his first of several trips to Japan. In September, Honey and I hosted a picnic at the governor's residence for Japanese families living and working in Tennessee.

In November 1979, nine months after our White House dinner, Honey, Cotham, and I traveled to Tokyo for dinner with the Chairman of Nissan Motor Corporation, Katsuji Kawamata and its CEO, Takashi Ishihara. A Nissan task force was concluding a six-year search for a US truck plant location. For some lucky state, this would mean thousands of good auto jobs. In those days, Tennessee had no car or truck assembly plant and only one significant auto parts supplier.[2]

Good news came almost exactly one year after our Tokyo dinner. At 11:30 a.m. on Thursday, October 30, 1980, Marvin Runyon, chief executive of Nissan North America, called.

"We're coming to Tennessee," he said.

Three years later, Nissan built its first truck in Smyrna, twenty-four miles south of Nashville. It became the highest-volume assembly plant in North America. In August 1985, General Motors announced it would locate its Saturn automobile plant forty-one miles from the Nissan plant. It became the largest GM plant in the world.

In 2005, Nissan moved its North American headquarters from California to Williamson County outside Nashville. In 2008, Volkswagen chose Chattanooga for its only North American manufacturing plant. And in September 2021, Ford Motor Company said it would build electric truck and electric vehicle battery assembly plants near Memphis at the 3,600-acre "Blue Oval City," described as "the most advanced, most efficient auto production complex in [the company's] 118-year history."[3]

These manufacturers—plus those who have located in adjacent states—have attracted nearly 1,000 suppliers to eighty-eight of Tennessee's ninety-five counties. In 2021, there were 140,000 auto jobs—one-third of all manufacturing jobs in Tennessee. As the automotive sector surged, family incomes did too.

* * *

How did a state that, in 1980, had almost no auto jobs suddenly become the fastest-growing state for auto jobs?

At first glance, Japan would seem an unlikely catalyst. Japan is a skinny country, literally on the other side of the world. Today in Tennessee is almost always tomorrow in Japan. This time difference left me sleepy for days.

Time and distance were not the only differences. The Japanese language is hard for English speakers. Buddhist temples instead of Baptist churches dot the hillsides. Manners are different. Never arrive late. Don't hug. Don't admire an object or a Japanese person will give it to you. Don't leave a tip—they'll think you forgot your money.

Most Japanese are physically smaller than Americans—and, because they eat raw fish, rice, and vegetables instead of fast food, they are healthier. More than once, I put into my suitcoat pocket an ominous-looking piece of squid or eel.

The inhabitants of Japan all look Japanese because almost all *are* Japanese. A person of any race or background can become an American by pledging allegiance to an idea. It is not possible to become Japanese in that way. Japanese people are so skeptical of the 2.6 percent of island residents who are foreigners that they have a word for them—*gaijin*.

Then there is "The War." Our 1979 Tokyo dinner came only thirty-four years after American atomic bombs devastated Nagasaki and Hiroshima. Mitsuya Goto, who attended that dinner as an interpreter, later gave me two miniature airplanes he had carved. They were replicas of General Jimmy Doolittle's carrier-based fighter planes that had flown over Nagoya, strafing railroad yards when Goto was a boy.

"The planes flew so low that I could see the faces of the pilots from the rooftop of my grandfather's house," Goto told me.

During a dinner in his honor at the Tennessee governor's residence, Nissan CEO Ishihara asked me about the silver service displayed on the sideboard along the wall of the dining room. I did not tell him that it was the captain's silver from the USS Tennessee, which the Japanese had bombed at Pearl Harbor. Most Japanese men we met who were more than fifty-five years old had fought in that war. Some Tennessee war veterans still had nightmares of death marches from Japanese prison camps in China.

Yet, some aspects of Japan we found familiar. Tokyo's latitude is about the same as Nashville's, so our climate, seasons, and love of nature are alike. Irises, azaleas, and maple leaves show their colors at the same time. The mist in Nikko's mountains reminded us of the Great Smokies. It seemed that every Japanese man we met in a bar could sing the "Tennessee Waltz," the first popular American song they had heard after the war.

Because their economy was based on exporting products made in Japan, the Japanese felt inexperienced and insecure away from home. Kawamata and Ishihara had only reluctantly become persuaded that, if Nissan did not build trucks in the United States, President Carter would impose tariffs that would make Japan-made vehicles too expensive to sell here.

Kawamata, seventy-four, a stout and genial bear of a man who had led Nissan to become Japan's second-largest carmaker, burst out laughing halfway through our dinner in 1979. Through the interpreter, I asked why.

"Because I am considering making in your state the largest investment ever outside of Japan, and I am twice as old as you are!" he replied.

In Japan, seniority and hierarchy reign. You always shake hands first with the Number One man and laugh *only* at his jokes. (There were no Number One women, then.) Kawamata must have been assuming that the governor was at the top of the state hierarchy in the same way he was at the top of Nissan.

From that conversation, I learned a lesson. Over the next eight years, I traveled eight more times to Japan, visiting four times with the prime minister, and dozens of times with ambassadors, government leaders, and business officials. I figured—correctly, as it turned out—that Japanese leaders expected to meet with the state's Number One person rather than with staff.

In those years, Japanese and Tennesseans knew almost nothing about one another. In 1979, after Commissioner Cotham had made his best pitch at the end of his seventh visit to Japan, a Japanese businessman smiled politely.

"Now, please tell me, Mr. Cotham. Just what *is* a Tennessee?" the businessman asked.

I had to figure out what would be the best way to approach the Japanese when all they knew about us was Jack Daniel's, Elvis, Brenda Lee, and the "Tennessee Waltz," and all we knew about them was "Madame Butterfly," Mount Fuji, and hot springs.

A photograph became my secret weapon.

CHAPTER 22

Bridge to the Sun

"When I come here, I feel at home."[1]

—**MASAHIKO ZAITSU, Nissan executive 1985**

Nashville to Tokyo. 1980–1986.

ON MY FIRST VISIT TO TOKYO, I introduced Tennessee to the Japanese with a photograph of the United States taken at night from a satellite.

"Where is Tennessee?" Katsuji Kawamata, the Nissan chairman, asked as he looked at the photograph of our country with all its lights on at night.

"Right in the middle of the lights," I said, pointing to Tennessee in the center of a brightly lit eastern United States with many dark areas between the Mississippi River and California.

Central location was Tennessee's first advantage in recruiting the auto industry. In the early 1900s, Henry Ford, Walter Chrysler, and Louis Chevrolet all invented cars in Detroit. It made sense to build the cars where they were invented because then the Midwest was at the center of the American population. That central location reduced the shipping costs of millions of vehicles. By 1979, the American population center had shifted from the Midwest to Kentucky and Tennessee—but the production of cars and trucks had not shifted with it. Nissan understood this.

The second major advantage Tennessee had was its right-to-work law, allowing workers to have a job without paying union dues. Kentucky and every other centrally located state north of Tennessee did not have one. The right-to-work law created a different labor environment. In his 1986 book, *The Reckoning*, David Halberstam recounts how an oligopoly composed of the United Auto Workers union and the Big Three—Ford, Chrysler, and General Motors—ignored the 1970s energy crisis and barreled ahead, paying high wages to make large and unreliable vehicles that were sold at high prices. This allowed small, affordable, and reliable Japanese and German cars and trucks to make their way into the American market.[2]

Nissan wanted to avoid the high costs and inefficiencies of the Midwestern labor environment. That meant no UAW. It also meant hiring Marvin Runyon, a Ford Motor Company vice president and Texas A&M graduate eager to return to the sunbelt.

"I want to combine the best of Japanese and American management philosophies to try to build the highest quality cars and trucks in North America," he'd said.

Runyon, who had once been a Ford assembly line worker, recruited a team of other Ford executives who had grown frustrated with the constraints imposed by Detroit's labor and management practices, and who also were eager to apply their skills at a start-from-scratch plant.

The third advantage was the Tennessee Valley Authority. The federally chartered utility's ability to offer large amounts of low-cost and reliable electricity was a major factor in bringing auto jobs to Tennessee. In February 2023, the chief executive officer of Ford Motor Company told me that TVA was the "decisive factor" in the location of Ford's massive West Tennessee facility.

Although almost every state east of the Mississippi River was pursuing the Nissan truck plant by the summer of 1980, the requirements for a central location and a right-to-work law had narrowed the final decision to Tennessee and Cartersville, Georgia. Tennessee started at a disadvantage. In November 1979, when I arrived for my first Tokyo visit, sixty-seven Japanese companies already located in Georgia were hosting a reception honoring Georgia Governor George Busbee. Marvin Runyon had let me know during his first visit to Tennessee that he and Busbee were close friends.[3] And President Carter, who was pushing the Japanese to make their cars and trucks in the United States, was the former governor of Georgia.

After realizing how uneasy the Japanese were about doing business outside their own country, my strategy was to create a fourth advantage by doing everything I could to make Nissan feel at home in Tennessee. During my first twenty-four months as governor, I spent eight working weeks solely on Japan relations—three weeks in Japan and the rest visiting with an endless stream of Japanese visitors to Tennessee—from the National Diet, newspapers, chambers of commerce, and Nissan. Masahiko Zaitsu, from Nissan's Los Angeles office, was a guest at the governor's residence eleven times in 1979 and 1980. Our children began to think of him as some sort of Japanese uncle.

And I paid close attention to anything Nissan CEO Takashi Ishihara said or wanted. Ishihara was large for a Japanese man.

"[He had] the fierceness of a rugby player and the precision of an accountant," the *New York Times* said.[4]

Ishihara was also a risk-taker and a hands-on executive. In January 1980, he drove to Dickson County to inspect the depth of rock to determine its suitability for heavy equipment. Then he identified 437 acres south of Nashville in Rutherford County that he wanted for the plant.

"Tennessee doesn't own that land. Maymee Cantrell does. Nissan would have to buy it from Maymee, and she does not want to sell," I tried to explain to Ishihara.

That conversation produced nightmares of Nissan going to Georgia, so I visited Maymee one chilly February morning at her home in Waverly. In her breakfast room, she served iced tea and key lime pie.

"Maymee, I hope you will let Nissan buy your land. It will tell the whole world that Tennessee is the best place to do business and bring jobs to people who need them," I said.

"I believe in what you are trying to do, but I've promised our caretaker, Mr. Ward, that he could live on the farm, and I won't break my promise," she said.

I found a different farm ten miles away that Mr. Ward could manage. Saying that satisfied her promise, and Maymee agreed to sell.

But four hundred acres weren't enough. Ishihara also wanted the 260-acre McClary farm adjacent to Maymee's. Mr. and Mrs. R.W. McClary were in their seventies. Their farm had been in the family for a century. We talked it over on a hot June night, rocking on their screened porch. They agreed to sell.

In 1983, when the first Nissan truck rolled off the line, I saw Katherine McClary as we both left the ceremony.

"How do you feel?" I asked her.

"We did the right thing for the people of the area. I know that. But if you really want to know the truth, I can't say it makes me happy to lose our farm," she said.

On July 14, 1980, I was attending the Republican National Convention in Detroit. Teachers' salaries were higher there, and universities were better funded. There were more research facilities. I was reminded of what a money magnet the auto industry is, collecting billions from all over America, and pouring most of those dollars into payrolls, taxes, parts, and services within 250 miles of their plants and headquarters. When I learned that Ishihara was making a surprise visit to Nashville, I canceled a meeting with the next American chief executive, Ronald Reagan, and flew home to see the Nissan CEO.

After Nissan decided to locate to Smyrna, an ugly incident at the plant's groundbreaking ceremony threatened to derail the project. On February 3, 1981, a cold and rainy Tuesday morning, hundreds of union workers—most from out of state—stood in the mud around the construction site, hurling rocks at police.

"Go home, Jap!" they shouted.

They were angry because Nissan was using a construction company that hired nonunion as well as union workers. Citing safety concerns, the highway patrol recommended that Speakers Wilder, McWherter, and I not attend. The Speakers did not attend. I did. When I arrived, it was clear that the fifty state troopers assigned to the incident were not one too many. The demonstrators had slashed the tires of the Nissan pickup truck Marvin Runyon was driving. They had spread nails on the ground. I had never been so disgusted.

I walked to the platform set up in the muddy field, grabbed the microphone, and reminded the audience of Mel Tillis's song "Detroit City"—about a Southerner working at an auto plant in Detroit who croons about wanting "to go home" and how, because of Nissan, Tennesseans would now not have to leave home to find jobs in auto plants.

Tennesseans watching television heard my words, saw the demonstrations, and became incensed. The legislature condemned the riots. Japanese watching TV saw that the demonstration had backfired, creating an even warmer welcome for them in Tennessee.

* * *

In the fall of 1984, I drove to Gwen Terasaki's home in Johnson City. She told me the story of her book, *Bridge to the Sun.* A half-century earlier, Gwen—a Tennessee girl—had married Terry Terasaki, the first secretary to the Japanese embassy in the United States.

"We hoped our love would help to build a rainbow of peace across the Pacific," she said.

After Pearl Harbor, the United States interned the Terasakis and their daughter, Mariko, in White Sulphur Springs, West Virginia, then shipped them to Tokyo. After the war, in 1947, Terry became ill and insisted that Gwen take Mariko to the US. Ten months later, Terry was dead.

"Now you can help build that bridge, Governor," Gwen said as I left her home.

We were working hard to build that bridge. The state created Saturday schools to help Japanese children keep up with mathematics and the Japanese language, and a Japan Center to assist families. Honey invited every Japanese family living in Tennessee to a picnic at the governor's residence. Brenda Lee, the tiny but big-voiced, red-headed singer who spent fifteen weeks each year in Japan, helped make the Japanese feel at home in Tennessee.

When Mr. and Mrs. Ishihara visited Tennessee, Honey and I drove them to Cades Cove in the Great Smoky Mountains. We spread a picnic lunch in the meadow near a spring by towering hemlocks. On the mile high mountains surrounding us, red maples displayed their autumn colors. I hoped that our Japanese friends would feel as at home in Cades Cove as we did when we visited Nikko in the mountains of Japan.

Honey and I began to feel even more at home on our visits to Japan. We both looked forward to mornings when we could run three miles around the Emperor's Palace, greet new friends in the massive lobby of the Imperial Hotel, or shop in the Ginza for Mikimoto pearls and new electronic wonders for our children.

In 1985, I asked Tennessee's Pulitzer Prize-winning state photographer with the improbable name Robin Hood to spend five months in Japan with his camera, capturing the unusual friendship developing between a Pacific Island nation and an inland American state. Robin's photographs were collected in the book, *Friends: Japanese and Tennesseans,* for which I wrote the text.

The pictures reveal profound differences, but they also show how Tennesseans found familiar glimpses of our own life deep within Japanese culture, comparing churches with pagodas, cherry blossoms in Franklin and azalea blossoms at the Nezu Shrine, quilters in Norris and Kyoto, the Grand Ole Opry's Grandpa Jones and a Kabuki actor, a Nashville farmer's market and a Tokyo fish and vegetable market.

At Christmas that year, Honey and I gave friends two of Robin's photographs. One was of the wild iris that is beloved in Japan. The other was of Rachel Jackson's iris garden at The Hermitage in Nashville.

In 1986, during my last trip to Tokyo as governor, I visited the son of the founder of Bridgestone Tire Company at his Tokyo home near the Imperial Palace. I expressed my appreciation for Bridgestone's plant near Nashville. On the coffee table next to Mr. Ishibashi's chair was a single book—*Friends: Japanese and Tennesseans.* That year, the former Japanese ambassador to the United States, Yoshio Ōkawara, estimated that 10 percent of all Japanese capital investment in the United States was in one state—Tennessee.

A *New York Times* reporter asked Masahiko Zaitsu why so many Japanese businesses had moved to Tennessee. His answer described what turned out to be our greatest advantage over other states—a relentless effort to welcome the Japanese to such a different country.

"When I come here, I feel at home," Zaitsu said.

* * *

My favorite part of this remarkable story is that as I write this book the Nissan plant sprawls across eight hundred acres of the farms where the

McClary children once played with the children of Maymee Cantrell's farm manager. The plant is only ten miles from Lascassas, where I spent the night on my walk in 1978 and Lillian Knight told me that she was afraid that she would never see her grandchildren because her "smart twin boys will never find a job around here."

In 2006, one of those boys, Ronnie Knight, became manager of the Nissan plant and its seven thousand employees. That same year, Ronnie's twin, Ricky, was a Nissan floor production manager.

And the grandson Lillian Knight was afraid she would never see was in his second year as a Nissan associate.

CHAPTER 23

The Sniper

"You'll have to decide whether to go ahead with the inauguration."

—TOM INGRAM, Chief of Staff, Friday, January 14, 1983

Nashville. Saturday, January 15, 1983.

I WORE A BULLETPROOF VEST during my second inaugural address.

"We think we've found a sniper in the Hermitage Hotel. He's in custody but he may have friends," Tom Ingram said on the day before the swearing-in.[1]

Before that conversation, it had been a great day. Visitors were arriving for the ceremony, which would be staged outdoors at noon on the legislative plaza between the Capitol and the Hermitage Hotel. Despite the bad national economy, I had won a second term when most Republican governors running for reelection had lost their jobs.

"What do you mean, a sniper?" I snapped, sounding like I was blaming Ingram for the bad news.

He told me the story.

"Last night, police picked up a man for using stolen credit cards. He had a rifle and a toolbox in his room at the Hermitage Hotel. We investigated because the man had written you a threatening letter and because of comments he had made about you in a book he was writing. The Secret

Service already was involved because of earlier letters he had written to Rosalynn Carter."

I sank in my chair. For the last four years, I had chafed under—and mostly ignored—security restrictions. This cooped up feeling had started on election night in 1978 with Opryland security guards and state troopers pushing aside swarming supporters and forming a tight circle around me until we could move to a comfortable place. Williamson County deputies began sleeping in our den, which disrupted life for a family with three children under the age of ten. Highway patrolmen drove us everywhere.

I caught myself taking out my frustration at the loss of privacy on the troopers. They were doing their best to stay out of my way in a job that paid them to be in the way. But I did not like the idea of hiding from people.

"Here is what else we found," Ingram continued.

"In addition to the rifle and toolbox, we found a snub-nosed .38 Smith & Wesson pistol with hollow-point bullets. The room did not face the legislative plaza where the inaugural will be, but with the tools, he could have easily broken into other rooms or gained access to the hotel roof.

"He had a passport application and an account book showing recent deposits of several thousand dollars. He had an airline ticket from Nashville to Washington at a time just after you are supposed to attend an event at the Hyatt Hotel."

I knew that governors received threats and that Louisiana's Governor Huey Long had been assassinated. After the 1970 election, I had heard Governor Ellington tell Governor-elect Dunn that he was going to build an iron fence around the governor's residence because a man had wandered in the front door one day with a loaded pistol.

Threatening letters had come to me, too, but I never read them. Staffers fielded those, as well as angry calls. I suppose that I should have worried about unhappy murderers who I kept locked up in the state prison after the FBI said they had paid cash for their pardon from Governor Blanton. The only time I was anxious was when a woman who had threatened our children appeared one Sunday morning, sitting in the church pew behind us. My plan for tomorrow was to put on my red-and-black plaid shirt, and do what I had done four years earlier—walk at the head of the inaugural parade. I did not want to avoid the people that I was elected to serve.

Saturday morning arrived clear and cold. I looked out from the inaugural platform across brightly colored hats perched on several hundred bundled onlookers, and across the legislative plaza to the Hermitage Hotel. Today, the hotel seemed taller. As the ceremony proceeded, sometimes it seemed like it was the only building on the square. The bulletproof vest under my black raincoat felt as large as shoulder pads under a football uniform, but no one seemed to notice. Behind me in the shadows around the top of the Capitol, I saw police sharpshooters. For the first time, I was worried.

"What if someone does fire a rifle and misses me, hitting our children, hitting anyone? Should I stop the ceremony to be safe?" I wondered.

I hurried through my address. The twenty-one cannon shots that ended the ceremony seemed to last forever. I left the stage and changed clothes, draping a loose red-and-black plaid jacket over my broadened shoulders, before walking to the head of the inaugural parade. Away from the plaza, I felt more relaxed, but I was glad when the day ended.

After that day, I put the sniper suspect—who stayed in jail on other charges—and most other security considerations out of my mind. My official duties during the second term remained the same as the first—open meetings, public events, and walking in the Mule Day parade. I finally agreed to allow a highway patrol car to follow the one in which I rode, to putting bulletproof glass in the window behind my desk at the Capitol, and to installing electronic eyes at the residence.

The only other security incident I can remember occurred years later during the Senate Obamacare debate.

"The senator deserves to be shot," a caller to my Nashville office said.

"Sir, that is the kind of comment that can cause the FBI to want to talk with you," a staff member replied.

"Oh, I don't want to shoot him. I just hope someone does," the caller said.

CHAPTER 24

Best Harmonica Player in the World

"Governor, I have just one question.
When are you going to go away and leave us alone?"

—REPRESENTATIVE ROBB ROBINSON,
Chairman of the House Transportation Committee

Nashville. 1983–1986.

On a pleasant September evening in 1985, Honey and I hosted General Motors executives at a dinner on the patio at the governor's residence.

We were celebrating their decision to locate the $3.5-billion Saturn automobile plant in Spring Hill. For a taste of Tennessee, Honey served fried okra, corn on the cob, biscuits, and Early's Tried & True Country Ham. As the sun drifted behind the white oaks on the front lawn, guests moved into the living room where Charlie McCoy performed on the harmonica and Andrew Jackson peered from his portrait above the fireplace.

When guests were leaving, a Nashville matron confronted me.

"Oh governor, I'm so embarrassed. What will these fine people from Michigan think of us? Why did you have that harmonica player? Why didn't you offer Chopin?" she asked.

"Why should I offer average Chopin when we have the best harmonica player in the world?" I replied.

The matron's complaint was a symptom of a persistent problem for Tennesseans in the early 1980s—a lack of self-confidence. Too often we ignored our strengths, wished we were what we were *not,* and doubted that we could compete with the best. Some Nashvillians worried about being labeled "Music City," although plenty of cities would have paid big money to corner that brand. Memphis ignored its Beale Street blues and agricultural heritage, wishing it were more like Nashville. Chattanooga was still recovering from Walter Cronkite's description of it in 1969 as "the dirtiest city in America."[1] Upper East Tennessee communities, which were nearer to Canada than to Memphis, felt ignored.

And then there was Knoxville. Despite being home to the nation's largest energy laboratory (Oak Ridge), biggest public utility (TVA), most popular national park (the Great Smokies), and a major research university (the University of Tennessee), Knoxvillians persisted in thinking that their city added up to less than the sum of its considerable parts, and instead kept reminding themselves that the *Wall Street Journal* had once referred to it as "a scruffy little city."[2]

"Do you like living here?" they would ask a newcomer as if they were pretty sure the newcomer would not.

This insecurity emanated from several sources. For African Americans, it was the residue of slavery. For White Middle and West Tennesseans, it was the defeat of their Confederate ancestors. For mountaineers, it was growing up being called hillbillies. When I was a boy, we would smash snowballs into the windshields of Ohio cars racing through Maryville toward the Florida sun. The cars would screech to a stop.

"You blasted little hillbillies. Go home to your mothers!" these sour Yankees would shout as we ran away.

In the 1930s, East Tennesseans' incomes were one-third of the national average. Most mountain people were poor—but they were proud. During a visit to Knoxville in the 1960s, television's *College Bowl* show asked its University of Tennessee audience to wear overalls. Insulted, the students showed up in tuxedos. Hurt feelings and repressed pride—among descendants of slaves, Confederates, and those labeled hillbillies—had created a state of citizens with low self-esteem and low aspirations.

My cure for low aspirations was to start winning. That is why I believed that coming in first in the Nissan competition in 1980—thirty-nine states put in bids for the plant—was as important as attracting its seven thousand jobs.

Winning the Saturn competition five years later made it two big "firsts" in a row. To build a small car that would compete with Japanese and German cars, the world's biggest corporation would make the largest one-time investment in US history.

Again, every state east of the Mississippi River wanted the plant. Governors began making fools of themselves, pitching their states to Phil Donahue's television talk show. The media frenzy became so intense that as many Americans could identify a Saturn as they could a Pontiac, even though not one Saturn had been built yet—and General Motors had been building Pontiacs since 1926.

In May 1985, I saw GM Chairman Smith at a Washington dinner.

"Do I need to go on the *Donahue* show?" I asked.

"Oh no. That's not the way we do it. We'll send our people in without anybody knowing it, find out what the people think, and option the land," he said.

Then he added, "It *would* be smart to pass the seat belt law."

Passing the seat belt law required hauling reluctant, freedom-loving legislators into the governor's office, one by one.

"You might want to rise above principle if you want auto jobs in your hometown," I explained to them.

Still, I looked for an opportunity to make Tennessee's case to General Motors. I knew that Nissan's choosing Tennessee would be either the kiss of death or the hook. In June, Senator Baker and I met with Smith in Memphis after he spoke at a United Way luncheon.

"Put your Saturn plant right next to the Nissan plant, and tell your union and your management, 'If the Japanese can do it here, you can do it too,'" I told Smith, pointing to a big map of Tennessee.

Six weeks later, GM did just that. On Tuesday, July 30, 1985, the company announced that it would locate the Saturn plant twenty miles from the Nissan plant. I wrote an ad and spent $450,000 of state money on a ten-day, full-page national newspaper advertising blitz.

"Well, Saturn finally found its home… in Spring Hill, Tennessee…. Saturn is here. Nissan is here. Where are you? Here's my phone number. 615-741-2001," the ad said.[3]

There was a third opportunity to win an auto plant first prize—Toyota. For three years, I had been trying to wrangle a meeting with Dr. Shoichiro Toyoda, the son of the company's founder. On the day in 1985 that GM announced its Saturn decision, Dr. Toyoda invited me to meet him in Toyota City.

I worried that Toyota would not want to locate its US plant in the same state as its rival, Nissan. To address that concern, I carried large color photographs of the Great Smoky Mountains, its flowers, and black bears to Toyota City.

I sat on one side of a long table. A dozen Japanese executives sat on the other with Dr. Toyoda at their center.

"Tennessee has mountains and flowers and black bears, just as Japan does," I said, displaying my photographs.

"Ahhhh, so," the Japanese said in unison.

"Our irises bloom in the spring and maples turn red in October, just like in Japan. You will feel at home," I said.

"Ahhhh, so."

"Our bears have territories, just like yours do."

"Ahhhh, so."

"Nissan has a territory near Nashville."

Scowls around the table.

"But we have a territory for Toyota two hundred miles from the Nissan plant, near the Great Smoky Mountains."

More scowls.

Toyota located its plant in Kentucky and hired 8,000 employees. A few months later, a Toyota executive met me at a governor's conference in Virginia.

"We have a small consolation prize, a Toyota supplier, Nippon Denso, for your hometown of Maryville. It has one hundred jobs—but it might grow," he said, bowing.

Nearly forty years later, in 2025, Denso, as the company now is called, employs 6,100 Tennesseans and is one of the most advanced auto parts suppliers in the world.

I counted our pursuit of auto plants as two home runs and a triple—a better batting average than any other state, a boost to Tennessee's prestige, and, more importantly, to our self-confidence.

* * *

Recruiting Saturn taught me that there was another opportunity for Tennessee to lead the country—build the best four-lane highways.

"Exactly how do you choose plant sites?" I asked GM executives in late 1985.

"For Saturn, we used three banks of computers that analyzed one thousand sites in thirty-eight states. We have a just-in-time delivery system for suppliers, so we look first for sites adjacent to high-quality four-lane highways," the executives said.

They also said that Saturn expected to have 650 suppliers within 250 miles of its Spring Hill plant. I wanted those suppliers to be in Tennessee, but I knew that if having the best four-lane highway system made the difference, Tennessee would be runner-up for most of those jobs.

The legislature and I already had enacted three road programs, but our highways were still far from the best. So, I asked the Department of Transportation to list all road projects that needed work. We drew up a plan ambitious enough to give Tennessee the country's best four-lane highway system.

On Monday, February 17, 1986, in my State of the State address, I proposed Tennessee's largest highway program since President Eisenhower started the interstate highway system. The proposal cost $2.8 billion and included 159 miles of new interstate projects, paid for 100 percent by state funds.

In one-on-one meetings in my office, I told legislators, "We want Saturn's six hundred and fifty suppliers. We want to say, 'Come to Tennessee. We're completing the best four-lane highway system so you can move your products where you need to move them and when you want to move them.' For fifteen dollars per motorist per year, less than the cost of one tank of gasoline, we can cut the time it takes to build these roads in half."

Such an ambitious plan startled legislators. They had been expecting a quiet election year session and wanted to go home early to campaign.

"You're not going to leave anything for me to do," grumbled House Speaker McWherter, who was running for governor.

But McWherter also made it possible to pass the bill.

"You and [Jim] Henry (the Republican house leader) get all thirty-eight Republicans to vote for it, and I'll find you thirteen Democrats—but one of them might not be me," he said.

That was all the help I needed from the burly Speaker. We had learned to trust each other during the bipartisan boot camp that led to my early swearing-in. About all one politician needs to know about another politician is exactly where he or she is. I could always count on McWherter to be where he said he would be.

Legislators asked if they would have to vote for a gas tax increase, something they despised.

"There are a lot of ways to pay the bill. Debt, taxes, tolls. We're not going to talk one minute about how to pay the bill until we decide what roads we need to build," I told them again and again.

Then, we constructed a map of Tennessee with 312 road projects drawn on it so legislators could go home and take credit for the new roads in their districts. Finally, to pay for the projects, we settled on an increase of four cents on the gas tax and three cents on diesel fuel.

Representative Lincoln Davis, who represented most of the rural Upper Cumberland counties, was one of the thirteen Democrats McWherter had identified to vote for the projects and the gas tax increase.

But Davis told me, "I can't vote for that. I'd get killed in the next election."

A week later, in his legislative district, he and I met with Overton County commissioners at the courthouse. I showed them the map with a new four-lane highway coming to the county and outlined the share of gas tax revenues that the county would receive to relieve property taxes.

After my presentation, one commissioner stood up in the back of the room.

"Lincoln, if you don't vote for it, we'll defeat you next time," the commissioner said.

Every Republican House member and just enough Democrats, including Davis but not McWherter, voted to enact the plan, 54–37–1. The Senate vote was 26–6. In November, Davis was reelected, and McWherter was elected governor.[4]

With the passage of the new law, the state was able to build the nation's best highways. It paid for this by doubling the gas tax instead of borrowing, leaving Tennessee as one of only six states with zero road debt. As a result, all gas tax revenue went for roads, not to pay interest on debt.

In 1991, the National Truckers Association said Tennessee had the country's best four-lane highway system.

"Driving from Tennessee into Arkansas is like driving from Heaven to Hell," the truckers said.

It was another confidence-building first for Tennesseans.

* * *

As I tried to persuade legislators and the public about what I was asking them to do, I began to pay more attention to how words were strung together—and I developed an aversion to official-ese.

As chairman of the federal agency that created the "National Assessment of Educational Progress," I insisted on renaming it "The Nation's Report Card." I admired the name "right-to-work law" because those four words win the argument before the argument starts. I saluted Memphis for changing its slogan from "Uniport" to "America's Distribution Center."

"Avoid jargon," the *Little Plaid Book* advises.

I noticed how few of my staff and visitors could explain themselves in jargon-free terms. I gave my communications staff (I called them "the "propagandists") Ezra Pound's book, *ABC of Reading*, and recommended his suggestions about spare writing, aggressive editing, and the differences between horrible and interesting writing. I also recommended William Strunk Jr. and E.B. White's *The Elements of Style*, *Ogilvy on Advertising*, and anything Hemingway wrote.

I worked with staff on headlines, first paragraphs, summaries, and bill names—which I am convinced contributed to more persuasive speeches, statements, and legislative successes. Democrats, who had large majorities in the legislature, joked about my obsession with words.

"A bunch of essay writers," was how House Speaker McWherter referred to us.

In his biography of the Speaker, McWherter's aide, Billy Stair, described in more detail how Democrats felt.

"Alexander's frequent use of labels and props became the subject of closed-door humor for legislators and the media. Annual budgets were called 'Bare Bones' or 'No Frills' proposals. Likewise, legislative initiatives were labeled 'Healthy Children,' 'Safe Growth,' or 'Master Teacher.' Many legislators made fun of what they felt was Alexander's preoccupation with the media," Stair wrote.

He went on.

"[The legislators] also conceded that Alexander's public relations efforts were more sophisticated and effective than those of any Tennessee governor in memory.... To counter the Tennessee Education Association's expected opposition to the Master Teacher program, Alexander engaged in a public relations blitz unlike any before witnessed in Tennessee... He provided a simple prop and an effective one-sentence description of his plan that stuck in the public consciousness. Holding up a penny, he would dramatically begin each speech, 'In Tennessee, not one Tennessee teacher is paid one penny more for doing a good job.'

"Thousands of Tennesseans who had little idea how Alexander's Master Teacher Program would work nonetheless became convinced that it was a good idea," Stair wrote.[5]

CHAPTER 25

Getting to Know Reagan

"Rule 216. Surround yourself with people who actually have done something."

—*LAMAR ALEXANDER'S LITTLE PLAID BOOK*

Nashville. 1979–1987.

As the 1980s began, 14.6 percent inflation, 18.4 percent home mortgage rates, and 9.7 percent unemployment hamstrung the American economy even as it was transforming itself.

Economists estimated that 10 percent of jobs were disappearing every year. That meant that, to grow family incomes each year, I would need to help the state replace about 200,000 disappearing jobs. Recruiting a few thousand auto jobs would not be nearly enough to achieve my number one goal.

Such turbulence could be bad news for a state already behind. *Or, perhaps good news,* I thought. While all the balls were in the air, there might be an opportunity to catch up instead of fall back. To better understand how to raise incomes in this changing environment, I invited John Naisbitt, the author of *Megatrends,* to meet with me and my Cabinet.

During an afternoon conversation in 1982 at the governor's residence, Naisbitt described an American economy moving from industrialization to information, from high touch to high tech. There was one takeaway from the meeting that I had not anticipated—the country still has to manufacture things. *If every other state is rushing from industry to information, maybe Tennessee should stick with being the best state for industry,* I thought. Manufacturing was our natural advantage, with our central location, right-to-work laws, and a willing workforce. So, we doubled down on policies to encourage industry, like low taxes, the best highways, removing the cap from bank interest rates to attract capital, and other business-friendly policies.

But that would not be enough. The brunt of Naisbitt's message was, if you want better jobs, you'll have to grow them, not just recruit them. Growing jobs requires skilled people. Most people learn their skills in schools. So, we set a new goal—to improve our colleges and have the best schools. That was ambitious—many said unrealistic—but there was no harm in aiming for the top.

In 1982, Speakers Wilder and McWherter visited my office.

"We think we need to take a look at education to see what needs to be done," Wilder said.

"Let's do it together," I answered.

That discussion launched the most important step we could take to improve the lives of Tennesseans. The three of us appointed a task force headed by Democrat Senate Education Committee Chairman Anna Belle Clement O'Brien, whom everyone called "Miss Anna Belle." She was a skilled partisan who was also known for working across the aisle. The sister of former Governor Clement, she was also a character.

"When I am laid out at my funeral, if there is cornbread in my hands, you'll know I'm dead because I *luvvvv* cornbread," Miss Anna Belle told friends.

On Friday, September 4, 2009, Jim Henry and I were the only two Republicans at her funeral. The casket was open, and cornbread was in her hands.

Tennessee had a long way to go. In 1982, one-third of our eighth graders didn't have eighth-grade-level skills, our high school dropout rate was one of the highest, one-fourth of college freshmen weren't prepared for college, teacher pay was low, and our public schools needed help.

In January 1983, at the outset of my second term as governor, I accepted most of Miss Anna Belle's task force recommendations, added a few, and asked legislators to enact a ten-point "Better Schools Program." For universities, these included $100 million endowments for Chairs of Excellence to attract faculty and $30 million annually for Centers of Excellence.

I asked McWherter to travel with me to visit North Carolina's residential high school for math and science. We decided that its $5 million price tag was too rich, and instead created summer Governor's Schools for gifted high school students in the arts, sciences, international studies, and humanities. Forty years later, there are eleven Governor's Schools that have broadened the horizons of tens of thousands of students, most of whom came from rural schools and most of whom then stayed in Tennessee for college. At Wilder's suggestion, I proposed creating a new state Board of Education.

I flew to Palo Alto, California, to visit Steve Jobs at Apple. Jobs was polite, intense, and curious about a Southern governor's new "Basic Skills First/Computer Skills Next" program. The next year, Tennessee became the first state to buy hundreds of new, bulky Macintosh computers to help all eighth graders become computer literate. Our initiative had one oversight—we trained students, but did not train their teachers.

The most controversial initiative of the "Better Schools Program" was the "Master Teacher Program," a career ladder and evaluation system. Everyone seemed to have a scheme for improving student achievement, but to me, it boiled down to parents and teachers. Since I did not know how to write a "Better *Parents* Program," I proposed a plan to reward better teachers and keep them in the classroom.

In 1983, not one state paid one teacher one penny more for teaching well. When colleges of education told me there was no way to pay teachers more based on their proficiency, I thought that was nonsense. Universities did it. IBM did it. I turned to Chester ("Checker") Finn Jr., a Vanderbilt University professor with whom I had worked on the Nixon White House staff.

He helped design a plan to offer teachers a $1,000 raise if they passed the National Teachers Exam (36,000 did). Instead of the standard nine-month teaching contract, teachers could also qualify for ten-, eleven-, or twelve-month contracts with up to $7,000 more a year in salary—*if* they succeeded on a state-designed evaluation. (Ten thousand eventually did.)

At a meeting on school reform in the fall of 1982, Texas Governor Bill Clements, a brash oilman, had challenged other Southern governors.

"When is one of you bastards going to get up the nerve to take on the NEA?" he asked.

Clements must have been talking to me. The Master Teacher debate provoked a brawl that attracted national attention. The enraged National Education Association even raised the dues of its Tennessee members to fight my plan to pay its members higher salaries. In the 1983 legislative session, the NEA won. Legislators dispatched my career ladder plan to a "graveyard" committee for further study, from which it would likely never return.

I was defeated, but not about to give up. I decided to resign as governor and run for reelection in a special election. I would ask the people the Master Teacher question—should Tennessee become the first state to pay teachers more for teaching well? The state attorney general quashed that idea, saying that I would be running for a third consecutive term and that the constitution only allowed two.

* * *

When my plan to resign didn't work, I brought out my secret weapon. Ronald Reagan agreed to come to Tennessee to tout the "Better Schools Program."

Reagan had become president as I was beginning my third year as governor. As his policies improved the national economy, Tennessee's economy improved at an even faster rate.

In 1981, I asked to meet with Reagan in the Oval Office to propose a grand swap—the federal government would take over all of Medicaid in exchange for states taking all of K–12 schools. That would make it clear who had the responsibility. This fit Reagan's unconventional brand of thinking, and he advocated for the swap, but the idea went nowhere.

He had the same sort of unconventional attitude toward national defense. He built up America's strength so he could reduce nuclear weapons—and do it unilaterally—hoping that the Soviets would follow. In 1985, after I led a People-to-People trip to Russia and China, I again asked to see the president and encouraged him to travel to Russia, where he had never been.

"One of my goals is to eliminate nuclear weapons entirely," he told me in that Oval Office meeting.

He asked me to head his "Presidential Commission on Outdoor Recreation Resources Review," called ORCC for short, which I did only after he agreed to change the name to plain English—"The President's Commission on Americans Outdoors."[1]

Over the years, I learned a lot from Ronald Reagan.

An early lesson came when he fired striking air traffic controllers.

"He told them he would fire them if they went on strike. They struck. He fired them and it made my job much easier," Secretary of State George Shultz told me. "After that, every world leader knew that Ronald Reagan would do what he said he would do."

One reason he was called "the great communicator" was that his words were usually his own. He would sit in the back of a campaign plane and make speech notes on cards in his special shorthand, according to his aide, Marty Anderson.

He ignored staff advice when he made his 1987 address at Berlin's Brandenburg Gate.

"Mr. Gorbachev, tear down this wall!" were Reagan's own words.

He also knew how to deliver lines others had written. He moved the world to tears at the fortieth anniversary of D-Day when he spoke of "the boys of Pointe du Hoc," and with his message of hope after the Challenger spacecraft exploded. Speechwriter Peggy Noonan wrote most of those words.

His acting skills benefitted Reagan, as Americans became more interested in how public figures look and perform on the screen. He wore clothes not just to cover himself but to look good. When we flew to Nashville on Air Force One, he took off his suit, hung it in the closet so it wouldn't get wrinkled, and put on jogging pants. He often kept a contact lens in one eye so he could read speech notes with the other.

At age fifty-five, he had come late enough to public life to have thought about what he wanted to do and say. He knew why he wanted to be president—to face down an evil empire abroad (the Soviet Union), and an arrogant empire at home (Washington, DC).

Reagan stuck to his guns and he supported Cabinet members who also did. His education secretary, Bill Bennett, told me that he had once walked into a Cabinet meeting expecting to be in trouble for media criticism of his conservative views.

"Well, what's wrong with the rest of you fellas?" Reagan asked as Bennett took his seat.

With his humor, he even made the press like him, even though most disagreed with him. At a Gridiron Dinner, Reagan strode in smiling, waited until the applause died down, and then said to the journalists, "Thank you very much. I know how hard to is to clap with your fingers crossed."

Of the presidents with whom I worked, Reagan seemed to best understand the need for mature, broad-gauged advisers. He created his own "team of rivals"[2] by selecting as vice president his principal primary opponent, George H.W. Bush, and then hiring Bush's campaign manager, Jim Baker, to be White House chief of staff. Eventually, he hired another primary opponent, Howard Baker, as chief of staff.

Reagan surrounded himself with advisers who had broad experience. They had lived and grown and fought and won and lost in a variety of life's arenas. They had learned to face challenges, unravel complexities, and survive. Such individuals were less likely to become lost in the Washington, DC, maze than someone without such experiences. Reagan was not afraid to hire strong people who had actually done something.

These men did for the president what Bryce Harlow said Eisenhower's Chief of Staff, Sherman Adams, did. "He kept the trash away from the president so he could concentrate on the crucial matters, and made sure it was all properly coordinated and staffed out before it reached the president."

"JFK did not have a chief of staff," Harlow said. "He ran the place like a country store. Lyndon Johnson was his own chief of staff, his own everything else."

Jimmy Carter came to Washington, DC, basically never having been there before, and brought with him a team of aides who also rarely had been there before. By the end of his term, Carter was turning to more experienced hands, but it was too late to salvage his presidency.

Reagan's experienced "team of rivals" helped save his presidency. In 1987, when Reagan fell into trouble over the Iran–Contra scandal, he telephoned Howard Baker, who was in Miami on a family vacation. Joy Baker answered the president's call.

"Where's Howard?" Reagan asked.

"At the zoo with the grandchildren," Joy Baker answered.

"Wait 'til he hears about the zoo I have for him," Reagan said.

Reagan made Baker his chief of staff and told him to get to the bottom of the scandal. Giving Baker that assignment was not without risk. Fourteen years earlier, Baker had helped bring down another Republican president: Richard Nixon.

"We are here to save the president, *if he deserves to be saved,*" Baker told A.B. Culvahouse Jr., the new White House counsel.

Reagan could be jovial. A surefire way to launch a conversation with him was to bring up horses. As a dinner companion, Honey found him charming. But Reagan was not an easy-going backslapper. He kept his distance—so much distance that his authorized biographer, Edmund Morris, found his subject "inscrutable."

Of the ten presidents with whom I worked, I found Ronald Reagan to be the one who best fit the job.

CHAPTER 26

"Not the Same State."

"Rule 147. Be proud of what you do best."

—LAMAR ALEXANDER'S LITTLE PLAID BOOK

Nashville. 1983–1986.

On Tuesday, June 14, 1983, I traveled with Ronald Reagan on Marine One, the presidential helicopter, from Nashville to Knoxville.

During the flight, the president brought up Senator Baker's plans to retire.

"Why don't you run for the Senate?" he asked.

"It's the middle of my second term," I said. "I have big plans. I want to finish the job."

Then, I added, "If I may say so, Mr. President, you never ran for the Senate while you were governor."

"No, I didn't," Reagan said, smiling.

My big plans for that day included visiting Farragut High School to build bipartisan support for another attempt to enact the "Better Schools Program." The event included a national teacher of the year, the state president of the teachers' union, and the legislature's Democrat Speakers, Wilder and McWherter.

"I'm committed to a merit pay concept because that's the American Way," McWherter said at the forum.

Reagan agreed. "There are plenty of outstanding teachers in Tennessee.... What we must do is find them, promote them, and hold them up as role models," the president said. A few weeks later, McWherter stepped in with a "Weakley County Amendment" to gather support from Democrats.

During the remainder of the summer, I traveled to several states, encouraging governors to emulate our Master Teacher Plan so that the National Education Association could not concentrate all its firepower on Tennessee. Checker Finn and I flew to Baltimore to meet with Albert Shanker, president of the NEA's rival union, the American Federation of Teachers.

When I accepted Shanker's invitation to address the union's annual convention in Los Angeles my mother warned, "Be careful, son."

She shouldn't have worried.

"If we have master plumbers, why can't we have master teachers?" Shanker told delegates.

In the fall, I launched a public relations blitz. I recruited Frank Clement, the former Democrat governor's son and Miss Anna Belle's nephew, to head Tennesseans for Better Schools. I hired Democrat Peter Hart and Republican Bob Teeter to poll the state, and then barnstormed, presenting the poll's favorable results and citizen petitions supporting the plan to legislators at public meetings in their districts.

In January 1984, I called legislators into a special session, during which they could consider only the "Better Schools Program." In February, in a remarkable display of bipartisanship, Florida's Democrat Governor Bob Graham stopped in Nashville to help persuade Miss Anna Belle to cast the decisive committee vote in favor of the program. Graham did this even though Florida and Tennessee were in a friendly competition to be the first to enact a pay-for-performance teacher plan.

On Tuesday, March 6, 1984, Tennessee became the first state to pay teachers more for teaching well. If those state stipends had kept up with inflation, at this writing, they would be worth more than twice as much. Many of the 10,000 Master Teachers who voluntarily climbed the career ladder have since told me that their higher salary and retirement pension paid for their children's college expenses.[1]

This flurry of education activity created a national buzz.

"Why Tennessee?" reporters asked the president of the new Saturn plant, Bill Hoglund.

"We liked Tennessee's location and work environment. And we liked Tennessee's commitment to excellence in education, especially to paying more for teaching well. That's our philosophy too," Hoglund said.

"National education news these days is generally divided into two parts: one half is Tennessee, California and Texas. The other half is everybody else." US Secretary of Education Bill Bennett said.

* * *

My final year as governor was 1986, and Tennessee was on a roll.

Family incomes were on their way up. The state's political leadership had worked hard to start winning, but another quiet force was driving the state's growing self-confidence and economic success. That was Tennessee "Homecoming '86." In my second term inaugural address in January 1983, I had asked each of the 3,000 places with names that Tennesseans call home to do three things—"(1) Define what is special about your community; (2) During 1986, celebrate that something special; and (3) Invite everyone who ever lived there to come home to join the celebration."

During my reelection campaign in 1982, my focus shifted from the state Capitol to communities. Honey and I had worked in forty-five "community days" on self-help projects ranging from new libraries to shelters for abused women. I had come to understand that communities—not governors—decide whether to fix schools and prepare for new jobs. Too often, Tennessee communities had set low goals.

I also knew that the guitarist Chet Atkins was right when he said, "Be careful where you aim, because you're likely to get there."

The homecoming idea was that if each town or city understood and celebrated its strengths, it was more likely to set and reach high goals. The state would prosper, community by community. The 1980 Memphis Jobs Conference and Chattanooga's "visioning process" were already showing that such thinking worked for big cities too.

When I explained this idea to legislators in 1983, they yawned. But during 1986, five thousand homecoming celebrations erupted in 540 communities—so many that I gave up trying to attend them. Knoxville's

Forest Brook neighborhood invited every family who had ever lived there to come home for a Fourth of July party. Fifty thousand Tennesseans greeted the Homecoming Train that crossed the state carrying Minnie Pearl, Alex Haley, Tennessee Ernie Ford, and Lynn Anderson. The train symbolized a new spirit.

Our logo, a quilted state flag draped over a rocking chair, symbolized the simplicity and honest lifestyle that drew so many thousands home.[2] New York City and Los Angeles advertising agencies asked for appointments. They were surprised by the power of the homecoming idea and wanted to know where it had come from. Iowa Governor Terry Branstad came to Nashville to learn more about what we were planning and launched Iowa "Homecoming '86."

Four decades later, Tennesseans still talked about that spirit. In 2024, the Halls community, population 2,255, published two volumes describing its 1986 Homecoming Celebration, when the town had invited veterans to come back to a now-abandoned World War II Air Force base to see a Fourth of July display of wartime aircraft. Their homecoming launched seventeen more years of air shows and a veterans' museum, "bringing much recognition and making all of us proud," Mayor Sammie Arnold said.

"There are not too many people who can point to an event and say, 'That changed our lives,' but it surely did," Patricia Higdon, the Halls Homecoming organizer, wrote to me forty years later. Historian Bill Carey has written about other long-lasting Homecoming successes, including Nashville's Southern Festival of Books which, in October 2024, attracted 25,000 people, including about two hundred authors and one hundred vendors.

Connie Dowell grew up in rural Cumberland County in a family that raised hogs, milked cows, and grew tobacco. She was embarrassed by Tennessee's *Beverly Hillbillies* television image. She watched classmates move away, and, eventually, she did too.

She reflected on those changes when, in 2009, she became Vanderbilt University's first Dean of Libraries.

"When I came back, it was not the same state," Connie Dowell said in 2009.

"On that walk across the state ... he had stayed with families like mine. He was hearing them say, 'Our children are leaving. We've got to have jobs and reasons to keep them here.' He listened to those people, and I see it in Homecoming. I wouldn't have imagined it," she told Keel Hunt in *Crossing the Aisle.*[3]

"The1986 Homecoming experience had imparted chiefly a new level of Tennessee pride of place," Hunt wrote.

* * *

Higher aspirations and increased confidence were not all it took to grow family incomes.

Elected officials had to do their part. The bipartisan boot camp that had preceded my early swearing-in forged relationships that made progress easier. From 1979 to 1986, each Wednesday morning at 7:30 a.m. during the legislative session, the state's leadership met in my office—the two Democrat Speakers, the Republican and Democrat leader of each house, the Republican Commissioner of Finance Administration, and myself. There was no staff. I would offer an agenda. We would then argue and hash out what we were going to do.

"You can say outside this room whatever you said inside, but you can't repeat what anyone else said," was the rule we faithfully followed.

At our last leadership meeting on Wednesday, April 30, 1986, this was the conversation:

> *Governor Alexander:* "I don't know in how many other states a Republican governor sits down with the Democrat and Republican legislative leaders and discusses the issues the way we have. We certainly have set the parameters and constructed the environment for whatever good has happened here. Without sounding too stuffy, I want to thank you for that."
>
> *Speaker McWherter:* "There is one thing I can say for sure—not once in eight years, never has anyone used anything said in one of these meetings in a political speech from the back of a pickup truck to embarrass one of us. I've been to meetings of Speakers of the House from all over the South. Some of the Speakers don't have any connection at all with the executive in their state, and usually they're all of one party."

Lieutenant Governor Wilder: "In some states, the Speakers don't even talk to each other."

McWherter: "I don't know if they do it in other states either, but I know that here, it has been very important."

Wilder: "This is the way to do things. Some people think it is smart politics to act mad and never talk to each other. That's the way some people do it. But these meetings have been good. They have been good for the state."

Data later showed that Wilder and McWherter were correct in their belief that our leadership meetings had been good for the state. During the following ten years, Tennesseans' per-capita incomes made a remarkable surge, spurting from 82 percent of the national average to 91 percent, according to calculations by Dean Marianne Wanamaker of the University of Tennessee's Howard H. Baker School of Public Policy and Public Affairs. For the next thirty years, incomes stayed at about 90 percent of the national average.

"It is clear from the data that something unique was going on that caused Tennessee to make that much progress compared with the rest of the country," Wanamaker said.

Compared to its Southern neighbors, Tennessee's progress was even more striking. When I walked across the state in 1978, Tennessee family incomes were the third lowest in the region. By 1995, when measured by per capita income, Tennessee was ahead of six Southern states.[4]

My hope had been that, as the national economy recovered, the steps we took would help Tennessee ride that wave and even exceed it. That did happen, although, in some ways, we had sailed against the wind. John Naisbitt had recommended a focus on high tech. Instead, we chased manufacturing. High tech still came our way. The Nissan and Saturn plants made cars and trucks with robots, and one-fourth the number of employees that once assembled vehicles in old plants in the Midwest. FedEx became a leading logistics company, hiring 30,000 Memphians and 500,000 worldwide. Four road programs made our highways the country's best (according to truckers) and helped grow auto suppliers from one in 1980 to nearly 1,000. Family incomes soared as auto jobs replaced textile jobs.

Naisbitt and MIT professor David Birch had emphasized that we needed to grow jobs instead of only recruiting them, so we focused on better schools and colleges. To advertise an "entrepreneurial hot spot," state funds built an interstate quality "Oak Ridge Corridor" to the nation's largest energy laboratory.

Talented people who grow jobs prefer to live in nice places. With that in mind, the state designated 10,000 miles of scenic highways, fixed up state parks, promoted conservation land trusts and greenways, built highways without billboards, and encouraged fishing, hunting, and boating on our many lakes and streams. The legislature appropriated funds for community orchestras, and I played the piano in concerts to raise more funds.

To attract tourists—and to entertain ourselves—the Memphis Jobs Conference and state dollars fixed up Beale Street, the Peabody Hotel, and the Orpheum Theatre. Elvis's Graceland attracted more visitors than the White House, Nashville became "Music City," Chattanooga built the largest aquarium between Baltimore and Miami, the Grizzlies and the Titans arrived, 146,000 race fans watched for crashes at Bristol Motor Speedway, while Opryland and Dollywood became two of the country's most popular theme parks.

All of this helped Tennessee make a bigger gain in relative personal income between 1985 and 1995 than any other Southern state, according to Dean Wanamaker.

PART SIX

Where Now?

1987 to 1989

"We've got to get out of here—a long way and for a long time, maybe six months. We need to be a family again, and you need some time to think about what to do with the rest of your life."

—HONEY ALEXANDER, summer of 1985

CHAPTER 27

Six Months Off

"Rule 211. Schedule family time before you schedule any other time."

—*LAMAR ALEXANDER'S LITTLE PLAID BOOK*

Nashville to Sydney. January–July 1987.

WE WERE SITTING AROUND the supper table in the governor's residence.

I was at the head. Honey commanded the other end, guarding the only exit to the television set. I watched while Honey led the children in conversation in the same practiced way a circus ringmaster performs when all the spotlights are on all the rings.

Suddenly, Honey ceased ringmastering and looked down the table squarely at me.

"We've got to get out of here," she said in her calm but direct way.

I sensed that I should join the conversation.

"No worry about that. The constitution kicks us out automatically, maybe a year and a half from today," I said.

"I mean *really* out of here, a long way away and for a long time, not just two or three weeks, maybe for six months," Honey said.

"Ho boy! Six months off from school," six-year-old Will shouted.

"Wrong," I said. "If we stay six months, you can enjoy going to school in another country."

"I hate school," Will said.

"You're not allowed to say 'hate,'" said Drew, who was almost sixteen.

Their mother said, "I was thinking of Paris, where you could improve your French, or Switzerland, or maybe even Australia, where it's warm and friendly, where kangaroos and koala bears live, and where it's too far away for anyone to come find Daddy. I was thinking of a place where we could get a clean break and a rest."

Her pronouncement produced a variety of negative reactions from both sides of the table.

"I've never heard of *one other family* talking about a six-month *family* vacation. It's embarrassing just to think about it. Besides, it would be my junior year, my most important year. I can't go," Drew said.

"What about my friends?" wailed twelve-year-old Kathryn. "I'd rather take ten exams than go to Australia for six months."

"Kangaroos are boring," Will chimed in, trying to keep up.

With that and other objections, all four children escaped into the TV room, leaving Honey and me alone. She moved from her end of the cluttered table to Leslee's chair, which was next to mine, and sat leaning forward on her elbows, her chin cupped in her hands. These moments after dinner—moments when just the two of us could talk—were precious. I tried hard to be home every night for supper. Governors in other states professed astonishment at this, and even said they were jealous.

"A few minutes of quality time with the children is much more important than some after-dinner speech," I would assure them. But after eight years of quality time spent pretty much only at the supper table, the children's chairs seemed to be a little more turned toward their mother's end of the table, and their backs turned even more toward mine. I was becoming aware that my greatest challenge in public life was leaving it with my reputation—and my family—intact.

Honey's hand touched mine.

"We do need a rest. We need some space and some reflection time, to see ourselves from another perspective. We need to get to know each other again," she said softly.

She got up and began to clear the table, then stopped and looked back.

"And you need some time to think about what to do with the rest of your life," she added.

"And what about you?" I asked.

She sighed.

"Well, I guess for a while it will be enough for me if we're a family again," she said.

Her determination for us to be a normal family included moving into the Residence in January 1979, with "three small children, dogs, guinea pigs, bikes, toys, and most important, hopes to make it a real home."

She insisted that Sunday remain family day.

"It's a quiet time for us. We work puzzles, play games, read, watch television, bake—normal things. No matter how exciting and challenging politics is, it's a lot of hard work and sacrifice, especially in terms of personal time and finances. This was Lamar's decision. This campaign was my gift to him. I support him but I won't be sorry when it's over," she told one interviewer.

Drew, ten, and Leslee, seven, struggled during the next eight years to develop their own teenage identities, while at the same time contending with their new identity as "the governor's children." Kathryn, five, clung to her mother and was less affected by this dual identity. Will, who was born in our fourth month in the Residence, knew no other existence, and seemed unaffected by our public life.

At age fourteen, after living eight years in a 15,500-square-foot mansion surrounded by an iron fence, Leslee wanted to go away to boarding school.

On her application form she had written:

> "Many teenagers might call their family a zoo, but I think the description particularly fits my family's situation. Perhaps a more specific view would be a wildlife refuge. We are different animals, wandering and discovering quietly, but being observed constantly. We have lived in a fishbowl these past eight years.
>
> "It has not been easy with my father as Governor. The family has been thrust into the public eye. We have learned a lot, though. We are all unique.
>
> "My younger brother, Will, reminds me of a kangaroo. He is feisty and assertive.
>
> "Kathryn, who is twelve, asks for attention by being flashy, but she leads those who choose to follow her. She reminds me of a peacock.
>
> "My older brother Drew is a panther, a loner. At the age of 17, he does things as he wishes and gets away with everything.

"I see myself as a brash monkey asserting her will where she can and sometimes not knowing where to stop.

"I characterize my father as an egret standing on one leg and viewing the world. Although powerful in government, he is withdrawn in family life.

"My mother is the lioness who keeps the family in hand and allows us to live and grow.

"I am looking forward to spending time in Australia with my family under normal circumstances."

—*Leslee Taylor Alexander*, age fourteen, January 9, 1987

* * *

When we arrived in Sydney on Australia Day, January 26, 1987, it seemed like America thirty years ago—or, as Mark Twain observed a century earlier, "an English city with American trimmings."[1]

The British are the ancestors of us both, making Australians our first cousins. A cargo of convicts settled Australia in 1788. They would have been on their way from London to Georgia had the American Revolution not succeeded, thereby denying the British the opportunity to send their prisoners to America. The governor-general explained this relationship at the 1987 Australian-American Bicentennial dinner.

"Our pioneers, like yours, were as unlikely a band as one could conceive. Your gold rush spilled into ours. Our constitution and our national park system has been built on yours. We read your prose and watch your plays and films. We even watch your terrible TV dramas," Sir Ninian Stephen said.

Still, Australia was different. Longer vacations. Smaller servings at dinner. Laid-back. Seasons in reverse. Looking up at the world from Down Under. Most startling were the breezes and the birds and the light.

We had rented a home in Mosman, looking down on Balmoral Beach. Each day, the sun warmed the hills, pulling air from the sea and creating a breeze that blew until midnight when the hills cooled again. The gentle wind spilled through our open glass door and swirled under the dinner table. Some nights I would be so sure that gusts were blowing up a storm that I would climb out of bed and open the window. I would listen to the wind and watch moonlight through swaying trees make dancing shadows on the walls. Beyond the trees, I could see the black water of Mosman Bay and, beyond that, the outline of buildings in Sydney speckled with shining dots.

We were far away from the life we had known—even airmail back then took eleven days to arrive from Nashville. It was far away enough that I comfortably could say, "No" when, one month after our arrival, President Reagan's new chief of staff, Howard Baker, telephoned in the middle of the night to ask me to come home and help save the presidency from "Iran-gate."

Nevertheless, for a while, politics kept creeping back into our lives. We spent a weekend with former Prime Minister Malcolm Fraser and his wife, Tamie, in Nareen, a sheep station four hours from Melbourne. At a Chester A. Arthur Society dinner in Sydney, I competed with Australian parliamentarians to determine who knew the most trivia about American presidents. The Australians always won. On April 28, a letter from Richard Nixon found its way to Sydney. "Your decision to take six months off... will give you and Honey a chance to recharge, and your children a mountaintop experience. I hope you will return to public life..." he wrote.

Despite such outbreaks of the political virus, I gradually began to see politics and government as a narrow slice of life and was embarrassed that it had consumed me so. Honey and I took computer lessons, learned to drive on the wrong side of the road, and to enjoy stage plays about life in Australia. We did so many "new first things" that gradually we began to create new patterns of life and sink into new ruts. I was becoming comfortable in a routine of learning new habits, rather than struggling to unlearn old ones. I was planning less and opening myself up to more.

We soaked up Australia. I took two-hour walks. On most days, Honey ran for three miles. We took a weeklong one-hundred-mile horse trek across the fabled Snowy Mountains. After a cruise to the Great Barrier Reef, we avoided tragedy when doctors at the Townsville Hospital decided that Will's overnight delirium was merely the result of swallowing mouthfuls of seasickness pills as we rolled through nine-foot waves.

In April, we flew ten hours north to Japan.

"The cherry blossoms will make me think of our dogwoods. The azaleas and tulips will be blooming. It will be beautiful running around the emperor's palace. I don't want to miss spring," Honey said.

Our busy lives helped avoid the nuclear family explosions that can accompany such thick family living.

* * *

On Tuesday morning, June 30, we arrived at the Sydney airport with seventeen suitcases and began a slow journey home, stopping in Bangkok, Beijing, and Moscow, then crossing the Berlin Wall at midnight on the train to Paris. Once back in Nashville, Will entertained other second-graders with stories of Australian adventures and plans to become an architect. Drew waited tables, practiced his guitar, and made arrangements to attend Kenyon College in Ohio. Kathryn's eighth-grade friends elected her captain of her class team. She had grown taller and wanted to be an actor. Leslee, now sixteen, had plans "to go riding horses in the Wyoming mountains next summer or something like that."

I had learned small things about living—to focus on the day and to start it with a few quiet minutes. My exercise became walking instead of running. I had lost twenty pounds without trying, and discovered that, in a family, it is more important just to be there, physically *and* mentally.

I also realized that I had jumped into some pretty deep water, reading Thomas Merton and other tomes on life's transitions, and then had come back up about where I jumped in. I found myself back on a familiar track. I was making daily lists of things to do.

In March of 1988, eight months after we came home from Australia, Honey and I took a long walk after supper. It was 7:00 p.m. and still light in Nashville. The evening was cool, about like it was in Sydney at that time of the year, although the seasons there were moving the other way. We wondered how much of our time in Australia we would remember in ten years.

Here's what we decided. We'll never forget the adventures, but what we'll treasure most is the memory that we were important enough to each other to actually manage to do it—to take six months off, while we still could, together.

CHAPTER 28

"Find the Good and Praise It."

"Rule 255. Know the name of and something special about each person in your office."

—*LAMAR ALEXANDER'S LITTLE PLAID BOOK*

On a freighter from Long Beach to Auckland. December 1987.

OUR FAMILY FIRST MET ALEX HALEY in 1980 at a reception in the governor's residence.

I can still see this genial bear of a man cradling our newborn son, Will. He was—at that moment—the world's most celebrated writer and I was governor of his native state. From that day, a friendship blossomed. No one in our family felt quite so important as when Alex would visit.

"Now, let me see that essay," he would say to Leslee or Kathryn.

"My, with just a little work, that could surely win a prize," he would say after reading it.

When Will was six, he began experimenting with a video camera.

"You have a real talent. I think I'll tell Steven Spielberg about you," Alex said.

No one who spent the night at the governor's residence—not even the president of the United States—created the stir among employees that Alex Haley did. He had time for each one. He wanted to know each of them just as much as they wanted to know him. He taught us to find the good and praise it.

In late 1987, I told Alex that I was having trouble finishing my book about our six months in Australia. He was about to leave on an eighteen-day voyage in a cargo freighter from Long Beach, California, to Sydney.

"Why don't you go with me? While I work on my new book, perhaps you can finish yours," he said.

These long voyages were the way Alex had found time to write *Roots* and *The Autobiography of Malcolm X,* two books that each sold six million copies. He had come to look forward to these long trips on cargo ships where there were no interruptions.

Three weeks before Christmas, we boarded the SS *Wellington.* Soon, we were far out in the Pacific, two of only eight passengers on a German freighter. During the day, we would write in our compartments. After dinner, we would climb to the second deck, admire the stars, and talk about what we were writing. My friend taught me yet another lesson.

"It helps to talk a story," Alex said.

Alex settled against the railing and began "talking" the story of his grandmother, a slave named Queen, and Queen's father, an Alabama plantation owner of Irish descent. Alex would practice a phrase and then polish it, all the while judging my reaction to each serving.

Stars danced as the freighter rolled, and Alex told me about writing *Roots.*

"It took twelve years, searching to find Kunta Kinte, to understand what those stories meant that I had heard as a boy on my grandma's front porch. For days, I rode in the belly of a ship, trying to imagine what it was like when one of every four of those captured Africans died in those hulls, trying to hear their shrieks in the wind. I dug and dug and kept trying to find a way to use all the research," Alex said.

"I was broke, down to eighteen cents and two cans of sardines. Once, standing on the stern of a ship just like this, I thought of jumping. The water seemed so inviting, so peaceful. It would be the end of my misery. I could see no way out of the mass of material that eventually became *Roots.*"

"What made you finish?" I asked.

"There came a time—maybe I was halfway done—when the book took over, just swept me ahead with it, something like a stream rushing. The book became itself, and I became merely the instrument that made it happen," he said.

Roots won a Pulitzer Prize and was translated into thirty-seven languages. During twelve years of research, Alex had "talked" the stories of *Roots* perhaps 1,000 times to one million listeners. In January of 1977, almost nine of ten Blacks and more than seven of ten Whites had watched at least one of the eight episodes of *Roots* on the ABC network, according to his biographer, Robert J. Norrell.

"What is it about *Roots* that has affected so many millions of people?" I asked Alex late one night on our voyage.

"Kunta Kinte's struggle for freedom, I think. It seems to help others struggling," he said.

When I heard Alex tell his grandma's stories, I began to pester my older relatives to learn what my ancestors had been doing seven generations earlier. When I heard how his Aunt Liz, rocking on the porch telling stories, "could knock a firefly out of the air at fifteen feet with an accurate stream of tobacco juice," my great-grandmother Sadie's snuffbox became a prize.

The more Alex's fame spread, the hungrier he seemed for his own roots. Quietly, he purchased Grandpa Palmer's house—the one with the front porch where he first heard the stories of Kunta Kinte. He paid for the upkeep of the graveyard where "Chicken George" is buried. It still has the fence down the middle—Whites buried on one side, Blacks on the other. The legislature and I made it a museum. In 1983, he bought a farm outside Knoxville, at the edge of the Great Smoky Mountains.

To Alex, everyone was a superstar. Walking in Knoxville, he met Joseph Rivera, discovered that he was an adult learning to read, and encouraged him. Within a few months, Joseph was the subject of an Alex Haley story in *Parade* magazine. Cabdrivers, university students, out-of-work neighbors—all might find themselves guests at the Haley farm seated at dinner next to, say, Oprah Winfrey or Quincy Jones.

Alex's best lesson was that the most important superstars of all were family.

It was Memorial Day, Monday, May 27, 1991—long called Decoration Day in the South, when families gather to place flowers on the graves of loved ones—when Alex and our oldest son, Drew, visited the Alabama cemetery of Alex's great-grandfather, the Irish Confederate Lieutenant Colonel James Jackson III.

Colonel Jackson's White descendants were there too.

"No! No!" one older family member shouted when the Jacksons learned that the African American celebrity, Alex Haley, was their cousin.

The younger ones asked for autographs. Not long afterward, Jackson family members were guests at Haley's Tennessee farm as a part of filming the *Alex Haley's Queen* TV miniseries.

* * *

I was in a meeting at Alex's farm in Norris on Monday, December 17, 1990, when President Bush telephoned to ask me to become US Secretary of Education. When that call caused our family to move to Washington, DC, I saw much less of Alex. But whenever I was on the spot—which was often—I often found myself thinking, "What would Alex say?"

When I would salute an outstanding school or teacher, I usually began in this way.

"My dear friend Alex Haley has a saying, which I am putting into practice today. 'Find the good and praise it.'"[1]

In the classrooms of Los Angeles, after the riots in the spring of 1992, I would try to help teachers struggling to find ways to help children of different backgrounds learn to respect one another—and how to respond if someone did not respect them. I told them how Alex handled such matters. How, because of his race, his jobs in the Coast Guard during World War II were limited to the kitchen and included serving coffee to the captain.

Then one day, the captain stopped reading his magazine and lifted his cup.

"There's a good article here by an Alex Haley. Same name as you," the captain said.

"I am the Alex Haley who wrote the article," the server said.

After that, there were fewer calls for coffee, many more for conversations with the author.

In September 1991, Alex, our son, Will, and I sweltered in 100-degree heat at the opening game of the University of Tennessee football season. Alex was breathing heavily, I noticed, perspiring more than even a slightly overweight, seventy-year-old diabetic with an impossible schedule should.

Five months later, Honey and I were in Memphis listening as the oldest daughter of Malcolm X spoke about an unwelcome call that had come on February 10, telling of Alex's passing.

"My first thought of my godfather was always of how he had said, 'Find the good and praise it.' And then I thought, one less call, one less trip, and we who have demanded so much of him might have had him for a few more precious years," she said.

I once told Alex that I hoped he would speak at my funeral because it would sound so good. I did not want to speak at his.

When my turn came I said, "He was God's storyteller. We loved him so much, we just used him up," I said.

A month after Alex died, I spoke at the Gridiron Dinner in Washington. I played the piano, sang satirical lyrics set to country music melodies, and closed in this way:

"My friend Alex Haley used to say, 'Find the good and praise it.' He especially liked to say that to people who were busy finding everything wrong with America. It was a powerful message coming from the grandson of slaves, from the man who wrote *The Autobiography of Malcolm X* and *Roots*.

"I used to think of it every time Alex told the story about John Newton, the slave trader, and how he saw the light and wrote one of the world's great hymns, 'Amazing Grace.'"

Then, I played "Amazing Grace."

I was not surprised earlier that year when Will, then in the seventh grade, told me he had chosen to read *Roots* for a class assignment. Some evenings, he and I read it together.

When we came to the page where slave traders surprised Kunta Kinte in the woods, Will sat straight up. When Kunta is struggling in the filth and death of the slave trader's hull, we struggled, too, trying to imagine it.

After we read and before I put out the lights, I often paused at Will's desk, where he kept the mounted plastic fish that arrived in the mail soon after he caught what Alex assured him was "the biggest catfish ever seen" in the Haley Farm pond. On the wooden base of this trophy, there was a strip of white paper carefully cut and taped, with a neatly penned inscription:

"To Will, my favorite fisherman. Alex Haley."

To Alex, everyone was a superstar.

PART SEVEN

Back to Washington, DC

1990 to 1993

"Washington, DC, is a sticky place. If you stay much longer, you will never go home. You can stay and leave, but you will keep bouncing back, as I did three times."

—BRYCE N. HARLOW,
Counselor to the president, 1970

CHAPTER 29

Innocent Until Nominated

"Rule 288. When you are invited to testify before Congress, don't do all the talking. Remember that you are there to give members of Congress an opportunity to appear on TV."

—LAMAR ALEXANDER'S LITTLE PLAID BOOK

Knoxville to Washington, DC. December 1990–March 1991.

IN A WHITE HOUSE MEETING on Tuesday, December 11, 1990, President George H.W. Bush's chief of staff, John H. Sununu, told Secretary of Education Lauro F. Cavazos Jr. that Bush wanted Cavazos to leave the Cabinet.

"A more forceful presence was needed at the helm of the Education Department...they needed to buttress Mr. Bush's assertion that he was the 'Education President,'" the *New York Times* reported.[1] The article noted that I was a possible replacement for Cavazos.

I was then president of the University of Tennessee. I had grown up cheering for the Volunteers and, while I was governor, I had persuaded the legislature to fund the university generously and been its board chairman. I was convinced that a rising university was key to a rising Tennessee. But my transition from governor to university president had not been easy. I learned quickly that watching a lot of baseball doesn't make you a major league shortstop.

"What was your hardest job? Governor, university president, education secretary, or senator?" people ask.

"Obviously you've never been a university president or you wouldn't ask a dumb question like that," I answer.

On Friday, July 1, 1988, when I arrived on campus, some faculty members were unhappy that I did not have a PhD. Others suggested that I had accepted the job as a political way station. Some alumni were leery of my undergraduate degree from Vanderbilt, UT's in-state rival.

Another early lesson was that the university presidency is not the forum for Moses's "let's all go this way" style of leadership that worked as governor. During my first month on the job, worried faculty Senate leaders visited my office.

"We are concerned that you may think that the result is more important than the process," the Senate president said.

"I *am* results-oriented," I said.

"We believe that the process is more important than the result," he said.

One former university president said, "The faculty regards a decision by the president as a request to form a study committee."

By the fall of 1990, I was settling into my third year as president, our family was moving to Knoxville, and the university was prospering. The freshman class included thirty-eight National Merit scholars, up fifteen from the previous year. Faculty salaries had moved from near the bottom to the midpoint for peer universities. I had appointed the first two African American UT vice presidents. Research dollars and the endowment were up.

Still, there must have been several faculty members who breathed a sigh of relief when word spread that President Bush had asked me to be US Secretary of Education, and that I had said yes.

Events had moved swiftly. Sununu's call came on a dreary Friday morning, December 14, 1990, only three days after Cavazos was fired.

"If the president were to ask, would you be willing to be education secretary?" Sununu asked.

"I would have to talk with Honey, but the answer is likely yes," I said, dreading the thought of breaking this news while she was preparing for our first Christmas in the Knoxville home she'd been remodeling for two years.

"Can you do the job without asking for more money?" Sununu asked.

"Yes. More money is a state responsibility," I said.

I reminded him that Tennessee had raised taxes to fund our "Better Schools Program," and that I had urged President Reagan to eliminate federal aid to schools in exchange for Washington, DC, paying the states' share of Medicaid.

"Are you in favor of school choice?" he asked.

"Yes," I answered.

Millions of college students (including many at UT) received federal vouchers, called Pell Grants, which they could use at any accredited college—public, private, or religious. Beginning with the GI Bill for veterans, federal scholarships had created choices for students as well as competition among colleges. If vouchers have created the best colleges, why not also use them to help create the best schools, I reasoned?

When Sununu hung up, I called Honey, who had already heard media speculation. She was fond of President Bush and had grown accustomed—or, perhaps resigned—to my meanderings through public life. I called Howard Baker, whom Sununu had already telephoned to check on me.

Sununu had recommended my nomination to the president.

"Well, Lamar Alexander was a governor, and when you want to do things right you always call the governors. That's exactly where that came from. Lamar was a governor interested in education, whose involvement in his state matched what the president wanted to do nationally," Sununu said later.[2]

I made one more call, to Doug Bailey, who was now publisher of *The Hotline*, a daily journal that faxed overnight headlines to political junkies. He suggested two questions to ask the president.

Before I could gather my thoughts, Bush called, asking if I would take the job. I asked Bailey's two questions.

"First, may I develop a strategy to help the country reach the six national education goals, subject to your approval?[3] And second, may I then recruit a team capable of carrying out such an ambitious undertaking, subject to your approval?" I asked.

"Of course," the president said.

I thanked him and accepted.

The next Tuesday, December 18, at a White House press conference, I stood at the president's side as he announced my nomination.

Making as much news as my nomination that Monday was Bush's decision to review an Education Department decision that essentially outlawed race-based scholarships.[4]

"My general disposition would be that when you're wandering through constitutional thickets that a warm heart and a little common sense are helpful," I told the media.[5]

My nomination and race-based scholarships were far from the most important matters on the president's mind that day. Six months earlier, Iraq had invaded Kuwait. The president had asked Congress to authorize the use of force to remove Iraqi forces. Iraq did not budge. On December 13, seven days before the press conference announcing my nomination, the American ambassador left Kuwait.

Following the press conference, the president's aides ushered me into the office of the White House chief of personnel, who handed me a list of political supporters that I would be expected to hire.

"Wait a minute. The president promised that that I could develop an education plan, subject to his approval, and then recruit a team, subject to his approval," I said.

"That's not the way we do it," the patronage chief said.

"Then, I'm leaving," I replied.

"You can't do that. The president just announced your appointment," the patronage chief said.

"Watch me."

I walked out of the White House and started recruiting. First on my list was David Kearns, the CEO who had led Xerox to win the coveted Malcolm Baldrige National Quality Award for excellence in performance. I asked Kearns to apply those same leadership skills to the Department of Education.

One month later, on January 17, 1991, at 3:00 p.m., the president convened a meeting in the White House Cabinet room to discuss testing. I was surprised that Bush would sit through such a dry hour-long meeting, although at one point, he did step out of the room for a few minutes.

After leaving the White House, a group of us flew to Knoxville for a retreat at Blackberry Farm, where we were to spend two days writing the education plan I had promised Bush. When we landed at about 7:15 p. m., everyone in the terminal was watching television.

The United States was bombing Baghdad. A few hours later, we watched the president speak to the nation. Later, I learned that the White House education meeting earlier that day was listed on the president's public schedule to divert media attention from military action. During his brief absence from the meeting, Bush had called Soviet Union President Mikhail Gorbachev to let him know that bombs were about to fall on Baghdad.

As the Gulf War fireworks began, our planning group worked late into the night on plans for a partnership between the president and governors to reach the six national education goals they had set in their 1989 education summit.[6]

* * *

In December, when I told Honey about President Bush's invitation to move to Washington, she had just completed her 1990 New Year's resolution to read the Bible from cover to cover. Her reinvigorated Christian charity helped sustain her good humor—mostly.

"When I die, I want you to make Lamar spread my ashes at all the houses he has made me live in," she told her friend, Molly Pratt, who was helping with the move.

At first, we had planned to remain in Knoxville until June, but the confirmation process picked up steam. We found a school in Washington for Kathryn, then sixteen, and Will, eleven, while Honey began looking at houses. Ultimately, we bought a home near the National Zoo.

Honey continued her work on the board of the Corporation for Public Broadcasting, joined the International Club, and began daily walks with female friends "Tunky" [Riley], "Bitsey" [Folger], Ettel [Valitasaris], Skila [Harris], and "Modsy" [Rooney], who, with Honey added, must have created the most unlikely collection of names in a strolling group in the history of the city.

"This has not been the most timely opportunity, let me put it that way, since we've had so many moves lately," Honey told the *Knoxville News Sentinel* in an interview on Sunday, February 10, 1991. "I used to have expectations. I'd say, 'Well, next year we're going to do such and such.' I don't do that anymore. I try to be as flexible as possible."

Honey went on.

"Lamar and I are not alike at all. Lamar is much more of a risk taker in some ways than I am; I'm more careful than he is. Yet on a physical basis I am more of a risk taker than he is. We have a child like him. Actually, we have several. The return to Washington after 20 years away is less a circle than a spiral. I hope it's headed up instead of down. I'm not sure," Honey said.

"I drove in Saturday with two dogs, one cat, one son and a bunch of boxes and suitcases. And we have basically moved. We have come up here. And it'll be mighty embarrassing if Lamar is not confirmed."

* * *

Neither Honey nor I was prepared for the Senate tradition of "innocent until nominated."

On Wednesday, February 6, 1991, Senator Ted Kennedy presided over my confirmation hearing. It began innocently enough, with Senators James Sasser and Al Gore, both Tennessee Democrats, introducing me. But, during questioning, Ohio Democrat Senator Howard Metzenbaum lived up to his reputation for cantankerousness.

"Governor, I have seen some newspaper stories concerning your financial situation. I don't think I'm fully prepared to inquire on that subject at the moment..." he said.

"Why, Howard, I think you just did," said Kansas Republican Senator Nancy Kassebaum.

I was taken aback.

"I'm fully prepared today to answer any question you have. My financial records have been an open book for fifteen years in Tennessee. They're well known. If you have a question, I'd be glad to answer it," I said.

Metzenbaum declined to say more, providing an opportunity for the media to speculate about what nefarious activities I might have undertaken.

For the next several weeks, Democrat staffers pored over my financial disclosures and answers to committee questionnaires. The media interest in my investments surprised me because I had disclosed most of it earlier. The questioners really were asking how I could have so much money. I tried to explain that Honey's family had money and that, when I was not in public office, she and I had helped found two successful businesses. In addition, the state attorney general, a Democrat, had approved the investments and transactions that were being questioned.[7]

The confirmation process ground to a halt. Senator Metzenbaum put a secret "hold" on my nomination. Such a hold often defeats a nomination because the majority leader does not want to take several days to complete the parliamentary maneuvers necessary to overcome the hold. Metzenbaum was doing his best to make sure that I could not help Bush become the "education president."

For the first time, it crossed my mind that the Senate's Democrat majority might not confirm me.

Meanwhile, President Bush was contemplating war.

I had seen the worry in his face. A half million coalition ground troops were prepared to invade Kuwait and Iraq. From World War II, Bush knew the horror of combat.

"How many hours do you sleep in the midst of this?" I asked the president.

"Eight hours. When you know what you are going to do, you sleep well," he replied.

On Saturday, February 23, the deadline for Iraq's withdrawal from Kuwait passed. At 8:00 p.m. Washington time, the ground war began. Five days later, the president announced that Kuwait was liberated.

The war ended with my nomination still dangling. Not knowing which way to turn, I asked to see Senator Warren Rudman of New Hampshire. I had met him in Nashville during my first year as governor when he and Tom Rath, who succeeded Rudman as state attorney general, had joined Indiana Senator Richard Lugar and his aide Mitch Daniels Jr. and Howard Baker in my office to discuss Baker's presidential campaign.

"Keep your mouth shut. You have no cards to play. Let me tell you a story," Rudman said. "In 1976, President Ford nominated me for the Interstate Commerce Commission. The Democratic senator from New Hampshire, John Durkin, put a hold on my nomination just like Metzenbaum is doing to you. I was twisting in the wind. People in New

Hampshire were asking, 'What's wrong with Warren? Did he beat his wife? Steal money? Do something indecent?'" he said.

"Did Durkin finally lift his hold?" I asked.

"No. I finally asked President Ford to withdraw my nomination and I ran against the SOB Durkin in the next election and beat him. That's how I became a United States senator," he said.

I took Rudman's advice and kept quiet.

Then, abruptly on Thursday, March 14, after a two-month delay, the Committee approved my nomination, 16–0. The next day, the Senate approved it by unanimous voice consent.

I never heard what broke the logjam.

CHAPTER 30

Could Bush Have Been Reelected?

"The president should have used 'America 2000' for his entire domestic agenda."

—JACK KEMP, HUD Secretary, September 1991

Washington, DC. March 1991, 1992.

SENATOR METZENBAUM'S HOLD ON MY NOMINATION created one huge advantage—it gave us time to prepare and launch an "American 2000" strategy to reach national education goals.

On Wednesday, March 20, 1991, about a week after my Senate confirmation, David Kearns, Checker Finn, and I met with Bush.

"This is the best proposal I've ever seen," the president told us.

Two days later, at the National Air and Space Museum, with Charles Lindbergh's monoplane as backdrop and eighty-five-year-old Judge John Minor Wisdom administering the oath, the president swore me in. He said he would nominate Kearns as deputy secretary.

One month later, President Bush launched "America 2000." It was a partnership between the president and governors to move America toward the six national education goals. It was a national strategy—not a federal program—that was designed to work community by community. Soon, more than 250 task forces were helping forty-six states develop comprehensive plans to achieve the goals, measure results, and create at least one new "break-the-mold" school.

As federal departments go, the Department of Education is small, with about 4,000 employees. Its main job is to distribute grants and loans to college students and to administer the federal grant programs that make up about 10 percent of spending on public schools. Most of the responsibility for 100,000 public schools is properly with states, communities, classroom teachers—and especially with parents. Schools can only help do what parents can't do as well, as University of Chicago Professor James Coleman said.

President Carter and the Democrat Congress had created this newest of all departments in 1979. Because it was new, the Education Secretary sat at the end of the table during Cabinet meetings and would have been the last in line to succeed the president if he died.

"If you wake up some morning and see me on television assuring you that everything is all right...you'd better worry, because it won't be," I told friends.

For perhaps the first time, the Department of Education became Washington's "hot" place to work. Metzenbaum's delaying tactics, Bush's permission, and Kearns' prestige allowed me to recruit a top flight team.[1] Lights burned late as we mobilized a complicated country to move toward ambitious goals. During the next eighteen months, I traveled to thirty-eight states, visiting 101 communities in almost every state, encouraging them to create "America 2000" coalitions. I visited California twenty times.

Democrats in Congress did not cooperate, but "America 2000" was still bipartisan because it was a partnership with governors. In June, I traveled with President and Mrs. Bush to Grand Junction to help Roy Romer, chairman of the Democratic Governors Association, kick off "Colorado 2000," the first of forty-four such state efforts.

The media took notice. My photo appeared on the cover of *Parade* magazine on August 25, with the question, "Can He Lead Our Schools to Excellence?" On September 16, a *Time* cover asked, "Can This Man Save Our Schools?"

* * *

The genesis of "America 2000" had occurred two decades earlier as I was beginning my second term as governor.

In 1983, a blue-ribbon commission appointed by Reagan Secretary of Education Terrel Bell produced "A Nation at Risk," a report that triggered a national alarm about what children knew and were able to do. By 1985–1986, governors did something they had never done before. They devoted an entire year together mainly focused on a single subject: school reform.

I was chairman of the National Governors Association then, and Bill Clinton was vice chairman. I was determined to change the education agenda, which had mostly concentrated on racial desegregation and money. We had a different approach, which we titled "Time for Results: The Governors' 1991 Report on Education." Fifty governors divided into task forces to consider issues from paying good teachers more to giving students more choices of schools.

In early 1988, pollster Bob Teeter invited me to meet with then Vice President Bush in the same West Wing office where I had worked with Bryce Harlow two decades earlier. Bush asked about the slogan I used to enact Tennessee's "Better Schools Program."

"Better schools mean better jobs. I like that phrase," the vice president said.

During his presidential campaign, his standard stump speech included, "I want to be the education president" and "Better schools mean better jobs."[2]

After Bush won in November 1988, he included me in a meeting with college presidents. We discussed a summit on education. I suggested limiting it to the president and governors. That summit—in September 1989—produced the first national education goals.[3] During 1990, progress toward the goals languished, accelerating Cavazos's departure and my arrival early the next year.

"America 2000" produced results soon after Bush launched it. By December 1991, I was hosting monthly "America 2000" satellite town meetings for more than 2,700 communities. "The Nation's Report Card" began announcing academic achievement results at the state level for the first time and developed learning benchmarks that created de facto national standards.

Sam Walton, then known as "the richest man in the world," invited me to a family meeting at his home in Bentonville, Arkansas, on a Saturday morning in February 1992. I recommended that the family support school choice and charter schools. At noon, the Walmart founder rose to his feet and abruptly ended the meeting so that the family could watch the Arkansas Razorbacks play basketball.

He also gave a boost to the most successful "America 2000" initiative. After our meeting, Walton gave earnings from his memoir to the New American Schools Development Corporation, the launch pad for "break-the-mold," start-from-scratch schools. This idea was like the first eight "outcome-based schools" that Minnesota created in 1991. These forerunners of today's charter schools gave teachers more freedom and parents more choices. Two months after our visit, Sam Walton died of cancer.

President and Mrs. Bush invited business leaders to Camp David to raise $100 million for New American schools. Teachers' union leader Albert Shanker chimed in, asking, "If we can have a Saturn auto plant, why not a Saturn school?" After Bill Clinton defeated Bush in November 1992, I wrote to 13,000 school districts, asking them to create at least one "break-the-mold" public charter school. Thirty years later, in 2023, there were 7,800 charter schools, about 8 percent of all American public schools.

Democrats in Congress, however, did not help.

They refused to appropriate $1 million for each congressional district to start one "break-the-mold" school. They would not approve a half billion dollars to give low-income families more school choices. Instead, Democrats rewrote the K–12 education law to increase federal control. I urged the president to veto the legislation because it would create "a national school board." Bush threatened a veto, and Congress did not pass the bill.[4]

* * *

Midafternoon on Wednesday, March 6, 1991, an entourage, including the presidential limousine, emerged from the White House grounds and sped toward the Capitol, where President Bush was to address a joint session of Congress.

It was four days after Iraq had agreed to end the Gulf War. Euphoria was so great that the Democrat Speaker broke tradition by congratulating the Republican president before introducing him. Bush's Gallup approval rating had risen to 89 percent, even higher than President Truman's after World War II.

I sat in a gallery seat, still waiting for the Senate to confirm my nomination. I recall feeling that I was witnessing a historic occasion, but also a missed opportunity to change the course of the Bush presidency.

As presidential speeches go, this one was brief at thirty-one minutes.

"The war is over," the president declared to bipartisan cheering.

"Tonight, I come to the House to speak about the world—the world after war," Bush said.

He did that, but he mostly spoke about the world *overseas*, a new world order. He was more than halfway through the speech before he mentioned that five weeks earlier, in his State of the Union address, he had called for "new initiatives... to prepare for the next American century."

But quickly, he returned to Iraq and the new world order.

I sat on the edge of my seat thinking, *If only the president would speak for just five minutes celebrating victory and then say, "Now, let's show the world and show ourselves that we can do as well at home as we just did overseas."* That was the missed opportunity.

I was not the only American feeling that way.

"President Bush goes before Congress and the country tonight as the most popular president in more than four decades but with voters still expressing great uncertainty about where he intends to lead the nation in the years ahead," David Broder had written the day before in the *Washington Post.*[5]

Twenty months later, in the November 1992 election, the most popular president in recent history won only 37 percent of the vote, and Bill Clinton won the presidency with 43 percent. Ross Perot won 19 percent.

There are many theories explaining Bush's dramatic decline. Biographer Jon Meacham cites a thyroid condition and an irregular heartbeat as factors affecting the president's mood and vigor.

Sometimes, depression accompanies success. As Emily Dickinson wrote, "Success is counted sweetest by those who ne'er succeed."

Even after winning a war, nations can become weary of leaders, as Winston Churchill found out after World War II. Some blame Bush's 1990 support of tax increases. Others point out that the recession that began in 1990 lingered through the presidential election—although the recession had officially ended in March of 1992.

Campaign leadership was in disarray, some said, and I agreed. In May 1992, I visited James Baker and asked him to resign as secretary of state and take over the campaign. A few months later, Baker agreed to become White House chief of staff, and also supervise the campaign. But it was too late. Bush seemed to be counting his days before returning to Texas, which is why his glance at his watch during his October debate with Clinton and Perot was talked about so much.

I believe the principal reason for Bush's loss was something else. The American people saw him as preoccupied with the world and out of touch at home. He would have had a fighting chance to be reelected if he had started to address those concerns during his March 6 address to Congress.

In late 1991, the president dispatched me to Omaha with five other Cabinet members on Air Force Two to kick off "Nebraska 2000." During the flight out, Housing and Urban Development Secretary Jack Kemp voiced his impatience with Bush's lack of attention to issues at home.

"The president should have used America 2000 for his entire domestic agenda," Kemp said.

This was not Kemp's first expression of impatience with Bush. During Cabinet meetings, the former Buffalo Bills quarterback would sit as long as he could stand it, listening to Secretary of the Treasury Nick Brady discussing classic economic policy. Then, in a voice better suited for barking out signals in the Bills' stadium, Kemp would launch into the merits of supply-side economics. The president would slump lower in his chair and, usually, after listening to Kemp for a while, adjourn the meeting.

This time, Bush should have listened. Using "America 2000" to describe the entire domestic agenda, then traveling the country advocating it, would have given the president his best chance for a second term.

Bush joked about seeing a light at the end of the tunnel that he hoped was not a train, paraphrasing a line from a song sung by the Nitty Gritty Dirt Band.

The train was indeed coming. Its engineer was Bill Clinton, promising to be "a domestic president," and its conductor was James Carville shouting, "It's the economy, stupid."

It wasn't that Bush didn't try. For a president who claimed to be uncomfortable with "the vision thing," his education agenda provided visionary leadership. Passage of the 1991 "Clean Air Act" amendments backed up his promise to be an "environment president." He signed the Americans with Disabilities Act.

Nonetheless, offering a domestic agenda was not George Bush's natural inclination. He was most comfortable with national security and foreign affairs, and, arguably, no president was better at it. His demeanor and skill in handling the disintegration of the Soviet Union and reunification of Germany, and his decisiveness, combined with restraint in the Gulf War, set a high standard. He had spent most of his adult life in Washington or overseas serving as a congressman, chairman of the Republican National Committee, ambassador to the United Nations, chief of the US Liaison Office in China, director of the CIA, and vice president of the United States.

In 1973, when Bush spoke to the Knox County, Tennessee, Lincoln Day dinner, he told 1,200 red-blooded activists, "Many ask why I would leave the job of United Nations ambassador to become chairman of the Republican National Committee?"

I was in the audience, thinking, *there must not be one single Republican in this room asking that question. They all believe that being Republican party national chairman is a better job than cavorting with foreigners at the United Nations.*

The American people sensed that George H.W. Bush was more at home in the world than he was in their homes. As it was becoming clear that Clinton would be Bush's opponent, I was invited to be the Republican speaker at the Saturday, March 28, 1992, Gridiron Dinner, a Washington event for journalists and their guests. Both Bush and Clinton were there.

When I heard that Texas Governor Ann Richards was to be the Democrat speaker, I knew right away that I was in trouble. Governor Richards could light up a room with her oratory, and she did that evening.

Before the governor began her address, she peered around the Capitol Hilton ballroom at the 1,000 black-tied big shots.

"So this is what y'all do up here on Sattidy nights," she finally said, bringing down the house.[6]

Instead of trying to compete with her by delivering an entertaining speech late in the evening to an audience composed mostly of old men who had drunk too much, I sang new lyrics to country tunes and played them on the piano.[7]

I didn't have to change lyrics at all when I sang about the number of arms that had held Bill Clinton to the tune Eddy Arnold made famous: "I really don't want to know."

For Bush, I made up lyrics to Curly Putman's tune, "Green, Green Grass of Home:"

"It's been so long since we have seen him, he's become a European. It's good to have the president back home."

Not everyone saw the train coming. In June of 1992, Honey and I attended a small Washington dinner party that included sophisticates who presumably knew a lot about politics, including PBS anchor Jim Lehrer and Admiral William Crowley, whom Clinton later appointed as ambassador to the British Isles. We dinner guests took a secret vote of whom we thought would win the election. Although Perot was then leading in the polls, twelve of us said Bush would win, seven said Perot, and five said Clinton.

Later that year, in October, I helicoptered with Bush and Howard Baker in Marine One to an education event in Baltimore. The news that day showed the economy picking up steam, but not enough. Both Bush and Baker were in their late sixties, members of the Greatest Generation and World War II veterans. (Bush distinguished himself as a combat pilot and Baker served on a Navy V-12 boat.) Neither could comprehend how the American people could prefer a "draft dodger" to Bush.

"Maybe it's a generational thing," they'd said.

* * *

Working with George H.W. Bush for twenty-two months was a privilege.

"He is the only man ever elected president by being nice," Bob Teeter once told me.

I am among the hundreds who have a stack of handwritten George Bush thank-you notes. He was an excellent executive, giving me free rein to come up with an education plan, to recruit a team, and to help implement it. As president, he set an admirable example, always correct in behavior, self-effacing, and putting the country ahead of himself.

He was devoted to Barbara Bush and, when seen up close, good humor ran through their relationship. One evening, the Bushes invited Honey and me to join them at Ford's Theatre. When we arrived, the Secret Service helped the president out of the limousine, while Barbara remained in the back seat.

"I'll get the door, George," Barbara said, and helped herself out of the vehicle.

Once, before the president was about to speak, I heard him whisper, "Bar, what should I talk about?"

"About five minutes, George," Barbara Bush replied.

On a bright day in late June 1992, walking across the White House south lawn to an event announcing his "GI Bill for Children" school choice program, Barbara looked at her husband.

"George, you have on the wrong coat," she said.

"No one will notice," the president said.

"You go change," she said.

He walked back to his second-floor White House quarters to find the matching coat while I waited with the first lady.

No one can say with certainty what change of circumstances might have altered the outcome of the 1992 presidential election. But I believe that, if, about five minutes into his March 6, 1991, address to Congress, George H.W. Bush had shifted gears and said to the American people, "Now, it's time to show the world and ourselves that we can accomplish as much at home as we did in Iraq"—and then, if he had followed Jack Kemp's advice and launched his domestic agenda as "America 2000," that he would have had a fighting chance of winning a second term.

When President Bush lost in November, I resolved to turn his missed opportunity into an opportunity of my own. I would run for president myself, using the leadership skills I had learned as governor and education secretary.

I would try to persuade a majority of Americans that, as proud as we were of our military strength, what we needed most was to expect less of Washington, DC, and more of ourselves.

PART EIGHT

The Ultimate Startup

1993 to 2000

"The difference between running for governor and running for president is the difference between eighth-grade basketball and the NBA finals."

—LAMAR ALEXANDER

CHAPTER 31

Remember Your ABCs

"'He's too much like me,' Clinton claimed."

—**DICK MORRIS, President Clinton's pollster**

Washington, DC. January 1993.

I CAN STILL REMEMBER THE FIRST TIME those eleven words came out of my mouth—"I will be a candidate for president of the United States."

It was early December 1992. I was attending a noisy White House party about four weeks after Governor Clinton had defeated President Bush. The crowd that had gathered to say goodbye extended from the East Room to the ground floor, where I was mingling with other Cabinet members and those who had contributed $100,000 or more to Bush's presidential campaign.

Glasses were clinking, the throng was thick, and the chatter was so loud that it was hard to carry on a conversation. The affair reeked of the kind of melancholy one feels at graduation when you know something important has ended and that it might be a long time before we see each other again.

I found myself face to face with a swarthy man. We introduced ourselves.

"I am the California Republican party's largest contributor," Sam Bamieh said.

"I am the Secretary of Education—for another few weeks," I said.

"What are you going to do next?" Bamieh asked.

Well, I thought to myself, *if I am ever going to say it, I might as well start now, with all these people with so much money in one place.*

So, I blurted it out.

"I'm going to be running for president," I said.

"President of *what*?" Bamieh asked loudly.

"President of the *United States*," I shouted over the noise.

When I realized that those words had actually come out with no adverse consequences, I began to repeat them to others who inquired about my future. Mostly, they nodded politely, as if I had said nothing more consequential than that I was moving to South Dakota to become a rancher. As politicians will, I considered such polite responses to be encouraging. Nevertheless, I had taken the most important first step in running for president, summoning the courage to say publicly the words, "I will be a candidate for president of the United States."

The presumptuousness of that goal never occurred to me. When I was growing up so many people had told me that I could be president that I eventually tried. In Maryville, I was so often encouraged and applauded, as well as insulated from the vagaries of the wide world, that I had no real understanding of what obstacles might limit my ambition.

Once the words are blurted out, the most important question for a presidential candidate to answer is, "Why are you running?"

This is harder to answer than it would seem.

In a televised interview on Sunday, November 4, 1979, CBS anchor Roger Mudd asked Senator Ted Kennedy, "Why do you want to be president?"

For nearly an hour, Kennedy fumbled through a non-answer to Mudd's question. Seven months later, on Wednesday, November 7, 1979, he dropped out of the race.

In August of 1987, shortly after our family returned to Nashville from six months in Australia, George and Barbara Bush invited Honey and me to the Opryland Hotel for a visit. The vice president was making his rounds before announcing his candidacy for president. My face was bronzed from long walks in Australia, I had lost twenty pounds, and my hair was a little long.

I asked Bush the question Mudd had asked Kennedy and that Honey had insisted I answer before dragging our family through a second campaign for governor—"Mr. Vice President, why are you running for president and what do you hope to accomplish?"

The question so flustered Bush that the visit soon ended. Later, he told his campaign manager, Lee Atwater, about my question.

"I think Lamar's been out in the sun too long. Do you think he's gone *zen*?" Bush asked Atwater.

One can imagine Ronald Reagan having no trouble answering my question.

"To put a harness on the Soviet Union and the federal government," Reagan would have said.

Bush had no such ideological underpinning. He believed that he was destined to put his country first and to serve it. He was uncomfortable with "the vision thing."

Despite my early struggles to say why I was running for governor, I did not have that problem when I ran for president. My mission was to persuade Americans to "expect less of Washington and more of ourselves." The overriding principle of my public career had been that more decisions should be made locally. As governor, I had urged President Reagan to turn schools over to the states in exchange for a federal takeover of Medicaid. As education secretary, I had urged President Bush to veto a "national school board."

I said over and over, "My purpose in running for president is to lead a revival of the American spirit the old-fashioned way—neighborhood-by-neighborhood, block-by-block, family-by-family. Make Congress a citizen legislature. Cut their pay and send them home. Launch a Great American Homecoming, community-by-community."

* * *

In the beginning, the founding fathers passed the job of president among themselves, pretending not to want it.

After that, a backwoodsman claimed it, then a rail-splitter, followed by a Tennessee tailor, a Missouri haberdasher, a Kansas solider, and then a Catholic kid from Boston. One would have to go to Cotulla, Texas, where the tree line disappears into prickly pear, to imagine what large horizons an elementary school teacher must have had to imagine that he, Lyndon B. Johnson, would one day be president of the United States.

Across the presidential stage then marched a Navy lieutenant, a peanut farmer, an actor, and the son of a privileged family, who was ousted by a boy from Hope, the product of a dysfunctional family. Then came a president's son, a community organizer, a reality show host, and a lawyer who had been elected to the US Senate at age twenty-nine.

When Americans vote for president, we search for a way to express our national ethic that anything is possible. The notion that any child might grow up to be president has become the most visible symbol of that ethic. In this land of entrepreneurs, the campaign for the American presidency is the ultimate startup, an enterprise that starts from scratch and can balloon to immense proportions.

Running for president is like scaling a cliff for three years in the dark to earn the privilege of shooting one three-point shot in a basketball game. Or walking across Niagara Falls as the wind sways the tightrope, and the crowd below yells, "Fall!" It requires years of effort, raising tens of millions of dollars, a thick hide, an outrageous ego, a forgiving family, loyal friends, a heavy dose of luck, and a strong sense of purpose.

"Given the nature of the primary process, you have to spend a lot of time running for president—two or four or maybe ten years. And who's to say that's bad?" Bob Teeter once said.

I spent most of six years.

* * *

My obstacle was Bill Clinton.

Both of us grew up in small towns in adjacent Southern states. Every other president had been born before World War II. Music was part of our growing up and, later on, our public lives. But early on, we prudently decided that neither of us played piano or saxophone well enough to go on tour, so we turned our attention to learning about politics and public service at the Tennessee and Arkansas Boys State and Boys Nation.

Each of us married talented women who attended New England colleges. Hillary Rodham of Chicago, Illinois graduated from Wellesley before heading to Yale Law School. Honey Buhler of Victoria, Texas, graduated from Smith. Both had a strong sense of public purpose, but different ambitions. Hillary not only wanted her husband to be in the White House, she wanted to be there too.

Honey had different goals.

"Do you really want to be the First Lady?" Larry King asked Honey on CNN during the 1996 New Hampshire presidential primary.

"No," she said.[1]

"What is the number one priority for the Alexander administration?" a reporter asked her shortly after my election as governor.

"My family. People don't expect me to say that," Honey had said.

Hillary had the zeal of a United Methodist missionary. Honey was happiest when organizing the neighborhood Easter egg hunt. Hillary's focus was education and health care. Honey's passion for families and children led to Tennessee's infant screening for a genetic defect causing intellectual disability. Her Healthy Children's Initiative, matching pediatricians with expectant mothers, drove prenatal deaths to our state's lowest level ever.

Bill and I both launched our political careers in 1974. Clinton was twenty-seven when he announced his run for Congress. I was thirty-three when I ran for governor. We both lost, but made comebacks. In 1976, Clinton was elected attorney general of Arkansas. Two years later, at age thirty-two, he was elected the country's youngest governor.

That same year, 1978, at thirty-eight, I won the Tennessee governorship. Hillary, Bill, Honey, and I began working together on education and other issues. Both of us learned to work with members of the opposite political party. And both of us relied on the grassroots instincts of a Tennessee Democrat, House Speaker Ned Ray McWherter.

"I tried to find ways to get Ned to Washington so I could talk with him," Clinton said.

According to Clinton, McWherter introduced him to Al Gore.

"You two should get together. Al here knows everything about everything. Bill can explain it so people can understand it," McWherter told them at the Tennessee governor's residence.

McWherter also relied on Clinton for advice.

"Ned asked me, 'How do you get a woman interested in you when you're eighty?' Tell her you're ninety," Clinton said at McWherter's funeral.

* * *

"Clinton is the first president who is actually a political consultant," political consultant Mike Murphy said.

Clinton had fine-tuned political instincts. He would gravitate toward anyone who might oppose or dislike him. He would gaze into the eyes of each person who caught his attention—especially if she was a pretty girl—with such focus that the object of his gaze felt certain no one else on earth was important. This habit made him late for meetings, but it also made him an effective campaigner.

Bill Clinton would work a crowd until he had met them all. He was like Minnie Pearl after a Grand Ole Opry performance, determined to sign every last autograph.

In January of 1993, Honey and I attended a reception for the newly elected president. Clinton walked up to us and, as was his habit, stayed to talk until aides pulled him away.

"I feel like I'm like the dog who caught the truck," he said before finally moving on.

Bill Clinton's leadership earned a mixed scorecard.

Sometimes he headed in the wrong direction. He turned Bush's "America 2000," a governor/community/private initiative, into "Goals 2000," a federally driven enterprise—and the beginnings of what I called a "national school board." His Hillarycare attempt at national health insurance was a complicated flop. He penalized the most productive Americans with higher taxes. His inexperience in foreign policy showed when he failed to provide enough force to avoid the massacre of eighteen American soldiers in Somalia, failed to intervene in the genocide in Rwanda, and failed to take decisive action against Al Qaeda.

Clinton's "bimbo eruptions"—the phrase his Little Rock campaign staff used to describe his sexual dalliances—set a poor moral example and interfered with his ability to govern. He embarrassed, disappointed, and lied to his most loyal supporters, causing the House to impeach him—and creating an awkwardness for Gore that probably contributed to his defeat in the 2000 presidential contest.

On the positive side, he helped move the Democrat Party toward the center so that it could win a national election. He was confident enough in that strategy to choose Gore, another Southern centrist, as his running mate. They won twice. As president, he stuck to what he had learned as governor about welfare reform, despite jeers from the left. He presided over the passage of the North American Free Trade Agreement. His bipartisan experience as governor prepared him to deal with Republicans in Washington.

These middle-of-the-road actions caused many in his party to criticize him as a "Democrat Eisenhower." He had promised to be a "domestic president," and he came as close to being one as our nation is ever likely to have. He was also lucky. The national debt came down for three years during his presidency, mainly as a result of tough decisions made by his predecessor, George H.W. Bush, and from the internet's boost to the economy.

For three decades, Bill Clinton and I swapped ideas as we traveled toward the same goal. He got there first, but "bimbo eruptions" that continued into the White House soiled his legacy. Nevertheless, on balance, he became a charismatic and effective first president of our generation—which leads to the story of how I spent the next three years running against him so I could be the *second.*

According to his pollster, Dick Morris, I was not the opponent that Clinton wanted for his reelection campaign in 1996.

"Lamar Alexander had two big converts in the White House—Bill Clinton and Al Gore. Other than Colin Powell, he was the one man Clinton didn't want to face in November," Morris wrote in *Behind the Oval Office.*[2]

"Both were Southern, both essentially moderate, both charming, telegenic, young, attractive, and former governors, and both had made education the theme of their governorships. For Clinton, it would have been like running against himself," Morris said.

Clinton preferred to run against Bob Dole, who would be seventy-three during his first year in office. Clinton had defeated one World War II veteran, and he thought he knew how to do it again. Clinton and Morris were planning TV ads depicting Dole as a grumpy old man who would take the country backward; Clinton would own the "bridge to the future." But Clinton was not my immediate problem. Dole was far ahead in polls of Republican primary voters.

I set out to persuade Republicans to "Remember your ABCs—Alexander Beats Clinton," arguing that I could offer a more reliable bridge to the future than Clinton could, and that Dole could not offer one at all.

* * *

On January 21, 1993, as Bill Clinton delivered his inaugural address, Honey and I drove our red Ford Explorer from Washington, DC, home to Nashville.

Four Bush Education Department staffers moved to Nashville to set up a political and fundraising operation.[3] I enlisted Ted Welch, a former Republican National Committee finance chairman, as chief volunteer fundraiser. Bob Dole had called Welch "the best fundraiser in America." In Tennessee, the most feared words in the English language were said to be, "Ted Welch is holding on line one."

The *Little Plaid Book* enshrines several Welch fundraising doctrines.

"Remember that early money helps the most, is appreciated the best, and remembered the longest.

"When raising money, don't forget to ask for the money.

"Never confuse pledges with money in the bank.

"Never take cash.

"Studies show that half a campaign's money is wasted; hire a campaign manager who can figure out which half."[4]

I joined Howard Baker's law firm, practicing just enough to justify my partnership and to earn a living until I announced my candidacy.

In May of 1993, I created the Republican Neighborhood Meeting, using the same technology that I had used as education secretary for "America 2000" satellite town meetings.

"We are pretty good at saying what we're against, not as good at painting a picture of what we want our country to be," I said. "The winning Republican strategy has the word populist written all over it. Paying teachers more for teaching well is populist and progressive because it challenges the establishment. We need to do more of that. That's where the great center of the Republican Party is. It's activist, best exemplified by Republican governors."

The monthly meetings became a sort of Republican choir practice. In eighteen months, they grew from 250 meeting sites to about 3,000. By November 1994, it reached nine million homes in over 500 cities. Every second Tuesday at 8:00 p.m., Republicans gathered at places like the dog track in Keene, New Hampshire, Big Dog's Brewing Company in Las Vegas, Smitty's in Little Rock, homes, community colleges—anywhere there was a satellite receiver or the meeting was carried on cable TV. This was all before people were using the internet. We called it "America's largest Republican meeting." My guests for each month's meeting included many who were, themselves, thinking of running for president.[5]

On Monday, July 4, 1994, the day after my fifty-fourth birthday, I set out from Nashville to drive 8,800 miles for eight weeks, circling the country. As I had done on my walk across Tennessee, I stayed in the homes of families I mostly had never met, and stayed up late talking with them and their neighbors.[6]

My first night was in the home of Fred Montgomery, Alex Haley's boyhood friend, right after the town had its first drive-by shooting. In Savannah, I stayed with the imposing Reverend Henry Delaney—"500 pounds of prophecy"—who had transformed a neighborhood dominated by crack homes. In Jennings, Louisiana, I stayed with a Cajun restaurant owner called "the Boudin King." In Dallas, I slept on the floor of Father Jerry Hill's homeless shelter, and in Los Angeles, spent the night with the principal of Roosevelt High School who told me that almost all of its four thousand students were undocumented Hispanics.

Senator Baker had also recruited to his law firm Lawrence Eagleburger, President Bush's Secretary of State. In October of 1995, the three of us traveled for three weeks to Great Britain, Israel, and Asia. The trip was for law firm business, but for me, it also provided a seminar in international affairs.

After our visit in London with Tony Blair, I understood how, two years later, he became prime minister. Blair's eloquence filled the small room in which we met.

In China, we visited President Jiang Zemin, who studied the three of us.

"Mr. Eagleburger, I know you. But, please excuse me, all the rest of you Americans look alike," China's president said, laughing.

In Israel, we saw Foreign Minister Shimon Peres and spent half an hour with Benjamin Netanyahu, who talked nonstop. At the end of a long day, we visited Prime Minister Yitzhak Rabin.

After seeing how weary Rabin was, Baker offered this lesson.

"A good rule of thumb is never to visit a great man after 6:00 p.m.," he said.

"What is your greatest worry?" Baker had asked Rabin.

"Terrorism," the prime minister answered.

The next month, on Saturday, November 4, a terrorist assassinated Rabin.

CHAPTER 32

Porkburger by Porkburger

"His red and black plaid shirt was not fit for a possum."

— **MIKE ROYKO,** ***Chicago Sun-Times*** **columnist**

Iowa. 1993–1995.

In Iowa, progress in a presidential campaign is measured porkburger by porkburger.

My visit to Mary Klink's farm in Eldora on a steamy July day offered a glimpse of what that is like. The corn was tall, the air was still, and the temperature was 100 degrees. After a covered dish lunch under a huge white oak, about three dozen of Mary's neighbors and I talked about jobs, families, schools, and what kind of country we could have. I wished that anyone cynical about the presidential process could have been a fly on the wall.

Mary knew Bob Dole well. He had been to the Klink farm twice. His photograph was on the wall with daughter, Renee, and her husband, Les, a former state senator. And while she liked Dole, Mary thought that George Bush was the nicest of the candidates who had been to the farmhouse. But she didn't like what Bush had done to Dole in the last days of the 1992 New Hampshire primary one bit. "I told him so when I saw him in Des Moines a few months later," she said.

Mary was already thinking about the next caucus night. She would wake up when it was pitch dark. The thermometer outside the kitchen window might say thirty below. The wind from the northwest would burn her face as she walked to the street to extract the *Des Moines Register* from its delivery box. Before 10:00 a.m., she would bake her favorite Norwegian cookies and arrange the cloth napkins and coffee mugs on the walnut table in the living room.

Mary had done this at her house in just this way on one very cold Monday every four years beginning with the first Iowa Republican caucus in 1976. It was that time of year when winter had gone on so long, it seemed that the cold would never break. It was when Iowans who could afford it fled to Florida until they could imagine that the black earth had become warm enough to plant. Others bundled their children and drove to the Holiday Inn in Eldora for the weekend, where there was a swimming pool so huge that it filled the halls with the scent of chlorine, there were games to play, and endless snacks in the vending machines.

She would be smiling to herself, knowing that only the hardiest Republicans would show up that night for coffee and cupcakes, and to cast their caucus votes for president. Mary Klink also knew that it was worth it because it meant the candidates would come to her farm. She could meet and size up for herself the person who would make the rules for trading her crops, managing her Social Security money, and whether to send her grandson, Justin, to fight a war.

Iowans like Mary Klink provide an opportunity for an unknown governor. For example, one cold Monday night, January 19, 1976, Walter Cronkite reported on CBS news, "It appears that Governor Robert Carter of Georgia has won [the Iowa caucuses]."[1]

Cronkite reappeared in a few minutes.

"Excuse me. That's Governor *James* Carter," Cronkite said.

The national media didn't know much about Jimmy Carter in 1976, but enough Iowans did.

When I began visiting Iowa in May 1993, I had been both a governor and a Cabinet secretary, but I was unknown to most Iowans. Honey did not enjoy being my smiling sidekick, so she visited eighty different Iowa communities on her own, introducing herself and tolerating the indignities of a presidential campaign.

"We've always campaigned separately," she told one interviewer. "Lamar's in New Hampshire. I'll probably be in Florida or Tennessee. If he's in Georgia, I could be in Iowa.... A campaign is always a very big endeavor. So, we might as well spread the two of us around and get the most out of it."

After studying candidates' wives at the Iowa State Fair in August, one Republican woman slipped Honey a handwritten note.

"Dear, may I offer some advice? Mrs. Gramm is a redbird. Mrs. Dole is a bluebird. Mrs. Lugar is a yellow bird. And you are a thrush. You need more color in your wardrobe," the note said.

After that, Honey bought several brightly colored scarves to wear.

In December 1994, the campaign team expanded.[2] Mike Murphy agreed to be creative, communications, and media consultant. Murphy, at thirty-two, was already at the top of his game. Just as Ted Welch gave the campaign financial credibility, Murphy gave it political credibility. He believed I could win the primary, but did not underestimate the difficulty of unseating President Clinton.

* * *

On Tuesday, February 28, 1995, wearing my red-and-black plaid shirt, I walked four blocks from 121 Ruth Street to Maryville High School, then on to the Blount County Courthouse, where I declared that I would be a candidate for president.

"Where I come from has everything to do with where I stand. Now is a good time to give another Republican outsider the opportunity to put some humility into the arrogant empire in Washington, DC," I said, invoking Maryville and Ronald Reagan.

I mailed a plaid shirt to each of the nation's major political columnists. The only one who replied was the *Washington Post's* David Broder, who thanked me and noted that he had given the shirt to charity.

In June, eight months before the Iowa caucus, Whit Ayres, a Presbyterian elder who never would shade the truth, wore his most severe countenance as he presented the results of his first poll of caucus voters.

"Governor..." he began.

Whit never called me "Governor," so I knew he must be about to reveal something ominous.

"Governor, this is the professional challenge of my career. Our survey says, Bob Dole 54 percent, Alexander 3 percent, margin of error 4 percent," Ayres said.

Now, put yourself in my shoes. I had been chairman of the nation's governors, secretary of education, university president, and had raised $5 million. By then, Honey and I had each visited Iowa maybe forty times. Bill Kristol of the *Weekly Standard* had said that I had "the best 1994" of all the candidates—and I was still fifty points behind Bob Dole.

On Thursday, July 6, 1995, I began a walk across New Hampshire, seventeen years after my 1,022-mile walk across Tennessee. I started in Concord, where those I met worried that my plaid shirt was too warm for the summer. I assured them it was cotton. After walking ten miles with supporters, handing out brochures, and talking with citizens, I scratched an X on the highway with red chalk. The next morning, I returned to the X to continue walking.

On one Saturday morning, New Hampshire Governor Steve Merrill (many said we had a striking resemblance) appeared wearing *his* red-and-black plaid shirt. We walked together through Manchester neighborhoods, knocking on doors, looking like twins, and startling homeowners. I completed the walk in several multiday chunks, finishing the last stretch a few days before the primary on Tuesday, February 20, 1996.

Meanwhile, the news from Iowa was improving. At the August 19 straw poll in Ames, Dole and Phil Gramm tied with 24 percent of the vote. I played "God Bless America" on the piano, urged delegates to "cut Congress's pay and send them home," and came in fourth with 11 percent behind Pat Buchanan.

My remarks caused a storm in Washington, DC.

"'Cut Their Pay and Send Them Home' has become the mother of all reforms. The opposition in Congress is virtually unanimous," *Roll Call* said.

"What happens when a blatantly political bit of demagoguery also happens to be a good idea?" journalist Jeff Greenfield asked.[3]

"It's hard to imagine a dumber idea," Norm Ornstein wrote.

A few pundits were encouraging.

"I wouldn't be surprised if it went to Lamar Alexander," John McLaughlin said on *The McLaughlin Group.*

"The latest inside-the-beltway favorite among the longshots is ... Alexander," the *National Journal* wrote.

Progress in Iowa also is measured in crowds of two or three. Once, Jimmy Carter and aide Jody Powell arrived for a political meeting in Le Mars, a town of 8,000 touted as the "Ice Cream Capital of the World" for its manufacturing of Blue Bunny ice cream. The only person there was a reporter. Powell rushed out on the main street, borrowed two passersby, and created a crowd.

I ate a lot of porkburgers in Clinton, Buena Vista County, Atlantic, Okoboji, and Pella, and shook a lot of hands, hoping that what had happened to Congressman Mo Udall would not happen to me.

"I'm Mo Udall and I'm running for president," the congressman had said when he walked into a barbershop.

"Yes, we know. We were just all laughing about that this morning!" the barber said.

Insofar as our children were concerned, the campaign's high point came in October on *Saturday Night Live's* cold open, "Halloween in New Hampshire." After comedian Norm Macdonald, as a very scary Bob Dole, had several doors slammed in his face, I knocked on a door wearing my plaid shirt and said in a friendly way, "I'm Lamar Alexander and I'm running for president." The door slammed in my face too.

In November, I made a quick trip to Washington to try to influence the "invisible primary," an informal collection of elected officials, fundraisers, media, and operatives who pronounce a consensus about who should be the nominees.

"If you dislike Washington, DC, so much, why do you want to come here?" *Washington Post* publisher Katharine Graham, a leader of the invisible primary, asked me at an editorial board meeting crowded with curious journalists.

I was "catch of the day" at a breakfast for three dozen journalists hosted by the *Christian Science Monitor*'s Godfrey Sperling. For a year, these reporters had ignored my trudging around Iowa and New Hampshire, and instead had written about "candidates" who did *not* run. My national coverage had been mostly on C-SPAN's *Road to the White House.*

"If you guys were sportswriters, you would show up during the last game of the Final Four and claim you'd covered the whole basketball season. This race will be over before you ever get there," I told them.

* * *

As 1996 began, Michael Lewis offered this estimate.

"Dole attracts veterans, cynics, and chronically risk averse; Buchanan attracts the angry rabble; [Alan] Keyes attracts moralists. I could only conclude that Alexander attracts people who use niceness to get what they want," he wrote in his book, *Trail Fever*.[4]

Dole and Forbes were *not* being nice. They were spending millions on TV attacking each other. Iowans were growing tired of both. Forbes had spent at least $16 million during the last few months of 1995, mostly going after Dole on television. All Forbes had to do to pay for his attack ads was write a check.

At the January 13, 1996, presidential forum in Des Moines, Dole stayed quiet while the other eight of us angled for attention. I challenged Forbes's obsession with a single flat tax rate and said it was a windfall for the rich.

"Your flat tax would be a disaster, a truly nutty idea, in the Jerry Brown tradition. [It's] right up there with the Great Pumpkin. Steve, the only thing you've ever run is a magazine you've inherited, and you raised the price of your magazine. Now, what would you do with taxes?" I asked.

On January 28, two weeks before the February 12 caucus, our campaign ran an ad during the Super Bowl.

"Remember your ABCs. Alexander Beats Clinton," it said.

National media began to show up. NBC's Tim Russert stood at the back of the room when I spoke to a packed house at the Rotary Club of Ankeny. ABC's Peter Jennings was in the doorway in Des Moines while I played the piano and Amy Grant sang the "Tennessee Waltz." David Broder was at the University of Iowa when a student wearing a red-and-black plaid shirt shouted, "A-B-C-D-E-F-G!"

"Alexander beats Clinton and Dole and even Forbes and Graham!" the student said.

On Tuesday, February 6, Phil Gramm lost the Louisiana caucus and dropped out of the race. Two days later, I won the "Iowa student mock caucus." On Friday night, I played the piano and sang the "Tennessee Waltz" to several hundred supporters in Des Moines. "Big Foot" national media stood at the back, chatting and giving the appearance that they were "covering the caucus," unlike young John Dickerson, who had spent weeks reporting my speeches to small audiences.

"I didn't know I was running against Perry Como," Dole cracked, reminding voters of our generational difference.

On Monday, the 12, the day of the caucus, Walter Isaacson, the *Time* magazine editor, evicted Dickerson, his own reporter, from the King Air turboprop plane in which we were barnstorming, and took the seat for himself. That night, in most of the 1,681 precinct caucuses, my supporters wore red-and-black plaid shirts. When the results were in, it was Dole 26, Buchanan 23, and Alexander 18 percent.

Honey and I boarded a small jet for Manchester, New Hampshire, with Isaacson occupying the seat that was to have been Dickerson's. My good showing put me on the cover of *Time,* along with Dole and Buchanan and on "Meet the Press" the next Sunday.

As the plane sped through the night, I thought about the McDonald's waitress I had met outside Des Moines two weeks earlier.

"Honey, it might be you. One's too old, one's too mean, one's too goofy, and honey, you might be the one!" she'd said.

CHAPTER 33

Toast

"If you're in the game long enough, you're going to be the toast of the town one day...and the next day, you'll be toast."

— **ALAN K. SIMPSON, US Senator (R-WY)**

"That's the way of politics: surging success or plunging defeat— a tempestuous way of life."

—**BRYCE HARLOW, Counselor to the president**

New Hampshire to Nashville. February–July 1996.

UNLIKE THE SUPER BOWL that ends each football season, the Super Bowl of Politics *kicks off* the presidential campaign season.

The presidential Super Bowl is a wild eight-day ride that begins with the Iowa caucus and ends with the New Hampshire primary. Historically, it determines which two of the three candidates who have made it out of Iowa will survive after New Hampshire.

At 3:00 a.m. on Tuesday, February 13, 1996, Tom Rath, my New Hampshire chairman, greeted our plane when it landed in 10-degree weather at the Manchester airport.

"You shouldn't have stayed up so late," I told Rath.

"We live for this," he said.

Things were looking up. Streets I had walked alone a few months earlier were now clogged with supporters. Cameras were everywhere. Clinton and Gore were afraid that I might defeat Dole, network journalists whispered. For the last year, the Democrat campaign had spent millions on TV portraying Dole as a creepy accomplice of Newt Gingrich. Now, the journalists said the president's campaign was slipping them unflattering information about my financial affairs and my proposal to abolish the Department of Education.

I won CNN's Thursday night debate, according to the network.

In a Manchester restaurant, I overheard ABC's Peter Jennings ask Fred Thompson,

"If Dole loses, who will we support?"

Instead of being happy about the new media attention, I was angry, because it had taken journalists so long to decide that I might win. During one early debate (before Senator Richard Lugar entered the race), I had peered down the stage at the other candidates. There was Dole, whose age made it hard to challenge Clinton's "bridge to the future"; Gramm, who "doesn't stand a chance," according to Richard Nixon's remark to reporter Monica Crowley; Forbes, an unsmiling publisher who had never been elected to anything; Congressman "Bullet Bob" Dornan; the polemicist Alan Keyes; and Des Moines businessman Morry Taylor.

There was also Pat Buchanan, with whom I had worked on Nixon's White House staff.

"Your trouble is that you're not an ideologue," Buchanan told me (meaning I couldn't win the primary).

"Your trouble is that you *are* an ideologue," I told him (meaning that he couldn't win the November general election).

Among these contestants, it seemed obvious that I could win, and I wondered why the media had not been able to see what I had seen. Whit Ayres said the voters were seeing it. His New Hampshire polls now showed me in third place at 18 percent, with Dole at 23 and Buchanan at 21. Dole's polls saw it too, according to the *Boston Globe*.

Dole adviser Don Sipple wrote in a private memo on February 13, the day after the Iowa caucus, "The threat is Alexander.... Forbes and Buchanan would never be accepted by the party, and winning New Hampshire would give Alexander enormous momentum."

On Saturday afternoon, when I returned to our hotel room, Honey was worried.

"You won't like what I've been seeing on television," she said.

Overnight, Dole replaced his anti-Buchanan TV ads with anti-Alexander ads featuring Governor Merrill, who had apparently hung his red-and-black plaid shirt in the closet. The ads accused "Liberal Lamar" of releasing convicts and raising taxes fifty times—never mind that Tennessee taxes were lower per capita than New Hampshire taxes.

"The Dole ad was as distorted as anything put on the airwaves in New Hampshire. The average voter saw these ads 12 times over the weekend... and the percentage of voters who thought Alexander was conservative went from 44 to 22 percent," the *Globe* reported.

"It was the most extraordinary five-day turnaround I have seen in seventeen years of polling. It was ugly, short, and brutal and not attractive to watch, but it worked," Bill McInturff, Dole's pollster, said.

By the time I saw the ads on Saturday, the deadline had passed for submitting new ads to rebut the charges on Manchester's WMUR-TV. Dole's negative barrage had damaged me, but it damaged him too.

* * *

On Tuesday, February 20, 1996, the night of the primary, the camera light turned red, and Dan Rather said to me and to eight million other Americans watching the returns, "Governor, we have what we call in the business a 'hot lead.' This just in from our CBS exit polls. We predict Buchanan the winner of the New Hampshire primary with 27 percent, Bob Dole second with 26 percent, and Lamar Alexander third with 23 percent.

"Governor, how do you feel?" Rather asked.

Rather was interviewing me during an 8:00 p.m. newsbreak just after polls had closed.

"Just great, Dan. I feel just great," I said.

But I was not telling the truth. I knew that coming in third in New Hampshire, even a close third, was a death sentence.

"Three out of Iowa and two out of New Hampshire," was the media's mantra.

Deep down, I knew that after three years of scratching, clawing, and coming close, the media would now predict that I would lose, making it impossible to raise money. Washington big shots would encourage me to drop out, and I would be gone within weeks.

That is what happened. I stumbled in South Dakota, then again in South Carolina and Georgia. I had nowhere to go.

Two weeks later, on Wednesday, March 6, I telephoned Honey, who was campaigning in Texas.

"It's over," I said.

* * *

During the weekend before the New Hampshire primary, journalists R.W. Apple and Robert Novak had predicted that I would win.

Jack Germond was blunter.

"If you don't win, it will be because of that SOB Forbes," Germond told me in a Manchester bar.

Germond's theory was that most of Forbes's votes (he got 12 percent) were anti-Dole votes that would have gone to me. That was even more likely to be true of the votes Senator Lugar received. Life is full of close calls. Any defensive back can explain how he could have intercepted the pass that would have won the game, if only he had been one step closer to the wide receiver.

Dole, who was still Senate Republican leader, had told reporter Bob Woodward that he was tired of being embarrassed.

"If I come in third in New Hampshire, I'm going back to the Senate," Dole said.

If Dole had dropped out, that would have meant Buchanan versus Alexander—with Forbes hanging around because of his money—a race that I believe I would have won.

Whit Ayres wrote a postmortem memo.

"My assessment is that, had Dole not gone negative on Lamar, Alexander would have passed Dole to come in second or first in New Hampshire. Subsequent primaries showed just how linked Alexander's numbers were to Dole's. When Dole went down in New Hampshire, Lamar went up. But when Dole went up, as in South Carolina, Lamar went down. In many ways, Lamar Alexander was the younger version of Bob Dole, the mainstream, credible Republican leader who spoke for the dominant group of somewhat conservative voters," Ayres wrote.

Two days after I dropped out, at a press conference in Knoxville, I presented Dole with a red-and-black plaid shirt. Senator Baker, who had never liked the shirt, stood beside me.

"I hope that's his last one," Baker muttered loudly.

Dole easily dispatched Buchanan and Forbes.

During the fall campaign, Clinton owned the "bridge to the future," and in November, defeated Dole handily. The Republican Party had the same problem in 1996 that the Democrats had in the 1980s—anyone who could win the November election couldn't win the party nomination.

"I suggest that you get a job and make all this money you're accused of having," Honey said when we returned to Nashville.

* * *

I delayed taking Honey's advice.

"It's my turn," I told her ten months later, in January 1997.

I had looked at history. No Republican since Eisenhower had won the nomination on the first try. In 1980, the first time Dole ran, he came in seventh in New Hampshire. Ronald Reagan won the nomination on his third try.

As William McGurn has written, "Republicans have a habit of running their primaries like an Elks lodge—with the nomination going to the member who had waited his turn."

As Clinton was being inaugurated for his second term, Ted Welch was on board, and I was in Iowa speaking to the Farm Bureau. One year later, on Wednesday, January 21, 1998, my second presidential campaign crashed—literally. A chartered Beechcraft Baron carrying campaign manager Brian Kennedy and me took off from Washington, DC, heading for a Republican dinner in Dover, Delaware.

Shortly after takeoff, one of the pilots said the wheels were not working properly. The pilots decided to land, but only one wheel would lower. One pilot lay down on the floor and tried manually to lower the stuck wheel, but had no success. Authorities diverted the plane to Richmond so that if there were to be a crash landing on one wheel, it would not be in the nation's capital. For three hours, the plane circled Richmond, burning fuel to reduce the chance of fire in a crash.

Word spread. National media began calling my friends to gather information for an obituary. Trucks spread foam on the runway. Fire trucks stood ready. Television cameras lined up to record the disaster.

As the pilot touched the runway on one wheel, I cracked open the door. Then, as the plane slowed, I pushed Kennedy out and jumped out after him. That seemed the safest course in case the plane flipped or caught fire. The plane swung wildly and skidded to a stop on the foam, headed in the opposite direction.

I telephoned Honey to tell her no one was hurt, chartered a Learjet, and flew to Delaware.

I told dinner guests, "For a number of months, I have been wanting to come to Delaware in the worst way—and I think I just did."

Meanwhile, Iowa Governor Terry Branstad and Arkansas Governor Mike Huckabee had signed up. We were raising money. On Wednesday, March 10, I announced my second presidential campaign in Nashville's Old Supreme Court Chamber.

This time, I wore a dark suit. After my first presidential campaign, I had written my *Little Plaid Book.* Rule No. 1 said, "Wear your red and black plaid shirt, but not when you announce for president."

It didn't work.

I had not taken into account the advantages that George W. Bush had—his name, his father's network of fundraisers, and his personal charm. While I was waiting in the St. Louis airport to connect on a TWA flight from Nashville to Cedar Rapids, Governor Bush would be travelling to Iowa on a corporate jet or receiving supporters in Austin. Even when he didn't attend Republican events, he was the most popular candidate mentioned.

"The Grim Reaper will be in Ames for some of the candidates," Pat Buchanan predicted before the August 14 Republican Straw Poll at Iowa State University.

The Grim Reaper was looking for me. Bush came in first. I was sixth. I flew home to Nashville, embarrassed and dispirited.

Two days later, on August 16, I announced the end of my campaign.

"This is my last campaign for public office," I said, declaring my retirement from politics for the second—and I assured everyone—final time.

"What would you change about the presidential process?" reporters asked.

"The rush to judgment and the $1,000 [contribution] limit will weed out most of the people who are likely to run for president," I said. "It's become a money media contest. And if we're not careful, we'll end up with a race between only the rich and the already famous.

"I mean, we might have Donald Trump versus the latest Powerball winner, with Cher as an Independent candidate. That's what we could look forward to in 2004."

Reporters laughed.

"Think of it as a reverse calling," my brother-in-law, the Reverend Bill Carl, told me. "Being president would be your great joy, but an authentic calling requires that the world agree with that and, just barely, it didn't."

* * *

Ten months later, Dick Cheney left a message on my office answering machine in Nashville.

I delayed returning the call until Wednesday, May 24, the day before Honey and I were to leave for a month on Nantucket Island. It would be our longest time together, just the two of us, since our honeymoon.

"Governor Bush would like to consider you as vice president," Cheney said.[1]

"I've put politics behind me. Surely there are other, better people," I said.

"The governor has told me to put race and gender and geography aside, and go for the person who would make the best president," he said.

"That must be a long list," I said.

"You try to make it. When you make a list of Republicans using that criteria who are tested, it is a short list," he said.

"How short?"

"A handful."

"How big is a handful?"

"I've got five fingers on my hand. How many have you got on yours?" Cheney said.

"Why don't you do it?" I said.

"It's not for me," he said.

I couldn't believe it. I was settling into a new life. I was contributing my papers to an archive.

"Do what you want to do," Honey said, but I knew that she had zero interest in more political adventures.

About noon on Memorial Day, Monday, May 29, I told Cheney that I would do it.

"I'll send you the papers. Fill them out and send them back, and later in the month, we'll get together," he said.

I asked A.B. Culvahouse Jr., the best lawyer I knew, to help with Cheney's questionnaires. On Wednesday, May 30, Cheney sent Culvahouse 200 questions. For two weeks, answering the questions stole days from the time Honey and I had planned to be together.

I felt the political virus returning.

"The foolishness has begun again," Honey said.

On Monday, July 3, my sixtieth birthday, Cheney met with Bush for three hours in Crawford, Texas. Barton Gellman, Cheney's biographer, writes that, in that meeting, Bush offered the vice presidency, Cheney accepted, and the deal was made. If so, that meant that for another three weeks, Bush and Cheney interviewed candidates for a vacancy that had already been filled.

On Monday, July 24, Bush called me.

"Thank you for letting me consider you for vice president. Give my love to Honey," he said.

The next day, Bush introduced Cheney at a campaign event in Austin.

A few days later, the eight boxes of my answers to Cheney's questionnaires arrived at Culvahouse's office unopened, with the straps around them still in place.

"My close association with the president goes back to when he asked me to lead the search for a vice-presidential nominee. That worked out pretty well," Cheney joked a few years later.

"The only cure for politics is embalming fluid," Georgia Senator Johnny Isakson had told me.

Surely, I thought, *my life in politics finally has ended—fortunately, without resorting to embalming fluid.*

PART NINE

The Most Exclusive Club

2001 to 2008

"The United States Senate is a terribly sought after post.... So the Senate is the ultimate goal of most every politician."

—SENATOR PRESCOTT BUSH,
from Jon Meacham's *Destiny and Power*[1]

CHAPTER 34

From 9/11 to the Senate

"Rule 123. If you want to be noticed, don't ride in a convertible with Dolly Parton."

—*LAMAR ALEXANDER'S LITTLE PLAID BOOK*

Cambridge, MA, to Washington, DC. September 2000–November 2002.

THE HARVARD DEAN'S CALL came in September of 2000, two months after George W. Bush had thanked me for being one of his vice-presidential prospects.

"We'd like for you to come to the Kennedy School. You could tell students what you learned about running for president. You would be Professor of the Practice, teach classes, attend faculty meetings, have a course assistant. You could go home on weekends," Dean Joseph S. Nye Jr. said.

"Thank you, but I'm afraid that doesn't fit my plans," I said.

After I put down the phone, I realized that I had no plans. I was drifting again. I had resumed my law practice, joined the boards of five internet education companies, become chairman of one, and lost money on all five. Then came a flood of offers to join nonprofit boards. I joined twenty.

That evening, I was watching an NBA game.

"Kobe [Bryant] would be a much better player if he'd quit trying so hard and let the game come to him," the broadcaster, Hubie Brown, said.

I decided that Hubie Brown's advice might be good for me too. The next morning, I called Dean Nye and accepted the professorship.

* * *

In January, 2001, when I arrived in Cambridge, I found that Harvard lived up to its liberal reputation. More than 90 percent of registered voters were Democrats. For many students and faculty, the Kennedy School served as a way station between the last Democrat campaign or administration and the next one. Matt Sonnesyn, one of the few Republican students, became my first course assistant.[1]

"We Republicans get the best education," he said, "because our views are constantly challenged and we have to learn to defend them."

At the same time, Harvard was an intellectual feast. I was fascinated by luncheons where faculty members challenged each other's work. Students were talented, ambitious, and kept me on my toes.

On Wednesday, January 31, 2001, at my first class for "The Ultimate Start-up: The American Presidential Campaign," I told thirty students that the goal was to come up with an ideal way to elect a president.

"A presidential campaign is like starting from scratch to create General Motors. And then, if you win, you've got to make a quick transition to a different responsibility, as George Bush just found out. Or, if you lose, it's all over, as Al Gore just found out," I told them.[2]

Teaching how to run for president was not what I wanted to do. Politics is high sport but it is only a means to an end—and that end is to understand our complicated country well enough to unite its citizens around ideas that most can accept. And I wanted to discuss with students what it means to be an American, a subject I had tried to make the foundation of my presidential campaigns. I sought out faculty members Harvey Mansfield, Robert Putnam, Samuel Huntington, and other scholars who had explored "the American character."

"We all wave the same flag, but what does the flag mean?" Huntington had asked.

On the presidential campaign trail, my answers to Huntington's question had produced a mixed response. Sometimes audiences stood when I said, "It is time to put the teaching of American history and civics back in its rightful place in our schools so our children can grow up learning what it means to be an American."

Other times, eyes glazed over, making me so frustrated that, one afternoon in the summer of 1999, when campaigning in Bedford, New Hampshire, I stood by myself on a small stage in an empty park.

"We are proud of where we have come from, but prouder of where we have come, prouder of saying, 'We are all Americans!'" I shouted.

No one heard it, but I felt better.

* * *

On Tuesday morning, September 11, as the fall semester was getting underway in Cambridge, I watched in horror as the television showed the second terrorist plane crashing into the Twin Towers.

I tried to call Kathryn, who was living in Brooklyn. I thought about how five years earlier, during the presidential race, no candidate except Senator Lugar had even mentioned terrorism. It was Friday before the first Southwest plane flew to Nashville. I was one of three passengers. Before boarding, I removed my shoes, some clothes, was patted down, searched, and delayed—experiencing for the first time the permanent indignity that a few terrorists had inflicted on tens of millions of travelers.

I watched the national conversation shift from what pulls us apart to what pulls us together. Suddenly, Americans were again saying that diversity is important, but that our greatest strength is something different.

"No other nation has so successfully combined people of different races and nations into a single culture,"[3] was how Margaret Thatcher explained it.

Throughout most of our country's life, the national conversation had been a public classroom for teaching belief in the principles that allowed citizens of all backgrounds to say, "We are all Americans." At the beginning of the twentieth century, as President Theodore Roosevelt was inveighing against "hyphenated Americanism," institutions from Boys and Girls Scouts to Kiwanis Clubs "Americanized" a surge of immigrants.

During World War II, President Franklin Roosevelt made sure that those who charged the beaches of Normandy knew they were fighting for Four Freedoms.

The chief Americanizing institution was the public school.

"The public school was created to help immigrant children learn the three Rs, and what it means to be an American, with a hope they would go home and teach their parents," American Federation of Teachers President Albert Shanker said.[4] *McGuffey's Readers* sold 120 million copies to create a common culture of literature, patriotic speeches, and historical references, according to Diane Ravitch.

But for forty years, the conversation about what it means to be an American had been heading in a different direction. New waves of immigration, new cultural attitudes, and new scholarships had been challenging the notion that the greatest accomplishment of the United States of America, after establishing freedom and democracy, had been to find a way to unite its diversity into one country. Public schools had become reluctant to teach core values because teachers were afraid to answer the question, "Whose values?"

Americans were ignoring the country's original motto—three Latin words engraved above the presiding officer's chair in the Senate, *E pluribus unum—Out of many, one.*

"We have too much *pluribus* and not enough *unum*," filmmaker Ken Burns said.

"If it were many out of one, we would be the United Nations, not the United States of America," Huntington wrote.

At least for a while, America's response to 9/11 was to celebrate unity over diversity. After 9/11, television did the Americanizing, displaying patriotic exercises, prayers in prime time, President Bush's visit to the Islamic Center, and NFL players reciting the Declaration of Independence.

At Thanksgiving, Bush spoke of "the American character."

At the Kennedy School, Al Gore said, "We should honor their memories by fighting for the values that bind us together as a country."

The Republican and Democrat presidential contestants of the previous year were saying the same thing, invoking a traditional, value-based national identity. Americans were listening.

* * *

Five months later, Samuel Huntington was a guest in the first class of the course that I had really wanted to teach, "The American Character and America's Government: Using the American Creed to Make Decisions."

Huntington told students that most of America's politics and government is first, about balancing values with which most of us agree, and second, dealing with the disappointment of not reaching the high goals that we have set for ourselves. That became the subject of my class.

I told the students about attending the 1992 Italian American dinner in Washington, DC. It was a boisterous affair, with men and women bursting with pride in their heritage. There were cheers for Scalia, the justice; Stallone, the actor; Tagliabue, the NFL commissioner; and Pelosi, the congresswoman. What struck me most about that evening was not the attendees' pride in their Italian heritage, it was their pride in being Americans. They were proud of where they had come from. They were prouder of where they were now.

I asked students to imagine what words they would put on a sign over the door as someone enters the United States. Among their suggestions were: *anything is possible, one starting line for everyone, busy, freedom-loving, getting rich, moralists, evangelists, laissez-faire, looking different, pulling together.*

These words *do* describe "the American character," I reminded them, but people in other countries have these traits too. What makes America exceptional is that it is the only country based upon an idea. That idea is spelled out in our Constitution and Declaration of Independence. It includes values such as equal opportunity, individualism, rule of law, liberty, life, happiness, freedom of speech and religion, separation of church and state, government of the people, and *E pluribus unum.*

All one has to do to become a citizen is swear allegiance to this American creed and to know something of how our democracy works. Becoming Japanese or French requires being born Japanese or French. Becoming an American has nothing to do with your birthplace, your religion, or the color of your skin.

September 11, 2001, had made these values vivid—2,763 deaths at the World Trade Center reminded us of life. Canceled flights, barricaded streets, and no classes were reminders of liberty; postponed NFL games and a closed Disneyland, of happiness; and suddenly closed borders reminded us that we are a nation of immigrants.

If you want to succeed in politics or government, I told students, you must learn to balance these values so you can create laws and policies that most legislators will vote for, and that most Americans will accept. In our classes, we set about doing that, resolving questions such as, "Should Congress enact faith-based legislation?" (pluralism vs. freedom of religion); "Should government vouchers pay for poor children to attend religious schools?" (equal opportunity vs. E pluribus unum vs. separation of church and state); "Should government pay for race-based scholarships?" (equal opportunity vs. E pluribus unum); "Should undocumented immigrants have driver's licenses?" (rule of law vs. equal opportunity); "Should English be our national language?" (E pluribus unum vs. liberty).

* * *

As 2002 began, it appeared that I might have an opportunity to put into practice what I had been teaching.

On Sunday afternoons in January and February, Bill Frist, then chairman of the Senate Republican Campaign Committee, would walk a block down Bowling Avenue from his Nashville home to ours. He showed Honey and me polls suggesting that if Fred Thompson did not run for reelection in November, I could win that Senate seat.

Nine years earlier, in January 1993, the last month I was education secretary, I had invited Fred to lunch at the White House, and encouraged him to run for the Senate. At six-foot-six with rugged looks, a booming voice, and a big laugh, Fred's appeal made other politicians envious. Campaigning with Fred Thompson was like sitting next to Dolly Parton—you can be sure no one is looking at you.

"If I'm elected, what do you suppose I could accomplish?" was the only question Fred asked at lunch.

He and I had grown up together in Republican politics.

"Fred and Lamar are both in Howard Baker's stable," someone had complained.

"Stable? Hell, we're in the same stall," Fred had replied.

In 1973, Fred was minority counsel to the Senate Watergate Committee. Later, he was the attorney for Marie Ragghianti, the truth-telling chairman of the Tennessee Board of Parole, fired by Governor Blanton during the pardons-for-cash scandal. In 1985, he played himself in the movie *Marie* with Sissy Spacek. That led to roles in forty movies and many more television appearances.

Fred was easygoing.

A reporter once wrote, "Senator Thompson roused himself to answer a question." Fred was not lazy—he had worked his way through college—but he did amble along. His seeming not to try was part of his appeal.

In 1993, he and I were talking in the living room of our Nashville home when Honey walked in.

"What are you two cooking up?" she asked.

"Fred is thinking about running for governor," I said.

"Well, Fred, if you do, you'll have to work," Honey said.

"Aw, Honey, I work," Fred said.

"No, Fred. I mean *really* work," Honey said.

In 1994, Fred was elected to the remaining two years of Vice President Gore's unexpired Senate term.

A Washington reporter once asked Fred if he missed making movies.

"Yeah, I miss the sincerity of Hollywood," he said. "I look forward to going back there, where my views are taken more seriously."

During the first week of March 2002, telephone lines buzzed with speculation that Fred might step down. Late Thursday afternoon, March 7, he called me.

"I don't have the heart for another six years," he said. The next day, he announced his decision.

That weekend, I asked Whit Ayers to conduct a poll, and I began recruiting a campaign team.[5] While Honey was hiking in the Smokies with girlfriends, Sunday media reported that I would be a candidate. When Honey came out of the mountains, Molly Pratt found her with a telephone call before I did.

"Honey, I think there's something you ought to know," Molly told her.

Our children were grown, and Honey looked forward to reuniting with friends in her Washington, DC, walking group. The next day, Monday, March 11, she and I drove to the state capitol, where I announced my candidacy for the Senate.

Six months after 9/11, I had no trouble answering Honey's question, "Why are you running and what do you hope to accomplish?"

"This is a dangerous time... that brings out the best in us. I will do whatever I can to capture this moment... to make our country permanently stronger," I said.

That afternoon, I flew back to Harvard to finish the semester.

Congressman Ed Bryant, age fifty-three, had been campaigning for a year, in the event Fred didn't run. Ayres's survey in mid-May showed that I was comfortably ahead of Bryant and would defeat the likely Democrat nominee, Congressman Bob Clement. Later in May, I returned to Tennessee to compete full-time in the August Republican primary.

I hauled out my red-and-black plaid shirt for one more campaign. I wanted the shirt to become a distraction for Bryant in the way a rodeo clown's costume diverts a charging bull.

Bryant attacked my shirt.

"Don't be plaid. Be solid for Bryant," his TV ads proclaimed.

"It's my turn," Bryant said.

I defended my shirt and said to Bryant, "We're not playing Red Rover here. We're at war and we have a country on the line. The issue is not whose turn it is, the issue is who is best prepared in these serious times, and who will offer the strongest support to the president."[6]

I made sure to deal with the appropriate "rats in the barn." Visiting the Grainger County Tomato Festival in July, I happened upon the reigning political savants from Hancock County.

"Boys, I'm afraid I might not get there before election day. Can you take care of me?" I asked.

"We'll get their votes or we'll kill their chickens," one said with a big laugh.

Later that month, I met with Monroe County Republican nominees for courthouse offices.

"Will you carry me on your ticket?" I asked. They said they would.

On Thursday, August 1, I won, 54 percent to 43 percent.

In 2002, Tennessee still was a competitive, two-party state. Clement had an 83 percent name recognition and was a member of a storied political family. But George W. Bush was leading the United States into war.

"If you elect Bob Clement, the first thing he will do is pick up Fred Thompson's desk and carry it across the aisle to the Democrat side of the Senate and sit it down between Hillary Clinton and Ted Kennedy and make it one vote harder for George W. Bush to lead our country and represent our values," I said over and over.

November 2, the Saturday before the general election, was a sunny day.

"With control of Congress and his brother's political future at stake, President Bush began a marathon campaign swing to rally the GOP faithful in ten states with razor close races," CNN reported.

Bush's first stop was at the Tri-Cities Regional airport, a visit designed to boost voter turnout in heavily Republican East Tennessee counties. Two days later, on the Monday night before the election, Frist's polls of Senate races showed: Norm Coleman + 1, John Sununu + 3, Elizabeth Dole + 4, John Thune and Tim Johnson tied, Saxby Chambliss + 1, Alexander + 10.

On the next day, we all but Thune won.

Frist's recruiting and Bush's leadership had paid off. Republicans flipped the Senate from a 51–49 Democrat majority to a 51–49 Republican majority. According to Frist, it remains the only midterm election in US history in which a sitting president's party captured a chamber of Congress that it did not already control.

Bryce Harlow had been right.

"Washington, DC, is a sticky place.... You will keep bouncing back," he had warned me two decades years earlier.

I was bouncing back—for the fourth time. But this time, I had been elected on my own.

CHAPTER 35

Running for Something

"Rule 115. Don't be a threat to every vacancy."
"When I see an empty throne, I feel an urge to sit on it."

—**NAPOLEON BONAPARTE,**
in *LAMAR ALEXANDER'S LITTLE PLAID BOOK*

Washington, DC. November 2006–December 2007.

A FIRST-GRADE TEACHER CAN SPOT a budding United States senator.

The child will be perched on a front row seat, leaning forward, waving a hand, insisting on being recognized. Often this hand-waver is elected class president, as I was in first grade at West Side Elementary School. Infected early with the thrill of politics, these precocious campaigners continue to run for office at school, church, or Boys and Girls State.

Admiring adults encourage them.

"Why, one day that child might grow up to be governor or even a United States senator," they say.

When a few actually do reach the Senate, their instinct is well developed: *Run for something.*

The problem is, by the time they become senators, there are not many more opportunities to run for something. That's why so many survey the chamber, evaluate competitors, and run for president.

"How many senators wake up every morning, look in the mirror and think about running for president?" reporters asked South Carolina Senator Ernest "Fritz" Hollings when he launched his presidential campaign in 1984.

"Every damn one. Every damn day," Hollings said.

Senators are impatient to run because they know that those who wait until the time is right are usually left waiting.

They rarely succeed.

"Since JFK, senators are zero for fifty-five running for president," Utah Senator Bob Bennett calculated in 2003.

"For a senator to be elected president, a senator would have to run against a senator," Senator Trent Lott said, which happened when Senator Obama defeated Senator McCain.

Senators can run for chairman of a committee. But not really. These posts go to the most senior member. Waiting for that opportunity can take a long time. For twenty years, Connecticut Senator Chris Dodd sat next in line on two major committees, waiting for senior members to leave. Such congestion explains why senators seem to be like vultures, always speculating on the health of those just ahead in seniority.

The remaining opportunity is to run for leader, or more accurately, to get in line to run for leader. This process can be torturous. In 1958, at age sixteen, when he was elected president of the student council at Louisville's duPont Manual High School, Mitch McConnell was determined to become a United States senator, he writes in his memoir. Three decades later, in 1984, when he was elected to the Senate, McConnell was determined to become its leader. Three more decades and one triple bypass heart surgery later, in 2015, he finally did.

The six of us Republicans and two Democrats who were elected new senators on Tuesday, November 5, 2002, barely had time to unpack when, one week after our election, we were thrust into voting for caucus leaders. This rush was deliberate. In a body of one hundred, whose members' first instinct is to run for something, incumbent leaders do not allow time for challenges to develop. This strategy is like a hurry-up football offense—snap the ball quickly before the opposing side can get ready.

Eight days later, on Wednesday, November 13, at 10:00 a.m. in the Mike Mansfield Room across the hall from the Senate chamber, I sat next to my former roommate, Lott, as fifty-one Republican senators unanimously and by secret ballot elected him leader, and therefore Senate Majority Leader.

Next, the caucus without dissent reelected McConnell, my friend of thirty years, as whip or "The Number Two Republican" (the media numbers these jobs to clarify the hierarchy). Then, down the line came unanimous elections of Number Three (conference chairman), Number Four (policy committee chairman), Number Five (assistant policy chairman), and chairman of the Republican Senate Senatorial Committee (who somehow escapes being numbered).

Advancement up this leadership ladder is rarely interrupted. In the Senate, *no one* voluntarily gives up power. To create more opportunities to run for something, the Republican caucus limits leaders Two through Five-to-six-year terms—but sometimes incumbents swap positions to avoid term limits.

* * *

A little more than one month later, Lott, the newly elected Majority Leader, *did* give up his power, although not happily. On Thursday evening, December 5, he spoke during a celebration of South Carolina Senator Strom Thurmond's one-hundredth birthday.

"I want to say this about my state: When Strom ran for president, we voted for him. We're proud of it. And if the rest of the country had followed our lead, we wouldn't have had all these problems over the years, either," Lott said to hundreds crowded into a hearing room.

These comments dredged up memories of Thurmond's 1948 segregationist presidential campaign. Jesse Jackson said Lott should resign as leader. Vice President Gore called on the Senate to censure Lott unless he apologized. Voices as disparate as the *Wall Street Journal*, Representative John Lewis, and William Kristol rebuked Lott, who said his words were "misconstrued" and apologized. Republican senators scheduled a January 6 meeting to decide their leader's fate.

Events moved faster than that. On Thursday night, December 20, Honey and I were in our back row pew at a Christmas service at Westminster Presbyterian Church in Nashville when congregation member Emily Reynolds, who Bill Frist soon would appoint secretary of the Senate, whispered that Frist would challenge Lott. The next day, Lott announced he would step down as leader.

The results were stunning. Instead of being the leader of the world's greatest deliberative body, Lott was suddenly without even a chairmanship. (Senator Rick Santorum gave up his Rules Committee chair so Lott could have something.) Frist became Senate Majority Leader, leapfrogging the Number Two and Three Republicans, McConnell and Santorum.

Lott and Frist were as different as night and day.

Lott, then sixty-one, was a career politician. His mother was a teacher and his father a pipefitter in Pascagoula, Mississippi. He was the student body president in high school and a cheerleader at Ole Miss. He was elected to Congress in 1972 and stayed there for thirty-four years.

Lott is an inveterate social animal—upbeat, mischievous, and garrulous. On a weekend visit to our Tennessee home with his wife, Tricia, and New Hampshire Senator Judd Gregg and his wife, Kathy, Lott was standing in the kitchen, holding forth, when he grabbed a handful of snacks from a bowl on the counter and stuffed them in his mouth—only to discover in mid-sentence that the snacks were cat food. He paused only briefly, and continued to expound.

Frist, then fifty, called himself a "citizen legislator," and pledged to serve only two terms. His career was in medicine. Despite his success in politics, it did not seem a natural fit. Born to a teacher and Nashville physician, he quarterbacked a high school championship football team, then headed to Princeton, Harvard, and Stanford, before returning to Nashville to establish Vanderbilt's Center for Heart and Lung Transplant Surgery.

Some early mornings, Senator Frist could be found at the National Zoo in Washington, DC, operating on gorilla hearts. During the August recess, he might be in Sudan operating on villagers. In 1998, when a gunman attacked the Capitol, he treated two police officers—and the gunman. He saved the life of David Petraeus when a Fort Campbell soldier accidentally shot the general in the chest. Frist would remind those who questioned his toughness, "I used to cut out hearts for a living."

In their different ways, both Lott and Frist were effective leaders. Both respected the Senate as an institution and worked across the aisle to solve hard problems. The two had something else in common. If doctors had been more actively diagnosing attention-deficit/hyperactivity disorder when Lott and Frist were in first grade in Pascagoula and Nashville, the two boys surely would both have been prime candidates for such a diagnosis. Both must have been perched on the front row, waving their hands, seeking attention. Everyone knew that one day they would run for something.

After Lott had stepped down as leader, I insisted he attend my January 4 swearing-in reception. He did, as he attended others, but he was hurt and angry.

"I was knifed in the back," he wrote in his memoir.

* * *

It is customary to dismiss members of Congress as an unfortunate collection of soothsayers, misfits, and incompetents. The American people hold only lobbyists and car salespeople in lower regard, according to a 2025 Gallup poll.[1]

One new senator joked, "I spent the first week looking around the Senate floor wondering how I got here, and the next week wondering how the rest of them got here."

Edward Everett Hale, the Senate chaplain in the early 1900s, was asked whether he prayed for senators.

"No, I look at the senators and pray for the country," he said.

Oklahoma humorist Will Rogers had a sobering response to such cynicism. Rogers was once listening to his neighbors complain about their congressman.

"He lies, cheats, and steals, runs around on his wife, and is generally no count," the neighbors said.

"Well, "Rogers said. "I know the congressman and I know the district and I think he pretty well represents the people of the district."

Over eighteen years, I served with about three hundred senators. I found them to be more accomplished and more interesting than most other random slices of the American population. Almost all were congenial. Most were purposeful. A few were exceptionally talented. Many had led fascinating lives.

Jim Inhofe (Oklahoma) flew a single-engine airplane around the world. Bill Nelson (Florida) flew in space. Ted Kennedy (Massachusetts) became more accomplished than his two Senate brothers in forging bipartisan agreements. Martha McSally (Arizona) was the first US woman to fly in combat. David Perdue (Georgia) turned around two troubled Fortune 500 companies. Ted Stevens (Alaska) was decorated for flying dangerous missions into China during World War II. Hillary Clinton (New York) served as US secretary of state.

Jim Bunning (Kentucky) was a baseball Hall of Fame pitcher. Ben Nighthorse Campbell (Colorado) was captain of the 1964 US Olympic judo team and an accomplished Native American jeweler. Kelly Ayotte (New Hampshire) was attorney general and later governor. John McCain (Arizona) spent five and a half years as a prisoner of war in Vietnam.

There is more.

Strom Thurmond (South Carolina) landed by glider in the D-Day invasion. Ben Sasse (Nebraska), Roy Blunt (Missouri), and John D. Rockefeller IV (West Virginia) were college presidents. Richard Lugar (Indiana), Cory Booker (New Jersey), and Paul Sarbanes (Maryland) were Rhodes Scholars. Barack Obama (Illinois) was president of the Harvard Law Review. Mitt Romney (Utah) was chief executive of the Salt Lake City Olympic Host Committee and governor of Massachusetts. Kyrsten Sinema (Arizona) was an Ironman Triathlete. There were many other former governors and several Supreme Court law clerks as well as Frist, the transplant surgeon.

Daniel Inouye of Hawaii won the Congressional Medal of Honor, the highest decoration for heroism in combat. After the Pearl Harbor bombing, he joined a US Army unit composed of soldiers of Japanese ancestry at a time when other Japanese Americans were being incarcerated in internment camps.

On Wednesday, July 11, 2012, Inouye, eighty-seven years old and having served in the Senate for half a century, spoke to a room overflowing with fifty senators at the weekly prayer breakfast.

"I had never shot a gun," he told his hushed audience. "But when I took my rifle to the target range, I was the best shot. I had developed no bad habits. I became a sniper. And I was good at it. My colleagues sometimes have asked me why, with my war experiences, I have voted against the war in Iraq and in Afghanistan. I said to them, 'I know what war is. I know what killing is. Some people count sheep while trying to sleep at night. I count the men I killed. I can remember them.'"

Both Inouye and Bob Dole were wounded in Italy. After the war, they met during rehabilitation at a Michigan hospital. In 1959, after Hawaiians elected Inouye to the US House, he sent a telegram to Dole in Kansas.

"I'm here. Where are you?" Inouye wrote. Two years later, Kansans elected Dole to the House, and in 1968, to the Senate.

Again, Inouye already was there, having arrived in 1963.

CHAPTER 36

Freshman Orientation

"Boy, there's nothing to it. You just rare back, start talking and eventually you'll think of something to say."

—AN "OLD BULL" SENATOR
to Virginia freshman John W. Warner

Washington, DC. 2003.

WITH OUR LEADERS ELECTED, we new members began figuring out how one goes about being a United States senator.

Since the Senate is a place for talking, most freshmen have mastered that skill before arriving—but public speaking is not a natural act. It takes all the gall one can muster. I can still recall one chilly Saturday morning in the autumn of 1966, watching with wonder as Howard Baker stood alone on the Grainger County courthouse steps, bellowing to an audience of thirty-five. Some were chewing and spitting, some were swapping knives, and others were gossiping. Almost no one was watching the speaker. But all of them expected Baker to keep on bellowing—if he was to be considered a serious candidate. I doubted that I could ever stand on courthouse steps and summon what it takes to speak like that—but eventually, with practice, I did.

The *Little Plaid Book* offers maxims to hone speaking skills. "Don't step on your applause lines. If you don't have any applause lines, borrow some.

Try not to let your tongue run faster than your brain. Be yourself, speak from the heart, and not for too long. If you want a standing ovation, seat a few friends in the front row. Consider yourself in trouble if you say, 'And now in conclusion', and the audience starts to applaud."

There is Margaret Thatcher's wisdom included in the book. "Never speak on a subject about which the audience knows more than you do."[1]

There is also the skill of *not* talking.

I learned that lesson when my turn came at a Thursday Republican lunch, where senators are introduced, one by one, to offer thoughts.

"Lamar will have something to say. New former governors usually do," said the host, Missouri Senator Kit Bond, himself a former governor.

I thanked Bond and declined to speak.

At first, at Thursday lunches, I either told a funny story or said nothing. In other settings, I was often the last to offer an opinion. There is not much competition among senators to say the least or be the last to speak. Years later, Arkansas Senator Tom Cotton told me that the best advice I gave him was to ration his words during Republican lunches. At the same time, wise senators listen to colleagues at lunch who know what they are talking about, as when Pat Toomey talked about financial matters or Richard Lugar discussed foreign affairs.

A senator who doesn't say much attracts attention in the same way that Mahatma Gandhi attracted attention in India because no one could find him. Benjamin Franklin used the technique of silence because he believed that others would suspect that he knew more than he did, according to his biographer Walter Isaacson. The champion modern-day practitioners of silence have been Dick Cheney and Mitch McConnell. When Vice President Cheney attended a Republican Senate luncheon, he almost always would decline to speak, so that when he did—for example, on interrogating terrorists—senators listened.

Sometimes, McConnell would simply ignore a question.

"I don't get in trouble for what I don't say," he would explain.

Then there is "Senate Small Talk," for which there is a protocol. A freshman learns not to bring up disagreeable issues during personal times, such as when a senator is in the gym, or in the green room waiting for a television interview, or sitting next to a colleague in an airplane, or even on the Senate floor. Small talk usually turns to football.

Mississippi Senator John Stennis offered one word of advice—"Travel."

"I went overseas only one time, and it was a mistake not to go more. You learn about the world and you learn about your colleagues," Stennis told Trent Lott.

Honey and I liked to travel with congressional delegations led by Alabama Senator Richard Shelby and his wife, Dr. Annette Shelby, a Georgetown University business professor. Their journeys on military aircraft combined a pleasant mix of official duties and cultural experiences.

I took Alaska's Ted Stevens' advice to visit the Senate gym every day. At age eighty-five, Stevens could be seen running up the Capitol steps on the way to vote, as well as running for reelection to his seventh term.

"Every senator who has been here for a long time, except for Byrd and Inouye, came down to the gym," Stevens told me. "This is much nicer than it used to be. In the old days, there was a radiator turned up high, and you splashed water on it to create steam. They would supply high-proof whiskey and juice and the senators would sit there and splash water, drinking and talking."

The gym, which Senator Ted Kennedy called the "Water Resources Committee," is behind a locked door that appears to be an entrance to a hearing room on the first floor of the Russell Senate Office Building. It is a place for developing bipartisan relationships. After leading a brutal Democrat campaign against Republicans in 2008, Senator Schumer began coming to the gym at 7:00 a.m., when most of us there were Republicans. Antagonism cooled, and gym visits became a useful time to swap information.

There were lessons to learn about committees.

"Get on a committee and stay there," was one. Too often, senators jumped among committees, losing seniority and postponing their opportunity to become chairman. A freshman soon learns that committee "hearings" should really be called "talkings," because senators usually consume their allotted five minutes making speeches instead of asking questions.

"Remove your nameplate when you leave a hearing," is another committee lesson. In one campaign, an opponent used photographs of a nameplate in front of an empty hearing room chair to charge that the senator was often absent.

Mississippi Congressman Jamie Whitten had advice about how to stay in office.

"Get a project and don't finish it," he told Trent Lott. In 1969, when I was working in the White House, I watched Whitten persuade Bryce Harlow to add a 234-mile Tennessee-Tombigbee Waterway to the president's budget. Constituents kept Whitten in office until the waterway was completed in 1984, and then for eleven more years.

What about voting on a controversial issue? "If a controversial bill is going to pass, vote 'No,'" Whitten said. "Those who are for it will be happy it passed. Those who are against it will be happy you voted no."

Utah Senator Bob Bennett offered a lesson about how to deal with a moral dilemma. For four years, the Senate debated whether to seat Reed Smoot of Utah, an apostle of the Mormon church. The difficulty was that Smoot had supported—but not practiced—polygamy, the custom of being married to more than one person at the same time.

On Wednesday, February 20, 1907, the Senate voted not to expel Smoot.

"As for me, I would rather have seated beside me in this chamber a polygamist who doesn't polyg than a monogamist who doesn't monog," said the senator who cast the deciding vote, according to Bennett.

Answering mail is crucial. After a few weeks in office, Georgia Senator Sam Nunn asked to see his senior colleague, Herman Talmadge.

"Senator Talmadge, I receive a lot of mail from nuts. I don't think I'll dignify their letters with a response," Nunn said.

"Sam. I'd be careful. The nut vote is about one third of the vote. You'll never get reelected if you lose the nut vote," Talmadge said.

* * *

How does one deal with the media?

Again, the *Little Plaid Book* has plenty of advice. "If you don't know the answer, say, 'I don't know.' Remember that 'yes' and 'no' are perfectly acceptable answers. Treat every friendly reporter as a reporter doing his or her job. Treat every unfriendly reporter as a reporter doing his or her job. If you want media coverage, pick a fight. If you want serious media coverage, pick a fight in Washington, DC. Don't stamp it 'confidential' unless you want it published."

I never paid attention to social media's torrent of prejudices, opinions, and insults. I asked my staff to let me know if there was something I needed to know. The only time I watched television news was in the gym in the mornings when I couldn't avoid it. There were two reasons for this. One, I was so immersed in politics and policy that if I had extra time, I preferred to watch sports, or read a book, or hike, or take a nap, or go to a play. Second, I had my own agenda, so what was reported daily about other agendas didn't make much difference to me—except when I needed to make tactical responses.

And, most cable news is the angry left shouting at the angry right, so that it was barely relevant to the way I spent my days and what I was trying to accomplish. The public must be disturbed by the news from Washington, DC, but they shouldn't be, because it has little to do with what most of us are doing every day, or at least with what I did every day.

I found out quickly that every senator has an equal vote. During my first four Senate years, Bill Frist was majority leader.

"I treat Lamar as an equal," Frist would say.

"And I treat Bill as majority leader," I would respond.

I usually added, "Having Bill Frist as majority leader is good for the country and not bad for Tennessee," echoing what Texans said when Lyndon Johnson was leader.

I nevertheless voted the way I wanted to vote, though I was careful not to surprise the leader.

"Keep it simple" is always good advice. Growing up in New Braunfels, Texas, Senator Bob Krueger heard Texas Senator Wilbert "Pappy" O'Daniel campaigning.

"My motto is the Golden Rule. I am against Communism, for segregation, and for the Ten Commandments," O'Daniel told voters.

* * *

One of the responsibilities of new members is to preside over Senate sessions. One would think that the Byzantine Senate rules would make presiding hard, but it is not. Sitting at her desk in front of the presiding officer, the parliamentarian turns and whispers to the presiding Senator the proper words.

"The clerk will report," or "without objection," or "the Senate stands in adjournment until 9:30 p.m. on Wednesday," she would whisper when I was presiding. Then, I would repeat the words as if I knew what I was talking about. The parliamentarian's role is so inconspicuous that the senator appears to be an expert. It is the most effective ventriloquist and puppet act since Edgar Bergen and Charlie McCarthy.

Presiding is the best way to absorb the concoction of rules, precedents, and mysteries that have accumulated since the first Senate convened in 1789.

When she was an intern, Lisa Murkowski watched from the gallery as senators conversed on the Senate floor.

"What are they talking about?" she asked her father, Senator Frank Murkowski.

"It doesn't matter what they are talking about. What matters is who is talking to whom," he said.

There is no better seat from which to study relationships as members arrive to vote. A presider can predict what is about to happen by watching body language and who is sitting alone, who is laughing and who is making up to whom. Usually, there is a scrum of senators in the center aisle deciding what will come next. Others surround them listening so they can know too.

I would not have heard Senator Robert C. Byrd's Father's Day and Flag Day speeches had I not been presiding, but I was glad that I did. Listening to senators debate is a good way to prepare for votes. Since no one except a senator is allowed to approach the chair, presiding is a refuge from phone calls and staff. Some senators answer mail while presiding, but in Senator Byrd's day, they risked being chastised. Byrd would also rise from his chair to demand that the presiding officer look at the senator who was speaking. Senators, in turn, are supposed to look at the presiding officer when speaking, but some address the C-SPAN cameras.

There are lessons to learn about decorum. The founders anticipated that fiery speeches in close quarters could lead to violence. To discourage such behavior, the Senate rules—first written by Thomas Jefferson when he was vice president of the United States and president of the Senate—go to great lengths to create civility.

Only one senator may speak at a time, and not until the presiding officer recognizes him or her. Senators may not interrupt and must address each other through the chair instead of directly. Senators refer to one another as "my friend," especially when they are not.

"Rule XIX" states that if a senator impugns a senator, or even another senator's home state, the presiding officer may warn the senator to calm down or to take a seat. Senators usually speak from behind their desks. They are also supposed to vote from behind their desks, too, but while I was there, only Kansas Senator Jerry Moran and I followed that rule.

Then there is the matter of what to wear. In early days, the dress code for the Senate floor was lax. "Texas Senator Sam Houston wore a sombrero and a waistcoat of panther hide with its hair still on," according to Robert Caro.[2] Today, ushers swoop down the aisle to chastise a senator who might be too casually dressed. To avoid swooping ushers, a poorly-dressed senator sometimes walks through a back door into the cloakroom and extends only an arm through the open door to the Senate floor and then votes with a thumb up or down.

More recently, challenges to the dress code created consternation. In 2019, the newly elected senator from Arizona, Kyrsten Sinema, a forty-two-year-old triathlete, created a stir when she arrived on the Senate floor with her athletic form fitted into dresses with bare shoulders. During COVID-19, when it was difficult for women to find places to get their hair done, Sinema wore brightly colored purple and orange wigs in the style of Dolly Parton. Senators murmured their disapproval to the leaders of the Rules Committee.

"I'm not about to touch that," committee leaders replied in a bipartisan way.

Despite her bare shoulders, or perhaps aided by it, Sinema became one of the most effective senators.

In 2023, Pennsylvania's new senator, John Fetterman, arrived on the floor wearing shorts with a hoodie draped over his six-foot-six frame. The Majority Leader, Senator Schumer, changed the dress code to accommodate Fetterman. This provoked a bipartisan rebuke, a resolution that quietly reinstated the code—for men. Apparently, senators were still unwilling to touch the issue of Sinema's shoulders.

The *Little Plaid Book* suggests, "Before running for any office, take a vow of humility." Not long after being elected, I drove home along the "Lamar Alexander Parkway," which the legislature had named after I was governor. I stopped at a market to buy orange juice, eggs, and bacon for the next morning's breakfast.

When I handed my credit card to the young woman behind the cash register, she examined it and then examined me.

"May I ask you a question?" she said.

"Of course," I said.

"Was you named after this road?" she asked.

* * *

"Make every day count," was my advice to freshman senators at their orientation. "It's hard to get here, hard to stay here and while you're here, you might as well try to accomplish something good for the country."

In June 2014, speaking at the senators' prayer breakfast, retired South Dakota Senator Tom Daschle offered the same advice.

"My major regret about my time as majority leader was not reminding myself every day of what a consequential position I held, and how much opportunity I had to make a difference," Daschle said.

He urged senators to remember a poem, "The Young Dead Soldiers Do Not Speak," that Archibald MacLeish, the Librarian of Congress, wrote in the 1940s after witnessing the burial of a soldier at Arlington National Cemetery. Its words are emblazoned on the World War I Memorial in Washington, DC.

"Our responsibility is to give meaning to those who gave their lives for our country," Daschle said.

CHAPTER 37

Eloquent Listening

"Rule 36. Be aware that what you are saying may not be what people are hearing you say."

—LAMAR ALEXANDER'S LITTLE PLAID BOOK

Washington, DC. 1967–2003.

THE ESSENCE OF THE UNITED STATES SENATE is relationships.

"It means learning to be an eloquent listener," Howard Baker said. "There is a difference between hearing and understanding what people say. You don't have to agree, but you have to hear what they've got to say. And if you do, the chances are much better that you'll be able to translate that into a useful position or even useful leadership. It means consult, consult, consult."

On July 14, 1998, at Trent Lott's "Leader's Lecture Series," Baker explained that "what really makes the Senate work ... is an understanding of human nature and an appreciation of the hearts as well as the minds, the frailties, as well as the strengths, of one's colleagues and one's constituents."

Working on Baker's staff, I watched him cultivate relationships mostly by showing courtesy to other senators. He would visit a colleague's office instead of expecting the colleague to come to his. He'd accept a telephone call from any senator, even while another senator was in his office. He'd cosponsor senators' bills. Solicit their advice. Allow them to speak before he did. Visit their states. Raise funds for their campaigns. Invite them with their spouses for weekend visits at his Tennessee home or to join him on overseas congressional delegation visits.

Baker worked across the aisle to achieve results. I had already learned to do the same. As governor, if I wanted to accomplish anything, I had to work with Democrat legislative majorities. In the Senate, it takes sixty senators to cut off debate and proceed to a vote on the most important bills—and never in history have there been sixty Republican senators.

In 1978, the fruits of Baker's relationship with Democrat Majority Leader Robert Byrd were on full display when, with only one vote more than the two-thirds needed, the Senate ratified, 68–32, the treaty to return control of the Panama Canal to that country.

The historia[illegible] McCullough told me, "At first, Baker and Byrd opposed the treaty, but both said, after reading my book on the canal, that they changed their minds and worked together to ratify it."

Byrd told me, "It never would have happened without Howard. We had to allow a vote on every senator's reservation to the treaty, and then we had to work together to defeat them all."

Another example of the Baker-Byrd relationship occurred in 1980, after Republicans gained twelve seats in the 1980 Reagan landslide, creating a Republican Senate majority, 53–46, with one Independent. This outcome stunned no one more than the imperious Democrat Majority Leader Byrd.

Shortly after the election, Baker walked to Byrd's elaborate suite of leadership offices. Byrd's rooms, according to Senate documents, "have groin-vaulted ceilings, monumental doors and windows in ornate cast-iron frames, carved marble fireplace mantels, and colorful and intricately patterned English floor tiles from Minton & Company.[1] The site is lighted by nickel-plated brass and crystal chandeliers.... There is a balcony with a spectacular view of the Mall and Capitol Dome."

"Byrd was in a state of shock," Baker told me later. "There had not been a Republican majority in twenty-five years, and he was not expecting this one. Byrd knew very well that now I could swap my current office for the Democrat leader's suite."

And Democrats could expect retribution. They had been stingy, allocating the Republican leader only two rooms.

After exchanging pleasantries, Baker softened Byrd up.

"Senator Byrd, I wonder if you would mind keeping your office and allowing me to make my office the majority leader's office?" Baker said.

There was silence.

"Why, Howard, of course. That would be most generous," Byrd said.

"There is one other thing. I will never know the Senate rules as well as you know them. I'll make a deal with you. I won't surprise you if you won't surprise me," Baker said.

"Let me think about it," Byrd replied.

The next day, Byrd agreed to Baker's no-surprises proposal. For the next four years, the two worked together in one of the most amicable and productive periods in recent Senate history. Senators reached agreements by unanimous consent and allowed legislation to come to the floor, be amended, and voted on in "the regular order."

Byrd had hardly outfoxed Baker. Adjacent to Baker's two leadership rooms was the bursar's suite, where staff members visited every two weeks, usually dressed nicely for the occasion, to pick up salaries in envelopes containing cash. Baker moved the bursar to a Senate office building and commandeered several rooms for himself.

In 1985, the Senate designated S-230, the entrance room to the Republican leader's suite, as the "Howard H. Baker Jr. Room." In 1989, it named Byrd's prized rooms, S-221 through S-224—which had helped to grease the operation of the Senate during the 1980s—in his honor.

Baker and Byrd were not the only party leaders who learned to work together. At a Senators-only prayer breakfast on Wednesday, August 1, 2012, Trent Lott described his relationship with Tom Daschle and how the two had worked together as leaders during the impeachment trial of President Clinton.

"Sometimes, we would slip into the back door of each other's office and say, 'I'm sorry.' We became friends, and now we and our wives see each other often.... When I heard on Sunday afternoon that the House had voted to impeach the president, I called Tom and said, 'Well, I guess it's in our lap now. How are we going to do this?'" Lott said. "We formed a committee of senators who made recommendations, and that fell flat. Then, we were in a scrum down on the floor one afternoon, and Senator

Nickles suggested we ought to try meeting in the Old Senate Chamber. That turned out to be a good idea."

Lott went on.

"I asked Danny Akaka to give a prayer. And then I asked Byrd to give some history, hoping he wouldn't talk too long. And then I had Connie Mack say a few words. That put us in the right mood. After a few people spoke, Phil Gramm made a proposal, and Ted Kennedy made a proposal. I walked over to Tom and said, 'It sounds to me like they said the same thing, although to tell the truth, I couldn't tell exactly what it was.' So, we asked some senators to write down whatever the Kennedy-Gramm proposal was, and that's the way we proceeded," Lott said.

* * *

When I arrived as a freshman, I already knew twenty-four of the one hundred senators, including Lott, McConnell, and Frist.[2] To start out with that many relationships in a body whose essence is relationships was an advantage. For example, in my first year as a senator Frist helped gain approval of a waiver that allowed me to serve on the education committee on which he was already serving. Without it, I never would have had the seniority ten years later to become its chairman.

An early order of business was selecting one of the one hundred mahogany desks in the imposing 114-foot-long Senate chamber. From behind these desks for more than two centuries, senators had stood up to presidents and to the runaway passions of the people. They had talked and talked until they resolved thorny national issues.

The first Senate chamber "was ideal for the ringing voices of eloquent men... an ornate, dramatic background for the forty-eight new mahogany desks—each with its silver-mounted inkwell and small bottle of blotting sand, each with a low-backed mahogany and red leather armchair—that were arranged in four rising arcs," Robert Caro wrote.[3]

In 1859, several of those desks and chairs moved to the new chamber. Galleries had filled to witness fiery speeches about taxing one section of the country to build canals in another; creating the federal judiciary; condemning the Mexican War; compromising to avert a civil war; rejecting presidential nominees; trying impeached presidents and chief justices;

killing the League of Nations; enacting Social Security, Medicare, and civil rights laws.

During my 2002 Senate campaign, I warned voters that the first thing Bob Clement would do would be to move Fred Thompson's desk over to the Democrat side. That was hyperbole. Clement, himself, would not have moved Thompson's desk—but Senate engineers would have.

This was how that worked. We new senators were given an opportunity to select desks of our choice. Some desks were unavailable—for example, the Republican leader's front-row desk on the right side of the center aisle (as you face the dais) and the Democrat leader's desk across the aisle. The party whips sit next to their leaders. Daniel Webster's desk goes to the senior senator from New Hampshire, even though Webster was also a Massachusetts senator.

I asked for Sam Houston's desk because of my admiration for the Texas senator who had grown up in Maryville—but his desk had not survived the move from the old chamber. So, I selected a desk once used by Howard Baker and then Fred Thompson. The next step was for the secretary of the Senate to arrange the desks reflecting the November election results. This required moving two desks to the Republican side so there would be fifty-one desks on the Republican side and forty-nine on the Democrat side including one Independent who caucused with Democrats. Then, by seniority, we chose the location of our desks.

Senators quickly took locations near the aisle and toward the front. Ted Kennedy continued to shout his speeches from the same back-row desk his two brothers had once occupied. Some chose the back row because they believed the blue-walled background improved their appearance on C-SPAN. Senators coveted front-row desks that placed the occupant at the center of conversations during votes. Since I was ninety-ninth in seniority, my first desk was in the middle on the far-right side of the chamber. Finally, engineers bolted the one hundred desks into their correct locations.

Over the years, I learned the importance of choosing good staff. Here are two lessons from the *Little Plaid Book*. "Don't think you're ready to host *Saturday Night Live* just because your staff laughs at your jokes. Be wary of the staff member laughing loudest at your jokes."

A Senate staff is more like a basketball team than a football team. Three or four five-star players can create a championship lineup. It is important to put the team on the field quickly. There are decisions to be made about mail, appointments, leadership elections, committee assignments, and office space that will have lasting consequences.

"Listen to your staff, but don't let them forget who works for whom," Senator Baker said.

Three decades later, I put it less gently to my staff, most of whom were in their twenties and thirties.

"These issues are big. You—and I—don't know much about them," I said. "So, I'm not interested in what *you* know. Your job is to find those who *do* know, so we can talk to them and learn from them."

A crucial early decision is choosing the right office manager. Hundreds of emails and letters poured in two months before my permanent Senate staff was in place. Some new senators never dig out of that early pile of messages and earn a reputation for inattention to their constituents. The office manager must also become an expert in arcane Senate rules and procedures that, if ignored, can lead toward an ethics committee violation. For that role, I hired an office manager who had set up six new senators' offices before she set up mine.

My chief of staff as governor took the same role in the Senate. He didn't know the Senate, but he knew my style of working with officials of both parties. He recruited a staff with more than sixty years of Senate experience.[4] My course assistant at the Kennedy School became legislative assistant. He helped put in place the practice of asking staff to make recommendations on issues balancing the principles of "the American character," just as I had asked my Harvard students to do.

The scheduler is more crucial than one might expect. Each week, there were hundreds of telephone calls and perhaps 300 requests for appointments. For that position, I hired Senator Thompson's scheduler, who was proper, shrewd, and had fifteen years of Senate experience. Her job was to apportion time—a fifteen-minute meeting, a five-minute "drop by," a meeting with senior staff, a phone call, a handshake, or a photograph at the weekly "Tennessee Tuesday" for as many as 200 constituents who might be in town. Most visitors only talked with the staff. This works surprisingly well, since most visitors know the staff does most of the legislative work.

To make visitors feel more at home, I asked John Rice Irwin to decorate the reception area with one hundred pioneer items from his Museum of Appalachia in Norris—such as a "fly minder," a guitar made out of matchsticks by "a prisoner who had a lot of time on his hands," and handcrafted musical instruments.

A skillful scheduler can make a casual visitor feel *very important*. In the summer of 1957, when I was a Boys Nation "senator," I dropped by the office of the real Tennessee senator, Estes Kefauver, although I doubted that such a famous person would have time to see me. Kefauver's waiting room was swarming with what appeared to be generals, political dignitaries, business tycoons, and potentates. To my surprise, the senator's scheduler whisked me through the swarm and into a chair in front of his desk.

"Where are you from?" Kefauver asked.

"Maryville," I said. And then, not knowing what else to say, I asked, "Do you know anyone in Maryville?"

"I know Verton Queener at Maryville College. He was my campaign manager," Kefauver said.

"Why, my mother bought Dr. Queener's Kimball piano for twenty-five dollars, and I practiced on it every morning after I delivered the *Knoxville Journal* and before I go to school," I said, providing the senator with more information than he could have possibly wanted.

Sometimes a scheduler has trouble with a persistent constituent.

"This is Maude from Madisonville. I need to talk to Estes," one caller to Kefauver's office said.

"I'm sorry, Maude. The Senator is not available. He's tied up on the floor," the scheduler said.

There was a pause.

"Well, untie the SOB and get him up off the floor and tell him Maude is on the phone and needs to talk to him," the caller said.

CHAPTER 38

Working with George W.

"Chapter I: Take your office seriously, but don't take yourself too seriously."

—LAMAR ALEXANDER'S LITTLE PLAID BOOK

Washington, DC. 2002–2005.

GEORGE W. BUSH'S ELECTION IN 2000 provided a platform for my election to the Senate two years later.

Bush came to Tennessee on a sunny Saturday, November 2, 2002, the weekend before I won my first Senate campaign. For the second morning in a row, there had been frost at our cabin. Still, last night it had been warm enough to sit outside, smoke a cigar, and listen for the whippoorwill.

Early that morning, I drove east to Tri-Cities Regional Airport. There, colorful leaves spread a glorious backdrop behind the hangar where 500 Republicans were waiting to greet the president. At 9:50 a.m. Bush appeared on stage—on time, smiling, and comfortable. Sitting next to him, I noticed redness in his eyes. I thought I saw tears. He told me that he had visited the family of a fallen soldier in nearby Elizabethton. After 9/11, the president had sent troops into combat, and he felt responsible for each one.[1]

Over the next six years, he made about five hundred such visits to 1,500 family members of American military men and women killed in action.

The families he visited sometimes added to his burden by telling him that they, too, felt he was responsible for their loved one's death.[2] Bush did not discuss these visits publicly. Like his father, he had no need to call attention to himself. Visits with grieving families were not about him.

But on this day, Bush was soon at ease, laughing and joking. His speech was decent, extolling Republican virtues, mispronouncing only a few words. He inquired about Honey, whom he had known in Texas. At about 11:00 a.m., after a big wave from the steps of Air Force One, he flew away to the next campaign stop. I thought then, as I believe now, that George W. Bush was the most "normal" of the ten presidents with whom I had worked.

Unlike Clinton, Obama, or his father, George W. was no Rhodes Scholar, Harvard Law Review president, or Phi Beta Kappa graduate. He earned Cs at Yale. His sense of "strategery" did not approach Nixon's. His Spanish speaking was only slightly less butchered than his Texas English. His father left Yale to become a war hero; George W. joined the National Guard. He did not possess the mystery of Reagan.

With George W., everything was up front. His pedigree was elite, but he did not act like it. He seemed comfortable in his own skin. He navigated having a United States senator for a grandfather, a president for a father, and a governor for a brother because he adored them. He welcomed being born on third base, treating it as an opportunity to steal home, instead of an excuse for a weekly therapy session.

When asked to name his favorite philosopher, he said, "Jesus. He changed my heart."

His answer seemed genuine. When the singer Bono visited the Oval Office in 2002 to talk about HIV/AIDS in Africa, he brought a gift—an Irish Bible. Bush laid the Bible on his desk and, for fifteen minutes, he and Bono discussed their faith. The president was skeptical of celebrities exploiting White House visits. But that discussion "broke the ice" and spurred a $120 billion HIV/AIDS investment that saved twenty-six million lives, according to Bush's Chief of Staff Joshua Bolten.

Before the visit, Bolten had briefed Bush.

"You *do* know who Bono is, don't you?" Bolten asked.

"Sure. He's the one married to Cher," Bush said.

"That's *Sonny* Bono," Bolten said, "and he's dead."

George W.'s head start in politics must have helped him avoid the quirky personality, shamelessness, and overbearing ambition that distort the personalities of most who start from scratch to run for president. Most of the rest of us in public life steel ourselves to the turmoil of the arena until it saps our capacity for empathy. George W. wore his feelings on his sleeve. He was the president with whom I would feel most comfortable attending a ball game or smoking a cigar at a campsite or on the second-floor balcony of the White House.

I was not the only senator who felt that way.

A Democrat senator told me in the gym, "I hate his policies, but I like him. I like him better than the others, Clinton or Carter."

* * *

As a rookie Senator in 2003, I had to scramble to accomplish anything, but it helped to have a friendly Republican president, a Senate majority, and a majority leader from Tennessee.

I had intended to make my "maiden address" on the importance of teaching American history and civics. Instead, only one month after I arrived, Democrats refused to allow a vote on Bush's court of appeals nominees. I was so disgusted that on Wednesday, February 12, 2003, I delivered my first floor remarks on the Democrats' maneuvering.

The president's three nominees were Charles Pickering, William Pryor, and Miguel Estrada. Democrats alleged racism against Pryor of Alabama and Pickering of Mississippi.

"This is grossly unfair," I said on the Senate floor.

I cited how Pickering, living in Mississippi in 1967, had testified against Samuel Bowers, the Imperial Wizard of the Ku Klux Klan, "whom Klan experts describe as the most dangerous man to ever don a white hood."[3] Pickering had kept his children in public schools when neighbors were enrolling theirs in "segregation academies."

I knew more about Pryor. Like me, he had been a law clerk for Judge Wisdom, the South's judicial champion of civil rights, and I knew of Wisdom's high regard for him. The unstated problem with Estrada, a former US Supreme Court law clerk and assistant solicitor general, was that Democrats suspected that Bush intended eventually to promote him to the

"Good luck. Tennessee and Indiana are the two states with the nut-cuttingest politics I know," President Nixon said in August 1970, when I told him that I was going home to manage Winfield Dunn's campaign for governor. In this photograph, it looks like I was warning Nixon that something bad was about to happen, which it was, but neither of us then could have imagined Watergate.

"Everett, if you won't come down and have a drink with me, I'm here to have one with you," President Johnson said when he arrived at Sen. Everett Dirksen's Capitol office late one afternoon in 1968. The two disappeared into a back office to negotiate the civil rights bill that was being crafted around a long table in Dirksen's outer office. I helped Sen. Baker draf amendments to the legislation and attended the April 11, 1968, White House bill signing when this photograph was taken.

"The intellectual competence of this man is probably the highest of any person ever to serve in the Oval Office," Bryce Harlow once told me about Nixon. In October 1969, sitting next to Pat Buchanan in a staff chair in the cabinet room during a congressional leadership meeting, I watched the president urge skeptical Republicans to act on the environment, which soon became as trendy as the Hula-Hoop. Watergate later destroyed what might have been one of the most consequential American presidencies.

"We'd like for you to be executive director of our presidential campaign," President Ford told me in the Oval Office on Tuesday, October 14, 1975, but I said, "No." After losing the 1974 governor's race, my job, marriage, and budget would not have survived another campaign. My tune changed after Jimmy Carter defeated Ford and brought with him a crew from Georgia who knew even less about Washington, DC, than he did. Republican prospects improved and, with Honey's approval, I ran again for governor.

I first met Ronald Reagan in April 1980, during his presidential campaign when the Reagans spent the night at the Tennessee governor's residence. Before that I thought that he was too old, too western, and too conservative to be president. Reagan was sixty-nine. I was thirty-nine, the youngest governor. My opinion changed the next day. At an 8 a.m. breakfast—6 a.m. on the West Coast—the California governor was sparkling and engaging. I was impressed by his executive demeanor and good humor.

Photo courtesy of Robin Hood

Nancy Reagan was choosy about who sat next to her husband. At White House dinners, she often placed Honey next to the president when protocol would have dictated another governor's spouse. Honey found Reagan to be a charming dinner companion. I found him to be the best suited to the job of the ten presidents with whom I worked. Robin Hood took this photo at Sen. Baker's Huntsville home in 1982.

Photo courtesy of the White House

"It is the American way. It is a simple American philosophy that dominates nearly every other profession. So why not this one?" President Reagan said when he visited Knoxville's Farragut High School on Tuesday, June 14, 1983, to lend support to my merit pay proposal for teachers. After the Nation Education Association defeated my first attempt, Reagan became my secret weapon for a successful second try, making Tennessee the first state to pay teachers more for teaching well.

Photo courtesy of the White House

"We start almost every day telling each other a funny little story. That's a lot of stories," Howard Baker said in 1988 after he took me to the White House chief of staff's customary 9 a.m. meeting with the president. It was reassuring that men with two of the biggest jobs in the world were comfortable enough with themselves, each other, and their responsibilities to begin the day in that easy way.

Photo courtesy of the White House

"Better Schools mean Better Jobs. I like that phrase," then–Vice President Bush told me in early 1988. Pollster Bob Teeter had invited me to meet with Bush in the same West Wing office in which I had worked with Bryce Harlow two decades earlier. After that meeting, Bush's presidential campaign stump speech included, "I want to be the education president" and "Better Schools mean Better Jobs."

"Patty: Thi(sic) is the product of your insturction(sic)," was the first sentence President George H. W. Bush ever typed on a computer. To set an example for others, I had asked him to take computer lessons from his secretary, Patty. He printed out his handiwork and gave it to me. Beneath the typo-filled sentence, the president had proudly written in longhand:

My first effort
George Bush
4-24-91

Photo courtesy of the White House

"The only problem I've got with Lamar is he has the propensity for working people to death. We've announced this Education 2000 just last week. He's been grinding away ever since he got in this job. And I have this ugly feeling that he's going to kill me," the president told one audience. In this photo from September 4, 1991, the president had dropped by my office in the Department of Education to make calls about the America 2000 education program to the governors of Maine and Maryland.

In 1986, Minnie Pearl introduced Bill Clinton and me at the Grand Ole Opry during a meeting of the National Governors' Association which we were leading together. Clinton and I had traveled parallel paths toward the same goal: to be the first in our generation to be president. When Clinton won that race to the top on Tuesday, November 3, 1992, he was forty-six. I was fifty-two then and already preparing to run against him four years later.

"It would have been like running against himself," President Clinton's pollster Dick Morris said, explaining why his client did not want me as his 1996 reelection opponent. I set out to persuade voters to "Remember Your ABC's"—Alexander Beats Clinton—arguing that I could offer a more reliable bridge to the future than Clinton could and that Bob Dole, who would be seventy-three during his first year in office, could not offer one at all. Clinton set a poor moral example, but he was the best politician of the presidents I knew and became an effective and charismatic chief executive.

"Wear your red and black plaid shirt, but not when you announce for President of the United States," became Rule No. 1 in my Little Plaid Book *after I dropped out of the 1996 presidential campaign. Walking across Tennessee I had earned the right to wear the shirt, but when I wore it running for president one columnist wrote that it "was not fit for a possum." In this 1996 photo from New Hampshire, Kathryn is on my right, Honey on my left, then Will, Bette Jo Buhler, and Leslee. Fred Thompson stands behind them.*

George W. Bush was the most "normal" of the presidents with whom I worked, the one with whom I felt the most comfortable attending a ball game or smoking a cigar on the second-floor balcony of the White House. He seemed to welcome being born on third base, treating it as an opportunity to steal home instead of as an excuse for a weekly therapy session. This photo is from Camp David in 2006.

The finest performance of George W. Bush's presidency came after Tuesday, September 11, 2001, when he restated American values and launched a "War on Terror" in Afghanistan. The next year, popular support for his leadership led to a Republican Senate majority, including my own election. Four years later, his "second term blues" led to a Democrat sweep and Obamacare.

Photo courtesy of the White House

"If you want to feel like the butler, try being vice president," Joe Biden told me in 2012. I began working in the Nixon White House in 1969 at a desk in Bryce Harlow's West Wing office fifty feet from the Oval Office. After six months, Harlow carved space from his secretary's office to create this cubbyhole office for me. When this photo was taken forty-three years later, the tiny office still was there and being used by then–Vice President Biden's chief of staff. Proximity to the Oval Office makes even a cubbyhole a prized possession.

Photo courtesy of the White House

"I'm going to work on [Sen. Tom] Harkin a little," President Obama said to me privately at the end of this late afternoon Oval Office meeting on Tuesday, July 16, 2013. During his first six years, Obama's majorities in congress, his ideology, and clumsiness in congressional relations led to few bipartisan legislative results. But this meeting was an encouraging sign. The president's push against Democrat liberals helped to enact our bipartisan law, saving students billions in interest rate loan payments.

Photo courtesy of Reuters; photograph by Jonathan Ernst

"Congratulations. You did what you said you would do," President Obama said to me before signing the "Every Student Succeeds Act" into law on Tuesday, December 10, 2015. "You did, too. It's a good way to work," I said. During my ride on Air Force One eleven months earlier the president had promised not to draw lines in the sand while I was negotiating the bill. My promise was, "I won't bring you a bill that you can't sign." Both of us had kept our word. He called the law "A Christmas Miracle."

Photo courtesy of the White House

"If it had just been you and me these eight years, everything would have been fine," President Obama told me on Tuesday, December 16, 2016, during his last month in office, as he signed the "21st Century Cures Act" on which we had worked together. It took a while to figure out how to work with Obama with whose liberal policies I disagreed but our relationship resulted in two laws that he called "Christmas Miracles" and that the Republican leader, Sen. McConnell, said were the most important of the 114th congress.

"Everyone in Tennessee loves me—except you, Lamar," President Trump told me when we inspected tornado damage in March 2020. Nevertheless, I learned to work with Trump, with whose views I mostly agreed—but with whose behavior and temperament I disagreed. We developed a relationship because he may have come to the same conclusion that I did: After the people decide who is president and who is senator, we should respect each other's office and do things together when we can.

Photo courtesy of Reuters; photograph by Jonathan Ernst

"It's your size. You may need it. Teddy Roosevelt said to 'speak softly and carry a big stick,'" I (wearing my plaid covid mask) said as I handed Trump a walking stick from my campaign for governor. On Friday, August 4, 2020, at the White House, the president had signed "The Great American Outdoors Act" produced by a surprising—some said unholy—alliance that I had helped engineer between Trump and eight hundred outdoors groups. It was the most important conservation law since Eisenhower—or, as Trump said, "Wouldn't you say ever*?"*

Photo courtesy of Robin Hood

In January 2021, we moved from Nashville to our cabin adjacent to Blackberry Farm in the foothills of the Smokies. Honey and I and Kries and Sandy Beall had purchased Blackberry in 1976 when it was a rundown bed and breakfast. Our goals were to protect the land near the national park, to create a "nice inn," and to have cabins for ourselves. Fifty years later, we and others have contributed nearly nine thousand acres to conservation land trusts, the Bealls own the Inn, and we Alexanders have our family cabin fifteen miles from Maryville, where I grew up.

Supreme Court, and they didn't want the first Hispanic American justice to be a Republican.

Led by Senator Schumer, Democrats had determined to filibuster the three nominees. As explained in the movie, *Mr. Smith Goes to Washington,* Senate rules then allowed one member to force senators to "talk their heads off" on a nomination or a bill, until sixty of them voted to cut off debate. Since there were only fifty-one Republican senators, if at least forty-one Democrats stuck with Schumer, there would not be sixty votes to proceed to the votes on confirmation.

The filibuster has its critics, but it provides the reason why the Senate has been our country's most valuable institution. When the president and the Senate majority are of the same party, a filibuster by minority Senators can restrain the president—and check the "tyranny of the majority" that the Frenchman Alexis de Tocqueville warned of in the early nineteenth century.

Schumer was doing something new. Senators always *could have* required sixty votes to approve a judicial nominee. They just never had done it—except in an odd case in 1968 involving LBJ's attempt to elevate Justice Abe Fortas to be chief justice. The Senate had even approved the controversial nomination of Justice Clarence Thomas in 1991, with not one Senator insisting on sixty votes. Then, Senators seemed to understand that, in a body of one hundred that operates by unanimous consent, a crucial part of making the place work is to refrain from exercising every power that the rules grant. Now, Democrats were throwing restraint to the winds.

Republicans reacted angrily, like parents confronting a teenage driver who had promised to behave then had come home drunk. Frist, the Senate leader, threatened to use his Republican majority to change the rules to allow fifty-one senators to confirm Bush's nominees. That would take away the Democrats' ability to block judicial nominations by insisting on sixty votes to end a filibuster. Frist's maneuver was called the "nuclear option," because Senate rules required sixty-seven votes—not fifty-one—to change the rules.

I disagreed with breaking the rules to change the rules. And I feared that using the "nuclear option" to eliminate the filibuster for judicial nominations would soon lead to destroying the filibuster for *legislation.* That would allow any bill to pass with just fifty-one votes. And that would make the Senate no different than the majoritarian House. The political passions of the moment would roar through both bodies like a freight train.

I proposed a solution.

"There is a way to avoid this train wreck. I have said I will never vote to filibuster [even a Democrat president's] judicial nominee. If six Democrats will join me, there will be no filibuster, no need for a rules change, and the Senate can get down to business," I said during forty-five minutes of remarks on the floor.

Another freshman, Arkansas Democrat Mark Pryor, and I went to work to build support. On April 14, I repeated my proposal. A bipartisan "gang" of fourteen senators negotiated a compromise that resulted in some confirmations and avoided, temporarily, the use of the "nuclear option."

"You know, you got this all started with your proposal," Frist told me. "The tigers are back in their cages for now. We'll see how it works."

It didn't work. The Senate soon plunged again into acrimony. Both parties began using the "nuclear option" to confirm judicial nominees by a majority vote.

Bridget Lipscomb, my legislative counsel, helped defend Pryor and Pickering against Democrats' charges of racism. Lipscomb, forty-two, was the first African American partner in a major Knoxville law firm when she became my first legislative staff member. In June 2004, the Bush Justice Department hired her as senior trial counsel.

While she was working for Bush, I recommended Lipscomb for a federal judge vacancy in East Tennessee. The White House said, "No." I kept pushing until Attorney General Alberto Gonzales came to my office. He told me that during an interview, Lipscomb had said she voted for Gore instead of Bush in 2000.

"But she supported me in my Senate race, and a Republican for mayor before that," I told the attorney general. "She was on the Senate floor defending the president's nominees. You have hired her as a senior litigator. How surprising is it that a talented Black Southern woman votes for Democrats as well as Republicans? I'm sure that some of the president's White nominees from the South have done the same."

As governor, I had appointed Tennessee's first Black Supreme Court justice and first Black chancellor. Neither would have survived a Republican purity test. I looked, instead, to demeanor, intelligence, and knowledge of the law, as well as to the importance of not having a lily-white judiciary and the opportunity to encourage Black lawyers to become Republicans.

Twenty years later, in December 2024, at a Christmas breakfast in Nashville, my former chief of staff, Tom Ingram, told Gonzales, who had become dean of Belmont University's School of Law, how disappointed I had been by Lipscomb's rejection. Gonzales wrote Lipscomb, "It appears that we missed on this one."

Lipscomb responded gracefully.

"I know that the stars have to be aligned for a judicial appointment, but I have had a storied legal career and am grateful for the support I have received," she replied to Gonzales.

* * *

On Thursday, March 4, in the midst of the nominations controversy, I delivered my official maiden address, offering legislation to create summer presidential academies for teachers of American history and civics. While I spoke, Senator Kennedy, against whom I had railed during my 2002 campaign, scurried around the floor, gathering twenty Democrat cosponsors, and later helped pass my bill.[4]

Despite my junior status, there were other legislative successes. In 2004, after a long day at a budget committee hearing, I became distressed that automatic spending increases for Medicare, Medicaid, and Social Security would drive out of the budget money for science and technology that was needed to keep the United States competitive. After the hearing, I walked to the National Academy of Sciences at the bottom of Capitol Hill.

"Most ideas in Washington fail for lack of the idea. If you will tell Congress the ten things in priority order that America must do to stay competitive, I believe we will enact them," I told the scientists. After a bipartisan request from four of us in Congress, the Academy created a commission that produced twenty recommendations.[5]

I asked senior senators to be principal sponsors and eventually lined up sixty cosponsors, including both the Republican and Democrat leaders. President Bush acknowledged our "America Competes" bill in his 2006 State of the Union address, and, in August 2007, three years after we began our effort, it became law, doubling the authorization for federal basic research funding.

During those negotiations, I learned a lesson about the difference between how American democracy and a totalitarian country respond to the same challenge. In 2005, I was part of a congressional delegation visiting China, led by Senators Stevens and Inouye. That year, China's President Hu Jintao announced his country's multiyear plan to become more competitive.

The Chinese put their plan in place instantly. It took the United States three years to make "America Competes" a law—and even longer to implement it.

* * *

In late January 2005, Congress recessed for two days so each political party could conduct its annual policy retreat. On Thursday, January 27, with the temperature below freezing, Republican senators, spouses, and staff shivered in buses outside the Hart Office Building until word came that our train had pulled into Union Station.

Black vehicles with shaded windows escorted our buses to the station. Then, commandos with automatic rifles and faces covered with black scarves created a corridor through which we walked to our train. It departed at 10:00 a.m., with more commandos along each side.

Six hours later, the train stopped in White Sulphur Springs, West Virginia. Another corridor of commandos formed, and we walked to The Greenbrier Resort, a massive watering place for visitors since Revolutionary times. A row of huge American flags guarded the entrance to the building, which looked like a shipwreck painted white.

The highlight of the weekend was to be President Bush's appearance. He arrived the next day, and began working a rope line of congressmen waiting for photos. In November, Bush had defeated John Kerry, and Republicans had increased their majorities in both houses of Congress. There were cheers when the president stepped to the podium.

In his remarks, Bush pointed the way as a chief executive should. For the first term, it had been tax cuts, "No Child Left Behind," $15 billion for AIDS, prescription drugs for Medicare, and freedom for Afghanistan and

Iraq. For the second term, it would be Social Security, immigration, more freedom, fewer junk lawsuits, and reining in the federal debt.

George W. had found his voice. As he walked out, he stopped forty feet from us and looked our way.

"Where's Honey?" he asked in a loud voice.

She waved, and the president left.

CHAPTER 39

Learning to Count

"Count carefully and often. Fifty-one votes today may be forty-nine tomorrow, so keep on counting."

—SENATOR HOWARD BAKER

Washington, DC. November 2006 to December 2007.

BILL FRIST'S COMMITMENT TO RETIRE from the Senate in 2006 created new opportunities to run for something.

Senator McConnell could now move up to the Senate majority leader position, leaving open his Number Two spot, whip. The Number Three Republican, Conference Chairman Rick Santorum, wanted to be Number Two—but there were a couple of twists.

The first twist was that Santorum had to be reelected in Pennsylvania, a swing state where the Bush presidency was wearing thin. There was a second twist, as well.

"Trent Lott may eventually get in the [whip] race," *Roll Call* predicted.

But it would have been unseemly for Lott to be gathering support for whip, based upon the expectation that his ally, Santorum, would lose his Senate seat. For me, that possibility presented an opportunity.

In early 2004, flying home from a congressional delegation trip to Europe, Senator Bob Bennett had moved over to the seat next to mine.

"Would you consider running for whip?" he asked.

That was like asking a five-year-old if he would consider trying chocolate ice cream. Bennett's encouragement was noteworthy because he was McConnell's deputy whip and confidante, suggesting that McConnell, when he moved up to leader, would prefer working with me as whip rather than with Santorum or Lott—although tight-lipped McConnell never would say that, himself.

McConnell did say, "In a leadership race, it is never too early to start."

So, I started early.

"You're doing a very Southern thing," Lott told me on the Senate floor, suggesting that Southerners are more conniving than other senators.

Eighteen months before the leadership election, I began one-on-one visits with my fifty Republican colleagues, some of whom did their best to avoid the meeting. Leadership contests are awkward affairs. Senators hate saying "no" or even "maybe" to a senator with whom they may have to work for another twenty years.

Leadership races are often close, and hurt feelings last for a long time. During these contests, senators squirm.

"I am already committed. I wish I had known you were running," is the easiest way to say "no" to a colleague running for leadership. My early start gained several commitments because it created an acceptable "I wish I had known ..." answer when the next candidate came calling.

Republican prospects for the 2006 November election looked grim. Support for the Iraq War had plummeted. Bush's approval rating had dropped so much that I asked the White House to keep the president out of Tennessee in the contest for Frist's seat between Democrat Harold Ford Jr. and Republican Bob Corker. Bush stayed away, but, validating my instinct, he did campaign for Virginia Senator George Allen, who then lost to Jim Webb, switching control of the chamber to Democrats, 51–49.

Sensing bad news coming, Frist and I had dispatched Tom Ingram to Tennessee to try to salvage the drifting Corker campaign. McConnell was so worried about losing the majority—and his opportunity to be the next majority leader—that he told Ingram to call him at 7:00 a.m. every morning with overnight poll results.

"Who on your staff do you want me to call?" Ingram asked.

"Call me," McConnell said.

On Tuesday, November 7, 2006, Corker won the closest Senate race in Tennessee history in the midst of a national Democrat sweep. Santorum lost his Pennsylvania race—and his opportunity to move up to McConnell's whip spot.

The next day, Wednesday, November 8, Lott announced his candidacy for whip. I told the media that I had enough votes to win. For a week, the back-and-forth was furious. Going into the vote on Wednesday, November 15, I had twenty-seven firm votes—or so I thought. When the Republican secretary opened the secret ballots, Lott won, 25 to 24.

Senators had been torn. They felt bad about voting against Lott after the Thurmond incident. Senator John Warner of Virginia, who had been a ringleader in deposing Lott, was an early supporter of my whip bid. I had worked for Warner on the 1968 Nixon campaign when Lott and I were roommates. A day before the vote, Warner switched to Lott.

"We all believe in redemption, thank God," Senator McCain said after the vote.

The power of redemption and Lott's experience in vote counting during his thirty-three years in Congress (compared to my four) gave him the win.

After the vote, I invited Lott to sit beside me at the weekly Republican caucus luncheon. I asked to be recognized and pledged to work with him.

"I will be writing twenty-seven thank-you notes for twenty-four votes," I told colleagues.

This produced laughter and applause.

Later, I asked Senator Baker, who had both lost and won leadership races by a single vote, whether any colleagues had ever misled him about their votes.

"Some," Baker replied.

To avoid such misunderstandings, Iowa Senator Chuck Grassley always showed his written secret ballot in advance to the senator to whom he promised a vote.

Oddly, my loss to Lott strengthened our friendship, which began before we were elected to anything. Honey and I continued to spend weekends with Lott and his wife, Tricia, and New Hampshire Senator Judd Gregg and his wife, Kathy, at our respective homes in Tennessee, Mississippi, and New Hampshire.

Politics is like throwing all the balls of life into the air. It creates an opportunity to meet and become acquainted with many interesting and talented people one would never meet in the normal silos of living. But in my experience, political life does not allow for the creation of many deep friendships. Many acquaintances, yes. Politics is a blood sport, and acquaintanceships, even cordial ones, rarely become close friendships. The most important of those in my life, of course, was Honey.

In truth, most of my best friendships are from before my time in politics.

* * *

One year later, on Monday, November 26, 2007, as senators were returning from Thanksgiving recess, Lott surprised everyone by announcing that he would resign his Senate seat by the end of the year. McConnell scheduled an election for two weeks later, on December 6, to settle the unexpected leadership reshuffling.

There was no opposition to Arizona's Jon Kyl moving up from the Number Three job into Lott's whip position. I announced my candidacy for Kyl's spot, chairman of the Republican conference. This time, I remembered Senator Baker's advice to "count carefully and often." Going into the election, I had a solid lead over North Carolina's Richard Burr. The emotion of the last leadership contest worked in my favor. Senators who had voted against me a year earlier were reluctant to do it again.

I won 31 to 16.

Politico reported, "In choosing a folksy moderate best known lately for trying to broker bipartisan compromises on the war in Iraq, Senate Republicans have at least for now embraced some middle ground in their leadership hierarchy."[1]

I told the media, "My job is to help our conference express our belief in a way that rallies Republicans but attracts Democrats and independents."

As my fifth year in the world's most exclusive club drew to a close, I had run for something twice, won the second time, and become conference chairman, a job the media described as "chief communications strategist and spokesman for Senate Republicans."

"Are you going to be a leadership senator or a maverick?" Fred Thompson had asked when I was elected to succeed him.

To lead as governor, I had to be a maverick—taking office three days early, traveling to Japan to find auto jobs, brawling with the teachers' union over merit pay, insisting on new taxes to keep road debt at zero, and enacting the Martin Luther King Jr. holiday when no Republican state senator would vote for it. And that's just part of a long list.

Becoming the Number Three Republican answered Fred Thompson's question, but in an ambivalent way. I was part of leadership, but I was still a maverick.

I had my own views, and I intended to use my new position to push them.

CHAPTER 40

Second-Term Blues

"Rule 97. If you're running for president, be prepared to answer a question like this: 'Sir, I'm ready to fight and die for my country. How have you prepared yourself to give the order?'"

"Rule 159. Be as committed to military men and women as military men and women are committed to our country."

—LAMAR ALEXANDER'S LITTLE PLAID BOOK

Washington, DC. 2005–2008.

George W. Bush's second term did not go as well as his first.

His immigration proposal could not overcome a Senate filibuster. Although he made sixty stops to sell his Social Security privatization plan, not one Democrat senator budged. I tried to cheer him up by telling him about my conversation with Chile's interior minister.

"What does the United States need to do to adopt Chile's privatization plan for retirement accounts?" I had asked the minister.

"You will need two things. Number one, our plan. Number two, our dictator," the minister had said, laughing.

Bush's expansion of the "War on Terror" to Iraq was coming under fire from even his closest supporters. I was among those growing uncomfortable. My concern had been simmering since at least May of 2004, when I attended a sendoff for the 278th Armored Cavalry Regiment, Tennessee's largest National Guard unit.

Three thousand men and women had completed their training and were headed for the northern border of Iraq. I visited with three deputy sheriffs from my home county and a fifty-five-year-old school superintendent from nearby Athens. I talked with a physician who was the mayor of Lexington and a sixty-one-year-old university administrator who had "gone to the top" of the Pentagon to obtain permission to go to Iraq. Their lives would be interrupted for eighteen months. They had children to raise, businesses to run, and mortgages to pay. They were genuinely at risk.

These members of the National Guard did not complain, but they had not expected this assignment. Most had signed up for weekend and summer training to put down a riot or to quell a disturbance in Haiti, not to have their legs blown off by a suicide bomb in a hot Arab country.

By March of the next year, death notices of Tennessee soldiers were crossing my desk more often. Newspapers reported that 1,600 Americans had been killed in Iraq. In the Republican conference, we were discussing $10 million in capital improvements for the amputee center at Walter Reed Hospital because, with better and quicker medical care, so many members of the military were surviving wounds, creating more amputees and more trauma.

George W. Bush had oversold his decision to enter Iraq. Information about weapons of mass destruction turned out to be wrong. There had been mistakes of judgment since his father's stunning victory—and then restraint—in the first Gulf War.

* * *

On Tuesday, March 22, 2005 I arrived in Baghdad, where I met with Lt. General David Petraeus in the Green Zone where several thousand Americans were working.

It was heavily fortified, but not entirely safe. Petraeus was impressive. I could see why the president had confidence in him. The general told me that twelve of the eighteen Iraqi provinces were relatively quiet, but he also said that the most popular TV show in Iraq featured criminals on the internet cutting off people's heads for one hundred dollars.

Among the wisest words in the *Little Plaid Book* are, "If you become cynical, visit a military base and have lunch with enlisted men and women." At lunch in Baghdad, I asked three Marines who had recently graduated from Tennessee high schools, "What do I need to know?"

"'Not much to know, sir. They shoot at us and we just shoot them back," Andrew Pottier of Savannah said.

And these young men are teenagers, I kept thinking for the rest of the day.

On Thursday afternoon, March 31, after coming home from Iraq, I drove to Knob Creek Baptist Church in Sevierville to attend the funeral of Sergeant Paul W. Thomason, III. He was the first to be killed in the 278th National Guard unit, whose soldiers I had helped send off only a year earlier.

It was a cloudy day, sixty degrees, with sprinkling rain. There was probably nothing Sergeant Thomason had yearned for more than the new warmth and green and rain in early spring in his Smoky Mountains—except for his wife and four children.

"Mommy, did that go on Daddy?" one of the four asked, as she reached to touch the bronze star that the adjutant general had handed to her mother.

Hearing "Taps" sound as a kneeling general presents an American flag to the widow of a fallen soldier is a heartrending experience.

The president was seriously off balance. But in a way, this was not surprising, I thought. At this stage of their presidencies, Clinton was being impeached and Reagan was dealing with Iran–Contra. Nixon was about to resign. Ford, Carter, and George H.W. Bush didn't have to face second-term blues because they had been defeated. LBJ chose not to run again.

And none of them had to deal with more than George W. Bush had been facing—9/11, wars in Afghanistan and Iraq, entitlement spending that was eating up 70 percent of the budget, so many hurricanes that the alphabet was exhausted, two top aides under grand jury investigation, and judicial nomination battles. Furthermore, none of those presidents had to cope with social media creating news cycles that demanded a 24/7 White House response.

Seven months later, on Friday, October 21, I visited wounded Tennessee soldiers at Walter Reed. First, I saw Sergeant Matthew Cantrell, from

Deer Lodge. He was also a member of the 278th, and had been wounded only ten days earlier. His wife, parents, and brother were with him.

"I was riding in an unarmored Humvee thirty-five miles north of Baghdad when we ran over an IED. There were four of us. The medic saved my life," he said.

Sergeant Cantrell was heavily sedated, and his legs were covered, but not amputated.

"I was there in Knoxville when you mustered up last spring, and at Camp Shelby too. Your unit is coming home at Camp Shelby on Monday," I told him.

I stopped by the room of Sergeant Richard Robertson, whose mother had asked that I visit him. He was sitting in a chair with a room full of family, including his wife and three-year-old daughter. He was cheerful and we talked about the Alabama–Tennessee football game the next day. He had served with Special Forces in the first Gulf War and had three tours in Iraq.

"We ran across an IED late one night, chasing foreign fighters near the Syrian border," he said.

"I am a paraplegic, sir, from about two inches below my waist down. But what I can do today compared with what I could do a month ago when I came here is amazing," he said.

* * *

At 4:30 p.m. on Wednesday, November 9, 2005, I joined a dozen of Senator McConnell's deputy whips for a social visit with President Bush in the White House's second-floor family quarters.

The afternoon was warm. We followed the president outside to the Truman balcony. Aides offered cigars. He took one, and so did I. The lights of the Jefferson Memorial twinkled against the gray sky.

The president spoke about Iraq in an animated way.

"We must win. We will win. We could win the war militarily and lose it because of a loss of morale. I know they are undermining my character. I'll hit them back at the right time, but not now. I hope you'll do it for me. Iraq is the issue. If we hadn't gone into Iraq, he [Saddam Hussein] would have gotten weapons and come after us. The issue in 2004 would have been, why didn't Bush do something about Saddam when he could—and they would have been right," he said.

The following month, at the annual White House Christmas reception, Senator Domenici asked Bush for a meeting to discuss putting our "America Competes" legislation in his budget. We met in the Oval Office at 2:00 p.m. on Thursday, December 15. The president had just visited with a group of Iraqi students.

"They were so impressive, so brave. Their biggest fear is that we will leave, and we won't," he said.

Bush moved to the fireplace where there were two wingback chairs. He sat in the one on the right. Senator Domenici sat in the other one, and Senator Bingaman, the top Democrat on the energy committee, and I sat on the couch.

Toward the end of the meeting, I spoke up.

"Mr. President, this is a good time to be thinking of your legacy," I said.

Bush nodded as if he had been thinking about it.

I continued, "Overseas, obviously, it will be your response to 9/11. Freedom in the Middle East. Maybe Iraq. At home, it will be tax cuts and education. 'America Competes' can be a part of that."

I went on.

"Even when there is a success in war, people tire of it and turn their attention home. I wish I had said this more directly to your father thirteen years ago. Rather than making a speech praising (Colin) Powell and (General Norman) Schwarzkopf at the end of the first Gulf War, I wanted him to say to the nation, 'Let's turn our attention to the work we have to do at home.' I hope you will make what you are doing at home the subject of your State of the Union address, and the focus of your next three years," I said.

Three months later, on Wednesday, March 15, 2006, former Secretary of State James Baker and Democrat Congressman Lee Hamilton announced they would chair an "Iraq Study Group," whose members included prominent Republicans. On December 6, the group reported that the situation in Iraq was "grave and deteriorating," and recommended getting combat troops out by the spring of 2008.

Bush's response was to launch a "surge."

"I've committed more than 20,000 additional American troops to Iraq," he announced.

The president invited me for a one-on-one visit in the Oval Office, during which he argued that the surge was necessary to end the war on honorable terms. I wasn't convinced. I had stayed in touch by telephone with James Baker, who encouraged me to keep our conversations private, saying that, as the study group leader, he was walking a personal tightrope. Baker was virtually a member of the Bush family, having been the senior Bush's closest adviser. He was the chief strategist in the legal effort that produced the 5–4 decision in the US Supreme Court that made George W. Bush president.

On Tuesday, June 5, 2007, with the support of seven Democrats and seven Republicans, Colorado Senator Ken Salazar and I introduced legislation requiring Bush to implement the study group's recommendations—essentially calling on the Iraqi government to establish a more unified country or face the consequences of a US troop withdrawal.

"This is the foremost issue facing our country. The 'Iraq Study Group' report is the most promising strategy for a solution—getting out of the combat business in Iraq and into the support, equipping, and training business in a prompt and honorable way," I told NPR.

"I think that the handwriting is on the wall, that we are going in a different direction in the fall," Senator McConnell said that same day.

* * *

In 2007, another damper depressed the public mood.

Mortgage-backed securities cratered in value, causing trouble for financial firms. In December, the nation entered a recession. By the fall of 2008, it was known as "The Great Recession." John McCain suspended his presidential campaign to help resolve the crisis. The House voted down Secretary of the Treasury Henry Paulson's proposal to bail out financial institutions, causing the Dow Jones Industrial Average to record its largest single-day point drop in history.

The next day, Paulson showed up at our Senate Republican lunch with a revised plan. He was an hour and a half late because of discussions with House Republicans. By the time he arrived, we had decided to support his proposal and were leaving the room. On Friday, October 3, 2008, the president signed the "Emergency Economic Stabilization Act."

"It sounded like a bailout of banks for the big boys, but it really saved Main Street people who would have lost their jobs, their savings, and their ability to make purchases. It would have been a genuine Depression," said Senator Gregg, who helped write the plan.

Voters did not agree with Gregg. They stopped me in airports to say they were mad about bailouts. They were anxious, too, about the recession and weary of the war in Iraq. This combination produced a political fever with calamitous consequences for Republicans.

Amidst the turbulence, a charismatic figure emerged, offering voters the opportunity to rid themselves of Bush's second-term blues and to elect the first African American president. On Tuesday, November 4, 2008, Barack Obama defeated McCain.

It was a sweep. Democrats not only had the presidency, they had the House and sixty Senate seats—the magic number necessary to allow them to pass any law or confirm any presidential nominee on which all sixty of them could agree.

CHAPTER 41

The End of Two-Party Competition

"Rule 202. Remember that most people who are nominated by Republicans serve by the grace of the Democrats. The reverse is also true. Your friends may elect you, but your job is to serve all the people."

—*LAMAR ALEXANDER'S LITTLE PLAID BOOK*

Nashville and Washington, DC. 2008, 2009.

THE DEMOCRAT SWEEP IN 2008 did not interfere with my reelection to a second term.

I had no opposition in the August primary. In November, I won 65 percent of the vote. Despite Obama's carrying majority African American Shelby County (Memphis) by 2 to 1, I carried it too. My winning Shelby County for the sixth time in over forty years showed that friendships among Black, as well as White, constituents can pay dividends for Republicans too.

The Tennessee election results seemed uneventful, but they marked the end of four decades of two-party competition in our state. McCain won Tennessee handily. Obama lost traditionally Democrat White voters in rural Middle and West Tennessee counties that African American Democrat Senate candidate Harold Ford Jr. had won just two years earlier.

Counties named for Democrat heroes Sam Houston and Andrew Jackson began switching from solid Democrat to solid Republican. Democrats dropped the names of Jefferson and Jackson from their annual dinners. Republican Lincoln Day dinners became Reagan Day dinners. A new polarization was underway.

"You need to know that some of us believe we're losing our country," a rural voter whispered.

The Great Recession, wealth disparities, community and family disintegration, exhausting wars on terror, and Obama's liberalism were prime sources of the anxiety. So was race, fueling feelings that had been stirring since the 1960s Great Society and civil rights laws. While for many, Obama's victory was an atonement for slavery, for others it stirred animosity. Fueling the fire, iPhone and Facebook made their debut, launching a "Digital Democracy" that allowed citizens to express their anxieties publicly, and with an immediacy and harshness that proved hard to absorb.

Beginning in 2008, Tennessee became as much a Republican one-party state as it had been a Democrat one-party state before the 1960s.

* * *

A restructuring of the political phenomenon known as "the base" helped produce this polarization.

When I began in politics in 1966, the East Tennessee Republican base was composed of voters who were patriotic, churchgoing, and leery of the federal government. Because most were descended from Civil War Lincolnites, they were generally pro-civil rights. The state party organization was the custodian of "the base." There were not many other intermediaries between an elected official and the voters. To stay in touch with "the base," candidates visited county Republican chairmen, commiserated with other "rats in the barn," attended Lincoln Day dinners, or went directly to the voters, as I had when I walked across the state.

During the 1970s and 1980s, new organizations inserted themselves between the elected official and the voter. They became the "new base." The state party was reduced to being a fundraising machine and producer of operatives who consumed most of the money raised.

This new Republican base grew up at first in Washington, DC, in reaction to a left-wing coalition of civil rights, anti-war, anti-gun, pro-choice, feminist, and environmental groups, as well as publications like *Mother Jones* that influenced the Democrat party. The right countered with The Heritage Foundation, the Cato Institute, the Free Congress Research and Education Foundation, Americans for Tax Reform, and political action groups like the Christian Coalition of America, the National Right to Life Committee, and the NRA. Neo-conservatives championed extending freedom through wars. Radio talk show hosts—and even an entire TV network, Fox News—spread the gospel.

This Washington, DC, "new base" did not affect me when I was first elected to office in 1978. I was a small-town, culturally conservative, anti-gambling, prayer-breakfast-sponsoring governor who twice vetoed requiring photos on driver's licenses because it smacked of too much government, fought the teachers' unions, and supported Second Amendment rights, even though I didn't hunt much. The issue of abortion rarely came up.

Then, "base" restructuring spread outside Washington, DC. Seen from Nashville, where I was working with a Democrat legislature on better schools and roads, clean water, and healthy children, Republican House Leader Newt Gingrich's confrontational politics made it look like activist Republican governors and nay-saying Republican members of Congress were not on the same team. Another difference was that congressional Republicans were winning elections, and Republican governors and legislators were not.

To discuss what, if anything, we still had in common, I invited Gingrich and two other House Republicans to join me and three other governors for a weekend at Blackberry Farm in July 1985.[1] As the weekend began, I told the group, "Washington issues are tremendously important and fascinating, but when we get together, that's all Republicans talk about. Democrat governors are running up and down the street proposing programs to improve schools, pick up the garbage, fix roads, and make children healthier—and they are getting elected."

When the session ended, we concluded that we, indeed, were on the same team.

"If I were in Congress, I would be voting 'no' to more federal control—as Newt is doing. And if he were governor, he would be hard at work fixing schools and roads and health care—as I'm doing," I said. Gingrich agreed.

We called that division of responsibility "The New Federalism"—resist federal control and solve problems locally. On *Firing Line*, William F. Buckley Jr. said the meeting was "a historic way station in Republican politics in the South."[2] Alabama Republican Party executive director Marty Conners and I started the Southern Republican Exchange, where Republican legislators, local officials, and campaign managers addressed bread-and-butter issues. They began winning elections.

In Washington, DC, Gingrich kept winning too. His "Contract with America" helped Republicans capture both houses of Congress in 1994. Running for president, I watched the "new base" spread as I drove to towns like Ottumwa, Iowa, trying to persuade Republicans that I was Christian enough, pro-life enough, and Second Amendment enough. In 2002, when I announced for the Senate, I said, "I have conservative principles and an independent attitude." That suited enough voters to elect me.

Once in the Senate, I found that many of my Republican colleagues were beginning their political conversations with issues that thrilled the "new base"—guns, prayer, abortion, marriage, and taxes. Others of us still went to church, preferred traditional marriage, were pro-life, and supported the Second Amendment, but didn't start our politics there.

* * *

In 2006, after I was elected Republican Conference chairman, Capitol Hill newspapers said I had become a "partisan attack dog." Most of my Republican colleagues laughed at that characterization. They viewed me more like columnist George Will did in 2009 when he wrote, "[Alexander is] a Tennessee Republican of mild mien ... in the Senate, he has been a model of the moderate Republicanism ... as valuable as it is scarce."[3]

I detested being described as "moderate," a lazy adjective typically applied to those who speak without shouting, work across the aisle to achieve results, and don't always toe the party line. This label describes style more than philosophy. Bill Bennett, the Reagan education secretary and conservative talk show host who chaired my 1996 presidential campaign, once told me, "You and I basically believe the same things and could make speeches saying the same things, and after the speeches, someone would say of me, 'What a good fire-breathing conservative.' And after you speak, the same people would say, 'What a nice, friendly fellow,'" Bennett said.

I especially resented self-righteous political pharisees who claimed to be a better Republican than I was, in the way someone might wander into Sunday school and claim to be a better Christian. I am a very Republican Republican, a bona fide Abraham Lincoln mountain Republican descended from Union soldiers who voted like they shot and who made certain that our congressional district had not elected a Democrat to Congress since Lincoln was president.

In the Senate, I learned pretty quickly that the division among Republicans was not one of moderates versus conservatives, but between conservatives who think their job is finished when they make a speech and conservatives who want to govern.

My priority of governing didn't suit the Washington, DC, political pharisees who had begun to infiltrate Tennessee Republicans. It didn't help that I had always worked with Democrats and tried to represent all Tennesseans. During 2009, I provided more ammunition by voting to support Obama 68 percent of the time, according to *Congressional Quarterly*.

There was a ready explanation for most of those votes "supporting Obama." I voted for appropriations bills since, as a committee member, I had helped write them. Forty percent of my votes in support of the president were to confirm his nominations. I believe that a president, having been elected by the people, is entitled to choose members of his administration, absent extraordinary circumstances.

But in politics, explanations rarely explain.

"There was a time when you could cast a difficult vote and go home and explain it to your constituents," New Mexico Senator Jeff Bingaman told me. "Nowadays, TV talkers and the special interest groups have already explained your vote before you have a chance to get home and explain it yourself."

I had won six statewide Republican primaries, more than any other Tennessean, but still some pharisees were calling me a RINO, a Republican

In Name Only. And soon, I would find out that social media influencers would be replacing "rats in the barn" as the preferred medium for political persuasion.

* * *

"Why is it that Tennessee has been producing more talented national leaders of both political parties than perhaps any other state?" *New York Times* correspondent Jonathan Martin asked me in 2015.

Martin was referring to the last half-century, when Tennessee politics churned out a stream of nationally prominent senators, governors, ambassadors, Cabinet officials, presidential candidates, two Senate majority leaders, and a vice president of the United States.

My answer was simple—two-party competition. The emergence of a strong Tennessee Republican Party during the 1960s had produced four decades of vigorous party competition. Just as talented athletes are drawn to the Southeastern Conference to compete against the best athletes, talented Republicans are attracted to two-party politics to compete with talented Democrats, and vice versa. Both want to be where the action is.

At least for a few years, these talented competitors chose public service over law, medicine, business, or other pursuits. As a result, they were usually propelled by purpose as well as ambition. When the election was over, two-party competition among such able and purposeful candidates produced better government.[4]

This had happened before. During the first half of the nineteenth century, contests between Democrats and Whigs sent a stream of Tennesseans to national prominence, including three presidents (Jackson, Polk, Johnson), a presidential candidate who had been governor of two states (Sam Houston), and a congressman who made a name for himself bear hunting in Tennessee and dying at the Alamo (Davy Crockett).

After the Civil War, Democrats ruled Tennessee, except in Lincolnite East Tennessee. One-party government mostly produced mediocre leadership, humdrum politics, backscratching, unaccountability, and occasional corruption.[5] A century of mediocre leadership is one reason why, in the 1960s, Tennessee had the third lowest family incomes of any state, its textile jobs were fleeing overseas, and it rarely ranked first in anything to brag about. Voter dissatisfaction with this state of affairs—especially among East and West Tennesseans who felt left out—fueled the rise of the statewide Republican Party.

With two political parties competing, Tennessee's economy became the fastest-growing in the South. Ken Burns celebrated our country music. Instead of companies struggling to persuade employees to move to Tennessee, many came on their own, looking for jobs in the state's "It" cities. Improving self-esteem pervaded the state. Two-party political competition had done its job, producing effective leaders who kept competing to create this success once they got into office.

The year 2008 ended four decades of vigorous two-party competition. Tennessee soon became one of forty states in which one political party controlled the governorship and both houses of the legislature or had enough power to block vetoes from the governor of the other party.[6] In other words, Tennesseans are among the 80 percent of Americans who live in a state where the minority party does *not* have a meaningful voice in government, according to the *Wall Street Journal*.[7]

In his memoir, Senator Everett Dirksen wrote that his practice was to adopt a "tentative position" on an issue from which he would then proceed to find a solution among competing views.[8] That skill made Dirksen the most powerful legislator of his time—although it attracted criticism for being unprincipled.

"One of my principles is flexibility," Dirksen would reply.

Dirksen might not survive in today's "Digital Democracy," which rewards politicians who stick to extreme positions to raise money and win primaries. There is not much reward for those who work in the problem-solving center, adjusting their initial positions until they agree. It should come as no surprise, then, that there is not much market for consensus.

"Show me the incentive, and I will show you the outcome," Berkshire-Hathaway vice chairman Charlie Munger said.[9]

Will Tennessee's new Republican one-party era provide incentives to attract candidates who will continue the progress of the last four decades, or will it encourage the kind of lackluster leadership, unaccountable government, occasional scandal, and economic stagnation that flourished during the Democrat one-party century before the 1960s?

It is too soon to know.

CHAPTER 42

Senator or Governor?

"A senator who has been a governor who tells you that he prefers being a senator will lie about other things."

—SENATOR MITCH MCCONNELL (R-KY)

Washington, DC. 2006–2020.

BOB CORKER WAS HAVING A HARD TIME deciding which job he wanted—senator or governor.

For two hours on a sunny March afternoon in 1993, Corker and I paced up and down the wide beaches at Hilton Head, South Carolina. As we navigated around children riding bicycles and building sandcastles, Corker debated with himself. Every half hour or so, we would turn and walk in the opposite direction. With each turn, Corker would change his mind. Would it be the Senate, the position that every politician dreams of? Or governor of his home state, the position that politicians who have had both jobs prefer?

Corker, a scrappy entrepreneur, chose the Senate. In what became a contest of wealthy, forty-two-year-old political rookies, Corker lost the August 1994 Republican primary to Dr. Bill Frist, who was then elected in November. The next year, Corker become chief operating officer of state government, and was then elected mayor of Chattanooga. In 2006, Frist retired and recruited Corker to try again. He won, and eventually became chairman of the Senate Foreign Relations Committee.

Ask Bob Corker today which of those positions he prefers and he will tell you mayor—because a mayor, like a governor, can make executive decisions with a more direct impact on the lives of those who elected him.

I came to feel the same way about the advantages of being governor instead of senator—eventually. In the summer of 1963, when I was an intern the office of US Attorney General Kennedy, Washington, DC, was the boiling pot of political action. In that era, the government doing something was the federal government. Four years later, when I followed Howard Baker to Washington, the action was still there. Lyndon Johnson was using the national government to fight the Viet Cong and poverty. Lady Bird was using it to plant flowers and ban billboards, and Washington bureaucrats were meddling in the most local of institutions—schools.

The most celebrated politicians of the day were young senators of both parties. Governors were thought of as keepers of the provinces. People in the nation's capital paid little attention to what was going on in "flyover country" between the coasts. After waiting for a long time in an outer office to see House Speaker Thomas "Tip" O'Neill Jr., Georgia Governor George Busbee, chairman of the National Governors Association, said he felt like "a school child waiting to see the principal."

In those days, I agreed with US Senator Prescott Bush, the father and grandfather of presidents and governors, who said, "...the Senate is the ultimate goal of most every politician."[1] Then, in 1970, after returning home to help Winfield Dunn become governor, I changed my tune. Supervising the transition of a 40,000-employee state government between Democrat Governor Buford Ellington and Republican Dunn, I began to understand how much difference a governor can make in everyday lives.

There are more famous senators than famous governors, since senators are seen more often on network television news, which is what makes one famous these days.

"Didn't governors used to be more vivid?" the humorist Roy Blount Jr. asked.

Governors may not be visible on the national news, but they are seen almost every day on local television. In their home states, governors are better known and have more prestige than senators. Senators swear an oath to the Constitution of the United States. Governors swear theirs to the constitutions of their states. A governor is *of* the state, while a United States Senator is *from* the state—an ambassador to an unpopular foreign land: Washington, DC. That is why, when the governor enters the room, others stand. Not so for senators.

"A governor in his own state outranks everyone except the president of the United States. Everyone. Even a former president or the queen of England," former Secretary of State Dean Rusk told me.

Like most who have held multiple offices, Edmund Muskie of Maine, a former governor who became senator and then secretary of state, insisted on being called "governor." Even presidents preferred being governor. At a White House dinner honoring governors in 1979, Jimmy Carter spoke wistfully of his time as governor of Georgia.

"I don't think I've ever spent a more exciting and challenging and delightful four years than I did as governor of Georgia. And as the different governors went by in the receiving line and I shook hands with you, I had a recurring sense that was hard for me at first to describe in one word. But I finally realized it was jealousy."[2]

Even presidents who have not been governors understand this sentiment.

"There is so much noise around Washington that it makes it difficult to reach across party lines and get results. It's gotten worse. The governor's job must be more enjoyable because there is less noise in states," President Obama told Tennessee Governor Bill Haslam in January 2015, during a private lunch in Knoxville that included Vice President Biden, Senator Corker, and me.

* * *

To understand why so many prefer being governor to senator, it is useful to compare what it takes to do each job.

A good governor needs the skills of both Moses and Count Basie. Just as Moses led the Israelites out of Egypt, a governor's job is to point the way—to see an urgent need, deliver a strategy to meet that need, and persuade at least half the people that he or she is right. I began to understand that leadership formula during my first year as governor. Count Basie led in a different way. He could sit down at the piano, tinkle a few keys, and pretty soon, an average group of musicians would be playing better than they ever had. Moses pointed the way, and Count Basie brought out the best in those around him.

An example of using Moses's leadership skills was the legislative battle to enact Tennessee's "Better Schools Program." The strategy was to be the nation's first program to pay teachers more for teaching well. To enact that strategy over the opposition of the teachers' union—which meant I had to persuade at least half the legislators I was right—I conducted a fifteen-month county-by-county campaign. In the hometowns of legislators, I presented them with petitions signed by thousands of their constituents and a poll showing voter approval of the program. Then, I called a special session, during which legislators could discuss only one subject—the "Better Schools Program."

From this experience, I learned the value of focus. A governor who focuses on a single objective and throws himself into it with everything he has for as long as it takes can usually wear everyone else out and get what he or she wants. For example, focusing an inordinate amount of my time on Japan over eight years helped attract Nissan, Bridgestone, and other auto jobs.[3]

The best Tennessee example of the Count Basie leadership style was "Homecoming '86," arguably our state's most transformative initiative during the 1980s. Hundreds of homecoming celebrations in 1986 caused Tennesseans, community by community, to celebrate what made them special, and then to set higher goals for themselves.

Instead of pointing the way, the Senate leader's job is more like managing a cemetery—lots of people under you, but no one is listening. Howard Baker and Trent Lott described it as herding cats or taming tigers. Operating the Senate is difficult because many decisions require the unanimous consent of all one hundred members. That allows one grumpy senator to pull the cord and jerk the train to a halt. Governors have a hard time fathoming how to get anything done in such chaos.

To accomplish something in the Senate requires skills akin to those of a drum major who recruits band members, selects the music, and sees to it that musicians march in formation, play off the same sheet of music, and don't wander into the ditch on either side of the road. A resourceful drum major will often select one or two soloists to march in front. Both senators and governors run for president, although voters usually prefer governors because they have been chief executives.

A senator's job is less stressful. A disaster may call a governor into action while senators are sound asleep. Senators will be debating, while governors stay up all night struggling with truckers' strikes and prison riots. Senators can spend as much money as they want; governors must balance budgets.

A governor sets his schedule and, by doing so, the schedule of others. The Senate schedule is a mess. The Senate is best understood as a composite of one hundred senators' schedules, relationships, emotions, issues, and events, constantly adjusting to constituent, lobbyist, media, and family pressures as it labors to extract an occasional result.

The Senate is a more leisurely existence. With modern air travel, it has become (until recently) a Monday night to Thursday night job, operating between frequent recesses. There are typically one-week recesses each month and a four-week break in August. During 2004, for example, I spent 180 nights in Washington, DC, and the rest in Tennessee or traveling.

The threat to cancel a Senate recess ("work period," senators prefer to call it) is the leader's most effective weapon for achieving a result—or an objecting senator's most effective tool for extracting a concession. When senators "smell the jet fumes" of airplanes headed home, they will agree to almost anything.

As a governor, I learned that I should either get ahead of the schedule or it would get ahead of me. So, at the beginning of the year, I would mark off days that staff were not allowed to schedule, including every Sunday, Thanksgiving weekend, and the week between Christmas and New Year's. Then, I made plans to attend every UT home football game and a few basketball games. Then, I set aside days that Honey and I might invite friends, including senators, to our home in the Smokies for the weekend.

Both jobs provide five-star assisted living. Governors live in government housing with staff, troopers drive them, and state airplanes fly them. Senators are not quite so pampered. Constituents seemed surprised that, as a senator, I flew commercial—usually tourist class.

Senators are hardly left to fend for themselves. They have their own gym and restaurant, an attending physician, human operators of automatic elevators that are reserved for senators only, a trolley to travel back and forth to votes, hideaway offices in the Capitol for naps, and overseas trips, during which every detail of travel is arranged by military personnel.

Both senators and governors have staff to open doors, answer mail, undertake research, and entertain visitors. When senators and governors leave office, they must learn all over again how to drive, make reservations, and place their own telephone calls.

Many senators are content to do little more than have their say. Having a say is part of a senator's job, but if all one wants to do is offer an opinion, it is less trouble to launch a podcast or appear on the radio or television than it is to win a Senate race. In a similar way, many governors are content with the lesser roles of being chief executive—smiling, visiting, receiving, convening, leaping out of helicopters, or pulling the cord on loud guns at National Guard camps, making clever statements that help defeat the other political party, and serving as state cheerleader. All these roles are sometimes useful, but they are not how a governor transforms his or her state.

Governors usually are pragmatists, setting agendas and trying to achieve results. Former governors despair of passing legislation in the Senate's "polite anarchy." Most eventually agree with the advice of the *Little Plaid Book,* "Don't expect legislators to set an agenda. That's the executive's job." And most become unhappy.

"Compared to the responsibility, work load, and excitement of the four years as governor, serving in the U.S. Senate initially seemed about as exciting as watching a stump rot," Henry Bellmon said after serving two Senate terms in between terms as governor of Oklahoma.[4]

When he retired in 2024, West Virginia Senator Joe Manchin was more blunt.

"The two years I was in the Senate knowing I could have still been governor [of West Virginia] were the most miserable years of my life," he said.[5]

Just as there are not many Mickey Mantles who can hit a baseball both left-handed and right-handed, there are not many switch-hitting governors able to be effective senators. Voters seem to sense this. Only nine senators serving in 2023 had also been governors. Nearly half had been former House members, who also had a hard time adjusting to the Senate, but for a different reason. They had to navigate the transition from a two-year term, majoritarian, ideological body to the six-year term, operate-by-unanimous-consent, consensus-driven Senate. For the same reason, members of Congress who later serve as governors are often failures because they try to impose Washington, DC's ideological parameters on a job that requires leadership and problem-solving.

The jobs of senator and governor have this aspect in common—they are two of the best jobs in the world. Both confer the privilege reserved for those who have been elected to public office—the most reliable opportunity to save and improve our republic and to unleash our country's potential to help the most people.

PART TEN

Working with Obama

2009 to 2017

"If it had just been you and me these eight years, everything would have been fine."

—PRESIDENT BARACK OBAMA,
Monday, December 12, 2016

CHAPTER 43

Marching Off a Cliff

"When do you suppose you children will stop playing in the sandbox?"

—HONEY ALEXANDER, Saturday, December 5, 2009

Washington, DC. December 2009.

WITH CHRISTMAS IN THE AIR, sixty Democrat senators, holding hands, marched toward a cliff.

They were determined to jump. (Republicans can jump off cliffs all at once too, but each one will have a style: Senator Cruz might belly flop, Senator Paul back flip, Senator Murkowski swan dive, and so on. Democrats, by their nature, perform in unison.)

The occasion for this jump would be the final vote on the "Affordable Care Act" or "Obamacare." The Great Recession, Iraq misfortunes, and eight years of a Republican president had handed Democrats the presidency, a House majority, and sixty senators—enough to make any law if they all jumped together.

To begin the year, Barack Obama had resisted his party's temptation to use its huge victory to overreach. In a bipartisan gesture, he chose three Republicans for his Cabinet. But on February 3, one of those, Senator Judd Gregg of New Hampshire, decided to stay in the Senate. A budget hawk, Gregg had become uneasy with Obama's $700 billion economic stimulus package and other looming leftish proposals.

Had Gregg not reversed course, Obama's efforts at working with Republicans might have been more successful. Gregg was the ablest Republican senator, having served as consigliere to three Republican leaders—Lott, Frist, and McConnell. I had gotten to know him during the 1996 presidential contest. That took a while. Getting to know Judd Gregg is like getting to know a stray dog—you don't get to know the dog. You let the dog get to know you. Gregg is as spare with words as he is of build. His flinty personality reflects his disdain for government spending.

In January of 2009, Gregg and his wife, Kathy, accompanied President George W. and Laura Bush during their last weekend at Camp David. The weekend produced conflicting advice about becoming Obama's secretary of commerce.

"Take the job," Bush's Chief of Staff Josh Bolten urged.

"He'll destroy you," Bush warned.

Gregg's wariness proved to be well-founded. During the remainder of 2009, President Obama assembled a team of professors, community organizers, and lawyers who had never managed much. They became a sort of *Harvard Law Review* editorial board for the White House, spinning out proposals for what the federal government should be doing, and seeming to want to do it all at once.

At a Washington, DC, dinner, I told James Baker, George H.W. Bush's secretary of state, that Obama needed one or two people like him.

"Obama needs an implementer," Baker said.

By December, the Obama administration announced it was dispatching 30,000 more troops to Afghanistan, beginning federal regulation of carbon, preparing to spend $180 billion in leftover bank bailout funds on creating jobs, and setting the pay of executives in private companies. The president proposed raising the debt ceiling by $1.9 trillion, which Gregg described as "like a drunken sailor asking to have the bar open all night."

Front and center was a $2.5 trillion plan to provide health insurance, and pay for it by reducing Medicare benefits and raising taxes. Providing federal government health care to all Americans was the holy grail of liberal Democrat politics. Despite the 1993 "Hillarycare" debacle, health care trumped other concerns such as the debt, border control, or outdated infrastructure.

If "Medicare for All" was the true Democrat mission, the true Republican mission was to *prevent* government-provided health insurance from turning America into a European-style socialist country. Democrats are barking up the wrong tree, Republicans said. The issue is not more health insurance—91 percent of Americans already have it, and some who are eligible won't apply for it. Half of Americans have health insurance on the job; most of the rest have Medicare or Medicaid.

The real issue, Republicans argued, is lower health care costs. Bring down the cost of health care and make insurance cheaper for everyone—and do it step-by-step, Republicans said.

The partisan lines were drawn.

* * *

Throughout 2009, Democrat Senate Finance Committee Chairman Max Baucus worked with Republicans to write a bipartisan health care bill.[1] The effort failed. The urge to do what political parties usually do after a sweeping victory—overreach—became overwhelming. Democrats could not waste this opportunity, even if it meant jumping off the cliff all by themselves.

Democrats seemed oblivious to the political consequences of passing Obamacare with only their votes. A December 11 CNN poll reported that Americans opposed the health care bill, 61 percent to 36 percent, making the historic vote look like an historic mistake.

Through December, for twenty-four consecutive days and four weekends, Democrats marched in lockstep. Senator Harry Reid, the majority leader, used his most reliable weapon—threatening to cancel the most sacred of all recesses: the Christmas break. Tempers became short. Spouses telephoned, incredulous.

Reid wore Democrats down. Cooped up like inmates, his troops negotiated behind closed doors and reassured one another. There were long lunch debates and a White House meeting with Obama. So many constituents complained that some offices stopped answering phones.

Reid cut deals for the reluctant. For Senator Ben Nelson, the "Cornhusker Kickback" would pay for 100 percent of Nebraskans' Medicaid. Senator Bill Nelson protected Florida's Medicare Advantage beneficiaries. Senator Landrieu strode to the floor to deny that she had swapped her vote for a $100 million Medicaid fix for her Louisiana constituents.

"It was a *three-hundred-million-dollar* fix," she said.

As conference chairman, I was "the Republican offensive coordinator," the media said.

That gave me easy access to the floor where I offered dire predictions.

"Higher taxes. Higher premiums. Cutting Grandma's Medicare."

I went on.

"This bill is historic in its arrogance—arrogance that we in Congress are wise enough to take this complex health system that serves 300 million Americans and think we can write a 2000-page bill and change so much of the economy all at once," I said.

Democrats marched on through weekend and midnight votes to force a final vote—but they marched with low energy. Republicans, by contrast, competed for floor time, eager to predict disaster. They predicted the most sweeping political revolution since 1994.

Christmas was approaching and there were signs of exhaustion. In the mornings, the gym was crowded with grumpy senators. For me, the saving grace was that after twelve straight days of exercising, I felt tightness in my muscles and relief from back pain.

On Friday, December 18, Republicans gathered in the Capitol's Strom Thurmond Room to prepare for five days of round-the-clock sessions for one hundred senators whose average age was sixty-three. Walking to the caucus room named for a senator who had served until he was one hundred, I imagined that the high-ceilinged, chandeliered corridor was the entrance to a mausoleum. Three Democrats were in wheelchairs—a reminder that their party could not lose one vote and still pass the bill.

On Saturday, December 19, at 5:45 a.m. streetlights illuminated falling snow as staff drove me to the Capitol in a four-wheeler so that I could be on the floor to object, if necessary, to Reid's procedural moves. During the morning, Senator McConnell objected to Senator Ben Nelson's request for nine minutes to explain his "yes" vote.

"I merely delayed his farewell address," McConnell explained.

On Sunday, December 20, a CBS van drove me through sixteen inches of snow to the *Face the Nation* studio.

"It is outrageous in the middle of a snowstorm to give us a 2,700-page bill yesterday, start voting literally in the middle of the night, and say let's pass it before we go home for Christmas," I said to three million viewers.

That night was the longest and coldest of the year.

Two days later, at the Republican policy lunch, Senator McCain told a Christmas story that softened hearts. On Christmas Eve in 1970, during two years of solitary confinement when he was a prisoner in Hanoi, a sympathetic guard untied the ropes around his arms and legs, and took him to a dirt yard for four hours of exercise in cold weather. While he was exercising, another guard drew a cross in the dirt, made sure McCain saw it, and then quietly covered it.

"How fortunate we are to live as we do in our country," McCain told us.

As he spoke, I remembered asking McCain to help when I was chairman of the annual Republican senators' fundraising dinner.

"I don't have time for that," he had said, and abruptly walked away.

McCain was notorious for similar run-ins with colleagues, but after that incident, I decided to chalk up his rudeness to five-and-a-half years in a Hanoi prison.

McCain was aware of his temper, and usually apologized.

"I don't expect to be elected Miss Congeniality," he would joke.

But after he lost the 2008 presidential race, McCain made the kind of adjustment that losing candidates don't make easily—and some never make.[2] He became relaxed, convivial, and went out of his way to accommodate senators. Unlike those who had merely lost a political race, John McCain knew what it was to withstand real adversity, and to then go on with life.

* * *

Relief swept through the corridors on Saturday, December 23, when the majority leader announced that the Senate would finish its business with votes the next day on passage of the health care bill and raising the debt ceiling for one month.

The galleries were full the next morning at 7:00 a.m. when I cast the first vote. It had been a century since the Senate had voted on Christmas Eve. Senator Byrd, ninety-two, arriving in a wheelchair, voted "aye," saying, "This is for my friend Ted [Kennedy]," who had died four months earlier.[3]

As voting concluded, Senator Sanders, the sixtieth vote, was nowhere to be found. At 7:16 a.m., he rushed through the door and shouted, "Aye!" to applause from his side of the aisle. The vice president announced the vote, 60–39, with all Democrats voting yes and all Republicans voting no. The only absence was Senator Bunning, the Hall of Fame baseball pitcher, who had returned to Kentucky to spend Christmas with his thirty-five grandchildren. The appeal of Christmas and family had overwhelmed partisanship, delaying tactics, and hard feelings. Exhausted senators cordially exchanged holiday plans.

Democrats had the power, and they had used it. There was nothing to stop them from jumping off the cliff all by themselves, so they did. At least for now, the Senate had finished its work and had handed the Obamacare hot potato to the House.

I boarded the 11:00 a.m. American flight to Nashville, arriving in time to put Honey's gifts under the Christmas tree, attend Christmas Eve services, and join carolers in the front yard of a friend recovering from surgery.

On Saturday, Honey and I drove east for two weeks at our mountain cabin. It was below freezing for the second day in a row. Mountaineers call this steady freeze the "killing season," the hardest time of winter when people and plants give up and die, and insects burrow deeper into the ground. When the killing season is too short and not so cold, strange things happen. Buds pop out. Flowers die young. Unusual insects appear. Things become confused. In the Senate, things become confused when the session is too long. And this had been the coldest and longest continuous session since the first Senate in 1789.

"I think the last few nights of not sleeping had to do with all those silly middle-of-the-night votes and your schedule the last month," Honey said after I slept late on Sunday.

CHAPTER 44

A Republican Chorus

"Rule 109. Never waste time listening to a politician tell you how he or she won an election. They rarely have a clue."

"Rule 259. Keep in mind that enough small steps in the right direction will still get you where you want to go."

—LAMAR ALEXANDER'S LITTLE PLAID BOOK

Washington, DC. 2009–2010.

A United States senator is a political accident—or the beneficiary of God's plan, depending on one's beliefs.

Senators have a hard time coming to grips with either explanation. Most are convinced that their own skills elected them. Their self-assurance complicated my leadership job—I was offering political advice to senators who were sure they didn't need it.

Undaunted, I charged ahead.

"I have two clients," I told my Republican colleagues.

"Number one, the leader and, number two, each of you. My goal is to help you succeed. I will lead a Republican chorus whose harmonizing will persuade at least half the voters that we're right and help pass laws and turn us into a majority."

Just hearing these goals caused some to put down their BlackBerries and listen. Senators were not accustomed to a colleague expressing more interest in them than in himself.

Our challenge was that President Obama had a national megaphone. Forty Republican senators broadcasting forty different messages were no match for a Democrat president's State of the Union address. Fortunately, the Obamacare debate provided an opportunity to narrow the president's advantage. In political discourse, it's easier to remind voters of what they are already thinking, rather than to introduce a new subject. Since polls showed 61 percent of voters disliked Obama's health care plan, our job was to remind voters of what they were already mad about—and to offer something better.

Offering something better presented a second challenge. The Senate has a hard time digesting comprehensive legislation.

"If you're waiting for Senator McConnell to roll in a wheelbarrow with our 2,700-page Republican comprehensive bill, it's not going to happen because we have come to the conclusion that Congress doesn't do comprehensive well," I said on the Senate floor.

Wall Street Journal columnist Peggy Noonan suggested why Americans distrust comprehensive laws.

"They're afraid the bills are big because there is something hidden in them," she told me.

A lesson from the past suggested a better way to write a bill. Kentucky Senator Henry Clay proposed the "Compromise of 1850" to avert the Civil War. His effort failed, broke Clay's health, and he retreated to Nantucket to recuperate. Illinois Senator Stephen A. Douglas then introduced Clay's compromise in sections, one by one. Every section passed, with Texan Sam Houston being the only senator to vote for all of them.

The Republican strategy, then, would be like that of Senator Douglas. We would not try to preach the whole Bible in one sermon. Instead, we would do it one chapter at a time, proceeding step-by-step. That would fit my bent as a conservative policy skeptic.

The Obama team had a different bent. Trained in elite universities to create large systems to solve enormous problems, they had been producing a flurry of 2,700-page solutions that were scaring the country. When the president said that Obamacare was a proxy for a debate about the role of the federal government in everyday life, Republicans wholeheartedly agreed—but thought it was a political kamikaze mission for Democrats, and worse, for the country.

"That sort of thinking works in a classroom, but our country is too complicated for that," I argued.

I had learned that the best way to accomplish something big is to set a clear goal and then to take manageable steps toward that goal. If you are an executive—a president, governor, or mayor—you can set the goal, identify steps, and throw yourself into that one thing.

This leadership style is harder, but still possible, for a legislator. For example, in 2005, at the request of several of us in Congress, the National Academies recommended twenty steps to preserve America's competitive economic advantage. In 2007, Congress enacted two-thirds of them. "America Competes" was a far-reaching law, but it was fashioned step-by-step.

As governor, my goal was raising family incomes. I moved toward that goal step-by-step, some steps minor, some larger—amending banking laws, defending right-to-work, keeping debt and taxes low, recruiting Japanese industry and auto plants, building better highways for auto parts suppliers, and a ten-step "Better Schools" plan. I did not try to turn Tennessee upside down all at once. Within a few years, we became the fastest growing Southern state in family incomes.

Step one of the Republican health care plan would be to enact small business health plans to cover more employees at a lower cost. Step two would be to put an end to junk lawsuits that drive up medical malpractice insurance costs. Next, allow selling insurance across state lines to increase competition and lower costs; expand health savings accounts; support wellness and prevention; reduce waste, fraud and abuse, and so on. The danger was, too many steps might add up to "McConnellcare," a Republican comprehensive health care law.

That was a scary thought for Mitch McConnell, because it might shift voter anger to Republicans.

* * *

A third challenge was persuading forty Republican soloists to sing off the same song sheet. An Oak Ridge Boys' gospel song captures the challenge:

> Nobody wants to play rhythm guitar behind Jesus
> Everybody wants to be the lead singer in the band
> I know it's hard to get a beat on what's divine
> When everybody's pushing for the head of the line.

Senators pushing for the head of the line don't listen well, especially to other senators. Rarely do they take written material back to their staff. So, I tried pictures, specifically, videos. Instead of making a speech at Tuesday policy lunches, I showed videos of senators, themselves, speaking, saying what I wanted them to say.

I was using an established management principle—catch someone doing something right. My theory was that senators who are skilled enough as talkers to elect themselves will occasionally say something that can help reelect them. And, like all good storytellers, senators repeat words and phrases that resonate and persuade.

Each week, staff scoured senators' television news clips and assembled the best in a four-minute video. I wrote slides emphasizing the message of the week. For the State of the Union, it was "Jobs. Debt. Terror. And stop right there." On energy, it was "Produce more. Use less."

For health care, there were many messages.

"This is the same turkey you didn't like in August, and you won't like it any better for Thanksgiving."

"Smells like a mackerel in the moonlight the longer it stays out there," came from Republican Governor Haley Barbour.

"The mother of all unfunded federal mandates," from Democrat Tennessee Governor Phil Bredesen.

At weekly caucus lunches, senators would stop eating and stare at the screen, watching for themselves to appear. Soon, Republican songbirds were warbling in tune, mostly motivated by fear of being overwhelmed by the Democrat majority of sixty.[1]

During 2009, on the Senate floor, Republicans said "step-by-step" 173 times, according to the Congressional Record. Also during 2009, I made forty-three floor speeches delivering Obamacare messages. Our efforts did not equal a State of the Union, but they spread our story.

* * *

After passing Obamacare on Christmas Eve of 2009, senators had gone home for twenty-six days.

After having been away for so long, I puttered and scratched like a cat on a bed, making a new place for myself. On Capitol Hill, there was much scratching and clawing and pushing and shoving for a few days as senators found their footing.

The Obamacare fight was not over. Pro-life House Democrats were unhappy with the Senate's abortion language.

"I don't believe there are the votes in House to pass the Senate bill," Senator Rockefeller said.

And there was a new challenge. Democrats had lost their sixtieth Senate vote, making it unlikely that the Senate would approve any House amendment to the bill the Senate had passed. On Tuesday, January 19, 2010, Scott Brown won a Massachusetts special election to fill Ted Kennedy's Senate seat. Brown became the forty-first Republican senator, arriving in Washington, DC, with lessons on a new technology, which he explained to his new colleagues, who were barely familiar with their BlackBerries. To attract voters, Brown had used Facebook, which had only been available for four years. By election day in 2010, Brown had 76,700 Facebook friends.

Facebook, combined with Twitter, introduced in July 2006, and the iPhone, introduced in 2007, transformed campaigns. These online technologies launched the "Digital Democracy," diminishing political parties and polarizing politics as candidates discovered that extreme remarks attract attention, raise money, and win races—especially primary races. I asked other Republican senators to deliver messages in the way Scott Brown had in Massachusetts.

Senator Schumer found it humorous that Brown had worked his way through law school as a model, had won *Cosmopolitan's* "America's Sexiest Man" contest, and had posed nude in the magazine's centerfold. Schumer did not find it so funny that Brown's arrival had deprived Democrats of their sixtieth vote.

The day after Brown's victory, Democrats acted as if there had been an unexpected death in the family.

"Don't gloat," McConnell muttered, as Republican leaders walked to a crowded press conference in front of the Capitol's Ohio Clock.

"Is the health care bill dead?" a reporter asked.

"I hope so," McConnell answered.

Democrats planned an end run. The House would pass an amended Obamacare bill and ask the Senate to approve it under budget rules. That required only fifty-one votes—but the Senate parliamentarian had to agree with the House amendment, which was unlikely. That meant House Democrats would be asked to vote for an unpopular bill that the Senate might not pass.

"We believe what the president is doing is asking House Democrats to hold hands, jump off a cliff and hope Harry Reid catches them," I told the media.

If the bill was dead, it would be the largest abrupt policy change in memory—but that was not all. Losing the sixtieth vote created a roadblock to Democrat changes in labor, taxation, environment, and energy laws. It encouraged Republican candidates and made Democrat members of Congress skittish about controversial votes.

Obamacare, for now, had stalled in the House.

* * *

On Wednesday evening, January 27, 2010, President Obama arrived at the Capitol to deliver his first State of the Union address.

I had invited Hal Hardin, the Democrat former US attorney whose telephone call had resulted in my early swearing-in as governor, to join me at the secretary of the Senate's traditional supper in S-211, the LBJ Room. The menu had not changed for twenty-six years—green beans, ham, and biscuits.

After supper, staff escorted guests to the gallery. Those of us on the president's escort committees walked to the anteroom where Obama waited. At first, he was pensive.

"These are dog years," the president said, referring to the difficulty of his job.

"Last year, I was pretty worried about where things stood in our country. We had some tough things going on. I put on a good face but wasn't sure what was going to happen. But we're alright now. It's just a matter of grinding it out."

Then, Obama relaxed and became engaging. He joked with Speaker John Boehner, whose face was always tanned.

"I'd have to stay in Hawaii for a week before I'm as dark as you," Obama said.

Thomas Jefferson believed that Presidents Washington and Adams's style of appearing in person to provide information to Congress was "speaking from the throne." So, between Jefferson in 1801 and Woodrow Wilson in 1913, presidents sent an annual message in writing. Since Lyndon Johnson delivered the first primetime televised State of the Union address in 1965, it has become a spectacle rivaled only by the Super Bowl and a few other events.

Viewers have become accustomed to the awkward, redundant ritual.

"Mister Speaker, the president of the United States," the sergeant-at-arms announced at 9:08 p.m., and led Obama and his escorts down the center aisle.

House members, some of whom had arrived two hours early, hoping to be seen by 50 million viewers, pushed and shoved to greet the president. During the president's address, the vice president and the Speaker sat behind him. Above them, golden eagles guarded a large clock. George Washington watched from a portrait on the left. Teleprompters stood in front. (In a 1993 Bill Clinton speech to Congress, teleprompters displayed the wrong speech, and the president winged it for an hour and ten minutes.)

I sat toward the front with other members of the leadership, Cabinet members, and Supreme Court justices. Reminiscent of the Kentucky Derby, women senators, decked out in brightly colored dresses, pants, and scarves, outshone the drabness of male senators in dark suits and ties.

The first applause erupted at 9:17 p.m., and, for the next hour, the chamber resembled a high school cheerleading camp. Republicans and Democrats bobbed up and down, applauding or not, depending on what the president said. I stood perhaps a dozen times. The president took full advantage of his megaphone, gesturing toward individuals in the gallery who served as props for his speech points. He raced through civil and gay rights, opposition to torture, equal pay for women, and other topics crammed into the address by insistent Cabinet members and special interest groups.

It would have been more effective to speak for half an hour only on jobs, debt, and terror, and stop right there, I thought as I drove home to Georgetown at 11:00 p.m. The next day, Bill Galston, who had helped create the centrist Democratic Leadership Council that led to the election of Clinton and Gore in 1992, summed up Obama's address.

"This speech was 90 percent stay the course and 10 percent 'let's reach out to Republicans,'" Galston said.[2]

CHAPTER 45

The Obamacare Summit

"The folks in the White House just must be kicking themselves right now."

—DAVID GERGEN, CNN, Thursday, February 25, 2010

Washington, DC. January–February 2010.

DURING AN NBC INTERVIEW before the Super Bowl on Sunday, February 7, 2010, President Obama made the surprise announcement that in two weeks, he would convene members of Congress in a bipartisan summit to discuss health care.

The president's announcement was either clumsy congressional relations or pure politics. The only prior notice that Senator McConnell received was a staff-to-staff call with no details, two hours before the television interview. If Obama had been serious about achieving a result, he would have announced the summit after the White House congressional leadership meeting that was already scheduled for the following Tuesday. At serious summits, with foreign leaders for example, matters are first worked out privately so they can then be announced publicly.

The next afternoon, McConnell chuckled when he talked to me about the president's Super Bowl announcement.

"Obama used your step-by-step phrase during the interview," he said.

"That just goes to show how a good phrase, repeated a lot, will get picked up, especially if nobody remembers where it came from," I said.

McConnell was suspicious.

"I'm not going to allow him to create a setting that puts Republican senators at a disadvantage," he said.

I made three suggestions to McConnell.

"First, you should be the symphony director and not the soloist. Introduce other senators to make our health care points so it is not a president versus McConnell reality show," I said. There was talk that Obama intended to make McConnell his foil during the upcoming 2010 elections, in the way President Clinton had made villains of Newt Gingrich and Bob Dole in 1995 and 1996.

"Second, no questions. Republican senators should respectfully state their views but not ask the president questions. This is not question time, with Republicans being supplicants at the fount of wisdom.

"Third, pick the best soloists without regard to leadership or committee rank to perform, and they should practice their parts," I said.

The White House had announced that there would be nine Democrats and twelve Republicans at the summit. McConnell would designate four senators. The president then posted his proposal for resolving differences between the Senate and the House Obamacare bills. Again, the president was setting the terms of the discussion without consultation.

McConnell called me on Monday, February 22.

"You're in," he said. "I want you to be part of the health care summit team. And, so you won't be surprised, I may ask you to present the overview for our side. Boehner may ask you to do it for his side as well. There's been a lot of interest from senators who want to participate. I'm picking McCain, you, and the two doctors [Barrasso and Coburn]."

On Thursday, February 25, 2010, I arrived at Blair House, across Pennsylvania Avenue from the White House. It is where President Truman and Secretary of State George Marshall worked with Republican Senator Arthur Vandenberg on the Marshall Plan for the reconstruction of Europe after World War II—which was apt symbolism for another bipartisan occasion.

The Garden Room was arranged with a square of tables, around which forty-four participants, including thirty-six members of Congress, sat. I was at the table to the president's left. Across from me were Democrat congressmen. More than eight million Americans were watching on television.

The president began shortly after 10:00 a.m., spoke for ten minutes, then turned to McConnell.

McConnell said, "John Boehner and I have selected Lamar Alexander of Tennessee to make our opening framing statement."

An outsider to Washington, DC's world of sharp elbows and self-promotion might not appreciate how unusual my role was that day. First, the Republican Senate and House leaders were giving up an opportunity to be front and center on a nationally televised event. Second, other senators were deferring to a single senator. Third, House Republicans—who, three years earlier, had vilified Republican senators on immigration—were allowing a senator to speak for them.

I had decided to use stories and examples, but to be firm and to speak directly to Obama.

"Mr. President, as a former governor, I also want to try to represent governors' views. They have a big stake in it," I said. "We believe we have a better idea. And that's ... reducing health care costs ... let's go step by step toward that goal ... we want you to succeed, because if you succeed our country succeeds. But we think to do that we have to start by taking the current bill and putting it on the shelf and starting from a clean sheet of paper ... our view, with all respect, is that this is a car that can't be recalled and fixed, and that we ought to start over."

I outlined why our step-by-step approach would be better than Obama's comprehensive approach. And finally, I asked him not jam the final bill through the Senate by a fifty-one-vote budget procedure. I spoke for about thirteen minutes. During my remarks, the president seemed uneasy, then annoyed, almost as if he wanted to cut me off. Perhaps he didn't realize that McConnell and Boehner had given me both the Senate and House allocations of speaking time.

Finally, the president spoke.

"Well, thank you, Lamar. Both I and Lamar went a little bit over our original allocated time. Not wanting to be a hypocrite, I wanted to give you some slack," Obama said.

During my remarks, I had said that individual premiums would go up under Obamacare.

Later during the discussion, the president said, "So, Lamar, when you mentioned earlier that premiums go up—that's just not the case, according to the Congressional Budget Office."

I replied, "The Congressional Budget Office report says that premiums will rise in the individual market as a result of the Senate bill."

"No, no, no—let me—and this is an example of where we've got to get our facts straight," Obama said.

"That's my point," I said.

After some back-and-forth I said, "Rather than argue with you in public about it, I'd like to put my facts down and give them to you." I felt that it was inappropriate to continue the dispute in public, given the respect Americans have for the office of the president.[1]

Senator Reid also was upset with the length of my remarks. As was Speaker Pelosi, it seemed.

"I'm not an expert on much, but I am on filibusters and we've got forty members of Congress here," Reid said.

McConnell interjected, "Republicans have used twenty-four minutes, and Democrats have used fifty-two minutes. Let's try to have as much balance as we can."

"That may be true, but I wasn't calculating my time because I am the president," said the president.

During the day, my conviction grew that the six-hour summit was a mistake for Obama and an opportunity for Republicans. Obama demonstrated that he was the smartest person in the room on health care, but everyone already knew that. What they didn't know was that Republicans could propose something better. If the president had not loaned us his megaphone, there was no other way Republicans could have commanded six hours of network television to present our story.

As the day wore on, the president spoke longer, interrupting, explaining, and demeaning Republican motives. By the time we'd finished, Obama had spoken longer than all the Republican participants together. He could have taken a lesson from Colonel Tom Parker, Elvis Presley's manager, who allowed Elvis to make only one movie a year to avoid overexposure.

A king who spends all day at the sausage factory looks less like a king at the end of the day.

* * *

One month later, on Tuesday, March 23, President Obama signed the "Affordable Care Act." Unlike Social Security, Medicare, Medicaid, and other major social programs, Obamacare had been a wholly partisan enterprise. Not one Republican voted for it. Democrats had overreached—jumping off the cliff all by themselves just because they could—thus initiating years of acrimony that poisoned the president's efforts to work with Republicans on clean energy, the budget deficit, open borders, crumbling infrastructure, and other pressing concerns.

The new health care law was not the only source of Obama's congressional problems. White House clumsiness broadened the partisan divide. For example, Obama had zero relationship with McConnell. During the eight years he was in office, McConnell recalls only a single one-on-one meeting with the president he called "Professor Obama."

This lack of collaboration between a president and congressional leaders of the opposite party was different than anything I'd witnessed in my experience. Lyndon Johnson understood that a Democrat president has to work with Senate Republicans, and that the place to start is with the Republican minority leader. LBJ called Everett Dirksen every day at 5:00 p.m., David Gergen told me. There were multiple calls on some days.

Senator Baker told me about one of those conversations that occurred during the writing of the "Civil Rights Act" of 1968.

Johnson had asked Dirksen, "Everett, wouldn't you like to be the Republican senator who provides the decisive sixty-seventh vote on the most important civil rights bill in history?"

"Yes, I would, Mr. President, and I would also like to get my constituent appointed to the Sixth Circuit Court of Appeals," Dirksen replied.

Four years earlier, in February 1964, Johnson urged Vice President Hubert Humphrey to reach out to Dirksen on an earlier civil rights bill, according to the Dirksen Congressional Center.

"The bill can't pass unless you get Ev Dirksen," Johnson told Humphrey. "You and I are going to get Ev. It's going to take time. We're going to get him. You make up your mind now that you've got to spend time with Ev Dirksen. You've got to let him have a piece of the action. He's got to look good all the time. Don't let those bomb throwers, now, talk you out of seeing Dirksen. You get in there to see Dirksen. You drink with Dirksen! You talk with Dirksen! You listen to Dirksen!"[2]

LBJ called that "reasoning together."

On the Nixon staff, I wrote memos for the president's bipartisan meetings with congressional leaders. Democrat House Speaker Tip O Neill Jr. once said Ronald Reagan was the "worst president in his lifetime," but the two liked each other. When Reagan was shot, the Speaker, one of the first visitors, went down on his knees to pray for his friend. Bill Clinton would telephone Republican leader Trent Lott late in the evening to discuss welfare legislation, at the same time Lott was trying to convict Clinton in an impeachment trial. After 9/11, George W. Bush met daily with leaders from both parties.

After the health care summit, I told Senator Reid that, as governor, I had once asked Tennessee House Speaker Ned McWherter, a Democrat, to help pass a massive highway bill.

"You get all the Republicans and I'll find you thirteen Democrats—and one of them might not be me," McWherter had said.

McWherter was as good as his word, and the bill became law.

I asked Reid, "Doesn't President Obama know that he doesn't need McConnell's support? He just needs his *cooperation* so the president can attract enough Republican votes to succeed. Does the Obama White House not want to work with us, or do they just not know how?"

"You know, he was only in the Senate for four years," Reid said.

During those four years, Obama did not seem to try very hard to learn about the Senate. Perhaps it was because he had his eye on the presidency. In November of 2004, Obama was one of nine newly elected senators who gathered in the Mansfield Room in the Capitol for freshman orientation. His new colleagues noticed that Obama would depart the room frequently for a scheduled press conference, leaving an aide to take notes. When Obama returned, he would ask a question and then soon leave again. He was the only freshman senator that year to decline Majority Leader Bill Frist's invitation to have lunch with the leader and a senior senator. During his time in the Senate, his legislative output boiled down to co-sponsoring bills.

Obama's arrival in the Senate was different than that of another ambitious freshman, Hillary Clinton, who had been elected four years earlier. I often saw Clinton trudging through Senate corridors carrying a briefcase stuffed with papers. The media, as well as her colleagues. noticed that even as a junior member, she was on time for committee meetings and was usually one of the few senators who remained until the end of a hearing. By the time Hillary Clinton and Barack Obama both ran for president in 2008, she had learned the ways of the Senate well enough to work with Republican colleagues to play a key role in passing significant legislation on foster care, children's health insurance, and campaign reform.

Clinton had become the more effective senator, but Obama had won the presidency.

CHAPTER 46

Leaving Leadership

"Either they're challenged or they retire or they die."

—DONALD RITCHIE, Senate historian[1]

Turtle River, Ontario, Canada. Wednesday, August 3, 2011.

SUMMER DAYS ARE LONG IN CANADA.

It was 9:00 p.m. when I filled my flask and pushed the kayak into the reeds. Pink spread across the black water as the sun set. I lit a cigar to discourage mosquitoes and paddled to the center of the lake. There were no stars, but a crescent moon hung in the sky. The water reflected trees along the shore. An afternoon rain had made the air smell clean. The only sounds were a stream pouring into the lake, frogs croaking, and a loon trilling.

It was dark by 10:00 p.m., so I paddled in, beached the kayak, and walked to our cabin. I sat in my rocking chair on the screened porch. The Senate had adjourned for its August break. This was the first of eighteen days in Canada, my longest visit since buying the fishing camp in 2002. I found a blanket and lay down on the porch swing, hoping to see the northern lights.

Honey would arrive in a few days, but the rest of the time, I would be alone with plenty of time to think—and I had a lot to think about.

After four years as chairman of the Republican Conference, I was thinking about resigning and spending my remaining Senate years outside of leadership. Voluntarily giving up power is rare in the traffic jam of ambitions that is the United States Senate.

* * *

My goal had always been to accomplish something good for the country, and working with Democrats to do that would be easier if I were liberated from leadership. On the other hand, being the Number Three Republican provided an opportunity to shape conference positions. It gave weight to my arguments on issues. Behind closed doors in leadership meetings, I could find out what was going on and say what I thought.

When I told Honey what I was thinking, she said, "You know, you like positions and titles. I'm not sure you'll be happy without a leadership position."

My fire for running for something was burning low, and I was tired of being the political messenger. Serving in leadership is not all that it's cracked up to be. My job was like asking forty-seven football coaches which play to call on the ten-yard line—they would never agree in time to call the play. There is only one good leadership job. McConnell had that one, and he wasn't going anywhere anytime soon. The other jobs boiled down to doing whatever McConnell wanted.

Here is how things worked. Before leadership meetings each Monday at 5:00 p.m. in his Capitol Building office, McConnell would meet with the whip to outline his strategy. Then, at 5:30 p.m., the two would outline strategy for the rest of us elected leaders, along with a few others that McConnell had invited to sit in. The next day at policy lunch, the leader would convey his strategy to the entire caucus. The ensuing discussion reminded me of a governor's budget going through the legislature—a lot of fuss and talk but not much change.

After lunch, members of the leadership would walk to the Ohio Clock in the Capitol corridor where, as the rest of us stood grimly behind him, McConnell would tell the media what he had told Republican senators. Finally, one by one, each of us would deliver the same message. I joked with McConnell about how we must have looked standing there.

"We should be called 'Mitch and the McConnells,' like the 1960s rock groups 'Dick Doo and The Don'ts' or 'Nelson and the Rockefellers,'" I said.

Not only was leader the only good leadership job, it was also a hard job. In addition to managing the floor and dealing with the vagaries of the Democrat leader, it required tending to conservative groups, recruiting candidates, raising millions for campaigns, and attending to each senator's needs.

Liberated from leadership, I could spend more time doing what I really wanted to do—reduce federal control of schools, lower student loan interest rates, simplify college aid application forms, fund national parks, make sure songwriters were paid fairly, and increase research and development for nuclear power and biomedical science. Leadership positions could be confining, and they sometimes made me testy. At one lunch, I responded sharply when a senator criticized me for voting for a clean air regulation on coal plants when most other Republicans had voted "no."

In his autobiography, Senator Kenneth McKellar compared the Senate to a university, and a senator to a faculty member. After serving in both, I concluded that the best job in a university is not president, but professor, and the best job in the Senate is not leader, but senator. Both the professor and the senator have a prestigious forum, long terms, plenty of help, and can say and do just about anything they want.

I thought of senators who did not have an elected leadership role but who led by the force of their personalities, including Judd Gregg and Kentucky's John Sherman Cooper, as well as Georgia's Richard B. Russell Jr. and Michigan's Philip A. Hart, whose names are on two of the three Senate office buildings. And I thought of Ted Kennedy.

Thirty-four years earlier, on Thursday, January 21, 1971, Senator Robert C. Byrd had toppled Kennedy from his perch as the Number Two Senate Democrat, 31–24. Kennedy was stunned. Afterward, he deflected pressure to run for president by saying that he wanted to finish in the Senate what his brothers had started. Kennedy told me that, in August of 1980, when his presidential prospects collapsed, he looked at his whip loss and the end of presidential ambitions as liberating him to work on the issues that he cared most about. His attitude became an example for me.

Kennedy helped pass my legislation to create summer academies for teachers of American history and civics. He and I worked with David McCullough to plan a memorial to President John Adams. In 2005, following Hurricane Katrina's devastation, we enacted private school vouchers for children whose schools had been destroyed. Only a Democrat with the strongest liberal credentials could have survived such an affront to voucher-hating teachers' unions. To maintain those credentials, Kennedy would stand red-faced at his back-row desk shouting liberal bromides. During my time in the Senate, he became the most productive legislator, eclipsing both brothers who had once occupied the same desk.

* * *

In Canada, I also had time to think more about whether to run for a third Senate term.

I thought first of Honey, who was dealing with various ailments and now, not coming to Washington, DC, much. My own health was good, despite back surgery in 2008 and the prospect of needing it again. I would be seventy-four if I were reelected in 2014, and eighty by the end of a third term. Eighty would seem to be the right time for my third retirement from politics, and surely this retirement would stick. I could avoid what Senator Bingaman had warned me were "the 3 Ds in connection with retirement—defeat, disgrace, and death."

During my first retirement from politics, after leaving the governor's office at age forty-six, I learned in Australia that it only takes about sixty days after leaving public office to remember that politics is only a minor slice of life. I worried now about using up the remaining years Honey and I had together.

"Serve two terms and get out," the *Little Plaid Book* says.

Two terms as governor is enough, but the Senate is a three-term job. It takes about eight years to accumulate enough seniority, respect, and experience to wield real influence. If I were to run for a third term, I would be in line to be senior Republican on education, health, and labor policy, as well as on energy appropriations—the issues I cared the most about.

At the end of eighteen days, I had caught more big walleye than I ever had before, and paddled my kayak almost every evening into the sunset. I had written down the story of *Chief Waki Waki Poo & the Swimming Pool Monster* that I had told hundreds of times to our children and grandchildren. I would make it a book for Christmas presents.

I had resolved to resign from leadership—but also to visit all ninety-five counties during the next twelve months to prepare to run for a third term.

* * *

Between votes on Thursday, September 15, 2011, I walked with Senator McConnell to his office, where I asked to have an "in the tomb" conversation.

"Telling McConnell a secret is like speaking into a tomb," his aide once told me.

I told McConnell of my plans and that I hoped we could keep our relationship intact, but that he did not need to invite me to sit at the leadership table.

"After you pull it off, it's hard to give it up," he said.

As we talked, he began to smile.

"I could tell you were chafing in the leadership role. I saw you lose your temper on Wednesday at the steering committee meeting over the coal and clean air matter, and I've never seen that before," he said.

McConnell had sensed that something was up. He offered to let me to continue to attend the weekly leadership meetings, but I resisted.

"You could be a leader among thirty-five or so senators of both parties who could be the basis of a result-oriented group," McConnell said.

He was careful to distinguish between "moderate" senators—Republicans who serve in Democrat states and Democrats who are elected in Republican states—and "pragmatic" senators.

"Some are here to make a point and some are here to make a difference," he said.

"I would like to work to create occasional coalitions of Democrats and Republicans to help the Senate function," I said. "That could make your leadership easier. We won't always agree, but I won't surprise you."

He offered two pieces of advice.

"Say that you are running for reelection. Around here, when you say you are leaving, people assume you're gone.

"And second, try to avoid doing things just to show you are moderate. Even if you are not in leadership, you don't want to do things that cause half the conference to tune you out when you speak," he said.

We walked back to the floor to vote. I felt a little let down, knowing that I was doing the right thing, but regretting the parts of the leadership experience that I would miss. Since 2005, when I began my first campaign for whip, I invested a lot of time trying to succeed in leadership. It reminded me of the time that I spent between 1993 and 1999 running for president. In both cases, I did not achieve my goal. On the other hand, I had aimed for the top, knowing that if I did, I would probably end up somewhere near the top.

* * *

The next morning at about 10:15 a.m., Senator Reid, obviously aware of what I was about to announce, concluded his opening remarks on the Senate floor by saying that no one had done more than I had behind-the-scenes to make the Senate work.

At about 10:20 a.m., following McConnell's leadership remarks, I asked for the floor.

"Next January, I will step down as chairman of the Senate Republican Conference. My goal has been to help the leader and each individual Republican senator to succeed, to look for consensus within our caucus, and to suggest our message.

"Stepping down from leadership will liberate me to spend more time working for results on the issues I care most about. I want to do more to make the Senate a more effective institution," I said.

I went on.

"There are different ways to provide leadership.... After nine years here, this is how I believe I can now make my greatest contribution.... I said to Tennesseans when I first ran for the Senate that I would serve with conservative principles and an independent attitude. I will continue to serve in that same way. I am a very Republican Republican. I intend to be more, not less, in the thick of resolving serious issues. And I plan to run for re-election in 2014."

My decision stunned some and, for others, launched a game of musical chairs. Senator Cornyn now had a clear path to succeed Senator Kyl, who was retiring. Senator Thune announced his candidacy for my position; Senator Barrasso declared for Thune's position; Senator Johnson then said he wanted Barrasso's position, and Senator Blunt said he did too. Senators pursuing vacancies proceeded more energetically than football fans who study obituaries, call widows, offer condolences, and ask if the deceased's season tickets are available.

A barrage of media attention poured forth.

The *Washington Post* spread a headline across its editorial page.

"Lamar Alexander: Liberated from Orthodoxy," it read.[2]

One pundit said, "Imagine Lyndon Johnson voluntarily leaving the Senate leadership—especially at a moment when his party seemed poised to win the majority."[3]

"It was a rare event—people here seldom give up power," Bob Schieffer said in his Sunday *Face the Nation* commentary.[4]

On the floor that next Monday evening, September 26, while waiting for a delayed vote, I walked over to McConnell.

"I would like to reapply for the leadership, and then resign again to see whether I can get as much good publicity as I have gotten during the last few days," I told him with a smile.

He laughed, and asked if he could see me after the vote.

After most senators had left, McConnell and I sat at two empty desks.

"I have been thinking of your new role," he said. "You can become the leader of what I would call the practical members of our caucus. I judge there are between twenty-eight and thirty-two, and they have no effective spokesman right now. There are seven or eight others that are pretty far to the right, and about another eight who are intimidated by those and the threat of a primary race. But the majority is practical."

I invited McConnell and his wife, Elaine, to dinner, and his security detail drove us to Flavio's in a black SUV. McConnell seemed to harbor no ill will at the barrage of weekend publicity that had presented me as a statesman and him as an uncompromising scoundrel. He usually derides senators who veer from the party line to "seek a favorable story in the style section of the *Post*."

He is much more comfortable as a poker-faced dealmaker working to obtain a legislative result. My style is to lead with a public agenda and try to persuade at least half the people I'm right. Despite our different styles, I was grateful to have such a friendship, especially because if my goal was to accomplish something important, I needed to be able to work with the Republican leader.

The decision to give up power is rare in the Senate, but for me, it was not hard. I was comfortable exchanging my seat at the table for more independence. Leadership races are perpetual. Someone is always running for something. No vacant office is safe. Even though I did my best not to let my ambition to move up distort my relationships with colleagues and sometimes my votes on issues, it, of course, did.

I was relieved to leave the quest for leadership behind me.

CHAPTER 47

Reasoning Together

"Bring in the whiskey and lock the doors and we'll get a result. And it wouldn't hurt to bring in a piano, too."

—SENATOR DEBBIE STABENOW (D-MI)[1]

Washington, DC. 2011–2013.

AFTER LEAVING LEADERSHIP, I was liberated to work on the issues I cared most about, finally able to spend my time doing what I believed a senator was supposed to do.

I joined bipartisan meetings to eliminate federal mandates on schools and to simplify the college student aid form. I organized "gangs" of senators to speed up the confirmation process for 1,400 presidential nominations, to fund the world's fastest computer, and "to see to it that our country has the best waterways and ports." I helped increase biomedical and energy research funding faster, by percentage, than any other part of the federal budget.[2]

I persisted—but largely failed—in a crusade to stop wind turbine subsidies. I argued that they make as much sense as going to war in sailboats when nuclear ships are available.

"Do you know that you are the only senator saying these things about wind turbines?" a *Wall Street Journal* reporter asked me.

My first objection was that, in supporting the giant turbines, climate activists were defacing landscapes conservationists had spent a century saving. At the same time, these activists were refusing to support nuclear power, which produced 60 percent of the carbon-free electricity in the US. In my Senate office, I hung a giant poster showing that just one wind turbine would fit into the 101,915-seat University of Tennessee football stadium, and that it was twice as tall as the skybox seats. The only place in our state where wind might work was along the tops of scenic ridges. TVA tried that, building the only wind farm in the Southeast, but abandoned the project because the wind didn't blow enough.

Climate change is a threat and nuclear power is the solution, I said over and over. In a 2009 speech at Oak Ridge, I proposed that the United States do again what it had done in the 1970s—build one hundred reactors. I persuaded the Republican caucus to support a "find more, use less" energy strategy that included building one hundred nuclear plants and electrifying half of America's cars and trucks. If the federal government had spent its extravagant wind subsidies on building nuclear plants, today there would be more clean electricity for artificial intelligence and less of a threat from climate change.

One might say that there was a pattern to my legislative prejudices. After listening to other airline passengers discuss life's intimate details on their cell phones, Senator Dianne Feinstein and I passed a law banning cell phone calls on commercial flights. To stop the racket of low-flying helicopters, I teamed with Senator Wyden to limit their flights over the Smokies and Oregon's Crater Lake National Park. With Senator McConnell's help, Senator Paul and I passed the "Freedom to Fish Act" to allow fishing below dams on the Cumberland River. I reminded those who wondered about this that fishing is best below a dam—and that more Tennesseans have fishing licenses than vote in Republican primaries.

Riding on the Senate subway to vote after the 2010 election, Senator Joe Lieberman and I discussed the lack of opportunity for senators to know one another across party lines. We agreed that one reason was because we spent so much time in team meetings. In the 1960s, when I was a staffer, party lunches were only on Tuesdays, and Senate families visited on weekends. Now, Republicans have lunch together on Tuesdays, Wednesdays, and Thursdays, and travel home on Mondays and Fridays. Lieberman and

I found one vacant hour—Tuesday breakfast—not already occupied by some Senate function, and invited senators to discuss issues on which we might agree. My chief of staff organized monthly bipartisan lunches for other chiefs.

Over eighteen years, Honey and I invited more than sixty Senate couples to spend the weekend at our home at Blackberry Farm. There was little political talk and much telling of bear stories and comparing of grandchildren. The formula for success in all these bipartisan settings was not different than in other walks of life. If you get to know one another, you might learn to trust each other, and you might even find something you can agree on.

The "gangs" that often formed across party lines to fashion compromises helped the Senate function, but they did not become permanent institutions.

"Gangs are like the volunteer fire department. When the bell rings, come if you can," Senator Lindsey Graham said.

So that senators could socialize after votes, Senator Schumer and I refurbished the Styles Bridges room in the Capitol. Creating a bipartisan setting with food and drink may seem trivial, but it struck at the heart of the Senate's dysfunction.

"Bring in the whiskey and lock the doors, and we'll get a result. And it wouldn't hurt to bring in a piano, too," Senator Stabenow said.

* * *

Most Republicans believed that President Obama was unsuccessful in congressional relations because he was so ideological. I disagreed. I believed that the problem was more of a lack of adeptness.

Obama was superior to most presidents in matters of policy, but not in human relations, which is the essence of politics and government. For example, the president asked to attend the Republican luncheon on Tuesday, May 25, 2010, where he spoke for twenty minutes about the "New START Treaty," immigration, and bipartisanship.

After the president spoke, Senator Corker rose.

"I got to tell you something. There's a degree of audacity in you being here today," Corker said to Obama. "If you look at your three major initiatives, they were almost all done on party-line votes. I feel we're all props here today. Just last week you engineered a very partisan vote. I would just like for you to explain to me, when you get up in the morning, and when you come over to lunch like this, how you reconcile that duplicity."[3]

Obama maintained his composure, launched into a ten-minute defense of his bipartisanship, and said he would be willing to be a one-term president if that would solve big problems. He did not seem to know that Corker had taken the most political risk of any senator in the Republican caucus to try to negotiate in a bipartisan solution on the financial regulation bill.

Then, Obama turned to me.

"Lamar, I think you would agree that, on education, I have done some things that my own party would not," he said.

"On education, Mr. President, except on student loans, I do agree," I said. "And I give you great credit."

It was an odd visit. There was no apparent reason for it. There was no discussion in advance to help create a result.

There was more clumsiness. In 2009, Mrs. Obama broke seventy-five years of tradition by inviting spouses to random White House dinners instead of hosting the "First Lady's Luncheon." Perhaps the Obamas had been in the Senate for such a short time that they didn't understand how much spouses looked forward to this annual ritual, and that random dinners were no substitute for building relationships at the "First Lady's Luncheon."

On Tuesday, June 29, 2010, fifteen Democrats and eight Republican senators waited patiently until the president arrived, twenty minutes late for a 10:50 a.m. White House energy meeting.

Toward the end of the discussion, I made a suggestion.

"The first priority should be to clean up the BP oil spill, then a mini-Manhattan Project to electrify half our cars and trucks, double the number of nuclear plants, double energy research, and pass the clean air bill that has fifteen bipartisan sponsors. These are things we can agree on," I said.

"I know these are your talking points, but this is not a meeting on the oil spill. On your clean energy points, we have some agreement..." Obama began to reply.

I interrupted.

"These are not my talking points, Mister President. These are my opinions," I said.

It was reminiscent of our exchange at the Obamacare summit. The meeting lasted until 12:30 p.m., with no consensus.

Small gestures could have helped Obama's relations with members of Congress. For example, he could have regularly attended the annual Alfalfa Club dinners, a century-old tradition of good-natured foolishness attracting 1,000 big shots from Warren Buffett to the chief justice of the Supreme Court. Such an audience might not seem as important for Obama as the media's Gridiron and White House Correspondents' dinners that the president did attend. But at the Alfalfa Club dinner, the Marine Band salutes veterans and the president makes closing remarks, after which he is honored with the only toast of the evening. From at least JFK to George W. Bush, presidents had attended, offering patriotic remarks and humor that "singed but did not burn." It was an opportunity for them to address a friendly audience of influential Americans who would then travel home, spreading the word about how impressive the president had been.

Typical of the evening's spoofing was Senator McConnell's introduction of me with these words in 2011 as the Alfalfa Club nominee for president:

> "A man who, in the middle of his career, spent six months living in Australia and no one knew he was gone.
>
> "A man not afraid to speak his own mind because he knows no one is listening.
>
> "A man, who, if you Google the word 'bland' prompts you with, 'Did you mean Lamar Alexander?'
>
> "A man so lacking in charisma that when the two of us are together, people listening cannot drive or operate heavy machinery."

For my acceptance speech, I played a nine-foot Steinway and sang new lyrics to country songs. For House Speaker John Boehner, I sang to "Crying Time." Boehner, who smoked incessantly and was always tanned, often ruined his tough guy image by crying in public.

The Speaker laughed and made an obscene gesture from his head table seat when I sang this verse:

"Well, its crying time again for Mister Speaker,
Could it be that Camel Light smoke in his eyes?
Who knows if he's just heard some sad, sad story
Or if he's reacting to some spray tan dye."

Obama did attend the Alfalfa Club dinner twice, in 2009 and 2012, but not attending regularly meant missed opportunities. They were small ones, but missed opportunities, nonetheless.

* * *

At the same time, there were encouraging signs of bipartisan progress.

On August 4, 2010, after I had publicly complimented Obama for supporting charter schools—which his teachers' union allies did not support—he telephoned me.

"I saw your remarks on my education program. I read it. And I appreciate it," the president said.

"You deserve support on this, Mr. President. You are not the first Democrat to advocate these policies, but you are the one most likely to be able to do the most about them," I said.

That same day, Obama invited McConnell to the White House for the first one-on-one meeting between the president and the Republican leader since Obama was inaugurated eighteen months earlier.

"It was constructive," McConnell said afterward, seeming surprised. "We agreed not to characterize each other's positions afterward. Maybe it is the first indication that he believes he will have to deal with us more."

Then, on Tuesday, July 16, 2013, Obama intervened to help our bipartisan legislation tying interest rates on eleven million student loans to the market rate. For undergraduate students, the bill would drop the rates from 6.8 percent, which was set in law, to the market rate of 3.86 percent. It also established a ceiling in case rates went back up. Massachusetts Senator Elizabeth Warren had been throwing up roadblocks.

The president invited bill sponsors from both political parties to a late afternoon Oval Office meeting.[4] Obama was masterful in quickly understanding the issue and gently letting Democrat education committee chairman, Iowa Senator Tom Harkin, know that he supported our proposal.

Obama seemed more comfortable working quietly on issues in this way with bipartisan groups of senators, figuring that a more visible role, as he said, "might hurt more than help."

Harkin was slow to come around.

The chairman told the president, "You'll have to pass the proposal with more Republican votes than Democrats."

"How many Republican votes will there be?" Obama asked.

"Thirty-five," Senator Coburn, a Republican, said.

When the meeting ended, Obama asked Harkin to stay for some one-on-one persuasion.

"I'm going to work on [Senator Tom] Harkin a little," President Obama said to me privately.

Because of Obama's push, one week later, he was able to sign the "Bipartisan Student Loan Certainty Act," saving students billions of dollars.

It was presidential leadership reminiscent of Lyndon Johnson's "reasoning together" with Everett Dirksen.

CHAPTER 48

Political Pharisees

"I am here to hook a big one."

— **LAURA INGRAHAM, Fox News host, Nashville, Saturday, July 26, 2014**

Turtle River, Ontario, Canada. Thursday, August 15, 2013.

THE INTERNET AT OUR FISHING CAMP had been off and on, so I hadn't seen the message from the day before until after I had caught enough walleye for supper.

Twenty county Tea Party groups had sent me a letter.

It said, "Unfortunately, our great nation can no longer afford compromise and bipartisanship, two traits for which you have become famous. We urge you to conclude your long and notable career by retiring with dignity instead of fighting against a serious conservative primary challenge."

For the next four days I focused on fishing, and then, on Monday, August 19, attempted a graceful response.

"I appreciate the suggestion, but if the people of Tennessee will allow it, I'd rather continue to serve—hopefully, with dignity. Washington needs more, not fewer, conservatives who know how to get a result," I wrote.

The Tea Party movement had surfaced in 2009 in opposition to Obamacare, Obama himself, big government, too much spending, and an assortment of other grievances. It was part populism, part conservatism, part libertarianism.

"And what about this whole business of the Tea Party? Is it going to prove to be a good thing?" Bob Schieffer asked me on *Face the Nation* in April 2010.[1]

I was optimistic.

"Well, I think any time Americans want to get out of their chairs and focus on jobs, debt, and terror, and checking a runaway government in Washington, we want them in our primaries," I told Schieffer. "We want them as our nominees. And we want them in the United States Senate. It provides diversity in our party. It makes us a bigger tent. Gives us a lot more energy, but I think the American people are really upset right now. And this election is going to have a lot of fresh faces, a lot of surprises."

The surprises began the next month, and they were not the ones I had hoped for. The Tea Party erupted as a force in the 2010 Republican Senate primaries, attracting new voters who too often nominated candidates that could not win general elections. My fear was that Tea Party nominees would seem so extreme that Independent voters in the general election would shy away, and Republicans would lose the opportunity to set the country on a more conservative course.

That is what happened. On May 8, Utah caucus goers denied a fourth term to Senator Bob Bennett. According to wire service stories, Bennett lost to Mike Lee because he was "not conservative enough," having voted for bank bailouts, sponsored a health care bill with an individual mandate, and secured earmark appropriations for his home state. *If that is a recipe for defeat, then I had better watch out,* I thought.

In November of 2010, Lee kept the Utah seat Republican, but in other states, Tea Partiers helped nominate three gaffe-prone right-wingers who lost seats that center-right candidates likely would have won.[2] McConnell was furious, concluding that he would never be majority leader if fringe candidates kept winning primaries and losing general elections. He began raising tens of millions to support incumbents and other center-right candidates.

Meanwhile, Heritage Action For America and the Senate Conservatives Fund had begun to "score" votes deemed not conservative enough—even before senators had cast them. Encouraged by these political pharisees,

Tennessee social media and talk radio began buzzing with my transgressions. In a Friday, October 12, 2012, letter, Chattanoogan Mark D. West listed my sins:

> TARP Bank Bailout and Fannie Mae and Freddie Mac Bailout, Cash for Clunkers, the START Treaty, Eric Holder for attorney general and Sonia Sotomayor for the Supreme Court, raising the debt ceiling, not opposing the Law of the Sea Treaty, and voting to enforce environmental regulations on coal plants.

Had West waited a few months, he could have added immigration reform.

The Senate Conservatives Fund, a Tea Party ally, began dredging up 2014 primary opponents for McConnell and other incumbents, including me. After my Canadian fishing trip, I took nothing for granted. A reelection campaign is not stepping from one perch to the next. It is starting all over and climbing from the bottom to the top. I visited all ninety-five counties and raised $3 million. I aired TV ads of my encounter with Obama at the health care summit, and touted the "Freedom to Fish Act" with Tea Party favorite Senator Paul.

"We need more conservatives who know to govern," Arkansas Governor Mike Huckabee said at a Murfreesboro rally, where he played bass guitar while I pounded out "Johnny B. Goode" on the keyboard.

My principal challenger was Joe Carr, a state legislator. Since no one knew much about him, I wasn't going to tell them. I never mentioned his name or ran a negative TV or radio ad.

On Tuesday, June 10, 2014, the same day that Senator Graham won his primary, a shocking upset overshadowed his victory. In a Virginia Republican primary, a Tea Party professor, Dave Brat, trounced House Majority Leader Eric Cantor, whose $2 million in negative advertising had made Brat credible. Sometimes, such expensive scorched earth campaigns work. For example, one month earlier, while conservative groups spent millions against him, McConnell—as he always had—spent millions throwing the kitchen sink at his opponent, winning 2–1.

I resisted the kitchen sink urge. I hoped to be able to say, after winning, that I had not pandered, not run negative ads, not changed my voting habits—and I did not want to advertise my opponent.

* * *

On Thursday, June 26, at age eighty-eight, Howard Baker died from complications of a stroke.

One week later, with the thermometer outdoors soaring toward ninety degrees, 140 mourners stuffed themselves into wooden pews at the First Presbyterian Church in Huntsville, population 1,238, the hometown that Baker had called "the Center of the Universe."

In the front rows were former Senator Nancy Kassebaum Baker, Vice President Biden, Senate leaders Reid and McConnell, Governor Haslam, Senator Corker, former Vice President Al Gore, and a dozen other former senators and governors.

The pastor told a story about how Baker, as a church elder, had sat through a long session meeting debating the cost of light bulbs.

After the session meeting the pastor had said, "Senator Baker, you're a busy man. You could have written a check for the light bulbs and saved yourself a lot of time."

"I thought it was important that the elders talk it out until we came to a conclusion that most of us were comfortable with," Baker had said, providing an apt metaphor for how the Senate is supposed to work.

I was the only other speaker.

Toward the end of my remarks, I said, "I have added a rule to my *Little Plaid Book*. 'When invited to speak at a funeral, remember to mention the deceased at least as often as yourself.' I have done my best to follow that rule today, but I hope you understand how difficult that is for me, as it would be for many of you.

"So, let me just get it out all at once. For the last half-century, Howard Baker has had more influence on my life than anyone outside my own family. He inspired me to help him build a two-party system. I babysat for Darek and Cissy. I met Honey at a softball game between the Baker staff and the John Tower staff. My favorite photograph of her is one Howard took at the Baker home when we were celebrating our marriage. Our daughter, Leslee, was flower girl at Darek and Karen's wedding. I occupy the same Senate office Howard once had in the Dirksen Senate office building. My desk on the Senate floor once was his."

I spoke for thirteen minutes.

Baker's service, simple and Presbyterian, lasted forty-five minutes. Afterward, Biden rushed up to me.

"I hope you'll give the eulogy at *my* funeral," the vice president said.

"Thank you, but can we wait until after the primary?" I replied, smiling.

* * *

The political cauldron was boiling. With Graham and McConnell renominated, the Tea Party focused its angling on three remaining big fish—Senator Cochran, Senator Roberts, and me.

Baker's governing style was a big part of what the Tea Party didn't like about me.

"[Carr and those opposing Alexander] are running against Baker's legacy—a culture of Republican politics that has married conservative principles with pragmatic attitudes about governing," Dan Balz wrote in the *Washington Post.*[3]

During July, even though "the outside money [had] largely stayed home" as the *Wall Street Journal* observed, the Tea Party and its Washington-based allies did their best to retire me.[4] The political pharisees and media outsiders kept coming. On Saturday, July 26, Fox News talk show host, Laura Ingraham, stormed into Nashville. The Associated Press reported Ingraham's arrival in detail.

"[She caused] 700 or so people in the ballroom [to] cheer and whoop and holler and leap to their feet... Before that, she lays into Alexander for a solid 27 minutes, mocking the senator for a campaign ad last year that touted his Freedom to Fish Act," the AP wrote.[5]

The fisherwoman from Fox News had apparently not heard about how many Tennessee Republicans like to fish below the dams.

On the weekend before the election, tens of thousands of unaccompanied children swarmed across the Southern border, propelling immigration to the top of Gallup's list of concerns. I was finding it hard to be conservative enough, even though I was endorsed by the National Right to Life Committee, had an A-rating from the NRA, and a 100 percent record with the US Chamber of Commerce.

Cochran withstood Tea Party negative advertising to win a July 25 runoff. Roberts won eleven days later. On Thursday, August 7, I won a seven-candidate primary with half the vote.[6]

The pharisee anglers had arrived too late. The last of the big fish had swum away. It was the first time in three election cycles that no Tea Party candidate had knocked off a Republican senator in a primary. In November, I won the general election, 2–1.

Nationally, Obamacare's unpopularity caused what often happens six years into a presidency—the opposition party wins Congress. Republicans would command 247 House and fifty-four Senate seats, the largest Republican majority in eighty-five years. I would become chairman of a policy committee and an appropriations subcommittee, and perhaps could accomplish something. But unlike the Democrat landslide six years earlier, Republicans would not have sixty senators.

Republicans could all jump off the cliff together and still need six Democrats to pass a bill.

And for the bill to become law, the Democrat president would have to sign it.

CHAPTER 49

A Ride on Air Force One

"Rule 260. Don't draw lines in the sand that you can't defend."

—LAMAR ALEXANDER'S LITTLE PLAID BOOK

Washington, DC, to Knoxville. Friday, January 9, 2015.

I INVITED MYSELF FOR A RIDE with Barack Obama on Air Force One.

The White House had announced over the weekend, "[the president] will travel to Tennessee to discuss new initiatives he will propose to help Americans go to college."[1]

I had waited for the invitation that usually comes when the president travels to a senator's state. After hearing nothing, I asked a member of my education staff, Hillary Knudsen, to get word to her uncle, White House Chief of Staff Denis McDonough, that I wanted to speak with him.

He called on Monday.

"I would be happy to travel with the president and say that education is an area where we can work together," I said.

When the invitation arrived, I began thinking about what I would say to Obama as we flew to Knoxville—if he gave me the opportunity.

The next morning, when my alarm rang, it was twenty-seven degrees and snowing, so I gave up any idea of a walk on the National Mall. The news was reporting that Obamacare was unpopular, the Tea Party pot was boiling, and the president's approval rating was dropping. To complicate

Obama's life even more, today the Senate would swear in twelve new Republicans, flipping the majority from 53–45 Democrat to 54–44 Republican. I would be sworn in for my third term.

More than that, after twelve years, I would chair the Senate Committee on Health, Education, Labor and Pensions and the Senate Appropriations Subcommittee on Energy and Water Development. I could create subcommittees, set budgets, allocate staff, and preside over and decide the subject of hearings and what witnesses to call. I could set the agenda on education and health—the two issues I cared the most about—and on the intersection of energy and environment concerns, the most interesting issues I dealt with.

I drove to the Dirksen Senate Office Building and parked in the same garage where I had parked forty-eight years earlier when I had been on Howard Baker's staff. At 7:30 a.m., I walked to the Capitol and escorted to the Senate floor my newly enlarged, seventy-one member staff. I told the staff that I expected them to be very good at what they did, which was the only way I could be good, but to remember that *they* had not been elected to anything.

CNN reported that morning, "A new Republican-led Congress means ... there actually may be a change in education policy coming. Lamar Alexander says his top priority is reforming 'No Child Left Behind,' the deeply unpopular federal education law which is long overdue for reauthorization."

The 2001 act imposing mandates on schools had become so unworkable that *Newsweek* called it "a law everyone wants to fix."[2] President George W. Bush was its architect. The law mandated tests, defined progress, and prescribed penalties for fifty million children and 3.4 million teachers in 100,000 public schools.

By the time Obama was elected, almost every school was labeled a "failing school" for not reaching Washington, DC's ambitious goals. Obama's education department issued waivers of the requirements, but with a catch—to obtain the waivers, many schools believed they had to adopt the Common Core curriculum and methods for evaluating teachers that the department had been promoting. This spectacle of schools playing "Mother, may I" with the Department of Education created a "national school board," as I called it, sent black helicopters flying among conservatives, enraged governors, and provoked teachers' unions.

If I had been a senator in 2001, I would have voted against "No Child Left Behind" because it was too much federal control. *Bush had been an impressive education governor of Texas, but then he tried to be the education governor of the United States,* I thought. I felt just as strongly about Tennessee reforms—paying teachers more for teaching well and more school choice—as he did about Texas reforms. But I had refused to dictate those policies from Washington, DC, when I was his father's education secretary.

My second priority was to streamline regulations on 6,000 colleges and universities, starting with the dreaded Free Application for Federal Student Aid (FAFSA), the 108-question application form. Its complexity was an obstacle to college for twenty million low-income students. Third would be the "21st Century Cures Act," a bill to move medical miracles more rapidly through the federal regulatory process. This would affect nearly every American.

Turning these priorities into law meant working with Obama and, until then, the president had not accomplished much working with Republicans.

I told NPR, "Six years earlier, Barack Obama arrived in a big wave, and the thing to watch when you win big is overreach, which is exactly what he did. They passed Obamacare with no Republican votes and, ever since, the Senate has been tied up in knots arguing whether to repeal and replace it."

Still, I believed there was hope.

"[Now] the important thing for him to remember is that the two years he's got left could be the most productive two years he has in terms of achieving a lasting consensus on things that make a difference," I added.

That was why I invited myself to fly to Knoxville on Air Force One. A ride with the president might provide an opportunity to discuss two bills that Obama later would call "Christmas Miracles" and that Republican Majority Leader McConnell would say were "the most important pieces of legislation in the 114th Congress."

* * *

Friday morning, January 9, was a sunny but frigid twenty-one degrees.

I arrived at Andrews Air Force base outside Washington, DC, at 9:30 a.m. Military personnel escorted me to the massive blue-and-white

Boeing 747 with the United States of America and the presidential seal emblazoned on its side. Because of recent back surgery, I asked an officer to carry my bag up the steps to the aircraft, which is three stories tall and three-fourths as long as a football field.

Upon entering the plane, I turned right and walked toward the back, passing the president's suite on my left, which included the "flying Oval Office," a bathroom with a shower—and a conference room. I walked on past the domestic policy adviser to the section where members of Congress sit.

On its three levels, the plane can accommodate seventy-six passengers plus a crew of twenty-six. There are six bathrooms, and two kitchens that can serve up to one hundred passengers. It has a medical suite that can serve as an operating room. Since it can be refueled in midair, Air Force One can carry the president anywhere in the world.

Senator Corker and Congressman Jimmy Duncan soon joined me. At 10:45 a.m., Air Force One lumbered into the air. Stewards offered waffles, chicken tenders, and fruit. We helped ourselves to souvenir packets of M&M candy boxes and packets of matches imprinted with "Air Force One."

About fifteen minutes into the flight, Obama, without his suit jacket, walked alone back to our compartment and sat across from us. We talked for twenty minutes. Corker, the new chairman of the Committee on Foreign Relations, discussed Iran and Syria with the president. They arranged a White House meeting to discuss sanctions on Iran.

Obama turned the conversation toward "No Child Left Behind," expressing frustration that he "got no credit for taking on traditional Democrat allies," such as the teachers' unions and on issues such as charter schools. I told him that, while I knew that his education secretary wanted Congress to move on higher education, I intended to first fix "No Child Left Behind," working with Washington state Democrat Senator Patty Murray, to produce a bipartisan bill.

"This won't be easy," I said. "It's a swamp with one hundred alligators lurking. Everyone's an expert. It is like being in a football stadium with one hundred thousand fans who know exactly which play to call—and who usually say so. We've been trying for six years and have failed. A Democrat senator told me our chances are less than five to one. Your education secretary says less than ten to one."

I went on.

"Mr. President, I have one request—that while we're working on the bill, you not issue statements drawing lines in the sand. That would sink the bill. You and I have differences over how much federal control should be returned to states, but I won't bring you a bill that you can't sign," I promised.

In turn, Obama promised not to threaten vetoes. That gave me what I needed to work on what would become the first "Christmas Miracle," a law the president would sign eleven months later.

As the president rose to return to his suite, I pulled the multi-page FAFSA application form out of my briefcase. He said he had filled it out himself. We agreed that, working together, we should be able to simplify it, as well as reauthorize the entire higher education law.

"I'll turn to higher education as soon as I get 'No Child Left Behind' out of Committee," I said.

* * *

We landed in Knoxville just before noon. The president motioned for Corker and me to descend the steps.

"You have just been reelected, so you can go first," Obama said to me, laughing.

The president understood that he had arrived in alien political territory, and that it would not be popular for a Republican to appear with him. I waved at the media and walked cautiously down the steep steps, grasping the railing. Obama then bounded down the steps, demonstrating how much more agile a fifty-three-year-old president is than a seventy-five-year-old senator with a bad back.

Cargo planes carrying the president's limousine, security vehicles, and other services had arrived earlier. So had Air Force Two, carrying the vice president and Mrs. Biden. The Bidens were the first to greet Obama at the bottom of the steps. That, by protocol, was incorrect. The home state governor outranks everyone except the current president, but today, Governor and Mrs. Bill Haslam stood second in the greeters' line. Later, when

I told Haslam he should have been first, he joked about it. The governor's consolation prize that day was to ride in the presidential limousine.

The president spoke to an enthusiastic audience that been waiting for an hour.

"Tennessee is...doing some really smart stuff," he said, praising Haslam for making Tennessee the first state to provide two years of free community college tuition.

Obama then offered his own plan for other states to do the same thing, but with more federal involvement and at a greater cost than the Tennessee model. He also gave a shout-out to my ten-year quest to simplify the FAFSA. Haslam had told him that the application form's complexity had become the major obstacle preventing students from taking advantage of the state's free tuition program.

"Let's get that done this year," Obama said. (It took five more years, and then the Biden administration bungled its implementation for four more.)

After the president's speech, White House stewards served a lunch of fish and vegetables in a heavily guarded airport room. Obama sat at one end of the dining table with Corker and me on either side of him. The governor was at the other end. Mrs. Haslam and the Bidens sat along the sides.

"Mr. President, you'll be a young man when you leave office," Corker asked. "What will you do with the rest of your life?"

"I'm not sure. I'll be fifty-nine. Twenty good years left. I'll have options. What attracts me most is working with and inspiring young people," Obama said.

Then, the president turned to the vice president.

"Joe here. He'll be seventy-eight. He'll be through," Obama said.

We all laughed. I changed the subject.

"I hope to enact '21st Century Cures.' Medical miracles are stuck for years in the regulatory process while patients are dying. We should fix that," I said.

Obama said, "My doctor was talking the other day about precision medicine. I've formed a group to take a look. What can we do about it?"

"We'll make precision medicine a part of '21st Century Cures.' We'll work together and do something really big," I said.

We then talked about developing medicines that allow individualized treatments for patients. I told him that Bill Frist and the Bipartisan Policy Center were helping, and he liked that.

That conversation gave me what I needed to maintain White House interest in "21st Century Cures." That and fixing "No Child Left Behind" would consume my attention for the remainder of Obama's term.

* * *

During his visit, Obama was engaged, relaxed, and confident—and bipartisan in his approach. During the first years of his presidency, Obama had not accomplished much working with Republicans. One reason was his ideology, such as sailing off in his Knoxville speech with a huge federal program for free college tuition rather than using the Tennessee model to help states do it at a lower cost. Second, he and his staff had seemed clumsy at making a deal.

On the other hand, I had seen the president "reason together" in the Oval Office two years earlier with a bipartisan group of senators, producing a law saving students billions in interest payments on loans. It would not have happened without his involvement.

Perhaps it could happen again with "No Child Left Behind" and "21st Century Cures."

CHAPTER 50

The Lady Might Be Right

"Rule 164. Remember that those closest to the problem usually can figure out the best way to solve the problem."

—LAMAR ALEXANDER'S LITTLE PLAID BOOK

Washington, DC. January–March 2015.

MY PLAN TO FIX "NO CHILD LEFT BEHIND" careened into a ditch within a week after I announced it.

On Tuesday, January 13, 2015, in a floor speech, I told senators what I had told the president on Air Force One.

"Fixing 'No Child Left Behind' will be first on the agenda for the education committee," I said.

Then, I distributed a "Chairman's Mark," or staff discussion draft, as a place to start. It proposed returning to the states decisions about schools that Presidents Clinton, George W. Bush, and Obama had transferred to Washington, DC.

"We've had a trend toward a national school board, and we need to reverse that trend," I said.

Our committee would conduct hearings on my draft and allow amendments. The bill would then go to the floor, where there would be more amendments, the Senate would debate and pass the amended bill, combine our efforts with the House in a conference, and send to the president bipartisan legislation he could sign. *That would be the obvious way to create a bipartisan bill,* I thought.

"Not so fast," said Senator Patty Murray, the committee's top Democrat. "We'll write a bill together, or we won't do it at all."

Washington state's senior senator was not to be taken lightly. The last legislator who did that was a male legislator in her home state.

"You're just a mom in tennis shoes," the legislator had told Murray, a kindergarten teacher, when she lobbied for preschool education. She ran against him, defeated him, later won the 1992 US Senate race, and was now the top Democrat on both the education policy and funding committees. To remind those who might underestimate her, she displayed a ceramic tennis shoe in her office. Because it took sixty votes to overcome a filibuster on the Senate floor, Murray could block any bill that I passed out of committee.

Murray was dead wrong, I believed, and I told my staff why.

"It's the chairman's prerogative to draft a bill and then allow the minority to amend it. That's the way to do a bipartisan bill," I said. "Our committee has spent six years and held twenty-four hearings to fix this law. Six more weeks should be plenty of time to finish the job. Democrats are just unhappy in the minority and want to make it hard for Republicans to govern."

Then, I thought about Howard Baker's admonition.

"Keep in mind that the other fellow (in this case, a lady) might be right," he always said.

On February 6, Murray and I announced that we would write a bill together.

I told the media, "I listened to her. I took her advice, and it was good advice. If you don't get a consensus, you don't get a result."

Murray also understood that sometimes the other *fellow* might be right. She had negotiated with Republican House Budget Committee Chairman Paul Ryan the funding agreement under which Congress was operating.

"On any piece of legislation I've ever worked on, if you walk in and say, 'These are my words, and not one of them is going to change,' then you're in the wrong business," she said. Taking Murray's advice was step one.

Step two was framing the issue. For this, I relied on former Democrat Representative George Miller's suggestion.

"Pass a lean bill. Fix the eight or nine problems with the law," Miller had said.

That made sense. Replacing the entire education act sounded too much like "repeal and replace Obamacare." That would create legislative indigestion and never succeed.

My third step was to build consensus by posing this question at the committee's first hearing: "Should we keep the federal requirement that students take seventeen standardized tests over twelve years, or let states decide?"

My preference had always been to send decisions about schools—including about the seventeen tests—back to the states. As governor, I had asked President Reagan to take over Medicaid in exchange for states taking responsibility for schools. In 1992, as secretary of education, I had urged President Bush to veto Democrat legislation creating a "national school board."

On January 25, *Time* reported that I was offering to keep the seventeen-test requirement in exchange for returning decisions about *what to do* about the test results to the states.[1]

Margaret Spellings, President George W. Bush's education secretary, came by my office to say that that she and other architects of "No Child Left Behind" regarded requiring the seventeen tests as the "Holy Grail."

"That's the whole point of the law," she argued. "If you don't test to high standards, how will you know whether students are learning? And if you don't break out the results in subgroups, how will you know whether you are leaving behind the Black kids, the Hispanic kids, or some other group? The states won't do it unless you make them do it," Spellings said.

Obama, civil rights and business groups, House Education Committee Chairman Bobby Scott (a Democrat from Virginia), and many education advocates felt the same way. On the other hand, governors and teachers were leading the national backlash against too much federal control—including the seventeen-test requirement. They believed classroom teachers knew best.

In a Valentine's weekend address on "No Child Left Behind," Obama did what he had promised to do on Air Force One—he drew no lines in the sand. Ten days later, I spent an hour with Murray. We came close to agreement, working as engineers instead of idealogues. I wanted to be able to tell Senator McConnell that he could put a bipartisan bill on the floor before March. We would be the only committee actually functioning toward a result.

While not much legislation was moving, there was plenty going on. For example, Senator Cotton had written an open letter to the leaders of Iran, reminding them that Obama's term would expire in two years and that senators who opposed any agreement the president might make on nuclear weapons would be around for longer. I overrode my staff's recommendation, and turned down three requests to sign the letter. It undermined the president's constitutional role in foreign affairs, even if I didn't agree with this president.

At least my refusal made one important person happy. On Tuesday morning, when the media was filled with criticism of the forty-seven Republicans who had signed the letter, I received this email from Honey, who rarely instructed me on public policy.

"Did you vote for that stupid letter to Iran?" she wrote.

* * *

As we approached the bill's mid-April committee markup, our efforts nearly ran off the tracks again.

This time, it was because of my objection to Murray's passion for a big federal preschool program.

"Expanding early education is the states' job," I said to Murray.

"From the start, he told me 'no way.' And I brought it up every minute. Every time. Every day," an unhappy Murray said.

A Republican staff member said, "I remember looking out the window and thinking, 'This is where the bill dies.'"

In early March, Murray and I attended a US Supreme Court argument on Obamacare. Afterward, we walked together to her Capitol office. I asked her to work with Senator Johnny Isakson of Georgia, who also shared Murray's passion for early education and had a warm relationship with Murray.

"If you two can work something out, I'll accept it," I said.

They hammered out an agreement on grant programs allowing states to expand preschool education. It was less than Murray wanted.

"Well, it's something," she said. "Johnny's involvement enabled Lamar to not own it, but to allow it, in a bipartisan way."

"We are making significant progress," Murray and I announced on Monday, March 9, prompting an invitation to visit the president.

We met in the Oval Office on Tuesday, March 24, where Obama outlined three provisions that he wanted in the bill. First, he said to keep the seventeen-test requirement. Second, add an early education program. *Both of those I can do,* I thought. His third request was harder from a federalism point of view. He wanted states to identify the bottom-performing 5 percent of schools, and be forced to take certain actions to improve them.

"I don't have the committee votes for your third request, but I'll put it in during our conference with the House, or I'll not bring you the bill," I told the president. "I promised you on Air Force One that I would only bring you a bill that you can sign."

Actually, I was glad to save something that Obama could claim credit for after the final Senate-House conference negotiations. I left the meeting more optimistic than I had been since the first time the president and I had met on "No Child Left Behind" five years earlier.

On Tuesday, April 7, I agreed to keep the seventeen tests. That made the president and all those who wanted the "Holy Grail" happy. Murray and I released our proposed legislation.

"We have found remarkable consensus about the urgent need to fix this broken law, and also on how to fix it," we said.

Our agreement proposed "fixing" the law by keeping the seventeen tests, disaggregating and reporting the results, but restoring to states and teachers the decision about *what to do* with the results. We would end the federal Common Core mandate and definition of teacher quality. We would restrict the secretary of education's authority to grant waivers of mandates on states in exchange for new mandates. This had been the secretary's tactic for creating, in effect, a "national school board." For Murray, the agreement authorized childhood planning grants.

"[It] would represent the largest devolution of federal control to states in a quarter-century," said a *Wall Street Journal* editorial.[2]

Still, alligators lurked.

Education experts said it would be two more years before we succeeded—if we succeeded. Unusual alliances were pushing for and against the Alexander-Murray bill. Republicans raised their eyebrows when they saw me at lunch in the senators' dining room with Randi Weingarten, president of the American Federation of Teachers (AFT), and then with Lily Eskelsen García, president of the National Education Association (NEA).

I had learned the hard way not to underestimate the influence of the teachers' unions. In 1983, the NEA had labeled me its Public Enemy Number One for pushing through Tennessee's merit pay plan for teachers. Now, I was inviting the union leaders to lunch because their members were tired of a "national school board."

So were governors, who, as a group, endorsed a proposed federal law for the first time in twenty years. The unions helped keep Democrat senators in line, while governors helped corral Republicans. On the other hand, a coalition of forty civil rights, human rights, and business groups lobbied for more federal control, as did the education secretaries of Obama and George W. Bush.

As chairman, I was acting more like an executive than a legislator, leading in the way I did as governor—One, *set a goal* (fix "No Child Left Behind"); Two, *develop a strategy to reach that goal* (keep the seventeen tests in exchange for sending most school decisions back to states); and Three, *persuade at least half the people that I was right* (endlessly repeating that goal and strategy until the consensus sunk in).

* * *

At the same time Senator Murray and I were making progress, turmoil within the Democratic leadership threatened my alliance with Murray.

While exercising during the Christmas recess, the majority leader, Senator Harry Reid, had fallen at home in Nevada, hitting his head on the kitchen cabinet. This led to the loss of the sight in his right eye. On Saturday, March 27, Reid announced that he would retire at the end of the next year.

Two days earlier, Reid had told Senator Schumer, the Number Two Democrat, about his retirement. Tipping off Schumer was a signal of Reid's choice. Schumer's opponent was Illinois Senator Richard Durbin, the Number Three Democrat. The two were Washington, DC, roommates, but as their rivalry intensified, they found separate living quarters.

"You know, I can't leave the boys alone," Murray, the Number Four leader, told me when she arrived late because of a long leadership meeting including Schumer and Durbin.

Since it was hard to imagine Durbin playing second fiddle when Schumer was leader, (although that is what eventually happened), Murray had become the wild card in the competition for the Number Two position. Her candidacy would create problems for me. Democrats competing for leadership kowtow to colleagues on the left—and our committee had a murderer's row of far-left members, including Vermont's Bernie Sanders and Massachusetts's Elizabeth Warren. If Murray were to move left, it would be harder to produce agreements that Republicans could support.

Schumer told me he'd secured votes from all but two caucus members within one day after Reid's announcement. It would have been hard for them to say "no." The Democrat leader has the power to appoint chairmen and members of committees, which is more authority than Republicans give our leader.

"I would like to help you strengthen the Senate," I told Schumer.

"I'm counting on that," he replied.

Reid and Schumer were close, but different.

"I made Schumer," Reid told me. "We're a good combination. He is strategic. I'm impulsive. He is very smart. Eight hundred on the SAT."

Reid, seventy-five, was wily, modest of manner and slight of build, which was more apparent when he received visitors while crouching in an oversized chair in the Democrat leader's cavernous Capitol office. He spoke in a rambling way and often at great length, in a voice so soft that it was hard to hear. He described his boyhood in Searchlight, Nevada, as a "town of four hundred and forty-five miners, ranchers, and prostitutes." He was a pro-life Mormon in a caucus of pro-choice senators.

Reid was mercurial, but we got along. Before bringing a bill to the floor, I would call on him in the Capitol. Typically, we would visit for twenty minutes or so, with Reid doing most of the talking, usually about matters other than my bill. Those visits always seemed to make passing the bill easier, and there were one hundred ways he could have made it harder—as he often did with other Republican proposals.

Schumer, sixty-four, was not only smart, he worked incessantly. Using his outdated flip phone, of which he had a dozen in reserve, he seemed to talk with every caucus member every day.

His weakness was political mischievousness.

He had a second handicap.

"Schumer doesn't like to tell people 'no,'" Reid said, although telling people "no" is what the leader spends most of his day doing.

Schumer seemed to agree with the state legislator who told him, "Being leader is like having twenty-five unpleasant conversations every day."

Schumer and I had developed an easy relationship. We would see each other in the gym at 7:00 a.m., sometimes swapping scheduling and legislative information. When each of us led the Rules committee, I arranged for him to have a prized room in the Capitol and he arranged for me to speak at the 2012 presidential inauguration. Occasionally, we carried messages between Reid and McConnell when they were at loggerheads.

I had urged both Schumer and McConnell to work together better than Reid and McConnell had. When leaders don't work well together, it is harder for other senators to cooperate. I had seen leaders cooperate—in the 1960s with Mansfield and Dirksen, in the 1970s and '80s with Byrd and Baker, and in the 1990s with Daschle and Lott.

"Baker had more moderates then, didn't he?" Schumer said, and he began to list them. "I see only four today and twelve traditional Republicans—you are one of them—and the rest are on the right."

"I'm a Lincoln Republican," I said.

"It's the same thing," he said.

Schumer and his wife, Iris, spent a weekend with Colorado Senator Michael Bennet and his wife, Susan, at our Smoky Mountain home. Dwight McCarter, the park ranger who took us hiking, called Schumer a "sweetheart."

It was surely the only time I'd ever heard that description applied to the hard-charging senator from Brooklyn.

CHAPTER 51

A Christmas Miracle

"So I was telling Lamar we should do this more often. . . .
[this is] a true bipartisan effort."

—**BARACK OBAMA, Thursday, December 10, 2015**

"It's a good result."

—**GEORGE W. BUSH, Monday, December 14, 2015**

"Sometimes you have to rise above principle
and do the right thing."

—**NASHVILLE TAXI DRIVER**

Washington, DC. April to December 2015.

By the time the Senate returned from its Easter recess, I had missed the spring display of cherry blossoms.

On Tuesday, April 14, our committee began a three-day markup of the Alexander-Murray bill fixing "No Child Left Behind." Senators had filed eighty-eight amendments, some so controversial that if the committee were to approve them, some senator would filibuster the bill and keep it from coming to the floor. There were amendments on sanctuary cities, on allowing states to opt out of the seventeen federally required tests, and on a fight over state funding formulas.

"Please exercise restraint in search of a result," I asked committee members.

After that plea, they withdrew twenty-one amendments, based upon my guarantee that each would receive a floor vote. As an example, Senator Scott and I withheld our school choice amendments. Senator Franken withheld his amendment to extend anti-discrimination laws.

The committee considered fifty-eight amendments and adopted nineteen.

On the third day, April 16, something dramatic and unexpected happened. Every one of the twenty-two committee members—from Elizabeth Warren to Rand Paul—voted to send the amended bill to the floor. After the vote, Maryland Democrat Senator Mikulski, a diminutive former social worker known for ferocity during debates, lauded the committee's "tone, tenor, and process" and my decision to write the bill with Murray.

"Had you thrown down the gauntlet, we would have just been fighting," Mikulski said.

Two weeks later, on Tuesday, April 28, Rhode Island Democrat Senator Sheldon Whitehouse walked up to me on the Senate floor.

"I ratted you out today," he said. "I told the state Chamber of Commerce that you had tears in your eyes when the vote on the education bill occurred, and that you were barely able to announce it. I told them it was refreshing to see a senator overcome with emotion by a unanimous vote and success, instead of putting a stake through another senator's heart. And the room erupted in applause."

That same day, Murray and I agreed to canvass committee members so that we could assure McConnell that we needed only one week to complete the bill on the floor.

"Floor time is the coin of the realm," McConnell had reminded us. The majority leader's only real power is to be recognized first when he rises to address the Senate, making him the only senator who can bring a bill to the floor. Senators consume weeks on "must pass" bills, such as those on national defense and appropriations. During the remaining few days, one unhappy senator can slow progress to a crawl. That is what makes floor time so precious.

On Thursday, June 25, before the bill came to the floor, I paid a courtesy call on the Democrat leader, Senator Reid. He suggested combining as many amendments as possible into a single manager's amendment, so they could be approved in a single vote.

On July 8, the House passed the "Student Success Act" by five votes. A week later, McConnell put the Alexander-Murray version of the education bill on the Senate floor, saying, "I'm doing this because the bill is bipartisan and I have confidence that it is good for the country, and that it is going to succeed."

Murray and I secured the consent of all one hundred senators to debate a long list of amendments, a practice that had not succeeded often since the 1980s. Senators who had withheld controversial amendments in committee got their floor votes. Each night, my staff and Murray's ate Shake Shack burgers or pizza together while processing hundreds of amendments, putting as many as possible into the bill to bolster support. We made sure that Democrats had at least as many as Republicans. As Reid had suggested, we saved many amendments for a manager's package.

"I've been here for four-and-a-half years, and this is the first time I understand how the Senate actually can work," Wisconsin Senator Ron Johnson told me as he watched the amendment process.

Just before Wednesday lunch, the floor was filled with senators waiting to vote to cut off debate and proceed to a final vote. After Senator Murray made her two-minute closing speech, I made mine:

> Mr. President, Senator Murray suggested that we work on this in a bipartisan way. I took her advice, and this is the result. We have had nearly one hundred amendments in committee and on the floor.... This is a law that everybody wants fixed. We have a consensus on how to fix it. Keep the measurements of academic achievement and turn the rest of it over to the states, the classroom teachers and others that are closest to the children....
>
> We reverse the trend toward the national school board. We end the Common Core mandate. We end the waivers with new mandates that the Department of Education is using to run public schools. We end DC evaluating teachers and [defining] adequate yearly progress....
>
> This gives us about eighty percent of what we want. A president named Reagan used to say, 'If you got eighty percent of what you wanted, you might take it and fight for the rest on another day.'... If you vote 'No,' we fix nothing.... Vote 'Yes' for local control of public schools.[1]

The next day, Thursday, July 16, by the lopsided tally of 81–17, senators cast the final vote for the amended bill.

"It's not brain surgery," I told the media. "It's basic human relations, listening to other people, accepting their ideas, and asking them to help you work toward a result."

At 3:00 p.m., I drove to Dulles International Airport. When I boarded the United Airlines flight to Knoxville, I found someone in my seat. I realized that I should have boarded a flight to *Nashville*. By then, United's Nashville flight had left. I apologized to the flight attendant, took an eighty-dollar taxi to Ronald Reagan Washington National Airport, and boarded a 7:40 p.m. American Airlines flight to Nashville. I must have been more affected by the week's events than I had suspected.

The next week, Murray and I exchanged bottles of wine and made an appointment to get back to work. There still were differences to work out with the House. And Obama's education secretary had told *Politico* he would "recommend veto of a mediocre bill."

* * *

Suddenly, on Friday, September 25, in a shock to our efforts, John Boehner resigned as House Speaker, the victim of turmoil on the right. In 2001, he had helped write "No Child Left Behind," and was supporting Education Chairman John Kline's work to fix it.

Since August, Senate and House conferees had been arguing over differences in their bills. On Thursday morning, October 22, Murray, Kline, Scott, and I set a goal to complete work in two weeks, and to give the new Speaker the opportunity to do something important.

That afternoon, Bill Gates came to my office. Common Core academic standards and teacher evaluations were the objects of much of his financial support. The last time we had visited, he did not seem to understand that Obama's Common Core push had aroused conspiracy theorists and turned Common Core into dirty words. Now, Gates had come to realize that such Washington, DC, mandates were counterproductive. Future battles would have to be waged in states.

"I believe we've won, but I guess I'm not supposed to say it out loud," Gates joked.

Four days later, on October 26, Republicans elected Paul Ryan to replace Boehner. The following Tuesday, Ryan visited the Senate Republican lunch.

"I want to do some old-fashioned legislating that produces results," he told senators.

I sat next to the new Speaker.

"John Kline and I have a result for you," I told him.

The Senate is like a giant steam locomotive—hard to start, but once it builds up speed, it's hard to stop. On Thursday, November 19, Senate and House conferees resolved their differences, 39–1, and reported their compromise.

"This shows what we can do when both parties work together," the new Speaker said.

On Wednesday, December 2, the House passed the conference agreement. One week later, on December 9, the Senate approved, 82–12. All "no" votes came from Republicans who wanted even less federal control.

Such a big vote for a contentious issue seems counterintuitive, but it is common. After "talking their heads off" and offering hundreds of amendments, senators often find a consensus that most can vote for and that most constituents will accept—although the big margin disguises how hard it has been to bring the warring parties into line. Putting together this 601-page bill had been a clinic on how to pass complex legislation in a divided government.

I summed up what had happened.

"This is a big Christmas present from the Senate and the House, and it's going down to the president, and I hope he wraps a big red ribbon around it and sends it out to one hundred million students and 3.4 million teachers in 100,000 public schools....[2] Six years ago, we passed a health care bill, and we're still arguing about it. Governors and teachers and communities can start implementing this bill to help children as soon as the president signs it. That's the way to govern a great big, complicated country like ours," I said.

* * *

The signing ceremony was held in the Eisenhower Executive Office Building auditorium because so many wanted to attend. When we walked on stage, the president hugged Patty Murray and spread credit around the room.

"A Christmas Miracle... So I was telling Lamar we should do this more often.... [this is] a true bipartisan effort, a reminder of what can be done when people enter into these issues in a spirit of listening and compromise," he said.[3]

President Obama signed this "Christmas Miracle" almost exactly twenty-five years after President George H.W. Bush nominated me to be secretary of education. Back then, we were encouraging—but not mandating—states and communities to create higher standards, better tests, and teacher evaluation systems. Now, twenty-five years later, we were unshackling states and school boards from federal mandates so they could design their own standards, tests, and evaluation systems.

Accolades spewed forth from unlikely sources.

"A new day in public education," said the AFT president. Later, the NEA gave its annual *Friend of Education Award* to Murray and me. Education Week noted the irony, calling me "the NEA's Best Frenemy."[4]

Jennifer Rubin wrote in the *Washington Post,* "It was telling that Alexander, regarded by the right-wing as some sort of squishy RINO, was responsible for the right's biggest victory in years."[5]

Newt Gingrich said on Fox News, "The biggest conservative education bill in at least twenty years."

Neither Murray nor I ever said privately or publicly, "I won."

* * *

The next Monday, December 14, I was working in my Nashville office when George W. Bush called at 11:00 a.m., precisely the time his assistant had promised. He was punctual, as was his father. Once, when I was a few minutes late for a Cabinet meeting, the first President Bush had looked up.

"Thanks for coming," he said.

After that, I arrived early.

George W. and I talked for fifteen minutes.

"I'm calling for two reasons. One, to congratulate you for your leadership on education. Second, to wish you a Merry Christmas," he said.

"We kept the best parts of what you did in 2001," I said. "And if Congress had done its job in 2007, there would not have been as much to fix."

"It's a good result," Bush replied.

CHAPTER 52

Barricade on the Train Track

"Rule 242. Don't waste time trying to make the pony express run faster or chasing trains that have already left the station."

—LAMAR ALEXANDER'S LITTLE PLAID BOOK

Washington, DC. November 2006–December 2007.

I KNEW RIGHT AWAY THAT "21st Century Cures" would help more people than any law I would ever work on, but that it was more complicated and would take twice as long as fixing "No Child Left Behind."

The "Cures bill," as I referred to it, was the second priority I had discussed with President Obama on Air Force One. I had seen medical miracles become stuck in regulations, cost so much, and take so long that patients died before treatments and cures arrived. I was now in a position to help change this.

At first, our bill was focused on speeding up the approval of tests, vaccines, and cures. Eventually, it included precision medicine and stem cell research, a "Cancer Moonshot," the opioid crisis, an overhaul of mental health agencies plus the "BRAIN Initiative" (Brain Research through Advancing Innovative Neurotechnologies®), and dozens of amendments to reduce health care costs.

The president had wasted no time following up our lunch conversation in Knoxville. Later that month, at a White House event, he proposed a $215 million project "to deliver the right treatments at the right time—every time—to the right person."

"This has bipartisan support," Obama said when he noticed me in the audience.

Early the next month, I had a lunch of clam chowder and grilled cheese sandwiches in the Senate dining room with the only senator who could bring the "Cures bill" to the floor.

"I'm looking for legislation that Democrats will not filibuster," Senator McConnell, the new majority leader, said.

The Senate was creeping along as Democrats, miserable in the minority, made it hard for Republicans to govern. My partnership with Murray on fixing "No Child Left Behind" was just about the only promising legislation. "Repeal and replace Obamacare" fireworks were still exploding, and most senators—including Murray—were unwilling to work on another major bipartisan health care law.

Murray did agree to less ambitious hearings on "biomedical innovations." The scientist Francis Collins testified on Tuesday, March 10, at the first hearing. He was director of the National Institutes of Health (NIH)—he called it the "National Institutes of Hope." Collins predicted the coming of "medical miracles," including an artificial pancreas for diabetes, nonaddictive pain medicines, a heart built from a patient's own cells, early detection or even prevention of Alzheimer's, and vaccines for HIV/AIDS, universal flu, and Zika.

In July, the House passed its "21st Century Cures Act." Trying to catch up, Murray and I agreed to complete our work on biomedical innovation by Thanksgiving.

We missed our deadline.

One reason we failed was that on Wednesday, October 21, Senator Warren showed up with an outlandish proposal that would become the major roadblock to the "Cures bill." She insisted that it include $6-12 billion in new NIH mandatory funding paid for by new taxes.

Warren was ignoring how Senate committees worked. The health committee that Murray and I led—and on which Warren served—sets policy. In other words, it specifies how much money *can* be spent, but lacks the power to spend it. That is the job of the appropriations committee. And it can't impose taxes—the finance committee does that.

The only way our committee could provide money for the National Institutes of Health was mandatory spending, a form of automatic annual spending. This was the reddest of red flags for the Republican budget hawks who now controlled Congress. Mandatory spending—mainly for Social Security, Medicaid, and Medicare—plus interest on the debt—accounted for three-fourths of all federal spending, and was the cause of the budget deficit. Not only was Warren's proposal a red flag, it was unnecessary. Congress was increasing NIH funding at a percentage rate twice that of national defense.

By the end of 2015, there was much hoopla over fixing "No Child Left Behind," but Warren's demand had become a barricade keeping the "21st Century Cures" train from moving down the track.

* * *

As 2016 began, Murray still would not join me in writing a "Cures bill."

Perhaps it was because she had been so busy fixing "No Child Left Behind." Perhaps it was because our staffs were now focused on higher education. Perhaps she did not want to confront Warren and Sanders while there was talk that the caucus might elect Murray whip.

Diligent and sharp-tongued, Warren, sixty-seven, would stride through corridors and onto the Senate floor as if she were late for a meeting. At hearings, she would consume five minutes of question time with a statement as aggressive and disciplined as she would have expected from her Harvard law students, leaving the witness only a few seconds to respond. I ignored her partisan comments at hearings, figuring that if I did not create conflict, she could make no news.

Sanders, seventy-four, could be affable, but he was a loner. During votes, he would wander on and off the Senate floor so quickly that he had little opportunity for the small talk that is the practiced art of mingling senators. Whenever Sanders spoke, his raspy voice was loud on behalf of those whose plight he championed. He had little tolerance for compromise, which made life awkward in a body where success depends upon working out differences.

Sanders and Warren presented both a long- and short-term problem for me. The long-term problem was that, if Murray were to be elected the

Number Two Democrat, she might have to give up her committee leadership. Next in line was Sanders. Once, when reporters asked Sanders if he could work with Republicans, he paused.

"Well, Lamaah. At least he's not a homophobe," he said.

Despite our polite relationship, it was hard to imagine finding much common ground with Sanders.

The short-term problem was that Sanders and Warren's influence was rising. Although he was not a Democrat—he was a Socialist—Sanders was a candidate for the 2016 Democrat presidential nomination. Warren had her eye on a presidential run in four years.

On our committee, Murray had more problems corralling Democrats than I did managing Republicans.

* * *

Finally, I settled on a familiar strategy—to move ahead "step-by step." I proposed creating a Senate "Cures bill" by approving nineteen bipartisan proposals, one at a time, and then attaching them to legislation already passed by the House.

On Tuesday, February 9, 2016, I chaired the first of three sessions to consider proposals ranging from FDA approval of medical devices to cures for rare diseases. Each one had at least one Democrat and one Republican cosponsor. The sessions went smoothly until Wednesday, March 9, when Warren showed up with an even more outlandish proposal for $50 billion in spending and taxes.

Murray and I plotted a response. We persuaded Warren to offer her amendment and then to withdraw it. That would avoid a vote that split the committee. I promised to work with Murray to cut mandatory funding from some other program and use those savings for the National Institutes of Health. I had no idea how to pull this off—but I had to come up with something.

Nevertheless, I confidently pronounced, "The 'Cures' train is moving down the track and it will reach the station. It has the House and the president on board, and soon it will have the Senate." I said this because senators knew that it was easier to attach their bills to legislation already on its way to becoming law. For example, Louisiana Republican Bill Cassidy,

Connecticut Democrat Chris Murphy, and their mental health proposal soon became passengers on the train.

I also wanted the vice president on board. President Obama had announced that "Joe" would lead a "Cancer Moonshot" in honor of his son, Beau, who had died of cancer. I telephoned Biden at 2:00 p.m. on Friday, February 12, after I had pulled over to the side of the road while driving from San Antonio to Cotulla, Texas, for an annual quail shooting trip with our son, Will. I asked the vice president to host a meeting on "Cures" with Murray and relevant House members.

"I want to pass the president's precision medicine initiative and your 'Cancer Moonshot,' but I'll need your help to get it done on our 'Cures bill,'" I said.

I continued.

"The problem is Elizabeth Warren. She says that there will be no 'Cures bill' unless we include fifty billion dollars of new mandatory funding and taxes. I have no way to do that. Even if I did, McConnell would never bring it to the floor."

Then, we had what Biden called a "Joe and Lamar" conversation.

"I have to tell you, there is no appetite in the White House for a clash with Elizabeth Warren. And there is a limit to what I can do. After I made a tax deal with McConnell, there is a joke around here that I am in the witness protection program," Biden said, laughing.

"I believe we can work this out. I think the White House trusts me," I said.

"It probably does you no good, but if there is one Republican the White House trusts, it would be you," he said.

"Where are you?" he asked.

"In Cotulla, Texas, where Lyndon Johnson taught elementary school," I said.

"The last time I was down there was when I went down on the Pedernales to LBJ's funeral. I guess I'm getting old," Biden said.

Will and I drove on to Cotulla to spend the weekend with Steve Smith and his sons, shooting quail and assorted varmints. South Texans celebrate killing a hog, coyote, and an armadillo as a "Texas Triple." Add a badger and it's a home run. The breeze was warm. There were no clouds. Mesquite and cactus created a desolate beauty. Drilling rigs were everywhere, but oil was down to thirty dollars a barrel, and hotels were empty. Ben's Western Wear still had my autographed Stetson on the wall next to George Strait's, but business was way off. As the sun set behind the ranch shack, I made margaritas and Steve made a campfire. We grilled prime beef and told stories until 10:30 p.m., when everyone fell into bed.

The next afternoon, we learned that Supreme Court Justice Antonin Scalia, seventy-nine, had died of a heart attack after an afternoon of shooting quail at a ranch six hours away from us. Senator McConnell had announced that the court vacancy would not be filled during 2016. McConnell's decision enraged Democrats, but it should not have been such a surprise. During presidential election years, senators always slowed down approval of judicial nominations. And, when the president and Senate majority were of different political parties, judicial nominations almost always stopped completely in presidential years. McConnell was doing what Senators Schumer and Biden had publicly said they would have done if George W. Bush had sent up a Supreme Court nominee in 2012, his reelection year.

Nevertheless, McConnell's decision plunged the Senate into more controversy and made it even harder to pass bipartisan legislation.

* * *

When I arrived at the Eisenhower Executive Office Building Auditorium on Thursday, February 25, staff ushered me to a front-row seat to watch the president lead a discussion on precision medicine. I was there to remind him to help with the "Cures bill."

Afterward, Obama invited me to walk with him to the Oval Office.

"If you need my help on the 'Cures bill,' let me know," he said.

After the photographer left, the president and I were alone, and he talked about what he really wanted to talk about—the Supreme Court vacancy.

"At least have a hearing. I am going to nominate a reasonable person," Obama said. "Anyway, I think I'm going to have a Democratic successor. I don't see how you got yourself into this fix," he said with a smile, referring to Donald Trump.

Two weeks later, at 5:00 p.m. on Wednesday, March 16, everyone necessary to make a deal—three House committee leaders, Murray, me, staff, maybe thirty in all—sat around a table in the vice president's office. Biden arrived in genial fashion, as was his custom, began the meeting at 5:05 p.m., and then talked nonstop until 5:30 p.m., saying "finally" three or four times, as was also his custom.

The House already had approved $9.3 billion in NIH mandatory funding, but then had "stolen" the savings that had been set aside to pay for it in order to pay for new spending in other legislation.

I told Biden, "We need your help to find $9.3 billion in savings or the Senate won't approve your moonshot and the president's precision medicine initiative."

At 6:00 p.m., the vice president was still talking. At 6:15 p.m., I stood up, passed out one-page summaries of our proposal, and ended the meeting.

At lunch on Monday, April 4, McConnell was not optimistic.

"I made all your arguments, and my staff still thinks mandatory funding is very hard," he said.

Still, McConnell had become interested in stem cell research and wanted an accomplishment to counter Democrats who were saying, "Do your job." (They were referring to his refusal to consider Obama's Supreme Court nominee.)

We finished our final committee markup on Wednesday, April 6. Eighteen separate biomedical innovation bills, "once bundled together, will form a companion to the House of Representative's mammoth 21st Century Cures bill," *Science* magazine reported.[1]

"I don't have any intention of taking the work product of this committee to the floor without having a bipartisan agreement ... about a surge of funding for the National Institutes of Health," I told the committee. "Without that agreement, we don't get this bill. But without this bill, we don't get mandatory funding either."

I said to myself, *"This is going to take some magic trick that creates mandatory funding that doesn't look like mandatory funding."*

I told Honey, "If I'm able to pull this off, that, by itself, will make serving eighteen years in the Senate worthwhile."

On Friday, April 1, I had described our progress to McConnell.

"It's good to have some good news," he said, which, for McConnell, was a rare burst of enthusiasm.

"Well, things are bound to get better," I said.

"I don't know. You know what McCain says. After the darkness, the black," McConnell cautioned.

"This could have been the start of a fruitful time in a capital barren of major policy accomplishments over the last few years," the *New York Times* said on April 29.[2]

Speaker Ryan was dubious.

"I'd say this is the most ideological president I've ever served with. He's very dogmatic in pursuit of his ideology, and therefore, I don't see a bridging of the gap because of the nature of this presidency," Ryan said.[3]

On May 23, I interviewed McConnell on C-SPAN about his memoir.

Afterward, he asked for a private talk.

"Basically, you've convinced me. I want to get it all done," he said. "Opioids, mental health, 'Cures.' The problem is, how? I've had two conversations with Ryan, and he said 'no' to mandatory spending."

I asked McConnell to set up a meeting with Ryan.

With that conversation, McConnell bought a ticket on the "Cures" train.

So, now I had nineteen bipartisan proposals. The train was about ready to head toward the station—but Elizabeth Warren's $50 billion barricade was still standing.

* * *

At 8:00 a.m., on Friday, May 27, a US Air Force Boeing 737 took off from Andrews Air Force Base, headed for Morocco.

I was leading a congressional fact-finding tour of African countries. The delegation included Democrat and Republican members crucial to bringing down Warren's barricade.[4] In Casablanca on Saturday evening, we drove to Rick's Café, which had been reconstructed to look as much as possible like it did in the movie *Casablanca.* It had a bar, a casino room, and a well-tuned mahogany grand piano.

"May I play one song on the piano?" I asked the owner.

"What would you play?" she asked.

"What would you expect?" I said, smiling.

So, after our meal of John Dory fish, she turned off the World War II music, and I played "As Time Goes By," the song Sam played and sang in the movie.[5]

During the remainder of the tour, and on the flight home to Andrews, delegation members debated mandatory spending.

When we arrived at midnight on Saturday, June 4, Warren's barricade still was blocking the track.

CHAPTER 53

A Second Christmas Miracle

"If you want to feel like the butler, try being vice president."

—**JOE BIDEN, Thursday, September 15, 2016**

"Rule 301. Remember that people will remember the last thing you do."

—***LAMAR ALEXANDER'S LITTLE PLAID BOOK***

Washington, DC. June–December, 2016.

"Last August, I was blind. Now, I can see," Doug Oliver told me.

Doctors had told Oliver, a fifty-four-year-old Nashville medical technician, that they had no cure for his blindness, but suggested that he search the internet for clinical trials of promising treatments. Oliver found one in Florida, where doctors injected stem cells from his hip into his eye. Three days later, his sight was 20/20 in one eye and 20/40 in the other. He regained his driver's license and drove to Washington, DC, to tell me his story.

During our conversation in my Senate office on Tuesday, June 21, 2016, it occurred to me that this treatment might help Harry Reid, now blind in one eye.

Later that day, I visited Reid in his Capitol office.

"I have been working on '21st Century Cures,' and I have run across something that may have a slight chance of helping you," I said.

I told him Oliver's story.

"If there is one half of one percent of a chance, I will reserve an hour for him," Reid said.

And then he stood up and gave me a hug.

"You don't know how much it means to me for you to even think of me like this," he said.

The next morning, Oliver spent an hour with Reid. I asked the staff not to tell anyone, that this was personal.

That same day, Wednesday, June 22, McConnell and I walked to Speaker Ryan's office for the meeting on the "Cures bill" that I had asked McConnell to request. During our discussion, Ryan's aide complained that I was creating mandatory spending. We argued for half an hour.

"This is likely to be the most important bill this year and we should find a way to do it," was the only thing McConnell said.

When the meeting ended, I told Ryan, "Thank you. I know these are hard discussions."

"This is my easiest meeting of the day," he said, laughing. On the House floor, Democrats were sitting in, demanding gun votes, and had even developed a way to filibuster. The Senate looked calm by comparison.

I walked with McConnell back to his office.

"I was feeling sorry for myself when I went over there, but after seeing what is going on in the House, I feel better. If the Speaker wants to do it, he will find a way. And if he doesn't, he won't," McConnell said.

The next day, Ryan announced that the "21st Century Cures Act" would be a part of his "agenda for the future," adding an important passenger to the train.

Doug Oliver had become something of a Capitol Hill sensation. I invited him to attend a Republican senators' luncheon that I hosted each summer. I served a Tennessee meal from Miss Mary Bobo's Boarding House in Lynchburg, including fried okra and chicken pie. Patrick Jaynes had driven from Knoxville with Grainger County tomatoes, and delivered a sack of nine to each senator's office.

"When are the tomatoes coming?" senators would begin asking each June. Some carried them home on weekends, as if there were no tomatoes grown anywhere except in Grainger County, Tennessee.

As Oliver told of regaining his eyesight, senators quit fiddling with their devices and listened.

Two weeks later, Ryan and House Budget Committee Chairman Tom Price approved language for an "NIH Innovation Fund." It was the magic I had hoped for. To satisfy Democrats, it would allow mandatory funding. To satisfy Republicans, it would not look like mandatory funding. To mollify appropriators, it would be for specific projects that Congress had to approve each year. And, to calm down budget hawks, the new spending had to be offset by reducing other spending.

Staff began calling Ryan's solution "fairy dust."

During these discussions, time ran out. It was a presidential election year and Congress had gone home for the August recess. The "Cures bill" was pushed off to September, but now Ryan had produced a way to remove Senator Warren's barricade—*if* I could get the White House to agree on spending reductions to offset the "fairy dust" additions to spending.

When Congress reconvened at the end of August, there were rumblings that Reid did not want to give McConnell more accomplishments, and that Schumer, anxious to lead a majority, did not want to give Republicans running for reelection something to crow about. I needed the president's help, but since May, I had not been able to reach him. I wanted to ask Obama to do what LBJ would have done—go to work *himself* to pass the bill.

On Friday, September 2, I telephoned Chief of Staff McDonough.

"The president told me that if I needed his help to let him know. Well, I need his help. I know he wants this to be part of his legacy, and I am trying to help him because I believe it is good for the country," I said.

"Let me work on it," McDonough said.

After two weeks of not hearing anything, I placed a call to the vice president. At about 12:30 p.m. on Thursday, September 15, I was in McConnell's office when my cell phone rang. It was Biden.

"Joe, '21st Century Cures' is stuck," I said. "I have money for the president's precision medicine, for your 'Cancer Moonshot,' for McConnell's stem cell research, for opioids, and for the 'BRAIN Initiative.' The mental health overhaul is in there. Paul Ryan has turned somersaults to accommodate Elizabeth Warren's spending demands. The House has already passed the bill, and Mitch is ready to put the Senate bill on the floor. I know that if I could explain this to the president, he would agree. All I need is for him to okay the spending we cut from Obamacare, then we can announce it, and pass it after the election."

I well knew that asking the president to cut funds from Obamacare was like asking him to sacrifice one of his children. I went on.

"I feel like the butler standing outside the Oval Office with a silver platter saying, 'Your order is here, sir' and the president won't open the door and take his order," I said.

"If you want to feel like the butler, try being vice president," Biden said, laughing. "Look, I'm a little behind the curve on this. I know that you're trying to help. Let me talk with Denis and the president about it."

Two weeks later, on Wednesday, September 21, Murray told me that she was ready to get a result. Now, she, too, was a passenger on the train. On Wednesday, September 28, the Senate recessed until after the election. McConnell, Ryan, Murray, and I all issued statements supporting "Cures." Nancy Pelosi climbed on board on October 19.

* * *

On Friday, November 4, a chilly autumn morning, I finished breakfast at our mountain cabin with Honey and our weekend guests, Bill and Tracy Frist, and walked to my office to wait for the telephone call I had asked for in May.

The White House operator called at 11:30 a.m. The president came on the line quickly.

"I'm with Bill Frist and we were talking about the '21st Century Cures' legislation," I said.

"He is a good person. Actually, given the way things have gone, it's kind of quaint to think of Bill Frist as Republican majority leader of the Senate," Obama said. "I appreciate that we have been working on trying to get something done on the 'Cures' legislation."

I tried the most persuasive argument I could think of.

"When I was in my last term as governor, my chief of staff told me that 'people will remember the last thing you do.' I never could get that out of my mind," I said.

"Hopefully, I'll have some good last things they can remember," Obama said.

I replied, "I hope one of them would be this—that in December, you can stand there in the White House and announce that, working with Congress, we have made a big step forward in precision medicine, the 'Cancer Moonshot,' the 'BRAIN Initiative,' fighting opioids, and that the last two Congresses, plus the 'Cures bill,' will have put forty-five billion new dollars into medical research."

"After this election, it would be important for the country to show that the place can work. I would like to do that," he said.

"I have a request," I said. "That you help us get an agreement by Monday so Paul Ryan can put the bill on the House floor and Mitch can put it on the Senate floor the week after Thanksgiving."

"I hear you. I appreciate the way you have worked on this. We have worked well together on things. I understand there are some issues in funding and we want to make sure the regenerative medicine section [meaning, the stem cell section] does not allow scams," Obama said.

"I agree, and our proposal takes that into account. The FDA has been difficult to work with," I said.

"The FDA needs updating. Okay, I will tell my team to recognize the importance of the Monday deadline, and to use flexibility in the last negotiations," he said.

I thanked the president and said goodbye, but he stopped me.

"Wait, wait, wait, I have something else," and he began talking about the election on the following Tuesday and his Supreme Court nomination of Merrick Garland.

"The scenario still is that Hillary is likely the next president and the Senate could teeter either way. I am concerned about the effect [that not considering Garland] will have on the Court and our institutional norms. If Hillary wins and there is still a Republican Senate elected, I think it is important to try to figure out how to have a hearing and a vote on Garland. Otherwise, it will lead to a post-inauguration determination not to confirm anybody she nominates for four years," he said. "If there is a Democratic Senate elected, they will apply the nuclear option and change the rules, with great damage to the country."

The president went on.

"Among the institutionalists, you have the most influence with McConnell. It would be hard to get a more conservative nominee by a Democratic president than Garland. My point is, very soon after the election, there is going to be a decision to make. It is important for an independent voice like yours to be heard. A lot is at stake here. We could end with a situation where no one could be appointed to the court unless one party controls both the presidency and the Senate."

I waited to speak until the president had finished.

"I want to be specific so I don't mislead you," I said. "First, I would be glad to have a conversation with Mitch after the election. Second, I don't believe Clinton, if she is president, should nominate justices until she first determines which ones Republicans would support. Third, I would not support a blanket refusal to block her nominees for four years."

Obama had been busy campaigning to elect Clinton, in addition to the responsibilities of his job. He had not, he said, "gotten down into the weeds" on the "Cures bill," as he had done when we worked together on student loans. I tried to turn the conversation back toward "Cures," but he continued to emphasize the Supreme Court.

We talked for a good twenty minutes.

* * *

Democrats were in a foul mood when Congress returned after the November 8 election.

They had expected a sweep and one came, but, for them, in the wrong direction. So, instead of another four years of Warren and Sanders pushing the administration further left, Donald Trump would be president. Republicans would control Congress, and Warren and Sanders would be relegated to disrupting their minority caucus—which they busily started doing. Democrats spent most of the week arguing about whether to pass the "Cures bill."

On Thursday, November 17, Murray came to my office. She had been elevated to Number Three in the Democrat leadership—but would keep the ranking position on our committee.

"You saved me from Bernie Sanders," I said with a smile.

We agreed that that "Cures" was on track for after Thanksgiving.

Schumer still was still on board, he said in a call. Warren was not.

"She is on the warpath, claiming that the bill did not include real money, trying to delay the vote and kill the bill," my staff reported.

The "Cures bill" had been one of the most lobbied bills ever, mobilizing more than 1,400 lobbyists. Hospitals and insurance companies fought disclosure. Safety advocates opposed faster approval of drugs and devices. Big Pharma did not want to pay more taxes. Doctors worried about stem cell quackery. Universities, medical schools, and citizens' groups pushed for research dollars. Advocates descended on senators' offices and contributed to campaigns.

On Tuesday, November 29, I spoke at the Republican policy lunch.

"For those who do not like the 'Cures bill,' I have a story. When Howard Baker was a freshman, he asked Maine's Republican Senator Margaret Chase Smith how she was going to vote on liberal Pennsylvania Democrat Joe Clark's amendment," I said.

"'Why, Howard, I *always* vote against Joe Clark,'" Mrs. Smith said.

"In this case, you can vote for 'Cures' because you will be voting against Elizabeth Warren," I said.

At 4:00 p.m., I walked to Harry Reid's office for my ritual visit before the next week's final vote.

"Does the bill do anything for stem cell trials?" Reid asked.

"Yes," I said.

"I have been staying in touch with Doug Oliver on this," Reid said.

In the gym, on Wednesday morning, November 30, Schumer said, "We'll have the votes."

That day, the House approved a new "Cures bill," incorporating the Senate's changes. It included Ryan's "fairy dust" spending. The vote was overwhelming, 392–26.

On Friday, December 2, as the House bill headed to the Senate, the *Wall Street Journal* observed that Warren "was having difficulty being an obstructionist on the 'Cures bill,' even in her own state."[1]

I telephoned Denis McDonough to thank him.

"I believe you and the president and I are now two for two," I told him.

"Three for three," he said, reminding me of Obama's role in the student loan law.

Biden called senators. Obama pushed the bill in his weekend address. On Monday, both McConnell and Reid supported the bill in leadership floor remarks.

The next week, on the Senate floor, Reid told the story of his visit with Doug Oliver.

"Senator Alexander introduced me to Doug Oliver, who was basically blind and now, because of work done by stem cells, he can see. Perhaps this bill would have passed without the senior senator from Tennessee but I doubt it. He and I have spoken about clinical trials. I'm hopeful that, in my lifetime, there will be something done to take care of retinas that are damaged," Reid said.

The Senate parliamentarian had discussed with Warren the Massachusetts senator's earlier vituperative floor remarks accusing senators who supported the "Cures bill" of "extortion." When Warren spoke again, Senator Sasse was in the chair, prepared to call her down for violating "Rule XIX," which states that "no senator in debate shall, directly or indirectly, by any form of words impute to another Senator or to other Senators any conduct or motive unworthy or unbecoming a Senator."[2]

On Wednesday, December 7, the vice president presided as the Senate voted 94–5 for the "21st Century Cures Act." Once again, the margin was no indication of how hard it had been to persuade passengers to board the "Cures" train, remove Warren's barricade, and move down the track to the station.

Six days later, on Tuesday the 13th, I arrived at the 17th Avenue entrance to the White House. Aides escorted me to the anteroom in the Eisenhower Executive Office Building, where I waited with members of Congress and cancer survivors for the president to sign a second "Christmas Miracle."

Obama arrived at 2:30 p.m., and began shaking hands.

"We're three for three. People remember the last thing you do," I said when he reached me.

"If it had just been you and me these eight years, everything would have been fine," the president said.

We walked together into the packed auditorium. Obama signed the law with several pens and distributed them to those on stage.

What none of us could have imagined that day was how soon the "21st Century Cures Act" would save lives. The next year, 2017, President Trump's FDA commissioner, Scott Gottlieb, interpreted the stem cell language in "Cures" to extend to an entirely new field of genetically engineered cell therapy involving the extraction of immune cells from a patient with cancer, genetically altering those cells to help them recognize and kill cancer cells, and then reinserting them in the patient to *cure the cancer.* Three years later, federal health agencies used "Cures" authority and funding to create tests, vaccines, and treatments to tame COVID-19, the worst pandemic in a century. And by 2025, there were examples of stem cell treatments in clinical trials to cure Type I diabetes and vastly improve Parkinson's disease.

A few weeks after the "Cures bill" became law, Doug Oliver came to my office and handed me his cane, the kind that blind people carry to avoiding bumping into walls or falling down.

"Here. I won't be needing this anymore. I want you to have it," he said.

Summing it up, during the journey of the "Cures bill," the president acted more like the chief legislator than the chief executive whose job it is to point the way, develop a strategy, and persuade half the people that he is right. Perhaps other issues had consumed his executive skills. Perhaps he believed that inserting himself more deeply into negotiations would "run off" Republicans, a concern he expressed to me more than once. Perhaps it was his scholarly temperament, or some combination of these explanations.

Nevertheless, from our conversation on Air Force One to the White House bill signings, Obama's word was good and his participation was indispensable to the results. And the Democrat president's legacy is burnished by enactment in a politically divided government of two "Christmas Miracles" that the Republican majority leader said were the most important laws of the 114th Congress.

PART ELEVEN

Finest Hour or Lack of Spine?

2017 to November 2020

"Elections belong to the people. It's their decision. If they decide to turn their back on the fire and burn their behinds, then they will just have to sit on their blisters."

—ATTRIBUTED TO ABRAHAM LINCOLN

CHAPTER 54

Shifting Gears

"By noon every day Donald Trump has done almost everything my mother said to never do."

—SENATOR ROY BLUNT (R-MO)

Washington, DC. 2017.

FOR EIGHT YEARS, I HAD LEARNED to work with a president with whose liberal views I mostly disagreed.

Now, I had to shift gears to learn to work with a president with whose views I mostly agreed—but with whose behavior and temperament I disagreed.

Donald J. Trump's descent down the Trump Tower escalator into politics was like nothing I had ever seen before—although I should have seen it coming. In 1955, when I was fifteen—about the time our family got its first television—comedians Minnie Pearl and Smiley Burnette rode in Maryville's annual Hillbilly Homecoming parade. They were big stars then. But the parade's biggest attraction was Francis the Talking Mule, who was starring in his own movie and comedy TV show.

Watching that parade, I began to understand the power of television. In 1960, even though Nixon sounded better on the radio, Kennedy won the presidential debate because he looked better on television. In college,

I read Daniel J. Boorstin's observation that television was making people "well-known for their well-knownness."

In 1967, as I arrived in Washington, DC, to work for Senator Baker, Marshall McLuhan was writing that the medium (television) was the message. During the 1980s, I watched Ronald Reagan's poise and appearance on television become a key to his political success. I learned that you are not important unless you are on television—and that, since television basically covers itself, if you want to be invited to be on television, it helps to already be on television.

Everyone seemed to be watching celebrities on some screen—and this was before social media. In 1992, when I was education secretary, I drove Will, then thirteen, to Baltimore to see the Orioles play at Camden Yards. Instead of watch[illegible] players on the field, many in the stands watched the game on a massive screen in center field.

Back in 1999, when I dropped out of the presidential race, I had made a prediction.

"If we're not careful, we'll end up with a race between only the rich and the already famous. I mean, we might have Donald Trump versus the latest Powerball winner, with Cher as an Independent candidate. That's what we could look forward to in 2004," I had said.

I had miscalculated Trump's arrival in politics by about a dozen years.

How Trump arrived was also a surprise. On rally stages, he clapped his hands for himself in the way that television show hosts do to encourage studio audiences to applaud. He disparaged John McCain's five-and-a-half years in a Hanoi prison, and criticized the pope. His inaugural address sounded more like Huey Long than either of the Bushes. He berated the prime minister of America's most reliable ally, Australia, and urged the Senate to "go nuclear" on his Supreme Court nominee. He said he would put tariffs on products made in Mexico.

My first White House lunch with Trump came on Thursday, February 9, 2017, three weeks after he became president. Just after noon, twelve senators—six Democrats and six Republicans—sat at an oval table in the Roosevelt Room. Stewards served salad, steak (the president liked his well-done), and chocolate cake for dessert.

Trump arrived at 12:45 p.m., shook hands all around, said he was "very" glad to see me, and sat at the center of the table across from the vice president. The occasion was to develop support for his Supreme Court nominee, Neil Gorsuch. Former New Hampshire Senator Kelly Ayotte was there because she was helping with the nomination.

The president's remarks quickly veered off topic. While the media still was in the room, he chided Ayotte, who, three months earlier, had lost her Senate seat by 600 votes, for failing to endorse him—although he lost the state by 2,736 votes. After the media left, the discussion rambled. Trump complained about voter fraud in the election that he had just won, and bragged about how well he had done in states he had carried. He said that Arnold Schwarzenegger had "ruined *Celebrity Apprentice*."

I offered a suggestion.

"Mr. President, because of your support in the Republican base, you could solve the immigration problem in the same way Nixon went to China," I said.

"We should do that. I like that very much," he said.

"We could start with the bill that the Senate passed four years ago in 2013. Sixty-eight of us voted for it, but the House never took it up," I said.

Two Republican senators at the lunch objected, and Trump changed his mind.

"I'm a rockstar in your state," he told Senator Bennet, a Democrat from Colorado.

He was agreeing to so many suggestions and ordering them done so fast that aides were scribbling furiously, trying to end the meeting, but the president was enjoying himself.

Somehow, he went off on Senator Elizabeth Warren and the next presidential election.

"Pocahontas is making an ass out of herself. I hope she gets nominated," he said, and began discussing Warren's high cheekbones and Native American ancestry.

But I saw another side to Trump. During his first two months in office, he nominated an impressive Supreme Court justice, proposed lower taxes, and ridiculed windmills as substitutes for nuclear power. He nominated well-qualified Cabinet officers with a conservative, pro-business bent. All of that appealed to me. Critics complained about his railing against Washington, DC, elites—but all forty-four presidents since George

Washington had done that and so had I. (Remember "cut their pay and send them home?") I even agreed with him on the well-done steak.

And, for all of Trump's bombast, a dose of his populism might be good medicine, I thought. Republican ideology had become ossified as Washington, DC, interest groups spun out litmus tests to raise money, control primaries, and maintain influence. He attracted Americans who had never before voted, a good thing in a democracy.

Trump had been elected by voters who were put off by an open Southern border, political correctness, elitism, and in-your-face identity and gender politics. Some were men who felt diminished by modern culture. Many were rural. Many lived paycheck to paycheck, and saw themselves as victims of hyper-globalism and capitalist forces beyond their control. Traveling the country during the last forty years, I, too, had been struck by how so few Americans amassed so much money, which was very different from the broad middle-income environment in which I had grown up.

In private meetings, Trump was gracious and often self-deprecating.

"Nobody knows more about grandstanding than I do," he told us at one senators' luncheon.

"I seem to get along better with the bad guys," he said of the Russian, North Korean, and Turkish presidents.

Another time he told us, "I never drink [alcohol], but can you imagine what I'd be like if I did?"

* * *

On Sunday, February 26, a little before midnight, two weeks after our lunch, the White House operator's call woke me up in Vienna, Austria, where I was attending a conference.

The president came on the line.

"It was good to see you at our lunch. You are more handsome in person than you are on television," he said, which I thought was a pretty strange way to start a conversation.

He thanked me for chairing hearings for two of his controversial Cabinet nominees. That seemed to be the purpose of his call. I brought up Obamacare.

"It was a big help for you to say on *60 Minutes* that Obamacare should be repealed and replaced, simultaneously," I said. Now that there were fifty-two Republican senators, some, including McConnell, wanted a repeal without first agreeing on a replacement.

"You don't tear down an old bridge before you build a new one," I said.

Then, I brought up the next week's annual meeting of the governors with the president.

"That's a rare opportunity," I said and described the "repair, repeal, and replace language" that I had been using to frame the Obamacare debate.

"Write it up. And I will say it just like you wrote it, and I will give you credit," he said.

I brought up our "Marketplace Fairness Act," which allowed states to tax goods sold over the internet in the same way they taxed goods sold in retail stores.

"That will appeal to governors. It could mean thirty billion dollars a year to states," I said.

"That much? I am for it. It is very unfair to main street businesses and other retailers to exempt internet sales. But I would call it internet fairness," Trump said.

After he hung up, I thought that, since Trump is such a successful brander, I would be wise to take his marketing advice. In the 1980s, Ronald Reagan was the Great Communicator, but in the twenty-first century, Trump left every other political communicator in the dust. In the new "Digital Democracy," he understood better than any public figure the third part of executive leadership—"persuade at least half the people you are right"—although it usually turned out to be somewhat less than half.

While the rest of us issued press releases to declining newspapers, his online tweets persuaded tens of millions. While we jabbered in the language of government, he wrote and spoke in plain English. His provocative outbursts earned seven times as much free cable TV coverage as our soundbites. We delivered scripted speeches to small audiences. His harangues at rallies drew thousands, creating a "circus comes to town" atmosphere reminiscent of nineteenth-century campaigns when candidates rode horses and delivered three-hour orations in town squares.

"I am able to speak with the people and the people can understand me," Trump said in Dallas in 2024.

As for the first parts of leadership—pointing the way and developing a strategy—Trump proved to be good at this too. Critics suggested that he had no views of his own, and sometimes, that seemed to be true. But he borrowed ideas—good and bad—from random places—*Fox and Friends*, rich developers, California entrepreneurs, senators, and anyone else who called his cell phone or wandered into the Oval Office.

His office had zero structure. It operated like a family business, with Trump as the hub and advisers competing for attention. Access to Trump was different than it was with the other nine presidents I had worked with. When I was a member of George H. W. Bush's Cabinet, I communicated with the president through the chief of staff. Presidential decisions came only after the staff secretariat had vetted them.

Not with Trump. He returned my calls promptly, sometimes within minutes. Often, he made decisions during those calls, acting on the last thing he heard—or the first thing—which often created trouble.

* * *

So, how does a United States senator go about working with a president with whose views he mostly agrees and with whose behavior and temperament he disagrees?

"To the people belongs the right of electing their Chief Magistrate," Andrew Jackson said in his First Annual Message to Congress.[1]

Abraham Lincoln agreed and offered a further observation.

"Elections belong to the people. It's their decision. If they decide to turn their back on the fire and burn their behinds, then they will just have to sit on their blisters," is attributed to Lincoln.

President Eisenhower said something similar about members of Congress for whom he had disdain.

"I ignore them as individuals and respect their offices," Ike once told Bryce Harlow.

I followed the path that Jackson, Lincoln, and Eisenhower had suggested. I voted against Trump's tariffs and against his attempt to build a border wall with funds Congress had appropriated for schools for military families. I voted to keep his war powers within constitutional limits. But I did not offer a daily commentary on his tweets and behavior. If I had done that, I never would have had time to do anything else. Plus, most of Washington, DC, was already preoccupied with offering those critiques.

Even when Trump and I disagreed, I stayed focused on the issues and treated the office of the presidency with respect. Trump did not like my independence, but he didn't criticize me publicly. I suppose that was because he may have come to the same conclusion that I did—whatever our differences, we should let the people decide who is president and who is senator, respect each other's offices, and work together when we can.

On Tuesday, June 6, 2017, I joined Senator Fred Thompson's family in the Oval Office when the president signed the law I sponsored naming the Nashville courthouse for the deceased senator.

"He was my one favorite *Law and Order* guy," Trump told Thompson's family.

And then he talked about me.

"We started off rough, but now we just love him," he told the Thompsons.

But then, he made a not-so-subtle comment to remind me not to stray.

"We never have had the base more energized in Tennessee than they are today," he said.

I switched the conversation to a different subject.

"I understand you're going to reappoint Francis Collins to head the National Institutes of Health," I said.

Some of Trump's friends were promoting zany candidates.

"Do you like him?" he asked, although I had recommended Collins to him several times before.

Trump often asks questions without waiting for an answer.

"I'm going to do it. I have a statement ready to go. I'm going to see him this afternoon. You can let him know," he said.

Three years later, Dr. Collins provided crucial leadership to implement the "21st Century Cures Act," and speed up testing, vaccines, and cures for COVID-19.

* * *

Donald Trump is notoriously thin-skinned—but not always, I found. For example, we disagreed publicly and privately—but politely—on tariffs, trade, and his constitutional authority.

I told him that high tariffs helped cause the Great Depression, would make Americans pay a big sales tax, and destroy auto jobs. He listened and didn't seem to mind the criticism—although I didn't persuade him otherwise.

On Tuesday, December 5, 2017, I was among several senators invited for a White House lunch to talk with Trump about trade. Entering the Cabinet Room, I spoke to US Trade Representative Robert Lighthizer, who has a fifteenth-century mercantilist view of trade—more exports, fewer imports. We talked about the president's threat to terminate the North American Free Trade Agreement (NAFTA).

"That is exactly what he plans to do," Lighthizer said.

Lighthizer began the meeting with an anachronistic defense of terminating NAFTA.

I interrupted.

"Mr. President, the US makes one million more cars today than in the year before NAFTA. Tennessee has nearly one thousand auto suppliers, and most of those jobs came after NAFTA," I said, and handed him a map showing 7 million auto jobs in the Southeastern states he had won in the election.

I went on.

"After 9/11, Detroit auto companies told President Bush, 'If you close the Canadian border for three days, there won't be a car built in the United States,'" I said.

"In order to get a good deal, I have to terminate NAFTA and make them think I'm serious," Trump said.

"The United States is rich, so we buy a lot," I said. "We're always going to have a trade deficit with Canada and Mexico. Focus on China and Japan. The trade deficit with Mexico and Canada is irrelevant. Don't build trade walls. Tell our trading partners, 'Do for us what we do for you,'" I said.

Senator Graham chimed in.

"A win is not sinking the stock market one thousand points, which you will do if you terminate NAFTA," he said.

"If the president concludes a new NAFTA agreement, whatever it is will pass the Senate," Lighthizer said.

"No, it won't, because I will oppose it and make sure it doesn't," I said.

Lighthizer's arguments were so off base that I thought someone needed to be aggressive.

As the meeting wound down, Trump laughed.

"So, what am I going to do now with all my plans? I had a NAFTA termination letter ready to sign until Secretary [Sonny] Perdue visited me this morning and talked me out of it—temporarily—because of what it would do to agriculture," he said. The agriculture secretary had told Trump that other countries would impose tariffs on American crops if he imposed tariffs on their products.

Two days later, Senator Sasse told me that he had been arguing with the president about trade.

"You sound like you're talking out of Lamar Alexander's playbook," Trump told Sasse.

Later that day, Tennessee Congressman Chuck Fleischmann called me with a message from Trump, whom he had seen the day before.

"I was very impressed with his knowledge of the subject matter and the way he conducted himself at a meeting with me. I want you to call him and tell him that," the president had said, according to Fleischmann.

Two years later, an even more explosive topic—a wall on the Southern border—again put me at odds with Trump. In February of 2019, the president declared a national emergency and said he would build a border wall with $3.6 billion that Congress had appropriated for building military barracks and schools.

"This is a gross abuse of presidential authority," I said on the Senate floor. "After a revolution against a king, our founders chose not to create a chief executive who could tax the people and spend their money any way he chose. The Constitution gave that responsibility exclusively to a Congress elected by the people, and every one of us US senators has taken an oath to support that Constitution. Separation of powers is a crucial constitutional imperative that goes to the very heart of our freedom. The late Justice Antonin Scalia said, 'Every tin horn dictator in the world today has a Bill of Rights. That's not what makes us free. What has made us free is our Constitution.'"

I set out to create what Senator McConnell labeled a "jailbreak," that would include at least twenty Republican senators opposing the declaration, enough to overturn a presidential veto when combined with

Democrat votes. When Department of Justice lawyers came to a Republican senators' lunch to plead the president's case, I told them that their argument "would have earned an 'F' in any respectable law school." Senators Rubio, Paul, Tillis, Isakson, Blunt, Cruz, and Lee, among others, joined in the criticism.

On March 13, I joined fifteen other Republican senators for a White House meeting I had requested on trade—but the issue of the day was the emergency declaration. The House had already voted it down, and the Senate was to vote the next day.

Trump was in a friendly mood and unhurried.

"Where should we start?" he asked. "We'll talk about whatever you want to talk about."

I was sitting directly across from the president and spoke up first, arguing that his steel and aluminum tariffs would raise the cost of cars and destroy auto jobs. Trump had assembled customs officials to tell us that there was a crisis on the border, but we all already agreed with that. The issue was the emergency declaration.

"I hope you'll vote with me, but vote for what you think is right," he said. There were no threats, no bluster. He allowed the meeting to run for nearly two hours.

The next day, I was one of twelve Republicans who voted to overturn the president's declaration—not enough of a jailbreak to overturn Trump's promised veto.

After the vote, I said, "There has never been an instance where the president asked for funding, Congress refused it, and the president then used the 'National Emergencies Act' to justify spending the money anyway. This is a dangerous precedent. If President Trump can build a wall when Congress has refused to provide the funding, then the next president can declare a national emergency and tear the wall down, or declare a climate change emergency and stop oil imports and offshore drilling. Our nation's founders gave to Congress the power to approve all spending so that the president would not have too much power."

No recriminations came from Trump—only praise for those who voted with him.

Perhaps the president's generous attitude was because he thought he didn't need my vote. Later, he vetoed the resolution, and two-thirds of the

Senate was unwilling to overturn his veto. The federal courts then ruled that the president had no constitutional authority to build the border wall with funds Congress had appropriated to build schools and barracks. The president responded by using other properly appropriated funds to build the wall—something I had suggested earlier and which, if he had done it, would have avoided all the constitutional fuss. Still, the episode illustrates Justice Scalia's observation that "what makes us free" is the separation of powers—the constitution's framework of checks and balances among branches of the federal government.

As the founders envisioned, if one branch—Congress—doesn't check the president, perhaps the other branch—the courts—will.

CHAPTER 55

A Wild Ride

"Well, people do like bipartisan. But the base doesn't. I'm getting pushback."

—**PRESIDENT TRUMP, November 18, 2018**

Washington, DC. 2017–2018.

DONALD TRUMP'S SUPPORTERS did not tolerate my independence as well as he did.

At a Southeastern Conference tournament basketball game, shortly after the vote on Trump's emergency declaration, a friend of forty years, sitting in the row in front of me, turned around and said, "I don't like you voting against the president on the border wall money."

"Congress appropriated that money to build schools for military children," I said. "I voted for the Constitution, not against the president."

As I was heading toward the checkout line in the Alcoa, Tennessee Kroger supermarket, an angry woman, probably sixty, with glasses and orange hair, confronted me.

"Why did you vote with those f***g Democrats on war powers?" she said.

"The president can defend the country, but Congress must declare war—if we are to have one," I said.

"He's not going to war. He should be able to do whatever he wants to do. He is defending us," she said.

My answer satisfied neither of the women.

Nor did Trump's detractors like my independence.

A college classmate emailed, "At long last, can't you speak out against this horrible president. Friends and relatives SHAME me for having been a friend of yours."

While I was walking Rufus, our Cavalier puppy, a neighbor glowered at both of us.

"We don't like your support for Trump," he said.

At Whole Foods, a woman ran up crying. Another shopper handed me a note.

"I have always supported you, but now I am disappointed," it said.

I started shopping at Publix.

My relationship with Trump had its ups and downs, but it created opportunities for accomplishments. I was a committee chairman, had been in Republican leadership, and could work with Democrats. Trump was a Republican president inclined to sign whatever I could produce.

My wildest legislative ride with Trump was an unsuccessful attempt to rein in costs for those who buy individual health insurance without government support—people like songwriters, farmers, and anyone who is self-employed. Only about 6 to 7 percent of Americans with health insurance buy such individual insurance—although that still is millions of people. To reduce these rates would mean amending Obamacare, something Republicans had tried to do one hundred times before with zero victories.

The ride began on Thursday, July 27, 2017, when the president called Senator McCain, urging him to vote "yes" on yet another attempt to repeal Obamacare. This was great irony—the senator, about whom Trump had said, "I like people who weren't captured," was the senator with the deciding vote on the issue the president cared most about. After the call, McCain walked onto the floor, turned his thumb down voting "no," and it was over.

I walked across the aisle to Senator Murray.

"I'll call you Monday and we can begin hearings in September on how to slow down rising rates in the individual market," I said.

Thus began a bipartisan rollercoaster ride that crashed nine months later. At first, Trump was not on board. Enraged by the failure to repeal Obamacare, he said McConnell was "ineffective," called senators "fools and quitters," and threatened to stop their subsidy for health insurance.

In September, Murray and I invited every senator to attend one of our four hearings about reining in health care costs. Sixty-eight did.

Then, obstacles appeared, including some from Republicans.

"Alexander is 'stealing our jurisdiction.... It's pretty hard to get excited about what he's doing,'" Senate Finance Committee Chairman Senator Orrin Hatch said.[1]

"There are several things I am willing to sacrifice my political career over, but this is not one of them," Speaker Ryan told McConnell.

Nevertheless, on Saturday morning, October 7, Trump jumped aboard our wild ride.

"I called Chuck Schumer yesterday to see if the Dems want to do a great health care bill. ObamaCare is badly broken, big premiums. Who knows!" the president tweeted.

Honey and I were on a congressional fact-finding tour near Aviano Air Base at the edge of the Alps in northern Italy. Hoping for a quiet dinner, we had walked to a restaurant named Porca l'Oca, which translated means "Crazy Goose"—an appropriate name for what was about to happen.

At 8:30 p.m., I was enjoying a glass of red wine when my cell phone rang. It was the White House. I walked out of the restaurant and sat on the curb in the dark until the operator announced, "The president of the United States."

I heard a familiar voice.

"Hello, Lamar. I want to talk to you about health care. I called Schumer today and told him that I might want to do a bipartisan deal. I think the block grant would be better than the Senate or House bill, don't you?" Trump said without pausing. "Maybe we can do something on an interim basis."

"I am working on something like that with Senator Murray," I said. "If you could just tell Schumer to tell Murray to take my last offer, we would have a deal. It would keep rates from going up in 2018 and bring them down in 2019."

"I'll put you in charge of this and you try to get an agreement," the president said.

That is not precisely the way our constitutional system of checks and balances is supposed to operate, I was thinking. *The people elected me to work with the president, not for him.*

"I'll stay in touch," I said.

I went back to the restaurant and jotted down notes on what the president had said. Honey and I walked to our hotel room and were in bed by 10:00 p.m., with sounds of a street food festival filling the room.

Saturday, October 14, was another bizarre day. At 1:00 p.m., we left Berlin for Wittenberg, Germany, where, five hundred years earlier, Martin Luther had tacked ninety-five theses on the Castle Church door. At 4:15 p.m., we were sitting in a pew when staff whispered that Senator Graham was on the phone with the president. They were on a golf course.

"If you want to get close to Trump, learn to play golf," Graham would joke. I walked outside, stood in the parking lot, and answered the phone.

"Tell him to give me four shots," Graham said as he handed his phone to the president.

I spoke first.

"I am doing what you asked me to do. I hope to have an agreement with Senator Murray by Monday. It will give states flexibility," I said. "It will avoid rising insurance costs. And next year, you can try, again, to repeal and replace Obamacare."

"That sounds good. I am one hundred percent behind you," he said.

Then, I offered some unsolicited advice, hoping to delay another futile attempt to repeal Obamacare.

"If a president, meaning you, focuses his full attention on one issue for as long as it takes, he can wear everybody else out. And that issue should be *tax reform* for the rest of the year," I said.

"Call me if you need my help," the president said.

That afternoon in Germany, it seemed like our wild ride might actually result in a law that cut the cost of individual health insurance for millions of Americans.

* * *

One month later, on Friday, November 3, Senator Murray and her husband, Rob, along with Senators Whitehouse and Hassan, arrived to spend the weekend in the Smokies with Honey and me. All three senators were Democrats on the health committee.

"Thank you for all you are doing with Murray on health care," a woman from Richmond said as we toured Blackberry Farm in a golf cart. She did not realize Murray was sitting next to me.

The media often linked our names.

"Is there a senator named Alexander Murray?" another woman asked.

It was a friendly weekend with little political talk. We did discuss making the Senate work better, something senators often discuss in private but rarely do anything about because of partisan pressure.

"After I did the Ryan-Murray budget deal and returned to Seattle, people greeted me at the airport with hugs, although they had no idea what was in the deal," Murray said. "They just liked to see people working together to get a result."

Two weeks after that, on Friday, November 17, Murray and I proposed my most popular bill that never became law. The Alexander-Murray legislation would cut some insurance rates by up to 40 percent and lower the deficit by $3.8 billion. Twelve Democrats and twelve Republicans cosponsored it. Trump had asked for it. Senator Schumer said every Democrat might vote for it.

The next morning at 8:30 a.m., I was about to speak at a media health care forum when my phone rang. It was the White House operator.

Sensing trouble, I spoke first.

"Mr. President, congratulations. I am about to tell the media that they underestimate you, that you engineered this bipartisan agreement *yourself*."

"Well, people do like bipartisan. But the base doesn't. I'm getting pushback," Trump said.

It sounded like someone had wandered into the Oval Office or called his cell phone or said on Fox News that a bipartisan bill was a bad idea, and that Republicans should try one more time to repeal Obamacare.

"Remember that you asked for this so people won't get hurt. It will create a bridge to repeal and replace Obamacare," I said.

"I'm not sure I can support it. I don't want to bail out insurance companies," he said.

"Our agreement doesn't bail them out. You don't have to support it. Just encourage the process you asked for," I said.

"I support you. I don't know whether you're going to run for reelection but I endorse you," he said.

"Thank you," I replied.

I brought the conversation to an end.

"I'm going in to speak now," I said. "I need for you to say that you encourage the process."

"That's no problem," Trump said.

I walked into the media conference.

"The president just called," I told them. "He said, number one, that he wanted to encourage the bipartisan agreement that Senator Murray and I announced yesterday. Number two, he intends to review it carefully to see if he wants to add anything. Number three, he is still for block grants sometime later, but he is going to focus on tax reform this year."

Within an hour, the president put out this tweet.[2]

"I am supportive of Lamar as a person & also of the process, but I can never support bailing out ins co's who have made a fortune w/ O'Care."

I am now going to leap to the end of this tale because what happened during the next four months is too byzantine to relate. Trump stuck to his guns in support of the Alexander-Murray bill—but not everyone else did. On Thursday, March 22, 2018, at 4:30 p.m. on the Senate floor, Senator Collins asked for consent to add Alexander-Murray to the appropriations bill. Senator Murray then *objected to her own bill* because Democrats opposed including an abortion compromise called the "Hyde Amendment,"[3] even though they had voted for that compromise hundreds of times before, and would vote for it again in the very appropriations bill to which Collins was trying to attach Alexander-Murray. Hundreds of hours of bipartisan work to lower health insurance rates went up in flames.

I had been so optimistic that I had bought bottles of "Alexander-Murray Scotch" to give to each health committee member. When the bill crashed, I decided to give it to them when I retired from the Senate.

I got over my disappointment quickly. I had learned early on to govern the same way I shot free throws in basketball—practice, do my best, then put the missed opportunities out of my mind. Focus on what comes next instead of what went wrong. Since amending Obamacare seemed impossible, I shifted gears to lowering health care costs. Experts had testified that as much as half of the money spent on health care is unnecessary.[4] And patients have no idea what their cost is.

Working with Murray and four other House and Senate committees, we produced legislation to end surprise medical billing for patients who are stuck with unexpected emergency room bills. "The Lower Health Care Costs Act" also included fifty-five bipartisan proposals.

Working with Senator Hatch, I engineered a law that helped songwriters earn a fair royalty on their music—a once-in-a-generation change in the copyright law.

"Only Trump could have done it," the president said when he signed the songwriters' bill at the White House in October 2018.

Ivanka Trump contributed to all these efforts. And she hosted a dinner in her home to help pass another bill that sent workforce policy decisions to states. Ivanka is striking in appearance, unpretentious, and well-informed. She was my most reliable conduit to the White House because I knew that the president would listen to her, and that she was the one aide he would never fire.

* * *

Earlier in 2018, during fifteen days in August at my Canadian fishing camp, I decided not to run for a fourth term.

"Serve in Washington, DC long enough to get vaccinated but not infected," the *Little Plaid Book* advises.

Already, I had been elected to more combined years as senator and governor than any other Tennessean. I preferred the Ted Williams example—hit a home run in your last at bat instead of hanging around until you have to be carried off the field.

Seventy is the sum of our years, or eighty, if we are strong, Psalms 90:10 teaches. I was nearly eighty. My health was good, but Honey's was not. *Before long, I may need to be with her all of the time,* I thought.

David Cleary had argued that I should stay, as loyal staff will. "There is work left to do. The Senate needs your voice. You could be reelected," he wrote in a memo. I had been tempted before to stay too long, but fortunately the Constitution had eliminated that temptation by barring my run for a third term as governor of Tennessee. In any event, I had two Senate years remaining, and there is no such thing as a lame duck, unless one acts like a lame duck.

I had been both in and out of public life, not always voluntarily. I had learned that politics is a narrow slice of life. There is much more. Paddling my kayak into the Canadian sunset with a cigar, enjoying my solitude, I thought of Emily Dickinson's poem:

> How dreary – to be – Somebody!
> How public – like a Frog –
> To tell one's name – the livelong June –
> To an admiring Bog!

At 7:25 a.m. on Monday, August 20, a single-engine Beaver float plane interrupted loon calls, landed on Bending Lake, and taxied to the dock. I loaded three bags and climbed into the right front seat. Flying to Fort Frances, I thought about my decision to retire, was happy that I had made it, and resolved not to say anything publicly about it until the end of the year.

Four months later, on Sunday, December 16, Honey and I were driving from our cabin to Nashville.

At 5:00 p.m., I placed a call to the White House. President Trump returned my call a half hour later.

He spoke before I could.

"You'll be serving another twenty years, I hope," Trump said.

"That's why I'm calling, Mr. President. I wanted to let you know in advance that I'm announcing tomorrow that I will not be a candidate for reelection."

"I'm sorry to hear that," he said.

"It's time to let someone else do it," I said. "I'll have two more good years, and we'll find things to work on together."

"Well, I should say congratulations, if that's your decision. We'll work on things for the next two years," he said.

The call lasted about ten minutes.

"I'll talk to you next week," he said.

CHAPTER 56

Trump Did It

"Rule 59. If it was a mistake and you did it, admit it and try not to do it again."

—LAMAR ALEXANDER'S LITTLE PLAID BOOK

Washington, DC. December 2019–January 20, 2020.

ONE OF MY FAVORITE SATURDAY PASTIMES is rummaging among items to be sold at the Case Antiques Auction in Knoxville.

At the Saturday, January 23, 2010 auction, for $400 I bought a book, *The Impeachment of Andrew Johnson*. Edmund G. Ross, who had been a Republican senator from Kansas, wrote the book in 1896, twenty-eight years after he cast the deciding vote to end impeachment proceedings against Democrat President Johnson. His vote made Kansas Republicans so angry that they ostracized and impoverished his family. A century later, the senator's independence earned a chapter in John F. Kennedy's book, *Profiles in Courage.*

At 1:10 p.m. on Tuesday, January 21, 2020, 152 years after Ross cast his decisive vote, I rose from the chair behind my desk on the front row of the Senate chamber for the arrival of John Roberts, chief justice of the Supreme Court. Sitting in a black robe behind the presiding officer's desk, beneath a plaque inscribed "In God We Trust," the chief justice announced in a voice weakened by a bad cold that the Senate would convene as a court of impeachment for the trial of Donald John Trump.

One month earlier, the House of Representatives had voted to impeach Trump based on his telephone call to the president of Ukraine, threatening to withhold military aid unless Ukraine announced an investigation into Joe Biden, Trump's 2020 presidential campaign opponent. No House Republican had voted to impeach Trump.

This would be only the third impeachment trial of a US president. The Senate acquitted Johnson in 1868 and Bill Clinton in 1998. Political passions of the day consumed both those trials, as they would this one.

Thus began the historic process that would continue through two weekends until I cast the decisive vote to end the proceedings.

* * *

The weekly Republican policy luncheon on Tuesday, December 17, 2019, in the Mike Mansfield Room, was the first devoted mainly to discussing the impeachment of President Trump. There was talk of a "motion to dismiss" and of a "summary judgment." That led me to make the first remarks that I had made to the caucus on the subject.

"We should avoid both phrases because we have a constitutional duty to be impartial, and to be *seen* as impartial, to hear the case and to be *seen* as hearing the case," I said. "To talk of 'motion to dismiss' and 'summary judgment' makes it appear as if we intend to do neither. Defeating a motion to proceed to the vote on conviction *after* the articles are presented, the arguments are made, and questions are asked is quite a different matter than a summary dismissal."

After lunch, I drove to the White House for a bill signing of legislation taking steps to simplify the burdensome college aid application form (the FAFSA). I had been working on this for fifteen years. Tim Scott and I were the only two senators present. The president told Scott and me that the impeachment was a "scam and a hoax," and gave each of us a six-page letter detailing why. He was furious about the impeachment but gracious during our visit. I rolled out the 108-question FAFSA form, and the president signed it as a souvenir.

I was thinking, *He is not going to like it when, during the trial, I—and perhaps several others—say that his phone call to President Zelenskyy was inappropriate for a president or for any elected official.* After the photographs, I talked with Ivanka Trump about the president's support after the impeachment trial for enacting the "Restore Our Parks Act" and legislation to end surprise medical billing.

On the next day, Wednesday, when voting ended at 7:00 p.m., I drove to The Prime Rib where I met Senator Feinstein for dinner. We sat in my favorite booth in the corner. As we were leaving, the pianist invited me to come over, and I played "(I Left My Heart) In San Francisco" for Feinstein. This produced applause from the diners and a kiss on my cheek from her. Although we had different opinions on many issues, we both knew how to achieve results, because she had been a mayor and I had been a governor. While we were having dinner, the House voted to impeach the president.

The next day, I flew home to East Tennessee where Honey and I spent the Christmas recess at our mountain cabin with our daughter, Leslee, and her husband, Paul. On Saturday, December 28, Paul and I drove to Knoxville, where we watched the University of Wisconsin trounce the University of Tennessee basketball team. When we returned to the cabin about 4:00 p.m., I felt sick.

At 7:02 p.m., I emailed my Vanderbilt doctors, saying, "I'm on my way to Maryville to the emergency room. Have had chills for the last three or four hours. Blood pressure has risen to 200/94 and my temperature has risen. My left leg is sore and tight. I have the same symptoms that I had the night before I went to George Washington University Hospital emergency room in October. I am wondering if I have a recurrence of infection."

Vanderbilt surgeon Herbert Schwartz emailed back, "Sounds like cellulitis. Antibiotics for sure."

I suggested to the Maryville doctors that I should go to the Vanderbilt University Medical Center on Monday.

"You're going tonight," they said. By 3:00 a.m. on Sunday morning, I was in the Critical Care Unit at Vanderbilt.

Dealing with the infection raised concerns about my return for the impeachment trial. On Wednesday, I was still in the hospital, but feeling better. Six days later, on Tuesday, January 7, the Senate was back in session, considering how to proceed with impeachment. I was recovering at home in Nashville, and now Honey was in the hospital at Vanderbilt with pneumonia.

Staff called to say that Senator McConnell wanted to see four senators—Collins, Romney, Murkowski, and me. He wanted to know, if he guarantees a vote on whether to allow additional witnesses, would we vote to table all Democrat amendments to his resolution governing impeachment proceedings?

On the next Monday, January 13, Honey was home, and I was on my way to Washington, DC, to prepare for the trial. The president tweeted that he wanted the articles of impeachment dismissed, which I had made clear to McConnell that I would not vote to do. And without my support, he did not have enough votes to pass a motion to dismiss.

Senator Collins had called a meeting for that afternoon with Murkowski, Romney, and me to discuss whether to allow the calling of more witnesses. I suggested that we should request a short meeting with McConnell to make sure that that we all understood each other. That "no surprises" meeting occurred the next day in the leader's office at 10:30 a.m. McConnell guaranteed a vote on whether to call more witnesses. The four of us promised to vote for his resolution. That agreement gave him all fifty-three Republican votes to proceed.

Walking through the halls after the meeting gave me an opportunity to frame the impeachment issue with reporters. The *Washington Post* reported my comments with this headline, "Top Senate Republicans reject Trump's renewed call for immediate dismissal of impeachment charges."[1]

Later that morning, I walked to the attending physician on the first floor of the Capitol, gave blood, and was measured for a compression sock, which I hoped would help with sitting for long periods during the trial. I already had a Senate-approved seat cushion and was looking for a Senate-approved stool that I could use to elevate my swollen leg.

At noon on Thursday, January 16, seven Democrat managers arrived from the House with two impeachment articles for President "Donald John Trump," an unfamiliar use of the president's middle name that was jarring. As Representative Adam Schiff read the articles from a podium, I sat in my usual seat at the end of the first row.

"The place is different, isn't it, when we are all in our seats?" Senator Feinstein said as she walked by.

During a break, Senators Blunt, Boozman, Capito, and I walked downstairs to the senators' dining room for iced tea and a meeting of our "Hillbilly Caucus." We occasionally got together with no rules, no officers, and no agenda. That day, we mainly told stories, among other things, about Jesse James's murder in Missouri.

I was back at my desk at 2:00 p.m. Gossip was that the chief justice had dinner with his family every night at 7:00 p.m., creating misplaced optimism that our trial days would end by 6:00 p.m. The sergeant-at-arms announced that, during the trial, all will be silent "on pain of imprisonment," which was the only threat that would keep senators from talking for such an extended period. The chief justice then swore us in with an oath of impartiality, which seemed a waste of time since half the senators already had announced how they would vote.

Then, the clerk read each senator's name in alphabetical order. I proceeded first to the well, and signed my name in the book offered by the secretary of the Senate. Every senator followed, forming a line as their names were called, four by four. The chamber was so cold that Senator Whitehouse and others wore their overcoats. At about 2:30 p.m., this process ended, and senators rushed to the airport, knowing that when we returned on Tuesday, we would be in Washington, DC, for the next three or four weeks, hearing the case from 1:00 p.m. to at least 6:00 p.m. every day.

Media coverage focused on whether I might be the fourth Republican who would vote to approve hearing more witnesses or asking for more documents, or, as some headlines put it, "to turn against Trump." My disposition was that I did not *expect* there to be a need for more evidence after the arguments were made, the questions were asked, and the record was considered, but I had decided to withhold judgment on that question until after I heard the arguments, questions, and answers.

On Friday, the *Wall Street Journal* ran this story:

As Senate Career Draws to End, Lamar Alexander Weighs Whether to Stick With Trump

WASHINGTON—He has complained about President Trump's tariffs, voted to block him from diverting military-construction

> funding to a border wall, and been at odds with the president's efforts to end health-insurance subsidies benefiting low-income people....
>
> Mr. Alexander—a Tennessee icon elected to the Senate in 2002 who has been governor, U.S. education secretary and presidential candidate—is hearing from all sides. He said in an interview that some Tennessee Republicans have written to him asking that he stand up more strongly against Mr. Trump. In Washington, members of his delegation have pulled him aside to complain that the House impeachment inquiry was unfair and to raise alarms about doing anything that legitimizes the process.[2]

On Monday, January 20, I emailed staff to expect an avalanche of emails and calls. I suggested that in their responses they use the statement that I would release later in the day. David Cleary, the chief of staff, doubted that my statement would be of much help.

"Right now, most people calling either want you to convict him or canonize him and don't even want us to talk. They just hang up," he said.

This was my statement released on Tuesday, as President Trump's impeachment trial began:

NASHVILLE, Tenn., January 21, 2020

> Just because the House proceedings were a circus that doesn't mean the Senate's trial needs to be.
>
> We have a constitutional duty to hear the case. That means to me, number one, hear the arguments on both sides, and not dismiss the case out of hand. Number two, ask our questions, consider the answers and study the record. Number three, be guaranteed a right to vote on whether we need additional evidence.
>
> Evidence could be documents; it could be witnesses; or there could be no need for additional evidence."
>
> The resolution I am supporting guarantees a vote on whether we need additional evidence at the appropriate time. Except for not including a motion to dismiss after senators have asked questions, the resolution establishes fundamentally the same rules that the Senate approved by a vote of 100-0 for the Clinton impeachment trial in 1999.

CHAPTER 57

Casting the Decisive Vote

"Rule 151. When stumped for an answer, ask yourself, 'What is the right thing to do?' Then do it."

—LAMAR ALEXANDER'S LITTLE PLAID BOOK

Washington, DC. Tuesday, January 21, 2020.

IT WAS TWENTY-TWO DEGREES in Nashville when I caught the 7:40 a.m. Southwest flight to Washington, DC, so that I could be in place for the opening of the impeachment trial.

Senators rose at 1:10 p.m. for the arrival of the chief justice. Senator McConnell offered a resolution governing how the trial would proceed, setting in motion a marathon of fifteen amendments by Senator Schumer, each of which could elicit up to two hours of debate.

The White House counsel said that the president had done nothing wrong, which, of course, was not true, unless you believe it is right for the president to withhold military aid to encourage the leader of another country to investigate the president's leading political opponent. Representative Schiff spoke for too long, arguing that the president believes he can do anything. Schiff would have done well to remember Senator Dirksen's advice to enjoy the luxury of an unexpressed thought. Or, as Louisiana Senator John Kennedy told the media, quoting Mark Twain, "Few sinners are saved after twenty minutes in a sermon."

The well of the Senate was congested with tables constructed for the occasion, and that's where the advocates sat. The president's counsel and seven others sat in front of Republican senators, filling the space so that it was impossible to exit the Senate from the door near my seat.

During the 3:00 p.m. break, I told Senator McConnell that I was just now appreciating that the House impeachment articles not only would remove the president from office, but would also prohibit him from running for reelection. That would take Trump's name off ballots already printed in many states, including the Iowa caucus which was only two weeks away.

During breaks, I walked to the Senate Reading Room behind the Senate floor where I could lie on a couch and elevate my leg. During the proceedings, I stood every hour or so and stretched. Schiff complained that McConnell's resolution did not guarantee allowing more witnesses or evidence—although I had made sure that the Senate would have the opportunity to vote on that question. All one hundred senators sat silently behind our desks, except when called upon to vote.

It was drip, drip, drip on Wednesday, as the House managers proved that Trump and Rudy Giuliani not only had asked Ukrainian President Zelenskyy to investigate the Bidens, but had threatened to withhold $391 million in military aid and a White House meeting with Trump if Ukraine did not announce a Biden investigation. The managers even played a video of Trump saying on television that China should investigate the Bidens. I thought more about what would happen if the Senate took away the country's right to vote for Trump this year. That would split the country. It would also produce chaos and turn the presidency over to the Democrats. *In a country where consent of the governed is a founding principle, the people, not the Senate, should make such a momentous decision,* I thought.

On the next day, Thursday, there was more evidence that Trump had pressured Zelenskyy to investigate Biden and had only released US military funding when Congress complained, or, as the House managers said, "when he got caught." I thought back to the morning last fall in the appropriations committee when Senator Durbin offered an amendment forcing release of military aid to Ukraine for the next year because Trump had not yet released the funds that Congress had approved for the current year.

This was news to most of us. There was a discussion to determine what was going on. Senator Graham then volunteered that the committee did not need to take action because this year's funds were "released last night." This sounded like Graham had sensed a problem and made a late-night call to the president. Having made his point, Durbin withdrew his amendment.

* * *

During the next several days, it seemed like every journalist was speculating that my vote would determine whether the Senate would require additional witnesses. I told the whip that I was undecided and said nothing, which increased speculation.

On Monday the 27th, I slept until 8:00 a.m., not feeling well enough to walk on the Mall. Senator Graham called. Overnight, the *New York Times* had reported that a new book from Trump's former National Security Adviser John Bolton said that Trump had told Ukraine that if it wanted aid it needed to announce an investigation of Biden. Graham said that if Bolton had direct testimony on such a quid pro quo, then the Senate should hear it. He proposed allowing as evidence whatever was in Bolton's book on that issue.

Later that day, at a Republican lunch, other senators said Graham's proposal was too complicated—but I was becoming more inclined to vote to allow more witnesses. The only other position I could take would be that even if the president did what he was accused of doing—which was now obvious—the House charges did not rise to the level of impeachable offenses.

Proceedings began at 1:00 p.m., with twenty-two hours and five minutes remaining for the president's team to make its argument. Ken Starr spoke for an hour. He said that this was a partisan impeachment that did not give the president due process, did not meet the high bar of impeachment, and would gravely divide the country.

Then, for an hour and a half, Alan Dershowitz argued that the founders intended for impeachment to be reserved for criminal-like actions that equated with bribery, treason, and other high crimes. He said that at the time of the Constitution, "misdemeanor" had a different meaning and included capital misdemeanors, for example, death for stealing a chicken. There are mere sins, he said, and then there are impeachable offenses. By the time Dershowitz finished, I had drifted back to my earlier thinking—that the people, not senators, should decide whether what Trump had done justified removing him from office and disqualifying him from running again.

On Tuesday, the media reported that McConnell did not have the votes necessary to block more witnesses. On Wednesday, the president had invited me to a White House trade bill signing. I thought it was inappropriate to go during the impeachment trial, and returned to my apartment to work on what would be the most important statement that I would ever make as a senator.

While I told no one, I had made my decision—there was no need for more witnesses to prove something already proven. I wanted my statement to explain both my vote on this witness question, and to frame an argument for other Republicans who also believed that what the president did was wrong, but not impeachable. I knew that every word would count when I was trying to persuade at least half of an angry and divided nation that I was right.

By midnight, my statement was ready but, to avoid last minute surprises, I decided not to announce my decision until the last question was answered on the following night. In addition, I like to write a statement and then let it cool, to make certain that I am comfortable with the decision as well as with the way I am expressing it.

On Thursday morning, the 30th, the Capitol Dome was shining in the rising sun when I walked on the Mall for forty minutes in the cold. On an institutional basis, I felt good about my decision. I would be protecting the Senate from perpetual impeachments of future presidents. That danger is real because, as soon as articles arrive from the House, the Senate *must* act on them, which means spending at least three to four weeks considering them impartially.

I was also struck by Dershowitz's argument that the country would not accept a decision removing Trump from office and from the 2020 ballot. An impeachment and conviction of a president is unlikely to be accepted unless there is enough of a consensus (as there was in Nixon's case) to persuade sixty-seven senators, as the founders wisely required.

I walked to the Mansfield Room, arriving in the midst of lunch for Republican senators as Senator McConnell was speaking.

"For those who came in late," he said—that meant me—"fifty-one votes is better than fifty, because fifty means that the chief justice would have to decide whether to vote to break a tie, thereby casting himself on one side or the other." Other senators made comments directed at "those who may not have decided," which, at that point, could only have been Romney, Collins, Murkowski, and me.

During an afternoon of questions from senators and answers from counsel, I passed the time at my desk reading again the book *Impeachment* by Jon Meacham, Peter Baker, and others. I showed Senator Lee, who sat next to me, a passage Meacham had quoted from Senator Ross's 1896 book about President Andrew Johnson's impeachment. Meacham's observation seemed to buttress my conclusion that President Trump did it, but that the people should decide what to do about what he did.

Meacham wrote:

> To Edmund Ross, the tool of impeachment was "a two-edged sword, which must be handled with consummate judgment and skill." To decline to use the weapon in the event of presidential lawbreaking would destroy the primacy of the rule of law. To deploy it in times of great political passion but without a clear violation of law, however, risked (and risks) pushing the American system in a parliamentary direction—a development that might have its virtues but which would be a definitive break from the original intent and the organic evolution of the of the constitutional order. For better or for worse, the framers intended America's to be a popular, not a legislative, government. The voters acting through the electoral process, not lawmakers in parliamentary setting, were to determine the occupant of the presidency.[1]

* * *

At 6:30 p.m., McConnell asked for consent for a forty-five-minute break for dinner.

Republicans drifted to the Mansfield Room, where Senator Crapo was serving Mexican food. I suggested to McConnell that he walk directly to his office, and that I would go first to the Mansfield Room and then out its back door to his office.

"This should minimize media attention," I said.

I walked into the room that is McConnell's working space. We sat down facing one another.

"I don't need more evidence to prove something that is already proven," I said.

I gave him my statement and asked him to keep it between us, because I intended to hear the final arguments tonight before announcing a decision. I walked back to the Mansfield Room through its back hall door. The media was roped off down the hall.

Senator Murkowski was in the food line.

"Do you want to talk?" she asked.

I suggested that we go to an elevator away from the media and up to my third-floor hideaway, Room 306. She followed with her food.

From the hideaway, we heard protesters shouting in the dark on the cold plaza. Beyond the shouting rose the brightly lit Supreme Court building. Murkowski sat on the couch eating chips and guacamole. I sat facing her, handed her my statement, and explained my reasoning.

"I have told only Mitch, so please hold the statement until the last question and answer tonight," I said.

She borrowed a manila envelope and put the statement inside.

"I do not like senators pushing me to vote one way or the other and I am not pushing you," I told her.

The impeachment court resumed at 7:45 p.m.

As the evening wore on, I made notes on the points that I would make explaining my decision to the media the next morning:

- The impeachment is partisan—compare it to the importance of making the 1968 "Civil Rights Act" bipartisan so the country would accept it
- The danger of perpetual impeachments
- Can't convict on just "inappropriate"
- If you have five witnesses to a hit-and-run accident, why do you need six?

- The Iowa caucus starting the presidential election is next Monday
- Don't use capital punishment for leaving scene of an accident

Lawyers answered the last senator's question at 10:40 p.m. Senator Risch and I took the elevator to the first floor and walked out the carriage entrance into the chilly night. Two dozen reporters and cameramen crowded around as we walked down the marble steps. They all wanted to know if I was ready to say how I would vote. Reynard Graham, a member of my staff, drove the car up near the steps. Risch pushed through the crowd and climbed into the back seat.

"What the hell is this all about?" he said.

I climbed into the front seat as reporters pushed cameras with bright lights close to my face.

"I'll have a decision soon," I said, and closed the door.

By 10:15 p.m., I was in my apartment. At 11:00 p.m., staff tweeted out my statement, not only to the media, but also to every Republican senator, their chiefs of staff, and legislative directors, giving them an opportunity to frame their arguments with mine in mind.

The tweets created an avalanche of coverage because my "no" vote was seen as decisive on the witness issue, since, at the same time, Senator Collins was announcing a "yes" vote and Senator Murkowski had not yet announced her decision. With my "no" vote counted, the tally would stand forty-nine to hear more evidence, and fifty to not hear more evidence. The motion to hear more evidence would fail.[2]

In my statement, I said:[3]

> There is no need for more evidence to prove that the president asked Ukraine to investigate Joe Biden and his son, Hunter; he said this on television on October 3, 2019, and during his July 25, 2019, telephone call with the president of Ukraine. There is no need for more evidence to conclude that the president withheld United States aid, at least in part, to pressure Ukraine to investigate the Bidens; the House managers have proved this with what they call a "mountain of overwhelming evidence."
>
> It was inappropriate for the president to ask a foreign leader to investigate his political opponent and to withhold United States aid to encourage that investigation... But the Constitution does not give

> the Senate the power to remove the president from office and ban him from this year's ballot simply for actions that are inappropriate.
>
> The question then is not whether the president did it, but whether the United States Senate or the American people should decide what to do about what he did. I believe that the Constitution provides that the people should make that decision in the presidential election that begins in Iowa on Monday.
>
> Even if the House charges were true, they do not meet the Constitution's "treason, bribery, or other high crimes and misdemeanors...."
>
> Let the people decide.

Assessing the events of that day in their book, *The Divider,* Peter Baker and Susan Glasser wrote, "Lamar Alexander had spoken and the trial of Donald Trump that was not really a trial would end."[4]

CHAPTER 58

"Let the People Decide."

"Lamar Alexander's Finest Hour: His vote against witnesses was rooted in constitutional wisdom."[1]

—***WALL STREET JOURNAL*** **EDITORIAL, Sunday, February 2, 2020**

"Mr. Alexander...was considered one of the Republicans most likely to grow a spine and cross the aisle. This was a misjudgment."[2]

—***NEW YORK TIMES*** **EDITORIAL, Sunday, February 2, 2020**

Washington, DC. Friday, January 31, 2020.

OVERNIGHT, MY STATEMENT PRODUCED a barrage of reactions.

Senator Lindsey Graham tweeted, "[Senator Alexander] most likely expressed the sentiments of the country as a whole as well as any single Senator possibly could."[3]

"You have shattered my faith in your integrity and incorruptibility," read an email from a former US Department of Education colleague.

"Since we already know the core of what happened...there was no need to hear from additional witnesses," wrote *National Review.*[4]

"Pathetic," stated an email from a Memphian.[5]

On Saturday, February 1, at 9:15 a.m., staff drove me to the NBC studios on Nebraska Avenue to tape *Meet the Press.*

I knew its host, Chuck Todd, because of our mutual admiration for Doug Bailey, who had been indispensable to my political career. Chuck began his career working for Bailey on *The Hotline*. For this broadcast, *Meet the Press* would attract more than three million viewers and be number one among Sunday shows. Still, it was not what it once was. When I was education secretary in 1991 and 1992, *Meet the Press* was an elaborate affair with champagne after the event and various network cameras waiting at the exit hoping to record "news" from that week's guest.

My interview was taped and would run the next morning in the last half of Sunday's show, as media coverage migrated toward that day's Super Bowl, Monday's Iowa caucus, and Tuesday's State of the Union address. By Wednesday, the Senate's acquittal of the president would be a headline, but not much of a story.

Later that day, after flying home to Nashville, I took a nap, not realizing how exhausted I was from the last two weeks. Afterward, when I went shopping for dinner, a child brought me a note from her mother saying that she had been a supporter but was "crushed" by my vote not to allow more witnesses.

So many have become so locked into their opinions that they are not able to consider another point of view. And because of such hardheadedness, a growing number of people completely tune out even considering divisive issues. In such an environment, it is hard to persuade anyone that I made a decision based upon principle rather than upon support for—or opposition to—the president.

Most of the media hardly know what to call the few senators who conduct themselves as I do, labeling me a "moderate" even though I have a thoroughly conservative voting record.

* * *

On Monday, February 3, I was back at the Capitol and at my desk when the chief justice arrived at 11:05 a.m. to preside over closing arguments. Senator Graham told me that he had talked twice with the president during the morning and that "Trump [was] pissed" at me and others who have said that "Trump did it." The Tuesday Republican policy lunch was subdued, with Senator McConnell thanking everyone. In the food line, McConnell told me that the president had mentioned to him his unhappiness with me and others who had said that he did something wrong.

"Get over it. You've won," McConnell said he had told Trump.

That evening, I attended my eighteenth and final State of the Union address as a senator. (I had attended two others as a Cabinet member.) President Trump, to the relief of Republicans, gave an upbeat speech detailing his accomplishments. He did not mention impeachment. The president's one-hour-and-fifteen-minute address was reminiscent of a *This Is Your Life* reality television show with the president introducing perhaps a dozen heroes and heroines in the gallery.

I sat next to Senator Romney.

"I believe this introducing people from the gallery started with Reagan, but Trump has taken it to a whole new level," Romney said.

When the president finished speaking about 10:25 p.m., I escaped through the side door, raced down the stairs to the first floor, and walked to the Senate side of the Capitol, avoiding most media and visitors. I reached my apartment at 11:00 p.m., issued a statement approving the speech, saw on the news that Joe Biden had come in third in the Iowa caucus reminding me of 1996 when I had come in third—and went to bed.

The next morning, at 9:00 a.m., I presided at the first of many briefings that Senator Murray and I would host on the coronavirus. The administration sent its top guns, including White House Chief of Staff Mick Mulvaney and Secretary of Health and Human Services Alex Azar.

"We meet twice a day and will continue until the virus is under control," Mulvaney assured senators.

I mentioned to Mulvaney that I would be talking at 11:00 a.m. to Secretary of the Interior Ryan Zinke about the "Restore Our Parks Act," and that I hoped to make it a priority in the Senate.

At 11:30 a.m., I walked to the Senate floor to take my turn, as senators made ten-minute speeches before the 4:00 p.m. impeachment vote. I repeated arguments from my statement two weeks earlier that had effectively ended the trial:

> The Constitution does not give the Senate the power to remove the president from office and ban him from this year's ballot simply for actions that are inappropriate. The question then is not whether the president did it, but whether the United States Senate or the American people should decide what to do about what he did. I believe that

> the Constitution clearly provides that the people should make that decision in the presidential election that began on Monday in Iowa.

At the Republican Steering Committee luncheon, I told the caucus that I hoped the House had learned a lesson.

"Don't do this again. Don't send us a half-baked, due-process-deficient, wholly partisan impeachment that seeks to make a weapon of perpetual impeachment, that immobilizes the Senate and the presidency, and elevates the House in a way that creates an imbalance among the institutions of government," I said.

During lunch, news came that Romney would vote guilty. Thus, as we went to vote, there were three positions: (1) Trump did it and it is impeachable—Democrats and Romney; (2) Trump did it, but it is not impeachable—the Alexander rule, which perhaps ten Republicans publicly adopted, and (3) Trump didn't do it and all is "perfect"—the public position of perhaps two-thirds of Republican senators, many of whom agreed with me but wouldn't say anything negative about the president.

Donald Trump Jr. immediately proposed kicking Romney out of the Republican Party.

At 4:00 p.m., senators, lawyers, and the House managers filed onto the Senate floor and took their seats. The Senate secretary shouted, "All rise," and the chief justice arrived.

The chamber was solemn. It felt like we were a jury waiting to announce a verdict in capital case when everyone knew the verdict would be acquittal. The clerk read the first Article of Impeachment.

The chief justice called for a vote.

"Senators, how say you? Is the respondent Donald John Trump guilty or not guilty? A roll call is required. The clerk will call the roll."

The clerk began reading names in alphabetical order.

"Mr. Alexander?" she said.

"Not guilty," I said loudly.

During the last few minutes, in my mind, I had run through whether or not I had doubts, and once again, concluded that I had none. After I voted, I listened for an unexpected vote. There was not one. Senator Romney voted "guilty." The final vote was forty-eight guilty, fifty-two not guilty.

Senator McConnell thanked the chief justice for his "evenhandedness," prompting applause on both sides of the aisle. At 4:40 p.m., the Court of Impeachment adjourned. I took the elevator to my third-floor hideaway and sent Senator Romney an email.

"Mitt. As you already well know, you never make a mistake doing what you believe is right. See you next week. Lamar," I wrote.

CHAPTER 59

An Excellent Relationship

"Everyone in Tennessee loves me—except you, Lamar."

—**PRESIDENT TRUMP, on Marine One,**
Wednesday, March 6, 2019

Nashville. Friday, March 6, 2020.

MARINE ONE, THE PRESIDENT'S HELICOPTER, was flying from Nashville to Cookeville above the devastation that a level-four tornado had caused four days earlier.

The news the day before had reported that a forty-four-year-old Franklin man had become the first Tennessean to test positive for coronavirus. President Trump turned to me, Governor Bill Lee, and Senator Marsha Blackburn.

"This virus came out of the blue. And we were headed toward the best job numbers anyone can remember. Who do you think I'll be running against?" he asked.

Without waiting for an answer, Trump mused about his support for Bill Hagerty, who was running to succeed me.

"My endorsement will help him. No one had ever heard of him until I endorsed him. I am twenty to zero on endorsements in primaries. Sometimes I hate to do it because it discourages other good Republicans," Trump said.

The president peered out the window at neat lawns and modest homes nestled among the hills.

"I love this state. I don't know why, really. It has the right kind of values. It would be a great place to raise children. And they like Trump," he said looking approvingly at Blackburn, an ardent supporter.

Then, he turned to me.

"Everyone in Tennessee loves me—except you, Lamar," Trump said.

"Mr. President, we have an excellent relationship," I replied.

An example of that "excellent relationship" was on display earlier that day when Air Force One landed in Nashville. Aides had ushered Blackburn and me to the president's dressing room in the front of the plane.

"You're welcome to come in here and primp with me," Trump said to Blackburn.

He was looking at the mirror and adjusting a "Make America Great Again" cap on his hair.

I saw an opportunity.

"Mr. President, what you are doing for the national parks with Senators Gardner and Daines is a home run," I said.

"It will help them, don't you think?" he asked.

"Yes, it will help them and you and most important, it is good for the country. It will be the most important conservation legislation since Teddy Roosevelt, and you will be doing something other presidents have been unable to do," I said. "Now, I have a recommendation for you, which will add the forest service and other public lands to the bill and attract support from the sportsmen. It will cost three billion more dollars."

"Do the sponsors want to do it? Does Mitch support it?" he asked.

"Yes. The other sponsors gave me the job of asking you to expand the bill. And if it were me, I would do it. As long as you're going to hit a home run, you might as well knock it way out of the park," I said.

"Then, let's do it," Trump said.

I had more to say.

"There is one downside. It's mandatory spending that's not offset by other savings and some Republicans won't like that," I said, motioning toward Blackburn.

"We can fix the budget during the next four years. I want to do the max," Trump said.

"Okay, we are going to introduce the bill on Monday. I will tell the other senators. They will be delighted," I said

I said this because, working with Trump on the Alexander-Murray health care bill, I saw him tempted to change his mind after he heard push-back from his retinue of supporters and advisers.

"Let's do the max," the president said again.

At 10:15 a.m., Secret Service agents opened the plane door, and the president prepared to descend the steps.

"Don't stumble and fall," he warned, and then said one more time, "I want to do the max."

Today was the first time I had seen the president since the impeachment proceedings one month earlier, when I had said that what he had done was wrong, but that it did not reach the constitutional standard for conviction—it was a "mere sin" and not an impeachable offense. Trump had told Senators McConnell and Graham that he did not like what I had said, but today he was cordial.

Without his support, the "Great American Outdoors Act"—expanded by our Air Force One conversation—would not have become what everyone later agreed was the most important conservation law since Eisenhower's presidency, or, as Trump said when he signed the bill, "at least since Teddy Roosevelt."

For the first time, a president would support using revenues from energy exploration on federal lands to maintain national parks and other public lands. The new law also included permanent funding for the Land and Water Conservation Fund, a proposal that Congress had been attempting to pass since LBJ's Rockefeller Commission recommended it in 1962.

The outdoors law had surmounted an intimidating array of obstacles—budgetary rules, the opposition of some Western Republicans who didn't want federal ownership of more land, demands of Louisiana Republicans for shore restoration funding, and the distaste of environmental groups for Trump, himself, and his support for more oil and gas drilling. Appropriators opposed losing their say over spending. Democrats were reluctant to give Trump a win during an election year, and Senator McConnell would have trouble finding time on the Senate floor to debate it.

Yet, on Tuesday morning, August 4, 2020, amidst celebration at the White House, the president signed the law that an unlikely—some said unholy—coalition of Trump and 800 environmental and outdoors groups from the Sierra Club to the National Rifle Association had persuaded a Republican Senate and a Democrat House to approve.

* * *

The journey of the "Great American Outdoors Act" began on Thursday, August 24, 2017, when Trump's interior secretary, Ryan Zinke, visited overnight at our home in the foothills of the Great Smoky Mountains.

He was the fifth interior secretary to stay at our cabin, beginning with Reagan's secretary, William Clark Jr. Zinke is an imposing figure. He did not mention his twenty-three years as a Navy SEAL, but when I asked, I learned that, for ten years, he was commander of SEAL Team Six, the special operations unit that later killed Osama Bin Laden. He had jumped from airplanes 871 times.

Zinke had persuaded Mick Mulvaney, Trump's conservative chief of staff and budget director, to do something no White House had ever before done—approve using revenues from energy exploration on federal land to pay for national park maintenance, instead of to reduce the national debt.

"Does the president know that Mulvaney agreed to this?" I asked.

"Mick agreed, and we need to pass the bill," was all Zinke would say.

I envisioned the former SEAL commander putting an armlock on the five-foot-seven-inch budget director and squeezing until he got a "yes." I also envisioned Zinke not telling Trump the whole story.

Zinke said he had asked to see me because his bill would have the best chance of passage if I would introduce it. He was preaching to the choir. Our home was two miles from the most visited national park. I had grown up hiking in the Smokies, gone on my first snipe hunt there, encountered my first bear, learned to make a fire without matches, and to cook pancakes with wild blueberries. With other families, Honey and I had created conservation easements to protect viewscapes and wildlife on nearly nine thousand acres of land adjacent to the park near Blackberry Farm.

Zinke's idea was not new to me. President Reagan's "Commission on Americans Outdoors," which I chaired in 1986, reiterated a 1962 recommendation of an LBJ commission for permanent funding for the Land and Water Conservation Fund. In my Senate campaigns, I had advocated using revenues from offshore drilling to buy conservation lands and, in 2006, had helped pass a law to allocate some revenues for that purpose.

"Match an environmental burden with an environmental benefit," I had argued.

I had seen the embarrassing condition of the Pearl Harbor memorial. The National Mall, where I took morning walks, was expensive to maintain. The National Park Service maintenance backlog was four times its annual appropriation. Zinke's proposal would eliminate that backlog in ten years.[1]

In March of 2018, I introduced Zinke's "Restore Our Parks Act" with three Democrats, three Republicans, and one Independent. Meanwhile, a "sense of ownership" issue erupted—a problem that has killed many bills. Senators Mark Warner, a Democrat, and Rob Portman, a Republican, had already introduced similar legislation. In April, when Zinke returned to our home for a second overnight visit, we agreed to try to combine the bills.

On June 26, at breakfast in the senators' dining room, I asked Portman to combine the bills and put his name as chief sponsor ahead of Warner's. He agreed, if Warner would agree. The next day, I walked to Warner's office. His staff was unhappy. They had not liked my bill competing with Warner-Portman. And now they heard that I wanted to make it *Portman-Warner.*

I asked to meet with Warner one-on-one.

"First, I'm afraid I've stepped on some toes. I introduced my bill because Zinke visited me last August and asked me to do it. I was only trying to get a result," I told Warner.

Then, I asked Warner to allow Portman to take his place as lead sponsor.

"We need a Republican as chief sponsor, especially one who has been the director of the Office of Management and Budget. The bill includes mandatory spending and Republicans don't like that. It has nothing to do with you. It has everything to do with having a Republican president and Republican Congress."

Then, I made a confession.

"Portman and I both have made plenty of speeches about how mandatory spending causes the budget deficit, but this time we're rising above principle to do the right thing," I said.

Warner agreed to play second fiddle to Portman, even though that meant giving up being lead sponsor of the most important conservation law in at least seventy years. After that, I always referred to the bill with both names, Portman-Warner. Warner was the most important of several senators who gave up their places in line to help the outdoors bill parade make it to the finish line. In June, we introduced the Portman-Warner-Alexander-King bill with thirty-three sponsors—nineteen Democrats and fourteen Republicans.

A similar House bill, led by Idaho Representative Mike Simpson, added permanent funding for the Land and Water Conservation Fund. Advocates wanted that provision in the Senate bill. I said no.

"Look, I've supported that fund for thirty-five years, but that's more baggage than the train can carry and still get to the station," I told them in my office.

Although I believed that the parks bill could not pass with the Conservation Fund in it, North Carolina Republican Senator Richard Burr and House Democrats made clear that our parks bill would not pass *without* it.

So, I changed my mind and included the Land and Water Conservation Fund, creating broader support from conservationists but more opposition from Westerners and budget hawks.

* * *

The Kavanaugh Supreme Court nomination, Trump's looming impeachment trial, and the approach of a presidential election year slowed down legislative action until the next year.

On Wednesday, February 5, 2020, as Trump's trial was ending, I sat next to Senator McConnell at the Republican Steering Committee luncheon.

"I want to come see you next week about bipartisan legislation," I said.

McConnell immediately brought up the parks bill. He had been studying it.

"I would like this to be my going-away present," I said.

"I would like to do it for you, but more importantly, for the country, because it is an important, bipartisan bill," he said.

He did not need convincing. He only wanted to know *how* to do it, given the opposition among many Republicans.

"I'll come see you with a plan," I said.

A week later, in his office, I described my plan to ensure that Trump, himself, was an advocate of Secretary Zinke's proposal.

"The best strategy is to take Daines and Gardner to see Trump and make it all political. Tell the president it is about their election and his," I said.

McConnell and I agreed to tie together the parks bill and the Land and Water Conservation Fund, and that he would take to the White House two Western Republican senators, Steve Daines of Montana and Cory Gardner of Colorado, both of whom were in the midst of difficult reelection campaigns.

"I'd better not take you, because you know how sensitive he is to any criticism," McConnell said, referring to what I had said earlier that month about Trump's telephone call to the Ukrainian president.

"Get sixty cosponsors if you can," he also told me.

Sixty were needed to overcome filibusters and budget points of order.

Two weeks later, on Thursday, February 27, McConnell, Daines, and Gardner met with Trump in the Roosevelt Room across from the Oval Office.

Gardner brought large photographs with him.

"This is the Black Canyon of Gunnison National Park," Gardner said.

"That's beautiful," Trump said.

"It's one of the most incredible overlooks. It would be terrible if someone put a casino there," Gardner said. (That was a risky statement, I told Gardner later, since Trump, himself, might have wanted to build a casino.)

Then, Gardner pointed to Teddy Roosevelt's portrait.

"If you support and sign this law, you'll be the greatest conservationist president since Teddy Roosevelt," Gardner said.

Trump leaned back, folded his arms, and looked into space.

"Wouldn't you say *ever*?" Trump asked.

After the meeting, Trump put out a tweet. "I am calling on Congress to send me a bill that fully and permanently funds the LWCF and restores our National Parks. When I sign it into law, it will be HISTORIC for our beautiful public lands. ALL thanks to @SenCoryGardner and @SteveDaines, two GREAT Conservative Leaders!""[2]

With this, Gardner and Daines marched into the lead of the outdoors bill parade. One week after my March 7 conversation with Trump on Air Force One, fifty-nine cosponsors introduced the expanded bill. In June, McConnell put it on the floor for two weeks. Ignoring the objection of Senator Lee, McConnell did not allow "killer amendments" that would have defeated the delicately compromised package.

Donald Trump often wears a scowl. But on Tuesday morning, August 4, 2020, when trumpets announced his arrival in the East Room of the White House, the president looked especially burdened, even though he was about to celebrate a great achievement. Having taken the mandatory COVID-19 test, and wearing my red-and-black plaid mask, I sat in the second row. As he presided, the president's mood improved. He compared himself first to Teddy Roosevelt and then to all presidents.

"I can't believe previous administrations didn't do this," he said.

The secretary of the interior joined in the praise.

"Thirty-five years ago to this day, President Reagan appointed a young governor of Tennessee to lead the 'Commission on Americans Outdoors' that recommended the Land and Water Conservation Fund, an idea first proposed in 1962. I added it up. Nine secretaries of the interior and ten secretaries of agriculture have worked on this... and only one president has gotten it done, and that is you," the secretary said to a beaming Trump.

"He's the only president, Democrat or Republican, it could have been done under," Senator Gardner said.

The White House did not invite Democrat members of Congress to the signing—a sour note on an otherwise joyous day, since Democrats had supplied much of the leadership and a majority of the votes for the bill. That night, in my apartment, I wrote thank-you notes to Democrat cosponsors and to Obama's Secretary of the Interior Sally Jewell, for her help in coordinating the coalition of outdoors groups.

* * *

The odyssey of the outdoors bill is an example of the split screen television that I have suggested viewers use to watch the Senate.

Most are drawn to the dysfunction screen, where headline-seekers take extreme positions to attract attention and raise money. Some viewers consider this high entertainment. Others watch and wonder how the republic can survive. Fortunately, another screen is available. On the function screen, one can see senators working across the aisle to resolve differences to create legislation that most senators can vote for and most voters will accept.

The fall of 2018 provided an example. On the dysfunction screen, senators were savaging Trump's Supreme Court nominee, Brett Kavanaugh, with such ferocity that parents wanted to hide their children to keep them from seeing the mayhem. At the same time, on the function screen, one could see seventy-two senators fashioning and voting for a law to address the opioid crisis.

These competing screens remind me of the Bristol Motor Speedway, where 146,000 spectators watch forty screaming stock cars race three inches apart at 100 miles per hour around a half-mile banked track. There are two kinds of Bristol fans. "Wreck fans" are there to watch for collisions. "Race fans" are there to see if a driver with the skill of Darrell Waltrip can win without a wreck. A skillful outcome at Bristol makes less news than a ten-car pileup—just as the Senate's function screen attracts less attention than the dysfunction screen.

Earlier, in chapter forty-one, when I compared the leadership styles of senators and governors, I wrote that viewers watching the function screen are unlikely to see senators exercising a governor's Moses "let's go this way" leadership style. That is the executive's job. In fact, if the president or the governor or mayor does *not* point the way, legislators are left to mill around like cattle, chewing their cuds and wondering which way to wander.

The Senate requires a different leadership style—one more like the drum major of a marching band who selects the music, recruits marchers, and sees to it that they march in formation, play off the same song sheet, and don't wander into a ditch. Sometimes, a resourceful drum major selects one or two soloists to march out front.

Drum major leadership is how the "Great Americans Outdoors" legislation became law. That is what we talked about when Senator Portman organized a supper at 6:30 p.m. on Tuesday, December 1, 2020, in the LBJ Room of the Capitol for Democrats and Republicans who had worked together to pass the "Outdoors Act."[3]

These were senators who followed two rules of the *Little Plaid Book*—"If you want to get something done, give someone else the credit," and, "Borrow good ideas and acknowledge them."

We swapped stories about pulling senators off planes to make sure there were votes to win procedural victories, and other political ins and outs of enacting two proposals that no one else had been able to turn into law. The evening was a reminder of what can happen when a bipartisan team marches in the right direction on an important issue.

We all agreed that, as with most successful Senate outcomes, when the "Great Americans Outdoors Act" parade finally reached its destination, it was impossible to say which of the many marchers had been most responsible for its success.

PART TWELVE

Heartbreak

November 2020 to December 2022

"I hope to see the spring flowers."

—HONEY ALEXANDER,
Sunday, November 22, 2020

CHAPTER 60

On My Knees

"To be able to eat Cheetos and drink Sancerre."

—HONEY, when doctors asked about her goals at the Vanderbilt Stallworth Rehabilitation Hospital, November 17, 2020

Mayo Clinic, Rochester, Minnesota. Wednesday, November 11, 2020.

"YOUR WIFE HAD A STROKE LAST NIGHT. We're taking her for a head scan to assess the damage."

It was the Mayo Clinic nurse calling. When the phone rang at 6:58 a.m. in my hotel room, I had hoped it might be Honey saying that she was feeling better. She always wakes up early. Instead, it was this terrible news.

I went down on my knees and asked God to help Honey.

Since her minor stroke in 2013, I had worried that stroke would be her downfall, and so had she. Yesterday, Mayo Clinic surgeons performed heart procedures that were designed to *prevent* a stroke. I had encouraged Honey to go to the Clinic because its heart doctors were said to be the "best in the world." One of her surgeons had coinvented the procedure. The previous night, they'd said that the results of the surgery were "perfect."

COVID-19 restrictions had kept me from spending the night in the hospital, or even going to visit. I telephoned a doctor, secured permission to go to her room, and arrived at 8:30 a.m. to find a devastated Honey. The stroke had affected her left side. Her left cheek drooped, making it hard to form her pretty smile. She could not speak clearly or move her left hand. Her left leg didn't work well. She was miserable and, despite her spunkiness, was having a hard time accepting this news. It did not help that her doctors said she was the victim of complications that occur only in 1 to 2 percent of cases.

I sent an update to our children and to Vanderbilt doctors.

"Honey will stay at Mayo Clinic until Tuesday. Then we will fly to Nashville, where she will be admitted to Vanderbilt's Stallworth Rehabilitation Hospital for 24-hour care. The doctors see improvement but say recovery is a 3–6 month process. She wanted me to tell you she misses and loves you and misses the grandchildren and Rufus, especially," I wrote.

When visitors' hours ended, I took a cab to a restaurant for dinner, returned to the hotel, and tried to sleep.

* * *

Nine days earlier, on Monday, November 2, Honey and I had flown from Knoxville to Rochester, Minnesota. It was the day before the presidential election.

It was a frantic time in a tumultuous year. The COVID-19 pandemic was worsening. Congress was rushing to finish its work before a new presidential term. In six weeks, I was about to retire from the Senate. Trump's reelection campaign was surging. But I felt certain he would lose, although, after his surprise win in 2016, I was not entirely sure.

On Thursday, the 5th, our second day at the Mayo Clinic and two days after the election, doctors had attempted Honey's heart procedures—but they were not successful. In the waiting room, I had watched TV. Election results were tilting toward Biden, but not settled. It was the same story on Friday—three days after the election.

The next morning, Saturday, November 7, the hospital allowed me to spend the day in Honey's room. Several events diverted our minds from medical matters. Honey and I sold our Nashville home. Beginning in January, we would live at our cabin in the foothills of the Smokies. Our daughter, Leslee, called to say that she and her husband bought a home near our cabin in Maryville. There was a third diversion. It was now four days after the election, the networks had not yet declared a winner, and President Trump was making noise that he would not accept the results if he lost.

I asked my staff to release this statement:

> After counting every valid vote and allowing courts to resolve disputes, it is important to respect and promptly accept the result. The orderly transfer or reaffirming of immense power after a presidential election is the most enduring symbol of our democracy.

By the end of Saturday, networks had all called the election for Biden.

On Tuesday, the 10th, I stayed in Honey's room while doctors made a second try at her heart procedures. Afraid that she might never leave the hospital alive, I wrote her obituary.

At 4:00 p.m., her surgeon called.

"We got a good result and she tolerated it well," he said.

When Honey returned, she told a different story.

"I've gone through hell," she said. She was very uncomfortable.

Honey's stroke occurred before dawn the next morning.

* * *

One day after her stroke, at 6:00 a.m. on Thursday, the 12th, Honey sent an email.

"I need you," she wrote.

I rushed to the hospital. We spent the day together. The previous day, she had mentioned the Serenity Prayer—"God, grant me the serenity to accept the things I cannot change, the courage to change the things I can, and the wisdom to know the difference." I Googled the prayer and read her its history.

Honey was sassy and spunky, but devastated and scared. When the doctors came by, she told them she loved them but hated what they had done to her. I left at 6:00 p.m. when visitors' hours ended. I spent Friday at the hospital, but doctors told me that COVID-19 had spiked and I could not come back until Tuesday.

During the weekend, Trump refused to concede. Most of the news was about the two Georgia Republican Senate candidates who were trying to convince voters that, with Biden as president, they were the only thing standing in the way of a total Democrat takeover, while Trump was claiming that *he* would be the next president.

Senator Schumer telephoned about Honey. I was so grateful that I had a hard time talking.

After fifteen days at the Mayo Clinic, the surgeons said, "Devices are in place and should significantly reduce the chance of another stroke." On December 17, a sunny, cold Tuesday, we flew home to Nashville. On the plane, Honey read for twenty minutes, then leaned back and slept, exhausted from two awful weeks. Patrick Jaynes and Leslee met us at the Nashville airport. Honey was overjoyed to see our dog, Rufus. The paramedic driving the ambulance allowed Rufus to ride to the Vanderbilt Stallworth Rehabilitation Hospital, where a stream of doctors and therapists began their examinations.

"What are your goals?" one asked.

"To be able to eat Cheetos and drink Sancerre," Honey said with her newly crooked smile.

Two days later, very early on Thursday, Honey called me at home in Nashville. Her voice sounded stronger. An impaired swallowing function limited what she could eat, so I brought her creamed potatoes, creamed spinach, and squash soup. The case manager told me that her target discharge date would be December 18, which coincided with my last Senate working day.

* * *

While Honey was trying to recover, President Trump was trying to ignore the election result.

I had set aside Friday, November 20, for farewell media interviews in Nashville at Curb Records, where our son, Drew, had worked for twenty-three years. On a wall, there is a photograph of Patti Page taken when I played the piano as she sang the "Tennessee Waltz" for a golden oldies recording in 2007.

I issued this statement:

> If there is any chance whatsoever that Joe Biden will be the next president, and it looks like he has a very good chance, the Trump Administration should provide the Biden team with all transition materials, resources, and meetings necessary to ensure a smooth transition so that both sides are ready on day one.... Recounting votes and resolving disputes after a close election is not unprecedented and should reassure Americans that election results are valid.
>
> Al Gore finally conceded 37 days after the 2000 election, and then made the best speech of his life accepting the result. My hope is that the loser of this presidential election will follow Al Gore's example, put the country first, congratulate the winner and help him to a good beginning of the new term.
>
> The prompt and orderly transfer or reaffirmation of immense power after a presidential election is the most enduring symbol of our democracy.[1]

Senator McConnell sent an email saying he liked the statement.

Pennsylvania Senator Pat Toomey sent a text expressing concern for Honey and asked that I call him "about what the president is trying to do and what our response should be."

When I telephoned Toomey, he told me, "The president is meeting today with Michigan legislators. He has also been talking with Pennsylvania legislators. They are talking about sending in a substitute slate of electors. This is crossing the line," Toomey said. "I don't think the legislators will do it, but this is a real concern. I suggest that we have a phone conversation with [White House Chief of Staff] Mark Meadows and tell him that if they do this, the Senate won't have fifty-one votes to approve it."

Toomey asked if I would join a noon conference call with Senators Collins, Romney, and Sasse.

At this point, the key dates remaining in the election certification process were Tuesday, December 8 (the "safe harbor" deadline, after which votes certified by states are considered conclusive), Monday, December 14 (electors vote in their states), Wednesday, December 23 (delivery of electors' certified votes to the Senate), and Wednesday, January 6, 2021 (joint session of the Senate and the House for counting the electoral votes).

On our conference call, Toomey, Sasse, Collins, Romney, and I all expressed concern that Trump's refusal to acknowledge the election results could damage the country in three ways: (1) keep Biden from being properly prepared to be president; (2) erode public confidence in democratic elections; and (3) overturn the result if Trump persuaded state legislators to substitute their own slate of delegates.

All agreed that it would be better to make a private call to Meadows. A public statement was what Trump would want—more controversy to persuade supporters that the election was stolen. Toomey tried to arrange a call, but the White House said Meadows was not available.

The next day, Toomey issued a statement declaring Biden president-elect.

"Toomey is no friend of mine," Trump said.

* * *

That afternoon, I drove to the Vanderbilt hospital with Rufus. Honey sat in a wheelchair in the courtyard sun, happy to see us, even with the construction noise next door. The next day, Sunday, we turned on the Titans–Ravens football game during my visit, even though Honey really doesn't enjoy football. She asked me "to snuggle" next to her in bed to watch it. She was afraid.

"I hope to see the spring flowers," she said.

I left at 4:40 p.m. that afternoon to drive to East Tennessee for a day of farewell interviews. I promised to return on Tuesday, and to be in Nashville for the rest of the week.

"We've been together all month," I reassured her.

"Not really. I've been in the hospital and you've been nearby," she said.

In Maryville the next day, Monday, November 23, I released this statement:

> Most states will certify their votes by December 8. Since it seems apparent that Joe Biden will be the president-elect, my hope is that President Trump will take pride in his considerable accomplishments, put the country first, and have a prompt and orderly transition to help the new administration succeed.
>
> When you are in public life, people remember the last thing you do.

* * *

On Thanksgiving Day—in a year that had been a disaster for our family, and, because of COVID-19, for many other families—I brought Rufus to visit with Honey in the hospital courtyard. They hugged and kissed until it became so cold that we went up to her room. We watched football and ate supper. Again, she asked me to lie down next to her, and she held my hand. She craved my companionship—and I craved hers.

The next day truly became the Black Friday after Thanksgiving.

Early that morning, the hospital emailed that, because of COVID-19, there could be no visitors. I felt sick. I had planned to spend the next three days with Honey before going back to the Senate. She would be at the hospital for another three weeks before we moved to East Tennessee. If the restriction was not lifted, I was afraid she could be without visitors, except for doctors, for that entire time. I telephoned to tell her about the visitors' ban. She said she understood, but I could tell she was shaken.

"Cavaliers By Crumley" had sent a photograph of our new puppy, which was to arrive in February. Honey had already named her "Clemmie."

I emailed Clemmie's photograph to Honey, and hoped that it might sound a happy note on Black Friday.

CHAPTER 61

Saying Goodbye

"No one misses anyone in politics. Politics is like quicksand. When you're gone, you're gone."

—SENATOR JUDD GREGG (R-NH)

Washington, DC. December, 2020.

THE SENATE HAD AGREED that I could deliver my farewell address at 10:30 a.m. on Wednesday, December 2, 2020.

I rehearsed it alone in my Dirksen Building office, then walked to the Senate floor, where Senator McConnell was about to begin his tribute. McConnell is known to be stoic. Someone once told President George W. Bush that McConnell was excited about the passage of a bill.

"How could you tell?" Bush had asked.

Senators already on the floor therefore saw something they did not expect—Mitch McConnell displaying great emotion.

"In a stirring scene on the normally staid Senate floor, Mr. Alexander...brought Senator Mitch McConnell, the majority leader and his close friend, to tears," the *New York Times* reported.[1]

McConnell's remarks reflected fifty years of friendship.

In 1970, when I was working in the Nixon White House, Senator Baker had told me, "You ought to get to know that smart young legislative assistant to [Kentucky Senator] Marlow Cook." That legislative assistant turned out to be McConnell.

When we both eventually reached the Senate ourselves, we would have a private dinner at a nice restaurant every few weeks, at which he would sometimes drink one gin martini—never more than one. One such dinner was scheduled for that night, and I was looking forward to it.

When McConnell completed his remarks, I walked to his desk, thanked him, and shook his hand.

"One martini tonight. Just one," he said quietly.

By then, most Republicans were at their desks. About half the Democrats were too. Because of COVID-19, every senator was wearing a mask. It was a large and bipartisan attendance for busy senators. Three years earlier, during most of Senator Reid's retirement speech, I was the only Republican senator on the floor.

At 10:30 a.m., I rose from the front-row corner desk that I had occupied since Senator Gregg retired in 2011. Fifty-three years earlier, I sat in a staff chair by that same desk while Baker delivered his maiden address.

A United States senator's two most significant speeches traditionally are the maiden speech and the farewell address. The first is an opportunity to tell the world what is most important to the new senator. In my maiden address, delivered nearly eighteen years earlier, I proposed—and Congress passed—summer "presidential academies" for outstanding teachers of American history. The farewell address is a time to reveal what the senator has learned while in office. I focused on a single subject—"Why our country needs a United States Senate."

As usual, I had written my own speech using lessons I learned over years of practice. I told stories, avoided sermonizing, minimized the use of the personal pronoun, and kept in mind Senator Dirksen's advice about enjoying the luxury of an unexpressed thought.

The reaction to my speech was generous, as is typical of remarks at a graduation, retirement, or funeral.

"There were so many tributes that votes were delayed," *Roll Call* tweeted.

"The citizens of this country will miss you in ways they do not fully appreciate," filmmaker Ken Burns emailed.

"Every Republican of this era will be defined, at least partly, in relation to how they interact with Donald Trump. But for Lamar, he's got a body of work that's long enough, and deep enough and bipartisan enough, that that's not the only thing that will be written about him," said Senator Brian Schatz, a Democrat from Hawaii.

The praise was not universal.

"Senator Alexander accomplished eighteen years of absolutely nothing. Just like most of his Republican colleagues," an MSNBC commentator said.

At 6:45 p.m., I rode with McConnell to The Prime Rib for the last of our occasional dinners. We each ordered our ritual Hendrick's gin martinis, straight up, which McConnell sipped slowly throughout the two-hour meal. Over Dover sole, fried potatoes, and creamed spinach, we swapped stories, told a few secrets, and enjoyed ourselves. He didn't ask for my vote. I didn't ask for his help, although I had a few bills that needed it during the last three weeks of the session.

He was amused that Georgia Republican Senate candidates were running television ads featuring his support for President Trump's judges.

"I told the staff to enjoy it. As soon as this is over, the base will be mad at me again because I will have to work with Biden," he said.

When I returned to my apartment, I telephoned Honey to let her know that I would be back in Nashville the next night, and that COVID-19 restrictions at Vanderbilt hospital had been relaxed so I could visit her. Then, I telephoned our son, Will. While we were talking, a call came from an unknown Washington, DC, number, which I normally would not answer.

I did take this one. To my surprise, it was the president-elect.

"I just wanted to call and let you know you are one of the good guys," Joe Biden said.

Biden was calling because I had talked in my farewell address about working with him on "21st Century Cures" legislation. After the call, I checked my email and found this message from our oldest son, Drew, which of all the day's tributes, meant the most. I printed, framed, and hung it by the door in my office at home:

> I watched the entire tribute.
> It was amazing.
> I'm so grateful to have you as my dad.

—Drew Alexander
President
Blair Branch Music, LLC

* * *

The *Little Plaid Book* offers this glimpse of what happens after you leave office—"When out of office, expect to be confused with wide receivers, newscasters, and country music singers." The book also suggests appropriate conduct. "Attend your successor's inauguration, but keep in mind that your role is approximately that of the corpse at the funeral—everybody just wants to look and make sure that it's you and that you're gone."

And, "Accept gracefully that you are out. Australians put it this way—*'Rooster today. Feather duster tomorrow.'*"

"We don't have a good way to say goodbye in the Senate," New Mexico Senator Pete Domenici told me when he retired in 2009. So, I hosted a goodbye dinner for Domenici at the Alibi Club in its dilapidated, narrow building three blocks from the White House. The Club was organized in 1884 as a "retreat where gentleman may associate without interference from process servers, publicity hounds, bill collectors, political satraps, and curious females."

Its name is derived from a sign above its pay telephone suggesting the amount of tip for the steward who answers when a wife calls looking for her husband:

Telephone tip re: Irate wives
Just Left $.25
On His Way $.50
Not Here $1.00
Who? $5.00

Club members have hosted significant gatherings in this setting. After World War II, Secretary of State George Marshall Jr. held meetings to plan the European reconstruction. In 1973, George H.W. Bush, then Republican Party chairman, and Bryce Harlow met there to try to calm down Nixon Cabinet members "who said they couldn't stand any more arrogant behavior by (Bob) Haldeman and (John) Ehrlichman," according to

Harlow. I hosted several dinners with senators—always including women senators—to encourage bipartisan behavior, which flourished during the dinner but usually disappeared soon afterward.

The day after my farewell address, Vice President Pence called to wish me well.

"I hope that the president will gracefully congratulate Biden if the electors vote for him," I told Pence.

"I will stand with the president," the vice president said.

In the afternoon, I delivered a "salute to the staff speech" and walked back to Hart Building 902 where eighty staffers had assembled, most of them wearing red-and-black plaid shirts. The next day, Friday, December 4, I walked to the basement of the Russell Office Building for my final appointment with Mario D'Angelo, who had first cut my hair in 1977 when I was on Senator Baker's leadership staff.

Life was rushing to a conclusion on many fronts. Retiring from politics again—and surely my political virus would be extinguished this time. Saying goodbye to senators. Finding jobs for staff. Shipping papers to the Vanderbilt archives. Moving out of my Washington, DC, apartment. Selling our Nashville home. Leaving friends in all those places.

The Senate session was ending too, but it was bringing good news. Senator McConnell and Speaker Pelosi announced that they had agreed to pass an omnibus appropriations bill before the year's end. That meant one more year of enacting spending priorities that I had helped to implement on the appropriations committee. As a result, over eight years, percentage increases of funding for science—mainly national laboratories—as well as funding for medical research, grew more than any other part of the budget.

The passage of this appropriations bill also created an opportunity to add difficult legislation that I had been pushing for years—ending surprise billing, simplifying student aid forms,[2] canceling $1.3 billion in debt for historically Black colleges, providing Pell Grants for prisoners, and funding community health centers. This demonstrated, once again, that the secret to creating a law is to have a bipartisan legislative proposal written, vetted, scored by the Congressional Budget Office, and sitting there waiting for a train to come along to carry it to the station. In this case, the train was the end-of-the-year "must-pass" funding bill.

* * *

On Wednesday, December 16, I spoke at the last senators' prayer breakfast of the year.

Like every other Senate meeting during COVID-19, it was virtual. At 8:30 a.m., I played hymns on a piano that the staff had moved into my office. I told stories of playing Mozart at age five and of playing "Amazing Grace" for Billy Graham's crusade. I had spoken at the prayer breakfast half a dozen times. In no other forum had I learned as much about the personal lives of senators.

At 10 a.m., as I presided for the last time over the Senate, Senator McConnell noted the absence of a quorum, and the clerk began a slow call of the roll. "Mr. Alexander" had been the first name called in alphabetical order several times a day for eight years—since January 3, 2013, when Senator Akaka of Hawaii retired. Next year, the clerk will start with "Ms. Baldwin." Not since the early 1800s has there not been a senator with a last name beginning with an "A."

Leaving the chamber on the way to my hideaway on the third floor, I strolled through corridors that I had walked for a half-century. On the walls are photographs of senators I had admired during the 1950s and 1960s—Goldwater sitting and Tower standing on the Capitol steps, so as to give the five-foot-four Tower more stature; Mansfield umpiring, Jack Kennedy catching, and "Scoop" Jackson swinging a baseball bat; Baker and Pearson at a hearing resting their chins on their hands, as senators will do.

I took the elevator down to the second floor. Turning left, I walked between the busts of Vice Presidents Nixon, Johnson, Truman, and Barkley. Heading for the rotunda, on the left, I passed the Mike Mansfield Room, the space the majority party uses for its meetings. On my right was S-230, the Howard H. Baker Jr. room, the entrance to the suite of the Republican leader, where I worked for a few months in 1977.

Across the hall was the Old Senate Chamber, where, from 1810 to 1859, senators forged compromises to try to hold the nation together. Now, senators hold leadership elections and other important meetings there. At one of those meetings, by chance, Mitt Romney sat at Sam Houston's desk. I reminded Romney that he and Houston are the only two Americans who have been governor of one state and senator of another.

On Thursday, December 12, in the second floor dining room of the Federal Reserve Building, I ordered a turkey and cheese sandwich for my lunch with chairman Jay Powell.

"I invited you today to thank you for what you did in 2012 to help me get confirmed," Powell said. He also thanked me for being one of two Republican senators to vote against a law limiting the Fed's independence.

"Senators who can't balance a budget can't be trusted to raise interest rates to control inflation," I told Powell.

On Thursday, December 17, I met with Sen. Schumer in his Capitol office. For years Capitol Hill newspapers had described me as "McConnell's friend and close to Schumer." But our relationship had gone downhill after he became Democrat leader in January of 2017. Our goodbye visit was cordial but brief. Schumer said he would get in touch with me about ideas for senate rules changes—but he never did.

At the end of that week, on Saturday, December 19, at 5:00 p.m., when the Senate had concluded its work for the year, I walked to Hart Office Building. A piano had been moved to the center of the atrium. The Senate had passed a resolution asking me to play Christmas carols. Senators were much in need of good cheer. The session had been contentious. Trump would not concede. Parties were brawling in the Georgia runoff. Tempers were hot.

As I played carols, word spread, and soon singing senators and staff hungry for bipartisan Christmas spirit filled seven floors of balconies above the atrium. Virginia Senator Tim Kaine, a Democrat, stepped forward with his harmonica. He and I had performed together three years earlier at a bluegrass festival in Bristol, a city that straddles the Virginia-Tennessee state line. This Christmas, we played "Go Tell It on the Mountain." There was a good feeling all around.

* * *

At 10:30 a.m. on Thursday, December 24, a nurse wheeled Honey to the entrance of the Vanderbilt Stallworth Rehabilitation Hospital where Patrick Jaynes and I were waiting.

I helped her into the front seat of a rented van, and we drove toward the mountains and home. For a while, Honey rode quietly. Then, she turned to me.

"I'm in a state of shock. This is my first time out of hospitals since we flew to the Mayo Clinic last month," she said.

It was late afternoon when we reached the long driveway to our Smoky Mountain cabin. Snow was falling on the ridges and fields. I built a fire and we ate a Texas barbecue supper. We listened to David McCullough's *The Wright Brothers* as we went to sleep together in our own bed for the first time in seven weeks.

It was Christmas Eve, and life seemed almost normal again.

CHAPTER 62

January 6, 2021

"How remarkable that this has survived for so long in such a complex country when so much power is at stake —this freedom to vote for our leaders and the restraint to respect the results."

—MY REMARKS at The Second Inauguration of Barack Obama. January 21, 2013

Washington, DC. Friday, January 8, 2021.

ON SUNDAY, JANUARY 3, 2021, I retired from the Senate and went home to Tennessee.

Three days later, on Wednesday, January 6, a mob of President Trump's supporters stormed the US Capitol, trying to interrupt the certification of Joe Biden's election. On Friday, January 8, I returned to Washington, DC, to receive my second COVID shot because the vaccine was not yet easily available in Maryville.

Arriving at about noon, I walked up the steps to the Senate side of the Capitol, following one path that the rioters had taken two days earlier. It was the end of a turbulent week of swearing in senators, the attack on the Capitol, and certifying the presidential election. Most members of Congress had fled for home.

Because the Capitol seemed deserted, the damage was more obvious. On the second floor, by the entrance to the Senate chamber, I saw shattered windows, pieces of glass on the floor, broken benches, and doors split open. Walking down the corridor, what I saw turned my stomach. I tried to imagine what I would have done had I been at my front row desk when rioters broke in while senators were debating a challenge to Arizona's electoral votes.

My first thought was that I would have been so angry that I would have stayed at my desk. Let the mob come. But surely the Capitol police would have persuaded me to follow other senators rushing from the Senate floor, down back steps, and through a tunnel to safety in Room 219 of the Hart Office Building.

"Hurry. Time is not our friend," Senator Roy Blunt remembers one officer urging again and again.

As rioters rushed up other steps to the second floor, one brave officer backed up slowly toward the Ohio Clock, distracting attention from senators escaping down the back steps. For six hours, most senators waited under guard in the Hart Building until police cleared the Capitol. During that time, seven of the fourteen Republicans who had announced that they would object to at least one state's certification of Biden's election changed their minds.

The rioters had entered the unlocked third floor gallery, climbed over chairs, leaped to the Senate floor, and opened doors to other rioters. Some climbed to the presiding officer's desk, taking selfies. Others broke into offices, pounded on doors, sprayed fire extinguishers and climbed statues.[1] A Nashville bartender was photographed climbing over chairs in the Senate gallery holding stolen zip ties that prosecutors said he planned to use as makeshift handcuffs.[2] Had I stayed, I might have found myself strapped to the chair at my desk or worse.

After my COVID shot, I retraced my steps through halls that the mob had roamed, and out a door that they had smashed. I drove to Dulles for the 6:15 p.m. flight to Knoxville. When I returned home, Honey was asleep.

I have recounted why I did not vote to convict President Trump in his first impeachment trial. The president's telephone call to encourage Ukraine's President Zelenskyy to investigate Biden, and then delaying military aid to prod Zelenskyy was grossly inappropriate. Nevertheless, I concluded that Trump's actions did not reach the constitutional requirement for the "high crime and misdemeanor" necessary for conviction.

Removing a president from office and taking him off ballots already printed for merely inappropriate actions seemed to me like imposing capital punishment for leaving the scene of an accident. The people, in an election, should decide what to do about the president's inappropriate conduct.

What happened on January 6 was different. Shortly after one that afternoon, at a rally near the White House, President Trump said to thousands marching down Pennsylvania Avenue to the Capitol, "We won this election, and we won it in a landslide.... If you don't fight like hell, you're not going to have a country anymore." The marchers' goal was to stop Congress from certifying electoral votes that states had already determined were accurate. Brandishing baseball bats, flagpoles, knives, guns, metal batons, and broken table legs, as many as 2,500 rioters engaged in hand-to-hand combat that injured 140 Capitol police officers.[3]

Court records show that one rioter was convicted of wrapping his arm around a police officer's neck, pulling him into the crowd, and yelling, "I got one." Another swung an American flag with a metal pole at officers. Still another wore brass knuckles, fighting with a police officer who was later hospitalized. One yelled at an officer, "You're going to die. Get out of the way."[4]

During his seventy-minute rally speech, Trump did say, "I know that everyone here will soon be marching over to the Capitol to peacefully and patriotically make your voices heard." But a few minutes after the speech, his staff told him the invasion of the Capitol was already underway. During the next three hours, the president's family, friends, and Fox News hosts encouraged him to call the mob off. But Trump did nothing, according to his former Chief of Staff in Congressional testimony. Finally, at 4:17 p.m., he tweeted a video telling the mob to "go home." At about 5:30 p.m., they did. By then the damage was done. At 8:06 p.m., senators returned to the Senate floor. After midnight, Congress certified Biden's election. Courts later sentenced 1,500 people for their part in the riot.

Sentencing one rioter who had climbed through a broken window, federal Judge Royce Lamberth, a Texas-born Reagan appointee known for his conservative views, said, "Having read dozens of indictments... I can say confidently: Nobody has been prosecuted for protected First Amendment activity. Nobody is being held hostage. Nobody has been made a prisoner of conscience. Every rioter is in the situation he or she is in because he or she broke the law."[5]

* * *

I knew something about an extraordinary transfer of power.

As I have written at the beginning of this book, four decades earlier legislative leaders had sworn me in three days early to oust a governor who was releasing prisoners in exchange for cash. Those leaders were Democrats, members of the opposite political party. They acted at the urging of another Democrat, the United States attorney. Before the swearing-in, all of us involved insisted that the state attorney general, also a Democrat, deliver his opinion that the state constitution and laws authorized it.

None of us wanted to participate in such an extraordinary transfer of power that looked like a coup, but we knew we had to do it to stop the governor from issuing pardons And we made certain that, unlike what would happen in Washington, DC, on January 6, 2021, Tennessee law authorized what we were doing.

On January 21, 2013, thirty-four years after my early swearing in as governor, I stood on the balcony of the US Capitol at President Obama's second inauguration. Assembled in front of me were one million Americans standing along the Mall from the Capitol to the Washington Monument. As senior Republican on the Rules Committee, I had one minute to address the crowd on this sunny and frigid morning.

Waiting to speak, I thought about a recent visit to Mt. Vernon when the tour guide told me what George Washington had said about the peaceful transfer of power.

Then I said:

> "Today we praise the American tradition of transferring or reaffirming immense power in the inauguration of the President of the United States. We do this in a peaceful, orderly way. There is no mob, no coup, no insurrection. This is a moment when millions stop and watch. A moment most of us always will remember. It is a moment that is the most conspicuous and enduring symbol of our democracy.... Our first president, George Washington, posed this question: 'What is most important, Washington asked, of this grand experiment, the

> United States?' Washington answered his own question in this way: 'Not the election of the first president, but the election of its second president. The transfer of power is what will separate our country from every other country in the world."

* * *

Eight years after my address at President Obama's second inauguration, President Trump refused to accept the 2020 election result even after his own United States Attorney General, Bill Barr, told him that the Department of Justice had found no fraud that would justify overturning the result. The Attorney General also said that he believed that Trump "knew well he lost the election."[6]

Barr issued an order allowing the ninety-three United States attorneys, most of whom Trump had appointed, to pursue any "substantial allegations" of voting irregularities in the presidential election. There were irregularities. There always are. But President Trump's attorney general and his US Attorneys did not find anything that would overturn the result. All fifty states and the District of Columbia, and then the Congress, certified the result. The Trump legal team filed more than sixty unsuccessful lawsuits trying to overturn that result.[7]

"[The rioters] told the world that the election was stolen, a claim for which no evidence has ever emerged," Judge Lamberth said.[8]

On Wednesday, January 6, 2021, President Trump encouraged a mob marching to the US Capitol to stop Congress from certifying Joe Biden's victory.[9] The acting head of the Capitol police testified that the crowd on the Capitol grounds became "well over 10,000" people. When about 800 of them actually entered the Capitol building it became "the most violent attack against the seat of government since the War of 1812," according to *USA Today*.[10]

In doing so, Trump undermined the United States Constitution and assaulted one of the most hallowed precepts and practices of the American Democracy, the peaceful transfer of power after an election. The president then ignored pleas to stop the rioters until it was too late.

If those actions do not constitute a "high crime or misdemeanor," I do not know what does.

CHAPTER 63

Our Best Years

". . . [L]ove one another; as I have loved you."

—JOHN 15:12

"All things bright and beautiful,
All creatures great and small,
All things wise and wonderful;
The Lord God made them all."

—CECIL FRANCES ALEXANDER

West Millers Cove. 2021 and 2022.

When we arrived at our cabin on Christmas Eve, it had seemed like life might be almost normal again.

But it would not be. Waiting for us was the first of Honey's round-the-clock helpers. Beginning on Christmas morning, a nurse came each day until I was trusted to take blood pressure and oxygen readings, and administer an assortment of medicines.

Two weeks later, I was working in my office thirty yards from the cabin when Honey called my cell phone.

"I'm in trouble," she said.

Honey had suffered a seizure. We rushed thirty miles to the University of Tennessee Medical center in Knoxville. The seizure caused a twitch in her left hand, obliterating all rehabilitation progress since November's stroke. Honey asked me to stay with her.

"I'm dying. When I'm gone, you'll need someone to be with you," she said.

When we went home on Friday, January 15, Honey wanted me with her constantly.

"Where are you going?" she would ask when I stepped on the porch to take a call.

We slept in the same bed almost every night for the next two years.

Honey's dependence was new. She had raised our first three children while I was walking across the state; traveled on her own to eighty Iowa towns during my presidential campaigns; and stayed in Tennessee alone many nights during my years in the Senate. I cherished my new time with her. Instead of Honey always doing something for me, maybe I could do something for her. The next two years became our best years.

We looked for things that she still *could* do. We listened to audiobooks by David McCullough, Stacy Schiff, and Jon Meacham. Watched any film we could find on television by Ken Burns. Swapped advice with the Blackberry Farm master gardener. Drove into town for physical therapy and to St. Andrew's Episcopal Church, where she struggled to her feet when the rector came to her pew to administer communion. With Rufus resting on her leg, we rode in the golf cart searching for sweet-smelling coreopsis. Her doctor granted permission to enjoy a "thimbleful" of Sancerre at 5:00 p.m. Sometimes, she asked for an additional "splash."

Her greatest love had been running. "My positive addiction," she had called it. She usually covered two to three miles a day, up to twenty-five miles a week—by the governor's residence, around the emperor's palace in Tokyo, along the sidewalks of Sydney, up and down mountain roads, between rows in soybean fields during a campaign stop. Now, she could barely walk, except in the pool at the Alcoa gym. When the weather warmed up, we lifted her into our pool where she could almost run.

Then, on a Nashville trip in October 2021 to attend the symphony, Honey used a wheelchair for the first time. After that, she rarely got out of it.

* * *

During Christmas week, our oldest child, Drew, fifty-two, fell ill during a trip to Key West. On Tuesday, December 28, I made a round trip by plane to take him to Vanderbilt Hospital, then returned to the cabin. Among other ailments, Drew had COVID-19.

"I could die tomorrow," he said on the flight home.

On Friday morning, we FaceTimed on my computer with the Vanderbilt intensive care nurse, in the way many families did during that time because of COVID-19's restrictions. Honey and I—with Leslee—watched our son take his last breath at 9:30 a.m.

"My baby. My baby," Honey cried.

On Sunday, January 9, we spread Drew's ashes in our family cemetery at Hesse Creek Chapel. We had not imagined that our child would be the first one of us to have a grave there. In June, we joined Drew's songwriter friends in Nashville to celebrate his life.

Despite Honey's bravest efforts, recovery became an illusion. It became more difficult for her to feed herself. In late August, our friend Charlotte Parish died. Honey wrote the family a note.

"I hope you can decipher this.... Oh dear, a stroke takes away so much, my penmanship...but it does not take away love," she scribbled, almost illegibly.

During September and October, all nine grandchildren came for a visit. In Nashville, she attended a fundraiser at the Honey Alexander Center, the new headquarters for Family & Children's Service. The next day, she tried on pretty dresses at her favorite Green Hills clothing store.

"It's the most normal I've felt in a long time," she told her helper.[1] Two weeks later, she wore one of those dresses to a banquet at which Leadership Nashville honored her for cofounding it. The next day, we attended "Drew Alexander Volunteer Day" at Second Harvest Food Bank, where Drew had spent lunch breaks feeding the homeless.

On Wednesday, October 12, six Nashville "girlfriends" drove to Blackberry Farm to celebrate Honey's seventy-seventh birthday dinner, complete with carrot cake.[2] On Saturday, October 22, her sister, Jessica, arrived. It was warm, a season Tennesseans call "Indian summer." We enjoyed a picnic by Hesse Creek and took long golf cart rides. We ate dinner on the porch.

On Thursday, October 27, the temperature rose to seventy-five degrees and Honey exercised for an hour in the pool.

"She was running in the water and didn't want to stop," her physical therapist told me.

"I need some air," Honey told Jessica after leaving the pool.

The two of them, with Rufus, took a golf cart ride. They had just returned to the cabin when I arrived from Nashville, where I had spent two days at the Vanderbilt archives. Leslee was at the cabin too.

"I brought your favorite salad from Nashville," I told Honey.

She corrected my pronunciation.

"Thank you, but it's *caprese* salad, Lamar," she said.

Those were her last words.

"Mom is sick," Leslee suddenly said.

We helped Honey to our bedroom. Her blood pressure was way too high. We rode in an ambulance to UT Hospital. The physician took a CT scan.

"I like to be truthful. She has had a massive hemorrhage on the left side of the brain. There is no way to recover from this," he said.

I told him that we had agreed to use no heroic measures. At 9:00 p.m., nurses moved her to the hospice unit.

That night, I slept next to Honey on the hospital bed and felt her quiet breathing. The next day, family members took turns reading poems and stories, talking and hoping that she knew the sound of our voices. When they had gone home, I sat by Honey on the bed. Her face was beautiful. She seemed at peace. At 8:30 p.m., I leaned over to kiss her. She seemed to not be breathing. The doctor listened for a heartbeat and pronounced Honey gone.

I called the children and lay down next to her until they arrived to say goodbye.

* * *

"On that last day, she was running in the water and didn't want to stop. She was running to heaven," the Reverend Bill Carl said at Honey's graveside service two weeks later.

At 9:45 a.m. on Saturday, November 12, as cold rain fell, sixty family members, friends, helpers, therapists, and physicians gathered outside Hesse Creek Chapel. Mourners moved along the stone walk bordered with Honey's Appalachian baskets filled with flowers. Inside, everyone squeezed together on wooden pews.

Will read from Isaiah, Leslee from Hebrews, and Kathryn from 2nd Timothy. Afterward, "Chariots of Fire" played while grandchildren carried baskets of flowers from the chapel to the gravesite next to Drew's.

On Honey's headstone were words from John 15:12, words that she said not even a stroke could take away:

"Love each other as I have loved you."

* * *

Now the cabin was quiet and my life was empty. I remembered little things from our lives and found tears in my eyes. I felt guilty about urging her to go to the "best doctors in the world," where procedures to prevent a stroke caused a stroke. About being in Nashville the night before she became sick. About politics making me a less attentive father and husband.

On Thursday evening, December 8, 2022, in Nashville, 300 friends gathered at the Honey Alexander Center. The next day, more than 600 assembled at Christ Church Cathedral for Honey's burial service.

The Reverend Lissa Smith, who had grown up with our children, spoke beautifully.

"When Honey got to Easter, never was there a greater 'alleluia.' Decorate tables, gather friends, best Easter egg hunt with actual coins and candy in the plastic eggs, lamb chops, potato salad, asparagus, and desserts galore," she said.

Our children and eight grandchildren read scriptures and prayers while the ninth, four-year-old Wynne, pronounced "Amen" after each prayer.

I was exhausted and my legs were tired. I drove to the flat, ate half a ham sandwich, tried to watch the Celtics play the Warriors, and was in bed by 9:00 p.m. I listened to David McCullough's *The Pioneers* on an audiobook, wishing Honey were lying next to me to hear it too.

I drifted off to sleep thinking of how grateful I was for these two years that Honey and I were almost always together. I hoped that during the last days of my life on earth, I could be as good and kind and loving as she was during all of hers.

EPILOGUE

It Takes Builders

"Any jackass can kick down a barn
but it takes a good carpenter to build one."

—SPEAKER SAM RAYBURN

Maryville, Tennessee. December 15, 2025.

As with the early months of Donald Trump's first term, there was much for me to like about the beginning of his second term.

The president controlled the southern border. There were fewer federal regulations, a tougher attitude toward Iran, less federal control of schools, more plans for nuclear plants, fewer ugly wind turbines, more pro-growth tax cuts and the culture of dividing Americans by gender and racial identity was on the run. I still agreed with the presidential preference for well-done steak.

But other Trump actions damaged the country. The most disturbing of these was his first: pardoning more than 1,500 members of the January 6, 2021 mob that stormed the US Capitol—including those who had assaulted at least 140 police officers.[1]

Then there were the chain saw cuts. This book began with the story of how Sen. Bill Frist worked with President George W. Bush to create PEPFAR, investing 120 billion federal dollars over twenty-three years to fight HIV and saving 26 million lives. That had not been easy. Congress did not like expanding foreign aid. Dr. Frist had to persuade the leading congressional critic of gays, North Carolina Sen. Jesse Helms, that helping those with HIV was "the Christian thing to do." South African President Thabo Mbeki delayed drug distribution because he read on the internet that "poverty" was the cause of HIV. In 2003, I was with Frist in Johannesburg when the Senator tried to persuade Mbeki that the internet was wrong and that delays were causing deaths.

Early in 2025, Elon Musk, President Trump' s billionaire cost cutter, waving a chain saw, slashed roughly 20,000 researchers, scientists, doctors, and staff from the US Department of Health and Human Services and eliminated more than 90 percent of USAID's humanitarian and developmental aid. "[PEPFAR] was decimated in the last 100 days," Frist said in Nashville on Tuesday, April 15, 2025. "When you interrupt people delivering the drugs and the supply chains, [people] die. None of us have ever seen anything quite like this . . .It is wrong."[2] Months later, much PEPFAR funding was restored, but the lives that had been lost could not be. (See the November 5, 2025 article by Atul Gawande in the *New Yorker* citing evidence that as of that date, the dismantling of USAID had already caused the deaths of 600,000 people, two thirds of them children.)[3]

Ten years earlier, on Tuesday, March 10, 2015 in testimony before the Senate Appropriations Committee, Francis Collins, head of the National Institutes of Health, had predicted that with adequate funding there soon could be "medical miracles," including an artificial pancreas for diabetes, non-addictive pain medicines, a heart built from a patient's own cells, early detecting or even prevention of Alzheimer's as well as vaccines for HIV, universal flu, and zika.

The chainsaw cuts swept into disarray thousands of research grants with promise for medical miracles. The cuts canceled hundreds of millions of dollars for cancer-related research and the new administration fired hundreds of employes who were moving those discoveries toward patients.[4] According to Collins, canceled grants included those supporting patients in clinical trials that might have cured their cancer.[5] Nine former acting directors of the Center for Disease Control said that HHS Secretary Robert F. Kennedy, Jr, had "...severely weakened programs designed to protect Americans from cancer, heart attacks, strokes, lead poisoning, injury, violence, and more."[6]

The promise of medical miracles exists, first, because of scientific research. For example, scientists have recently discovered how to extract immune cells from a patient with cancer, genetically alter those cells to help them recognize and cure cancer cells, and then reinsert them into the patient and *cure* the cancer.

The promise exists, second, because, after World War II, the federal government began pouring funds into basic scientific research. As a result, the US has most of the best research universities and no other country has anything like our seventeen national laboratories. That federal funding has led to biomedical discoveries, economic growth, a stronger national defense, and much of what we know about AI. For example, after helping to build the nuclear bomb that won World War II the Oak Ridge National Laboratory near my home supplied radioisotopes for cancer therapy and hosted research on the world's fastest computer.

For decades, millions of the world's brightest students have competed to conduct their research in American universities and laboratories. When I visit Oak Ridge, I see an exhibit of flags of seventy-four countries from which scientists who work there have come. Those who stay have helped make America the scientific world leader. The past two directors of Oak Ridge were born in India and Canada.

After the 1989 Tiananmen Square massacre, I encouraged President George H.W. Bush's decision to punish China by granting permanent residency to 30,000 Chinese students then studying at American universities. This exodus of Chinese brainpower has produced American citizens who are among today's leaders in US business and science. Some foreign students return home, but they take with them an understanding of capitalism and democracy.

In early 2025, as the Trump administration began revoking visas of international students, a *Nature* Magazine poll estimated that "approximately 75 percent of U.S. researchers were considering leaving the country." Because of the chainsaw cuts, scientists were accepting invitations to rebuild their work in more reliable countries.[7]

Ironically, the cuts didn't save much money. The federal deficit is mostly caused by entitlement programs that grow automatically—such as social security, Medicare, and Medicaid—plus interest on the national debt, all of which adds up to about three fourths of federal spending. NIH is a tiny fraction of the total federal budget.[8]

As his second term began, I was disappointed to see President Trump backtrack on two of his most important first term accomplishments on which he and I had worked together. Chapter 59 tells the story of the "Great American Outdoors Act" which Trump proudly called "the most important conservation law since Teddy Roosevelt." The law's goal was to make a significant cut in the $23 Billion national park maintenance backlog. Yet, at the beginning of Trump's second term, he eliminated thousands of national park maintenance jobs.

During his second term, HHS Secretary RFK, Jr. disparaged and limited access to the COVID vaccine, a first-term accomplishment that saved tens of millions of lives and won a Nobel Prize in 2023 for the scientists whose research helped to create it. Trump's "Operation Warp Speed" accelerating development, manufacturing, and distribution of the vaccine must be the fastest, boldest, and most successful federal government enterprise since the Manhattan project built the "atom bomb." This approach also is the strongest candidate to fight future pandemics or acts of terrorism. And, new research has discovered that the vaccine also helps fight cancer: patients with advanced lung or skin cancer who received an mRNA COVID vaccine within 100 days of starting immunotherapy saw a boost in survival time.[9]

Then there was this inconsistency: at the same time Trump was trying to reduce federal control of k-12 schools, he was trying to put the federal government in charge of higher education. His "Compact for Excellence in Higher Education" proposed creating, in effect, a national governing board for 6,000 US colleges and universities. In exchange for federal dollars, the compact would impose strict guidelines on student admissions, grading, testing, and the hiring of faculty, as well as set tuition, define free speech, and limit the number of international students.

* * *

To me, the most disappointing difference between the first and second Trump terms was not what Trump did, but what the senate majority *did not* do: Republican senators rarely checked abuse of presidential authority.

Senators should want the president to succeed so the country can succeed, but senators do not swear an oath to support the president. Their oath is to support and defend the US Constitution, specifically to guard legislative authority over spending, the right to declare war, taxes, and tariffs.

Yet Republicans did little when the president refused to spend research dollars congress had appropriated, spent dollars that congress did not appropriate, canceled $5 billion in foreign aid, blended his family business with official business, launched a "War" against Venezuela, deployed the US military to police American cities and established tariffs that soared to the highest level since the Great Depression.[10]

Neither did Republican senators say much when the president undermined free speech and the rule of law by ordering his Attorney General to punish specific universities, government employees, law firms, and others who had disagreed with him. "We seem to be moving rapidly toward a justice system in which the president essentially gets to decide who should be in prison." Gerard Baker wrote in the *Wall Street Journal.*[11] "If you're a political enemy, we'll come up with a crime to fit your punishment. If you're a friend, we will annul your crimes."

"They did it first" was the schoolyard excuse offered for this conduct. That ignored the schoolteacher's lesson, "Two wrongs don't make a right." Such moral relativism flew in the face of decades of Justice Department independence from the White House. President Carter's Attorney general Griffin Bell once told me that Carter ordered him to prosecute a Texas case that Bell believed would put the defendant in violation of the constitution's ban on double jeopardy. The Attorney General refused and wrote a letter of resignation. The president was angry, but backed down, thus preserving, for then, the independence of the Department of Justice.

To all of this, Republican Senators barely murmured. In the summer of 2025, one historian, comparing events in the United States to ancient history, observed privately that "as the Roman Republic collapsed, the senate continued to meet, but it was a shell of itself."

Except for Rand Paul. The Kentucky Republican became the most consistent defender of the senate's constitutional authority—and he announced his impatience with his colleagues.

"I'm just tired of always being the whipping boy" Paul said. "I'm tired of [being] the only one that has any guts to stand up and tell the president the truth. So these Republicans, they need to man up and they need to say, 'We're going to vote no because of this reason,'" he continued. "And they need to tell the president. But so far, what I'm hearing is rumbling and griping and wanting me to do their job for them."[12]

During Trump's first term, Republican senators had been more assertive. When the president's first budget proposed a 22 percent across the board cut in NIH funding,[13] several of us in both political parties continued to increase funding for NIH over eight years at a rate faster than any other part of the federal budget.[14]

Also in the first term, on Friday, February 15, 2019, Trump declared a "national emergency" and set out to build more border wall using $3.6 billion Congress had appropriated for military barracks and schools. At least twenty Republican senators objected. Two weeks later on the senate floor I said, "After the American Revolution against a king, our founders chose not to create a Chief Executive with the power to tax the people and spend their money any way he chooses."

Then I read to the senate the words of Antonin Scalia, the Supreme Court Justice Republicans most revere.

"Every tin horn dictator in the world today has a Bill of Rights. That's not what makes us free. What has made us free is our Constitution," Scalia had said. "The word constitution...means structure. That's why the framers debated not the Bill of Rights but rather the structure of the federal government. The genius of the American constitutional system is the dispersal of power. Once power is centralized in one person, or one part [of government] a Bill of Rights is just words of paper."[15]

On Thursday, March 14, 2019, one day after meeting with Trump at the White House, I voted with eleven other Republican senators and all Democrats to approve a House-passed resolution overturning the president's action. Trump vetoed the resolution, but the courts ruled that he had abused his authority.

In the first year of Trump's second term, when senators returned to Washington from their August recess, Sen. Paul found that he was not standing alone. In a free speech showdown, Senator Ted Cruz said the Federal Communications Commission chairman acted "like 'mafioso'" when the chairman's threat caused the ABC network to fire (temporarily) comedian Jimmy Kimmel for anti-Trump comments.[16] Five Republican senators voted to terminate Trump's tariffs on Brazil.[17] Wyoming's John Barrasso, an orthopedic surgeon, told Secretary Kennedy he had "grown deeply concerned about your handling of the vaccines."[18] Sen. Susan Collins said not spending money appropriated by congress was "a clear violation of the law."[19]

Kentucky's Mitch McConnell said that President Vladimir V. Putin of Russia had "spent the entire year trying to play President Trump for a fool," and added that if Mr. Trump's top negotiators were "more concerned with appeasing Putin than securing real peace[in the war with Ukraine], then the president ought to find new advisers."[20]

There were other signs of life in the senate Republican caucus. Armed Services Chairman Roger Wicker scheduled a "vigorous oversight" hearing on media reports that Secretary of Defense Pete Hegseth had ordered killing survivors of a strike on a drug-smuggling vessel in the Caribbean Sea.[21]

Sen. Thom Tillis said, "If it is substantiated, whoever made that order needs to get the hell out of Washington."[22] And Alaska's Lisa Murkowski condemned as "flat out wrong:" the administration's investigation into Democratic Arizona Sen. Mark Kelly for posting a video urging troops to "refuse illegal orders."[23]

The most encouraging sign of Republican senators' newfound assertiveness came after Trump wrote online that the senate should "TERMINATE THE FILIBUSTER NOW, END THE RIDICULOUS SHUTDOWN IMMEDIATELY." Also in capital letters, the president explained why he felt that way: "AND THEN, MOST IMPORTANTLY, PASS EVERY WONDERFUL REPUBLICAN POLICY THAT WE HAVE DREAMT OF FOR YEARS BUT NEVER GOTTEN."

The filibuster is the senate's best-known tradition, described in the movie *Mr. Smith Goes to Washington* as "Democracy's finest show," each senator's "right to talk [his or her] head off" until they come to a conclusion. Here is how it works: under senate rules, before legislating can start, a single filibustering senator can insist that sixty of the one hundred senators vote to stop the talking.

Here is why the filibuster is important: it forces senators to come to agreement on controversial issues that most of them can vote for and that most Americans can accept. A filibuster can restrain the president and can check the "tyranny of the majority"—a danger to the American democracy that the Frenchman Alexis de Tocqueville warned of in the early nineteenth century.

Make your own list of what "WONDERFUL REPUBLICAN POLICY" on guns, abortion, tariffs, taxes, use of the military, or immigration might become law if a Senate majority, like the House of Representatives, could pass any Trump proposal. Make a second list, too—of the policies that you'd see under a Democrat president when power shifts: DC statehood, gun bans, court packing, government-run health care, and the end of state right-to-work laws. That is why Presidents Obama and Biden also wanted to get rid of the filibuster even though they had supported it as senators. All presidents like to see their proposals roar through congress like a freight train.

Republican Senate Majority Leader John Thune offered two reasons not to terminate the filibuster.

"The votes aren't there," he said.

His second reason was better.

"Bad idea," Thune said and his Republican colleagues agreed, standing up to the president.[24]

During 2025, the federal courts provided the most effective check on executive actions. According to various trackers of the legal system, as of November, judges had entered over 200 orders to temporarily or permanently stop administration actions.

As the year ended, both political parties seemed to be well aware of this book's argument that the surest way to change the course of the country is to be elected to public office. Both parties spent millions as Democrats won governors races in Virginia and New Jersey and came within nine points of winning a special election in a Tennessee congressional district that Trump had won by twenty-two points. And legislatures in both red and blue states were gerrymandering congressional districts trying to gain an advantage in the 2026 congressional elections.

* * *

On Wednesday afternoon, May 15, 2019, I sat in a front-row pew at St. Luke's United Methodist Church in Indianapolis during a memorial service for Republican Sen. Richard Lugar.

Sen. Sam Nunn, a Georgia Democrat who had worked with Lugar to reduce nuclear weapons, delivered the eulogy.

"As a very young man, Dick achieved the rank of Eagle Scout," Nunn said. "He lived the scout law."

Nunn then listed the law's twelve principles: "Trustworthy. Loyal. Helpful. Friendly. Courteous. Kind. Obedient. Cheerful. Thrifty. Brave. Clean and Reverent."

As Nunn ticked them off, one-by-one, I was wondering, "How well are the rest of us in public life—from President Trump to the mayor of Maryville—living up to those principles?"

Over the years, I have concluded that character and temperament are the most important traits for anyone holding public office. I learned this growing up—in my home, church, scout troop, and school. My piano teacher made sure I knew the motto of Dr. Shinichi Suzuki, the violinist and music teacher: "Character first. Ability second."

Judge Wisdom and Sen. Baker reinforced these values. So did seeing firsthand the stress and the scope of responsibilities of the ten presidents with whom I worked. I am a conservative—a very Republican Republican—but character and temperament matter more to me in choosing a public official than whether that person leans left or right.

Some tell me that putting such a premium on character is naïve. I tell them Bryce Harlow's story about the time President Eisenhower's cabinet was divided and Ike asked, "Well, what would be the *right* thing to do?" If a president who was also the Supreme Allied Commander in World War II could make decisions on that basis, perhaps the rest of us could too.

Today's Digital Democracy discourages putting a premium on character. Instead, it creates an incentive to use coarse language to advocate extreme views on social media to attract attention, raise money, and win primary elections. The uproarious condition in which we find our public discourse therefore should come as no surprise. The public figures who attract the most social media followers continue to be the shrillest and the loudest, turning the national conversation into "screaming, sound bites, and slogans," according to the late FedEx founder Fred Smith.[25]

"Show me the incentive and I'll show you the outcome," Berkshire Hathaway vice chairman Charlie Munger used to say. Today's outcome is because there is not much incentive for forging the kind of consensus that founded and built our Republic. And without consensus, instability, radicalization, and politically-inspired violence make it harder to keep the Republic.

What can we do?

A good place to start is with the 519,682 Americans—from president to school board member—who are already elected to public office and the millions who work with them. Their character, temperament, and language can set a tone.

Still, the most talented prospects for the next generation of officeholders may ask, "Why should I run in an atmosphere that rewards extremists shouting obscenities instead of candidates who want to govern?"

The answer is that campaigns in our Digital Democracy are not easy. I believe that it takes fighting fire with fire. Since social media is the root of the problem, social media must be a part of the solution. I do not mean trying to defeat one's opponent by adopting an even more extreme position or using even coarser language. Instead, use social media messages to attract into primaries more voters who prefer candidates who want to govern instead of those who think their job is done when they finish a speech. Today as few as 5 percent of registered voters—mostly those attracted by extreme views on the left or right—choose primary winners. That leaves those who prefer a candidate who wants to govern with no one to vote for in the general election.

The unpleasant truth is that "if your political views are center left or center right—and a majority of us have such views—your vote doesn't count," former Sen. Ben Sasse has said.[26] The internet democracy has disenfranchised you. You are in the majority in the middle and you are left out. You have lost your opportunity to participate in the founders' vision of a Republic with enlightened voters electing well-meaning men and women to public office and trusting them to make decisions that are in the best interest of the voters.

Adjusting to changes in methods of communication is not a new skill. Five centuries ago, the Catholic Church feared that the first printing press would create books too dangerous to put in the hands of people. Since then, we have learned to live with radio, telephones, movies, and television. Now the worry is that social media will destroy our Republic—and if it does not, artificial intelligence will. We will just have to learn to live with both.

This is no great insight. It is basic politics—message, money, media and votes. If you really want to change things jump in feet first, get your hands dirty, raise and spend campaign funds, absorb the indignities, and join in the messy process.

For our future, it is encouraging that there are one million scouters—now both girls and boys—who are reciting the twelve principles of the law that Sen. Lugar lived by. Our founders expected that such civic activity in homes, churches, and schools would teach values that would temper the exercise of our constitutional freedoms.

But these young Americans are skeptical. "Students today want to change public policy, but they don't like government," says Dr. Marianne Wanamaker, Dean of the Howard H. Baker, Jr. School of Public Affairs and Public Policy at the University of Tennessee Knoxville. That is why administrators avoided the word "government" when naming the Baker School.

I heard the same message from American history teachers when I escorted them to the senate floor when the senate was not in session. Wandering the chamber, some teachers would search for Daniel Webster's desk. Others examined the back row desk that three Kennedy brothers used. Tennesseans wanted to see where Senators Baker, Thompson and I had scratched our names into the drawer of the desk that we all used.

I would point out the desk of Jefferson Davis, a Mississippian who resigned the senate to become president of the Confederacy. During the Civil War, a union soldier drew his bayonet and began chopping the desk that Davis had used. A doorkeeper stopped him.

"You are here to save the Union, not to destroy it," the doorkeeper said.

That story often would prompt a teacher to ask "My students want to know, what will it take to save the Union today?"

"You might teach them that at these desks senators helped build our country," I would answer. "When George Washington was President,

Connecticut Sen. Oliver Ellsworth's legislation created the federal courts. To try to hold the nation together, Missouri's Thomas Hart Benton championed the transcontinental railroad and Kentucky's Henry Clay sponsored the Missouri Compromise among free and slave-holding states. Your students can thank Vermont Sen. Justin Morrill for the land grant colleges they will attend. And give a shout out to Utah Sen. Reed Smoot for authorizing the national park system that we call "America's best idea". After World War II, Michigan Sen. Arthur Vandenberg helped create the Marshall Plan to rebuild Europe."

I would go on.

"Every state has sent builders to these desks. Take Tennessee senators, for example. Andrew Johnson's 'Homestead Act' made land free to citizens moving westward. Cordell Hill's 'Reciprocal Trade Law' reduced tariffs and created a system of trade with other countries. Kenneth McKellar hid $2 Billion in the appropriations bill to build the nuclear bomb that won World War II. Albert Gore Sr. sponsored the law that built the world's most ambitious interstate highway program. And Howard Baker helped to write the Clean Air and Clean Water laws."

I continued.

"It takes builders. Our republic is more likely to survive if your students also become builders. And I hope you will help them understand that the best way to change the direction of our country is to be a builder *in public office.* When former Tennessee Gov. Bill Haslam teaches Baker School students, he tells them that he has been surprised at how much more he accomplished in public office than he can in private life.

"Inspire your students to become a part of a project to save and improve our Republic. They don't have to become a Senator at one of these desks. They can be a school board member or a legislator or work for someone elected to a local office. They can be a citizen politician in their hometowns for a few years. After all, our country works from the bottom up."

Often, as our visit was about to end, a teacher would ask, "What would you like for us to tell our students about being a United States Senator?"

"Please tell them, I would say, "that after seeing public life from almost every angle for a long time, I have learned that the best way to help the largest number of people—and to keep our Republic from falling apart—is to be elected to public office or go to work for someone who has been.

"Tell them that I have been able to wake up every day thinking I might be able to do something good for my state or country and go to bed most nights thinking that I had."

Acknowledgments

WHENEVER THINGS LOOKED BLEAK, whether it was trouble with an obstinate senator, a presidential election, or a war, I often heard Senator Howard H. Baker Jr. assure worried constituents that "the Republic will survive." In this year of his one-hundredth birthday, I thank Senator Baker for the title of the prologue and for his example, decency, and friendship that inspired me to spend five years writing this book to try to persuade readers that, despite the indignities that come with it, the most reliable way to help the most people—and to help the Republic survive in our contentious Digital Democracy—is to be elected to public office or go to work for someone who has been.

I am grateful to Jon Meacham for lending his talent for prose to the foreword, for tolerating my questions about how to write a personal history, and for leading me to a gifted editor and agent, Will Murphy. Hopefully, Will's experience, skill, and patience squeezed my verbosity into a more readable story. Liz Wolgemuth, my Senate communications director who stuck with me from start to finish on this project, was of indispensable help and offered numerous useful insights.

I thank Anthony Ziccardi, Aleigha Koss, and their team at Post Hill Press for guiding me through the maze of book publishing. Julie Tate was invaluable for her fact-checking.

I am especially grateful to Robin Hood, the Pulitzer prize-winning photographer with the improbable name, and his technical assistant, Med Dement, for contributing the cover photograph as well as other photographs and for helping to arrange the displays of photographs inserted within the book. I thank Annie Leibovitz for allowing me to purchase the photograph she made of Honey and me during the 1996 presidential campaign. It perfectly captures that moment in our lives.

I selected other photos for this book from among thousands that have come my way. Some came from the White House or from Tennesssee's Division of Photographic Services. A few I purchased from newspapers, wire services, the Nashville Public Library, or from the photographer directly. The rest are photographs that friends gave us to enjoy. I have tried to identify every contributor. To everyone who contributed, I say, "Thanks." In addition to Robin Hood, those include Harry Butler, Bill Welch, Keel Hunt, and Cyndy Waters. To anyone I have missed, I apologize.

Throughout my work on this memoir, I have relied upon the staff of the Vanderbilt University Archives, who have spent the last eight years cataloging and placing online papers and photographs from my life. My special thanks to the university librarian, Jon Shaw, and to Zach Johnson, associate director of Digital Special Collections, and his associates for invaluable assistance. The daily diary that I kept during 2005 and during my last dozen years in the Senate proved indispensable in providing documentation for dates, events, conversations, and stories that I have included in the book.

Several friends read sections of the manuscript and offered comments. For this I thank Victor Ashe, Roy Blunt, Josh Bolten, Adam Buckalew, Jane and Bill Carl, David Cleary, Francis Collins, John Danielson, Daniel Diermeier, Checker Finn, Bill Frist, Lindsay Garcia, Scott Gottlieb, Grace Graham, Judd Gregg, Hal Hardin, Skila Harris, Barney Haynes, Tom Ingram, Patrick Jaynes, Debby and Bill Koch, Keel Hunt, Ed Lampert, Jon Meacham, Bruno Manno, Trent Lott, Bill Mowry, Charles Overby, Brian Reisinger, Ross Sandler, Ben Sasse, Lindsey Seidman, John Sergent, Steve Smith, Deepak Srivastava, the late Paul Tagliabue, Marianne Wannamaker, Agnes Warfield-Blanc, and Andy Wisdom. Of course, only I am responsible for what I have written.

Polly Walker, my assistant, kept manuscripts flowing and, as always, made life easier.

A superior staff can bring out the best in a public official. Staff members an also help an office holder keep his feet on the ground. Whenever my staff felt I had gotten too big for my britches as governor, they would suggest that I put on my red-and-black plaid shirt, go take a walk, and get over it.

I was fortunate to work with a superior staff from the beginning to the end of my public career. There is no way fully to acknowledge the hundreds with whom I worked in campaigns or in state government, at the University of Tennessee or in the US Department of Education, presidential campaigns, and the Senate. Hopefully, each one will realize that this volume is a thank you and celebration of his or her public service.

During eighteen years as a senator, I worked with 370 staff members on campaigns and in Tennessee or Washington, DC, Senate offices—not to mention 433 interns. On December 4, 2020, the day after my farewell address, I delivered a "Salute to the Staff speech" on the Senate floor, then walked to the Hart Office Building where eighty staffers had assembled in Room 902, most of them wearing red-and-black plaid shirts.

This is what said to them.

"When I say superior staff—here's what I mean: Superior in being what Senator Baker called an 'eloquent listener'—understanding that the constituent on the phone line might be right—or that other staffer in the other office might be right. Superior in courtesy to the Tennesseans for whom we work. Superior in insight. Superior in resolving complex issues and wrapping up the result in a nice package ready for passage, which usually will be at some unexpected moment. And superior in writing and speaking plain English that persuades at least half the people we're right. Also—superior in working well together so that we have a good time while we're working."

Unlike almost every other Senate office, at the suggestion of Chief of Staff David Cleary, I created a single team composed of personal, office, and committee staff, Washington, DC, and state staff. This arrangement improved communication, cohesiveness and produced better results.

On the day I retired from the Senate, January 3, 2021, David Cleary was still on the job, Allison Martin was legislative director and counsel, Liz Wolgemuth was advising on communications, Grace Graham and Lindsey Seidman were heading up health care policy, and Patrick Jaynes was the state staff director.

These are the names of the 364 other Senate staff members with whom I worked: Keith Abraham, Halee Ackerman, Hayley Alexander, Abbey Allen, Stacy (Cline) Amin, Carrie Apostolou, Sarah Arbes, Katie Argo, Jen Armstrong, Abby Atkins, Margaret Atkinson, Jill Bader-Thompson,

Jake Baker, Brandon Ball, Aaron Baluczynski, Andy Banducci, Kristin Bannerman-Herrmann, Kathryn Bell, Bailee Beshires, Anthony Birch, Jeremy Boshwit, Lyndsay Botts, Jennifer Boyer, Charlie Brereton, Kelly Brexler, Palmer Brigham, Justine Brittain, Louie Brogdon, Austin Bryan, Adam Buckalew, Brenda Buescher, Ace Burch, Jonathan Burke, Andrew Burnett, David Campbell, Will Campbell, Victoria (Souza) Campbell Meredith Carter, Laura Chambers-Crist, Robbie Champion, Jane Chedester, Stephanie Chivers, Sarah Chu, Joseph Cody, Chris Connolly, Molly Conway, Mary Catherine Cook, Hannah Cornwell, Margaret Coulter, Tom Craig, Sydney Crawford, Starling Crossan, Joseph Cwiklinski, Lucas DaPieve, Ashton Davies, Elizabeth Davis, Adam DeMella, Evan Dixon, Christine Dodd, Kay Durham, Emily Durnin, Jennifer Ellis, Grant English, Seth Ephrussi, Greg Facchiano, Sarah Fairchild, Anna Catherine Feaster, Qur'an Folsom, Kyle (Hicks) Fortson, Harrison Fox Jr., Emily France, Evann Freeman, Lindsey Fryer, Alice Ganier, Kitty Ganier, Lindsay Garcia, Jaime Garden, Nick Geale, Elizabeth Gibson, Randall Gibson Jr., Houston Goddard, Meredith Good-Cohn, Laura Ray Goodrich, Carolyn Gorman, Elizabeth Gorman, Reynard Graham, John Grant, Jon Grayson, Sarah Greene, Sharon Hagget, Daniel Hale, Jeremy Harrell, Brandon Harrison, Heather Hatcher, Jenn Hatfield, Taylor Haulsee, Crystal Hayslett, Faye Head, William Heartsill, Alicia Hennie, Richard Hertling, John Herzog, Laura (Lefler) Herzog, Kai Hirabayashi, Madison Hite, Jessica Holliday, Alexanderia Honeycutt, Derek Horne, Elizabeth Howell, Haley Hudler, Kara Huffstutter, Jones Hussey, Jordan Hynes, Joel Igelhart, Neena Imam, Tom Ingram, Charlotte Jackson, Jill Jaynes, Jim Jeffries, Lora Jobe, Tonya Johnson, Madeline Jurch, Nora Khalil, Lina Kilani, Kimberly Kirkpatrick, Emily Kirlin, Katherine Knight, Bill Knudsen, Hillary Knudson, Page Kranbuhl, Andrew LaCasse, Lesley Landrum, Mary-Sumpter Lapinski, Trey Lefler, Jeff Lewis, Bridget Lipscomb, Rachel Littleton, Anne Locke, Brett Logan, Linda Long, Ryan Loskarn, Molly Lukic, Nick Magallanes, Christina Mandreucci, Molly Marsh, Misty Marshall, David McAdam, Meghan McCully, Paul McKernan, Mackensie (Burt) McKernan, Bobby McMillin, Virginia (Heppner) McMillin, Kayla McMurry, Brett Meeks, Michael Merrell, Will Meyer IV, Latonya Miller, Meade Miller-Carlisle, Scot Montrey, Lana Moore, Bob Moran, David Morgenstern, Jennifer Moroney, Nicole Morse, Brandon Morton, Kim Morton, Jeff Muhs,

Patrick Murray, Katie Neal, Beth Nelson, Anna Newton, Laura Marks O'Brien, Andrew Offenburger, Katie Oglesby, Peter Oppenheim, Tyler Owens, Mary Parkerson, Will Patterson, Debbie Paul, Megan Paulsen, Austin Payne, Constance Payne, Laura Pence, Kelly Perry, Morgan Petty, Melissa Pfaff, Charlie Phelps Jr., Lee Pitts, Alexia Poe, Greg Proseus, Erin Reif, Brian Reisinger, Sarah Rittling, John Rivard, Michelle Rodriguez, Adam Rondinone, Kristin Rosa, Kristyn Royster, Marguerite (Sallee) Kondracke, Bonnie Sansonetti, Sandra SawanLara, Conrad Schatte, Lowell Schiller, Michael Schulz, Lauren (Davies) Schwensen, Kelly Scott, Sharon Segner, Meyer Seligman, Erin Shea, Trina (Eager) Shiffman, Tyler Shrive, Aliza (Fishbein) Silver, Tiffany Smith, Kathleen Smith, LaShawnda Smith, Rhonda Smithson, Charles Snodgrass, Matt Sonnesyn, Daniel Soto, Kristin (Nelson) Spiridon, Riley Stamper, Daniel Stanley, Matthew Stern, Deborah Sturdivant, Bill Sullivan, Carey Sullivan, Curtis Swager, Caroline Taylor, Rhonda Thames, Josh Thomas, Nathan Thomas, Kristi Thompson, Sean Thurman, Kara Townsend, Diane Tran, Bill Tucker, Harvey Valentine, Tim Valentine, Curtis Vann, Matt Varino, Andy Vogt, Sandra Wade, Jack Wells, Marty West, Mitch Whalen, Rob Wharton, Louann White, Donovan Whiteside, Brent Wiles, Samantha Williams, Mary Wooldridge, Liz Wroe, Sharon Yecies, and Alicyn York.

My greatest debt is to my family, first to Honey, to whom this work is dedicated for reasons that I hope are apparent on almost every page, and then to our four children—Drew, Leslee, Kathryn, and Will—who campaigned, supported, and accompanied me on my meanderings through a public life despite inconvenience to their lives.

This book is possible only because of the love, inspiration, and support of Flo and Andy Alexander, two teachers with six generations of roots in the mountains of Tennessee, and the citizens of Maryville who launched me on the trajectory that became this story.

Appendix A

This was my address to the senate on Wednesday, July 15, 2015 urging senators to vote to cut off debate and pass the Alexander-Murray bill fixing the "No Child Left Behind" law.

"Mr. President, Senator Murray suggested we work on this in a bipartisan way. I took her advice, it was good advice, and this is the result. We have had nearly one hundred amendments in committee and on the floor. I thank the Majority Leader and the Democratic Leader for creating an environment in which we could do that.

"This is a law that everybody wants fixed. We have a consensus on how to fix it. Keep the measurements of academic achievement and turn the rest of it over to the states, the classroom teachers and others that are closest to the children. That's what the governors, that's what the superintendents, that's what the teachers' organizations have said to us.

"Now, in the last few years, we've created a national school board in this country. That has made it harder to have better teaching, harder to set higher standards, harder to have real accountability. So, we changed that. We reverse the trend toward the national school board. We end the Common Core mandate. We end the waivers with new mandates that the Department of Education is using to run public schools. We end DC evaluating teachers and [defining] adequate yearly progress....

"This gives us about eighty percent of what we want. A president named Reagan used to say, 'If you got eighty percent of what you wanted, you might take it and fight for the rest on another day.'

"If we vote 'No' today, that means we leave the Common Core mandate right where it is. That means Education Department waivers are still running your schools. That means that Adequate Yearly

Progress is determined from Washington, DC, and Washington, DC, is evaluating your teachers.

"If you vote 'No,' we fix nothing.

"So vote 'Yes.'

"Do what the governors, do what the superintendents, and do what the teachers say we ought to do. They all agree. This is the most important step in that direction we've had in twenty-five years. Let's not miss the opportunity.

"Vote to restore to the people closest to the children the responsibility for their education.

"Vote 'Yes' for local control of public schools."

Appendix B

This was my statement released to the media at 11 p.m. on Thursday, January 30, 2020, explaining why I would vote the next day not to allow more evidence in President Trump's impeachment trial, effectively ending the trial:

"I worked with other senators to make sure that we have the right to ask for more documents and witnesses, but there is no need for more evidence to prove something that has already been proven and that does not meet the United States Constitution's high bar for an impeachable offense.

"There is no need for more evidence to prove that the president asked Ukraine to investigate Joe Biden and his son, Hunter; he said this on television on October 3, 2019, and during his July 25, 2019, telephone call with the president of Ukraine. There is no need for more evidence to conclude that the president withheld United States aid, at least in part, to pressure Ukraine to investigate the Bidens; the House managers have proved this with what they call a 'mountain of overwhelming evidence.' There is no need to consider further the frivolous second article of impeachment that would remove the president for asserting his constitutional prerogative to protect confidential conversations with his close advisers.

"It was inappropriate for the president to ask a foreign leader to investigate his political opponent and to withhold United States aid to encourage that investigation. When elected officials inappropriately interfere with such investigations, it undermines the principle of equal justice under the law. But the Constitution does not give the Senate the power to remove the president from office and ban him from this year's ballot simply for actions that are inappropriate.

"The question then is not whether the president did it, but whether the United States Senate or the American people should decide what to do about what he did. I believe that the Constitution provides that the people should make that decision in the presidential election that begins in Iowa on Monday.

"The Senate has spent nine long days considering this 'mountain' of evidence, the arguments of the House managers and the president's lawyers, their answers to senators' questions, and the House record. Even if the House charges were true, they do not meet the Constitution's 'treason, bribery, or other high crimes and misdemeanors' standard for an impeachable offense.

"The framers believed that there should never, ever be a partisan impeachment. That is why the Constitution requires a 2/3 vote of the Senate for conviction. Yet not one House Republican voted for these articles. If this shallow, hurried, and wholly partisan impeachment were to succeed, it would rip the country apart, pouring gasoline on the fire of cultural divisions that already exist. It would create the weapon of perpetual impeachment to be used against future presidents whenever the House of Representatives is of a different political party.

"Our founding documents provide for duly elected presidents who serve with 'the consent of the governed,' not at the pleasure of the United States Congress.

"Let the people decide."

Appendix C

I had written President Nixon complimenting him on his remarks at a meeting of Republican governors a few weeks before we left for Australia. This was his response on April 28, 1987. *(Letter follows on pp. 512–513.)*

RICHARD NIXON

April 28, 1987

26 FEDERAL PLAZA
NEW YORK CITY

Dear Lamar,

Of the literally thousands of letters I have received during the forty years I have been in the political arena, I can think of none whihc I enjoyed and appreciated more than the one you sent me from Australia.

You are right on target in your very perceptive observations about my staff. They often disagreed on issues, but this gave me the benefit of well-thought out options when I had to make tough decisions. Whatever one may think of them, they shared one characteristic in common, they were heavyweights. Too often today advisors to public officials are sycophants who are very good at buttering up the boss but who aren't effective in giving him the advice he needs to hear.

Harlow, of course, was one of a kind. There will never be another one like him. I vividly remember meeting him in 1947 on the handball court in the old House office building. He was a fierce competitor, but a completely gracious gentleman at the same time. I only wish he could have written his memoirs during his last difficult years. But whenever I suggested that he do so, he begged off on the ground that he didn't think it was honorable for a staff member to reveal confidences about the "Boss" and his staff or his colleagues. As I am sure you will agree, there is not much of that type of honor around these days, particularly in the White House!

Appendix C

Page 2
The Honorable Lamar Alexander
April 28, 1987

Your comments on Julie's book were most generous. Pat and I naturally are very proud of her and Tricia. It is very difficult for children of celebrities to grow up and not make fools of themselves at some time in their lives. We are very fortunate in that respect as you are.

I think your decision to take six months off was nothing short of brilliant. It will give Honey and you a chance to recharge your batteries and gain a different perspective after so many years of devoted public service. But even more important, you are giving your children a mountain top experience. I am sure that like you they all read history. Now they will have an opportunity to see it -- at Pearl Harbor, at Hiroshima, in China, Thailand, Australia, and other far away places.

I would not be so presumptous as to suggest what you should do in the future. But as an interested public citizen, I hope that you will be able to return to public life in some capacity. There are a lot of good men and women in our party but very few that I would classify as heavyweights. You are one who definitely rates that distinction.

Pat joins me in sending our warm regards to you, Honey, and the children.

Sincerely,

The Honorable
Lamar Alexander

Endnotes

Foreword by Jon Meacham

1 John Parish, "Hitting The Road: Alexander Finds Walk Educates," *The Jackson Sun*, April 24, 1978.
2 William Bennett, "Alexander Campaign No Cakewalk," *The Commercial Appeal*, April 16, 1978.
3 Quoteresearch, "Quote Origin: You Should Share the Passion and Action of Your Time at Peril of Being Judged Not To Have Lived," Quote Investigator, March 30, 2015, https://quoteinvestigator.com/2015/03/30/passion/.
4 "First Inaugural Address," Abraham Lincoln Online, Accessed 2020, https://www.abrahamlincolnonline.org/lincoln/speeches/1inaug.htm.

Author's Note

1 See: Robin Hood and Barry Parker, *The Tennesseans*, (Thomas Nelson Publishers, 1981); Keel Hunt, *Coup: The Day the Democrats Ousted Their Governor, Put Republican Lamar Alexander in Office Early, and Stopped a Pardon Scandal*, (Vanderbilt University Press, Nashville, 2013). See the chapter I wrote, "My View of the Coup," in the expanded version, published in 2017; Lamar Alexander, *Steps Along the Way*, (Thomas Nelson Publishers, 1986); Lamar Alexander, *Friends: Japanese and Tennesseans. A Model of U.S.-Japan Cooperation*, (Kodansha International, Tokyo, 1986); Lamar Alexander, *Six Months Off: An American Family's Australian Adventure*, (William Morrow, 1988); Lamar Alexander, *We Know What to Do*, (William Morrow, 1995); Carolynn Reid-Wallace; Lamar Alexander (ed.); Chester E. Finn, Jr, (ed.); and David M. Abshire (ed.), *The New Promise of American Life*, (Hudson Institute, 1995); Lamar Alexander, *Lamar Alexander's Little Plaid Book*, (Rutledge Hill Press, 1998); and Lamar Alexander, *Chief Waki Waki Poo & the Swimming Pool Monster*, (2012).

Prologue

1 GovFacts, "What is PEPFAR and Why Does It Matter?," GovFacts.org, November 21, 2025, https://govfacts.org/explainer/what-is-pepfar-and-why-does-it-matter/.
2 An observation of journalist Fareed Zakaria.

3 Rick Moran, "'A Republic if You Can Keep It.' The American Experiment Has Never Been in Greater Danger," *The Federal Observer*, July 19, 2025, https://federalobserver.com/2025/07/19/a-republic-if-you-can-keep-it-the-american-experiment-has-never-been-in-greater-danger/.
4 Doris Kearns Goodwin, *Team of Rivals: The Political Genius of Abraham Lincoln* (New York: Simon & Schuster, 2005) XIX.
5 "Benjamin Franklin: On the Constitution (1787)," American Rhetoric, https://www.americanrhetoric.com/speeches/benfranklin1787.htm.
6 "Ken Burns' 2015 Address," Washington University in St. Louis, May 15, 2015, https://commencement-archive.wustl.edu/speakers-honorees/speakers/ken-burns-address-2015/.
7 Margo McCutcheon, "A Rayburnism a Day Keeps the Memory Alive: Sam Rayburn Quotes," Texas Historical Commission, January 5, 2022, https://thc.texas.gov/blog/rayburnism-day-keeps-memory-alive-sam-rayburn-quotes.
8 Seth Motel, "Who Runs for Office? A Profile of the 2%," Pew Research Center, September3,2014,https://www.pewresearch.org/short-reads/2014/09/03/who-runs-for-office-a-profile-of-the-2/.

Chapter 1

1 The definitive account of these events is in the book by Keel Hunt, *Coup: The Day the Democrats Ousted Their Governor, Put Republican Lamar Alexander in Office Early, and Stopped a Pardon Scandal* (Nashville: Vanderbilt University Press, 2013). The expanded edition, published in 2017, includes my account of the early swearing-in, written in 1986, from which parts of this chapter are taken. See also: Keel Hunt, *Crossing the Aisle: How Bipartisanship Brought Tennessee to the Twenty-First Century and Could Save America* (Nashville: Vanderbilt University Press, 2018); Lamar Alexander, *Six Months Off: An American Family's Australian Adventure* (New York: William Morrow & Co., 1988) 55–66; Lamar Alexander, *Steps Along the Way: A Governor's Scrapbook* (Nashville: Thomas Nelson Publishers, 1986) 21–28; Judge William C. Koch Jr., "They Were Tennesseans First," *Nashville Bar Journal*, as cited in Congress.gov, "Congressional Record," March 26, 2007, https://www.govinfo.gov/content/pkg/CRECB-2007-pt6/html/CRECB-2007-pt6-issue-2007-03-26.htm; "Three Days Early: The Role of Lawyers in the Early Swearing-In of Governor Lamar Alexander on January 17, 1979," Harry Phillips American Inn of Court Program presented January 18, 2005 1:42:15, 2005-01-18, spc-mss0734-s15-ss14-g0096, Box: A-V 146. Lamar Alexander Papers, MSS.0734. Vanderbilt University Special Collections and University Archives. Sources also include the author's own recollections along with conversations with Hal Hardin.

Chapter 2

1 Keel Hunt, *Coup: The Day the Democrats Ousted Their Governor, Put Republican Lamar Alexander in Office Early, and Stopped a Pardon Scandal* (Nashville: Vanderbilt University Press, 2013) 91.

2 "NAFUSA Remarks," NAFUSA.org, October 26, 2018, https://nafusa.org/wp-content/uploads/2018/12/Doug-Jones-NAFUSA-remarks-2018.pdf.

Chapter 3

1 Mary Leidig, "The Mountain Q&A – Lamar Alexander: Hero for the American Outdoors," *Blue Ridge Country*, December 21, 2021, https://blueridgecountry.com/departments/guest-column/lamar-alexander-q-and-a/.

Chapter 4

1 Caleb Franz, *The Conductor: The Story of Rev. John Rankin, Abolitionism's Essential Founding Father* (Nashville: Post Hill Press, 2024) 17.

Chapter 5

1 As referenced in: Vicky Brantley, "Week of Sept. 25: Wisdom is Standing Firm in Decisions of Faith," The North Georgia Conference, September 17, 2011, https://www.ngumc.org/newsdetail/70273.

Chapter 6

1 Rev. Dr. Martin Luther King Jr., "Commencement Address for Oberlin College," Martin Luther King, Jr. at Oberlin, June 1965, https://www2.oberlin.edu/external/EOG/BlackHistoryMonth/MLK/CommAddress.html.

2 *The Vanderbilt Hustler,* March 24, 2006, Vanderbilt University, accessed December 15, 2025, https://www.jstor.org/stable/community.34450632?seq=4.

3 *The Vanderbilt Hustler,* January 12, 1962, Vanderbilt University, accessed December 16, 2025, https://www.jstor.org/stable/community.34451246?seq=1.

4 *The Vanderbilt Hustler,* February 16, 1962, Vanderbilt University, accessed December 16, 2025, https://www.jstor.org/stable/community.34450484?seq=1.

5 A. Lamar Alexander Jr., Note, *En Banc Hearings in the Federal Courts of Appeals: Accommodating Institutional Responsibilities (Part 1)*, 40 N.Y.U. L. Rev. (1965). Federal Courts of Appeal judges usually sit in panels of three. Occasionally, in important cases, all appellate judges of a circuit sit together or *en banc*.

Chapter 7

1 Frank T. Read, "The Penman of the Court: A Tribute to John Minor Wisdom," *Tulane Law Review* 60, no. 2 (1985): 1, https://www.tulanelawreview.org/pub/volume60/issue2/the-penman-of-the-court-a-tribute-to-john-minor-wisdom.

2 Allen D. Black, "Judge Wisdom, the Great Teacher and Careful Writer," *The Yale Law Journal* 109, no. 6 (2000): 1267–1272, https://www.jstor.org/stable/797464.

3 As cited by J. Woodford Howard Jr., "Commentary on Selecting Federal Judges," *Kentucky Law Journal* 77, no. 3 (1989): 621, https://files.core.ac.uk/download/232591210.pdf.

Chapter 9

1 The Knoxville lawyers who commiserated with the rats in the barn were Claude Robertson, George W. Morton, and Robert Campbell.

2 For instance, in Nashville at the Tennessee Voters Council and in Memphis campaigning with Lieutenant George W. Lee, Baker developed a friendship with the Reverend Ben Hooks, the eventual head of the national NAACP, and his wife, Frances. Sarah Moore Greene of Knoxville, a National NAACP board member, was a leader in the Baker campaign.

Chapter 10

1 William Haltom, "The Luxury of an Unexpressed Thought," *TBA Law Blog* 54, no. 3 (2018), https://www.tba.org/?pg=LawBlog&blAction=showEntry&blogEntry=30262.

2 Julian E. Zelizer, *The Fierce Urgency of Now: Lyndon Johnson, Congress, and the Battle for the Great Society* (London: Penguin Books, 2015) 236.

Chapter 14

1 Of the initial White House staff group that met at the Pierre Hotel on December 19, 1968—Harlow, Haldeman, Kissinger, Moynihan, Burns, Buchanan, and Ehrlichman—three of them (Harlow, Moynihan, and Burns) were being moved to the sidelines. The two with zero Washington experience had moved front and center—Haldeman, the adman and Ehrlichman, the land use lawyer.

Chapter 16

1 I recruited Gary Sisco from Congressman Robin Beard's office to be campaign manager. Tom Ingram and Marc Lavine handled press. Wendy Beasley and Emily Smith ran the office. F. Clifton White, Barry Goldwater's consultant, became mine. Howard Baker's television guru, Sam Newman, produced TV ads. Charlie Roll was pollster. Sandy Beall, Graham Hunter, J. Ronnie Greer, Tommy Anderson, Jane Chedester, and Tom Beasley handled schedule and politics. After I won the primary, Ted Welch took charge of fundraising. There were many volunteers from the Baker and Dunn campaigns.

Chapter 17

1 Roy Blount Jr., *Crackers* (Athens: University of Georgia Press, 1998) 13.

2 Katharine Q. Seelye, "John Deardourff, 71, a Leading G.O.P. Consultant, Dies," *New York Times,* December 29, 2004, https://www.nytimes.com/2004/12/29/politics/john-deardourff-71-a-leading-gop-consultant-dies.html.

3 Tom Gillespie, Terry Tabors, Bill Dickinson, and Kevin Kleinfelter were the band members. Jay Julian was the University of Tennessee band director.

Chapter 19

1 I did not want to be accused of skipping even one mile of my walk. The idea already had enough skeptics. So, on a Saturday in March, a few weeks after the truck hit me, instead of taking Southern Airways back to Nashville for the weekend, I returned to my "X" on Newport's Main Street, and hiked to Morristown, making up the twenty miles I had missed.

Chapter 20

1 Debby Patterson (later Debby Koch), who was for eight years deputy press secretary, took on the considerable task of arranging and coordinating my appearances at all these concerts. Julia and Bill Gibbons were key staff members.

After the Blanton episode, *Tennessean* editor John Seigenthaler advised me to hire as press secretary "someone who everyone knows is incorruptible and tell him he can walk into any meeting you have." I hired John M. Parish, a crusty reporter from the *Jackson Sun,* and that was the way we operated for eight years. Parish was the columnist who had observed during my 1974 race for governor that "some people thought Lamar Alexander, an Eastern educated lawyer, was a stuffed shirt..."

2 "[Charles M. Alexander's] love for congregational singing and the response that people gave him wherever he went so inspired me that I prayed that God would someday enable me to have the same privilege. His humble and gracious attitude and genuine love for the souls of men and women have always inspired me, and in a very humble way I have tried to emulate some of his wonderful characteristics and gracious demeanor with the large choirs that he conducted and the greater motivation of ministering spiritually to the choristers, too." Letter from Cliff Barrows to Lamar Alexander, July 13, 2005.

Chapter 21

1 Joe Concha, "Carter Says He Regrets Doing Away with 'Hail to the Chief' During His Presidency," *The Hill,* October 14, 2018, https://thehill.com/homenews/media/411368-carter-says-he-regrets-doing-away-with-hail-to-the-chief-during-his-presidency/.

2 From 1914 until 1958, a Ford plant in Memphis produced Model Ts, sedans, and coupes. At its peak, the plant had over 1,200 employees. "It closed in 1958

because of the Edsel Ford disaster," according to historian Bill Carey. In Nashville, The Marathon Motor Works built automobiles between 1909 and 1914.

3 Sadhana Shenvekar, "Blue Oval City Becomes Largest Assembly Plant Of Ford For Electric Vehicles," EMobility+, September 29, 2021, https://emobilityplus.com/2021/09/29/blue-oval-city-becomes-largest-assembly-plant-of-ford-for-electric-vehicles/.

Chapter 22

1 Timothy J. Minchin, *America's Other Automakers: A History of the Foreign-Owned Automotive Sector in the United States* (Athens: University of Georgia Press, 2021) 63.

2 David Halberstam, *The Reckoning* (New York: William Morrow & Co., 1986).

3 When Runyon threatened that Nissan might go to Georgia, I asked Bill Sansom, the commissioner of transportation, to lead the state's negotiations with Runyon. Sansom's business background and personality matched Runyon's, the two worked well together, and Runyon and Nissan settled happily in Tennessee.

4 Douglas Martin, "Takashi Ishihara, 91, Dies; Led Nissan's Rise," *New York Times,* January 6, 2004, https://www.nytimes.com/2004/01/06/business/takashi-ishihara-91-dies-led-nissan-s-rise.html.

Chapter 23

1 Commissioner of Safety Gene Roberts told Ingram about the sniper.

Chapter 24

1 Charles Love, "On the Prowl: The New Chattanooga," The Alley Cat, June 17, 2018, https://thealleycatblog.com/the-new-chattanooga/.

2 Leon Daniel, "'What If You Gave A World's Fair and Nobody Came?' UPI, June 4, 1981, https://www.upi.com/Archives/1981/06/04/What-If-You-Gave-A-Worlds-Fair-And-Nobody/1073360475200/.

3 While I wrote the copy for this ad campaign, the creativity and talent of Hank Dye and Eric Ericson proved invaluable—as it was later for Tennessee "Homecoming '86."

4 Davis's vote for the highway bill and gas tax did not end his political career. Ultimately, he moved from the state house to the state senate and then to the United States House of Representatives to represent his district until 2011.

5 Billy Stair, *McWherter: The Life and Career of Ned McWherter* (Billy Stair, October 12, 2011).

Chapter 25

1 LBJ's Outdoor Recreation Resources Review Commission, chaired by Laurance Rockefeller in 1962, had recommended a number of federal actions, including the Land and Water Conservation Fund, "National Wild and Scenic Rivers Act," and establishing a Bureau of Outdoor Recreation. Our report to Reagan, completed in 1986, focused on actions outside Washington, DC, including land trusts, greenways, and scenic highways. With one dissenting vote, we reiterated support for the Land and Water Conservation Fund, which finally became law in the "Great American Outdoors Act" that I helped enact in 2020. Victor Ashe, later Knoxville's mayor, was executive director of the commission.

2 From Doris Kearns Goodwin's book, *Team of Rivals.*

Chapter 26

1 In 1984, Hank Dye of the Dye, Van Mol & Lawrence ad agency, suggested a quilted Tennessee flag for a logo. I wanted something warmer. "Drop it over a fence. Tack it to a barn. Try a rocking chair," I said. According to Keel Hunt, Dan Brawner, art director at the agency, made the first drawing of the "rocking chair and flag" that became a perfect symbol.

2 In his September 2025 column in *Tennessee Magazine,* Bill Carey wrote about how the "Halls Homecoming '86 was such a success that it led to annual air shows. By the late 1990s, these air shows were attended by as many as 30,000 people and featured B-17s, P-51s, and other World-War-II-era aircraft." Bill Carey, "12 Things Started During Homecoming '86 That Still Exist," *Tennessee Magazine,* September 1, 2025, https://www.tnmagazine.org/12-things-started-during-homecoming-86-that-still-exist/. In his August column, Carey wrote about parades, reunions, and the passenger train associated with Homecoming '86. Bill Carey, "Homecoming '86 Celebrated in Every Corner of Tennessee," *Tennessee Magazine,* August 1, 2025, https://www.tnmagazine.org/12-things-started-during-homecoming-86-that-still-exist/. https://www.tnmagazine.org/homecoming-86-celebrated-in-every-corner-of-tennessee/.

3 Keel Hunt, *Crossing the Aisle: How Bipartisanship Brought Tennessee to the Twenty-First Century and Could Save America* (Nashville: Vanderbilt University Press, 2018).

4 These were Mississippi, Arkansas, Alabama, South Carolina, Kentucky, and Louisiana, according to Baker School calculations. Three decades later, in 2024, Tennessee had moved slightly ahead of North Carolina and trailed only Virginia and Florida among Southern states. "Although many Southern states did catch up to the rest of the country between 1985–1995, the rise in relative income was not automatic or guaranteed," Dean Wanamaker said. "Over this period, Kentucky went from 78 to 82 percent of national average per capita income. Arkansas went from 76 to 79 percent. Alabama from 79 to 84 percent."

Chapter 27

1 Mark Twain, *Following the Equator* (Los Angeles: American Publishing Company, 1897) 125.

Chapter 28

1 Perhaps Alex was compressing the words of the Olympic sprinter Jesse Owens, who said, "Find the good. It's all around you. Find it, showcase it, and you'll start believing it." "Jesse Owens Quotes," AZQuotes.com, https://www.azquotes.com/author/11205-Jesse_Owens#google_vignette.

Chapter 29

1 Maureen Dowd, "Cavazos Quits as Education Chief Amid Pressure From White House," *New York Times,* December 13, 1990, https://www.nytimes.com/1990/12/13/us/cavazos-quits-as-education-chief-amid-pressure-from-white-house.html.

2 "John H. Sununu Oral History (06/2000)," UVA Miller Center, June 8, 2000, https://millercenter.org/the-presidency/presidential-oral-histories/john-h-sununu-oral-history-062000.

3 President Bush's summit with governors in Charlottesville in 1989 adopted six national education goals: to have every child start school ready to learn, achieve a high school graduation rate of at least 90 percent, have every adult American be literate and skilled, have US students be first in the world in math and science achievement, have every school be free of drugs and violence, and to promote a transformation of the education system. Students would become competent in core subjects: math, science, English, history, and geography.

4 Maureen Dowd, "President Orders Aide to Review New Minority Scholarship Policy," *New York Times,* December 15, 1990, https://www.nytimes.com/1990/12/15/us/president-orders-aide-to-review-new-minority-scholarship-policy.html#:~:text=Trying%20to%20quell%20an%20angry,designated%20solely%20for%20minority%20students.

5 Lori Santos, "Bush Picks Alexander to Replace Cavazos," UPI, December 17, 1990, https://www.upi.com/amp/Archives/1990/12/17/Bush-picks-Alexander-to-replace-Cavazos/9342661410000/.

6 The group included Kearns, who, after a call from Bush, had agreed to become deputy secretary of education; Vanderbilt professor Chester "Checker" Finn, with whom I had worked when he was assistant to Pat Moynihan in the Nixon White House, and again when he was a Vanderbilt University professor and helped develop Tennessee's Master Teacher program; former New Jersey state education commissioner Saul Cooperman; education wise man Denis Doyle; and University of Tennessee vice presidents Michael Nettles and John Rudley. Doug Bailey was also there, and suggested a name for the plan: America 2000. The brainstorming and development process continued for several weeks, much

of it in Vanderbilt's cramped Washington, DC, office, with Finn and two employees of the Education Department, Bruno Manno and Scott Hamilton. It involved dozens of others—for example, Columbia University professor Diane Ravitch and Alcoa chief executive Paul O'Neill.

7 In 1976, before I was governor, Honey and I co-founded and bought 51 percent of Blackberry Farm, which, by the time of my Senate hearing, was on its way to becoming "the best place...to stay in America," according to a Tuesday, August 9, 2016, *New York Times* article. (See: Kim Severson, "A Widow Takes the Helm at Blackberry Farm," *New York Times*, August 9, 2016, https://www.nytimes.com/2016/08/10/dining/blackberry-farm-mary-celeste-beall.html.) In 1983, I used the proceeds from selling my shares in Ruby Tuesday, Inc. to buy 12 percent of the shares in a Knoxville food manufacturing company that did no government business but produced a good income for our family. In 1987, after I was governor, Honey and I co-founded and bought 40 percent of the shares of Corporate Child Care, Inc., which merged with its competitor, Bright Horizons, to become the world's largest provider of worksite day care. While I was governor, Honey purchased shares in a company that managed prisons, although she sold the shares at market value when the company said it would try to do business with Tennessee. The prison company never had a state contract while I was governor. The University of Tennessee spent $67,000 for gatherings at Blackberry Farm, although the university paid market price for meals entertaining donors. While I was a United States senator, I bought and sold no shares of stock and I served on no boards—public or nonprofit. Honey placed her assets in a blind trust over which she exercised no control. The trust publicly reported its investment activity annually.

Chapter 30

1 Although David Kearns and I had read Diane Ravitch's books and articles on education history, we had never met her until we flew to New York and recruited her to become assistant secretary for research. Carolynn Reid-Wallace came from City University of New York to head postsecondary activities, and IBM executive Don Laidlaw agreed to head the human resources and management. Washington, DC, attorney Jeff Martin became legal counsel. White House Director of Cabinet Affairs Steve Danzansky came aboard as chief of staff, and Vanderbilt University Associate Vice Chancellor Leslye Arsht, along with Etta Fielek, directed communications. Lanny Griffith arrived from the White House to head state and local relations; Bruno Manno, a Bill Bennett recruit to the department, became Assistant Secretary for Policy and Planning; Bob Okun agreed to head Congressional relations. I asked Bill Hansen, another able employee already there, to head the administration of the Department. Agnes Warfield came from the Department of State and promptly added Stephanie Fitzgerald and Stacey Lukens to her crack scheduling team. Former Labor Secretary Ann McLaughlin Korologos

agreed to be president of the New American Schools Development Corporation. Former US Chamber of Commerce President Ed Donley founded and chaired the nonprofit "America 2000" coalition. We enlisted a number of talented men and women already working in the Department, such as Manno and Becky Campoverde, who liked what we were planning and also liked all the presidential attention. Sondra Morris, who had been my executive assistant both in the governor's office and at the University of Tennessee, came to Washington, DC, with me. Either Kevin Phillips or Kirk Blalock traveled with me to thirty-eight states. And John Danielson was a special assistant.

2 Bruno V. Manno, "George H.W. Bush: The Education President," Walton Family Foundation, December 7, 2018, https://www.waltonfamilyfoundation.org/stories/k-12-education/george-h-w-bush-the-education-president; "Better Schools Mean Better Jobs," The Ripon Society, November 18, 2013, https://riponsociety.org/2013/11/better-schools-mean-better-jobs/.

3 Some said they were pie in the sky because they declared, among other things, that students would reach competency in English, math, science, history, and geography by the year 2000.

4 The next three presidents—Clinton, George W. Bush, and Barack Obama—all increased federal control of schools. In 2015, as a senator, I helped reverse that trend by engineering the passage of legislation that this was the "largest devolution of federal power to the states in a quarter of a century," according to the *Wall Street Journal*. That 2015 law thus restored the balance between federal and state responsibility for schools that President George H.W. Bush had put in place two decades earlier—that is, the federal government would advocate national goals, higher standards, and better testing and teaching, but would leave to states, communities, and teachers decisions about how to accomplish that.

5 David Broder and Richard Morin, "Bush Popularity Surges With Gulf Victory," *Washington Post*, March 5, 1991, https://www.washingtonpost.com/archive/politics/1991/03/06/bush-popularity-surges-with-gulf-victory/40a154e7-7668-409c-b89c-4bebb2c2a159/.

6 "Remarks to the Washington Gridiron," Texas State Library and Archives Commission, March 28, 1992, https://www.tsl.texas.gov/governors/modern/richards-gridiron-1.html.

7 Landon Parvin helped write the lyrics.

Chapter 31

1 Congress.gov. "Congressional Record Volume 168, Number 199: Honoring the Life of Leslee Kathryn Buhler Alexander," December 21, 2022, https://www.govinfo.gov/content/pkg/CREC-2022-12-21/html/CREC-2022-12-21-pt1-PgH9915.htm.

2 Richard Morris, *Behind the Oval Office: Winning the Presidency in the Nineties* (New York: Random House, 1997).

3 They were Agnes Warfield, Stacey Lukens, Kevin Phillips, and John Danielson soon to be joined by Stephanie Fitzgerald, Jim and Karin Jonas, Rob and Ann Gluck, Kay Durham, Phil Musser, Linus Catignani, Daniel Casse, Stephanie Chivers, Buckley Carlson and Lewis Lavine. John Tolsma, a Duke University student, traveled with Honey.

4 I learned another fundraising lesson during my losing 1974 campaign for governor—recruit a finance chairman whose motivation is good government and who has so much money that there is nothing that a governor can do for him or her. Jim Haslam, founder of the Pilot Company, fit that bill perfectly. During my 1978 and 1982 campaigns for governor, Haslam served as a shield between me and those who might want something. For example, in 1981, banker Jake Butcher, promoter of the Knoxville World's Fair, asked Haslam to urge me to sign a bill allowing the Knoxville airport authority to serve liquor by the drink. The airport was located in Blount County, which did not allow liquor by the drink. I opposed the bill because I believe in local control. "Tell him to sign the bill," Butcher told Haslam. "Jake, he's going to veto it," Haslam replied. "You're his finance chairman. Tell him to sign it," Butcher said. "That's not how we do things," Haslam said.

Butcher couldn't believe it. I vetoed the bill. Butcher became the Democrat nominee for governor the next year and went to prison for "kiting banks" in 1985. Susan Simons of Nashville, whose only experience raising money had been for cultural events, became deputy to Haslam. When I was elected, I named her commissioner of the Alcoholic Beverage Commission, which had been rife with corruption. Governor Blanton, himself, went to jail for selling whiskey licenses. Despite a lack of government experience, she did the job so well that she earned the nickname "Dragon Lady." Simons was one of six women that I appointed to Cabinet positions, which equaled the total number of women who had served in Cabinet positions since Tennessee became a state in 1796. In all of my campaigns, Lew Conner Jr. was a trusted friend, tolerant law partner, and willing fundraiser. Beginning with my 1996 campaign for President Steve Smith, he stepped into the shoes of Ted Welch and Jim Haslam and eventually became the Tennessee Republican Party leading fundraiser.

5 These included Governors Tommy Thompson, John Engler, and Pete Wilson; Senator Dole; Bill Bennett, Jack Kemp, and Steve Forbes.

6 While I did a lot of the driving, John Danielson, Scott Hamilton, Rob Gluck, Drew Alexander and Lewis Lavine accompanied me and drove on various parts of the trip.

Chapter 32

1 https://www.wsj.com/articles/SB935706968331620326?gaa_at=eafs&gaa_n=AWEtsqd_YyxxvmiC1hx9A-ansQgqeIEpygibKmXMPJgHe47ltLuCX-Pe-xpEo9aKt1MM%3D&gaa_ts=692ba9b4&gaa_sig=7JtYZxgoByuB-

KqFjIzHmU8OuAFp6feefzcwAZ9A6OcgccXgc2lUw1j45l0VaXrZdpAhX-JP3NgOcl4ukVbLeXiA%3D%3D.

2 Dan and Colleen Pero, who had been instrumental in Governor John Engler's election, bought a home in Nashville. Dan would be campaign manager. Colleen would be legal counsel and in charge of getting my name on the ballot in fifty states. Dan brought with him Jim Brandell, Margaret Murphy, and Michigan Republican Party Communications Director Bryan Flood who with Mark Merritt handled campaign communications. Daniel Casse from the *Weekly Standard* and Jessica Gavora arrived to supervise policy.

3 Senator Mitch, "Cut Their Pay and Send Them Home," The Heritage Foundation, October3,1994,https://www.heritage.org/report/cut-their-pay-and-send-them-home.

4 Michael Lewis, *Trail Fever* (New York: Random House Value Publishing, 1998) 79.

Chapter 33

1 I had been asked before to run for vice president. In the spring of 1996, while our family was vacationing in Hilton Head, Ross Perot flew from Dallas for visit. Even after an hour's conversation, I was not sure why he had come. A few days later, Perot telephoned. "I am calling to ask you to be my vice-presidential running mate on the Independent ticket," he said. "Thank you, Ross, but I can't do that. I'm a Republican," I said. "I thought that's what you might say," he replied.

Part 9

1 Jon Meacham, *Destiny and Power: The American Odyssey of George Herbert Walker Bush* (New York: Random House, 2015) 112.

Chapter 34

1 Jane Alonso was my second course assistant. She later served as legislative assistant to Maine Senator Susan Collins.

2 The class met on Mondays and Wednesdays. Guests participated by telephone or in person. The guests were an assortment of campaign veterans, from Mike Huckabee to Hamilton Jordan, Mike Murphy to Donna Brazile. Other guests were Governor Terry Branstad, President Reagan's speechwriter, Peter Hannaford, and NFL Commissioner Paul Tagliabue. From my campaigns came Doug Bailey, Daniel Casse, Ted Welch, Dan Pero, and Tom Rath. Students also heard from journalists David Nyhan and Jules Witcover.

3 "Speech at Hoover Institution Lunch," Margaret Thatcher Foundation, March 8, 1991, https://www.margaretthatcher.org/document/108264.

4 "Congressional Record—Senate (S11677)," November 20, 2004, https://www.congress.gov/108/crec/2004/11/20/CREC-2004-11-20-pt1-PgS11677.pdf.

5 Susie Alcorn, a former Bryant aide, became campaign manager. David Kustoff became chairman of the general election campaign. Patrick Jaynes and Jane Chedester worked in East Tennessee politics. Mike Murphy was busy with other campaigns but recruited Kim Alfano to produce television ads. Kevin Phillips and Josh Holly coordinated media. Ted Welch and Jim Haslam headed fundraising with Stephanie Fitzgerald as finance director and Kim Kaegi as consultant. Kim became my chief finance director during my time in the Senate. Lewis Lavine helped with planning. Molly Pratt traveled with Honey. During the summer, Will Alexander brought to Tennessee several University of Texas classmates to help with campaigning. Others pitching in included Lindsay Ward, Matt Sonnesyn, Stephanie Chivers, Michael Schultz, Mandy Ziegler, Katie Ogelsby, Justin Mitchell, Jon Michael, Houston Goddard, Rebecca Ayers, Will Barret, and Kay Durham, among many others.

6 Joel Roberts, "Tennessee Waltz Turns Into A Slugfest," CBS News, July 26, 2002, https://www.cbsnews.com/news/tennessee-waltz-turns-into-a-slugfest/.

Chapter 35

1 Lydia Saad, "Americans' Ratings of U.S. Professions Stay Historically Low," Gallup, January 13, 2025, https://news.gallup.com/poll/655106/americans-ratings-professions-stay-historically-low.aspx.

Chapter 36

1 Lamar Alexander, *Lamar Alexander's Little Plaid Book* (Nashville: Rutledge Hill Press, 1998) 14.

2 Robert A. Caro, "'Master of the Senate'" *New York Times,* April 28, 2002, https://www.nytimes.com/2002/04/28/books/chapters/master-of-the-senate.html.

Chapter 37

1 "The U.S. Senate Democratic Leader's Suite," United States Senate, Accessed November 30, 2025, https://www.senate.gov/art-artifacts/publications/pdf/room-democratic-leader-suite.pdf.

2 During the 1968 Nixon campaign, I had worked for John Warner and recruited Thad Cochran to head Mississippi's Nixon-Agnew citizens organization. In the Nixon White House, I had worked with North Carolina's Elizabeth Dole, then a consumer affairs assistant, and had met every Saturday morning with Utah's Bob Bennett when he was in charge of congressional relations for the transportation department. In 1980, Indiana's Richard Lugar and I worked together on Baker's presidential campaign.

At governors' conferences, I got to know West Virginia's Jay Rockefeller, Florida's Bob Graham, Missouri's Kit Bond, and New Hampshire's John Sununu (whose father was governor then). Jim Inhofe was the mayor of Tulsa, and I was a governor in 1982 when President Reagan appointed us both to the federal US Advisory Commission on Intergovernmental Relations.

Utah's Orrin Hatch and Ted Kennedy were in charge of the Senate education committee when I was education secretary. Running for president in 1995 and 1996, I competed against Judd Gregg as he led Bob Dole's campaign; campaigned with Oklahoma's Don Nickles; stayed in the home of Olympia Snowe and her husband, then Maine Governor John "Jock" McKernan; and met Maine's Susan Collins when she was running for governor.

3 Robert A. Caro, *Master of the Senate: The Years of Lyndon Johnson* (Toronto: Penguin Random House, 2002).

4 Tom Ingram was chief of staff—and the first staff member—and Alice Rolli, who had been my Senate campaign manager, was the second. Lindsey Ward (now Seidman), who had worked in the campaign, became a legislative aide and stayed for eighteen years. Trina Tyrer was office manager, Rich Hertling, and Matt Sonnesyn were legislative assistants. Matt had been my Harvard course assistant. Bonnie Sansonetti was the scheduler.

Chapter 38

1 Interview with Bush's Deputy Chief of Staff, Joseph Hagin. See: Peter Baker, "Bush keeps his war anguish hidden," NBC News, September 24, 2006. https://www.nbcnews.com/id/wbna14991955

2 Interview with Bush's Deputy Chief of Staff, Joseph Hagin. See: Peter Baker, "Bush Keeps His War Anguish Hidden," NBC News, September 24, 2006, https://www.nbcnews.com/id/wbna14991955.

3 Adam Cohen, "Widow And The Wizard," *Time,* May 18, 1998, https://time.com/archive/6732779/widow-and-the-wizard/.

4 Roger Wicker of Mississippi and Marsha Blackburn of Tennessee, who later became senators, helped pass the bill in the House.

5 The request came from Senator Jeff Bingaman and Representative Bart Gordon on the Democrat side. The Republicans were Congressman Sherwood Boehlert and me.

Chapter 39

1 John Bresnahan, "Alexander wins Senate GOP Conference chairmanship," *Politico,* December 6, 2007, https://www.politico.com/blogs/politico-now/2007/12/alexander-wins-senate-gop-conference-chairmanship-004514. The quote, along with the following two are taken from the same article.

Chapter 41

1 I had telephoned Trent Lott to invite him to send a House Republican delegation to Blackberry Farm, but he had a scheduling conflict and handed the job off to Newt Gingrich, later the first Republican Speaker in two generations. Gingrich

brought with him two other members of the Conservative Opportunity Society, Carroll Campbell Jr. of South Carolina (later governor) and Connie Mack of Florida (later a senator). I invited three other governors—Pennsylvania's Dick Thornburgh, New Hampshire's John Sununu, and North Carolina's Jim Martin. I also invited two consultants, Doug Bailey and Bob Teeter.

2 "How the States Turned Right," The James Madison Institute, September 28, 2015, https://jamesmadison.org/how-the-states-turned-right/.

3 George F. Will, "Will: Obama Rushing Through Too Many Policies," *Newsweek*, December 4, 2009, https://www.newsweek.com/will-obama-rushing-through-too-many-policies-75605.

4 My early campaigns attracted to politics many talented and entrepreneurial young friends who later founded and built significant business enterprises. These included Sandy Beall (Ruby Tuesday, Inc. and Blackberry Farm), Tom Beasley (Corrections Corporation of America, Education Corporation of America), Sam Furrow (Furrow Auction Company), Graham Hunter (Custom Foods of America), M. Lee Smith (*Tennessee Journal*), David White (Approach 13-30), Chris Whittle (Whittle Communications, Edison Schools—now EdisonLearning), Phillip Moffitt (bought *Esquire* magazine with Whittle and became its CEO), Marguerite Sallee (Corporate Child Care, later Bright Horizons), and Brad Martin (Corporate Child Care, bought Saks and became its CEO and later became executive chairman of FedEx). Talented young Democrats were entrepreneurial too. Phil Bredesen founded a health care company before he was mayor of Nashville, and a solar energy company after he was governor.

5 There was an interruption of one-party doldrums in 1910 when Democrats split over prohibition of whiskey and Tennesseans elected Republican Governor Ben Hooper, an orphan from Newport. This happened again in 1920 when Republican presidential candidate Warren G. Harding swept all but five Tennessee counties, propelling into the governor's office seventy-one-year-old Republican Alf Taylor. Democrat legislators promptly took most of Governor Taylor's powers away for two years until voters could elect a Democrat, Austin Peay. This burst of two-party competition produced one of the state's most effective governors. Among other things, Peay hauled legislators twice by train to East Tennessee to persuade them to appropriate $2 million to buy land and donate it to the federal government to create the Great Smoky Mountains National Park.

6 At the time of this writing, parties are competing to redraw congressional seats for maximum political advantage, further weakening the influence of minority parties. See: Aaron Zitner, "America Is Fracturing Into Red and Blue Nations, Redistricting Fight Shows," *Wall Street Journal,* August 8, 2025, https://www.wsj.com/politics/us-gerrymandering-political-divide-a2a83a28?mod=itp_wsj.

7 In 2025, Missouri Senator Roy Blunt described to me the same changes he had seen during four decades in public office. "In 1979, twenty-seven states had a

Republican US senator and a Democrat US senator. Today, it is three," he said. "When George W. Bush was elected president, there were thirty 'battleground states'—states that determined the winner. In the last three elections, there were seven. When I started, we could define ourselves. Now, your national party defines you. And now it's all about the primary, and that attracts a different kind of candidate. Someone who can be elected by the 5 percent of the registered voters who vote in that primary. Today, even the candidate for lieutenant governor of Missouri is running against China and to secure the border." Blunt went on. "Most senators who retired during the last two cycles would usually vote to make something happen if there was a chance that it could. Their successors vote 'no.' Voting 'yes' would mean supporting an agreement that inevitably includes provisions that hard core primary voters don't like," Blunt said.

8 Everett Dirksen, *The Education of a Senator* (Champaign: University of Illinois Press, 1998).

9 Jack Kelly, "Follow The Incentives And That Will Tell You Everything You Need To Know About A Company's Culture," *Forbes*, August 18, 2023, https://www.forbes.com/sites/jackkelly/2023/08/18/follow-the-incentives-and-that-will-tell-you-everything-you-need-to-know-about-a-companys-culture/.

Chapter 42

1 Jon Meacham, *Destiny and Power: The American Odyssey of George Herbert Walker Bush* (New York: Random House, 2015) 112.

2 "Toasts at a White House Dinner Honoring Governors Attending the National Governors' Association Winter Session," The American Presidency Project, February 27, 1979, https://www.presidency.ucsb.edu/documents/toasts-white-house-dinner-honoring-governors-attending-the-national-governors-association.

3 A focused, Moses-type leadership style can produce results on narrower objectives. In 2000, roadbuilders told Tennessee Governor Sundquist that their machinery had unearthed a strange substance near the town of Gray. That substance contained remains of mastodons and saber-toothed tigers. The governor rerouted the road and preserved one of the most important fossil sites in North America. "One reason we have governors is to make exceptions when they need to be made," Arizona Governor Bruce Babbitt once told me. Another example was when I persuaded the legislature to ban billboards on 152 miles of new Tennessee interstate highways paid for by the state, and to ban new billboards and junkyards on thousands of miles of roads to scenic places. Those are the kind of things a governor can do.

4 David Zizzo, "Henry Louis Bellmon," *The Oklahoman*, April 18, 1999, https://www.oklahoman.com/story/news/1999/04/18/henry-louis-bellmon/62245890007/.

5 Michelle Cottle, "Joe Manchin Has Some Unsolicited Advice for Kamala Harris and the Democrats," *New York Times*, August 18, 2024, https://www.nytimes.com/2024/08/18/opinion/joe-manchin-kamala-harris.html.

Chapter 43

1 These included Gregg, Mike Enzi, Bob Bennett, Chuck Grassley, Olympia Snowe, Lindsey Graham, and me.

2 In a cloakroom conversation between presidential nominees, Senator George McGovern told Senator Barry Goldwater, "It's a good thing both of us were defeated so badly or we never would have gotten over it."

3 Governor Deval Patrick had appointed Paul G. Kirk Jr., to the vacancy created by Kennedy's death. Kirk was a former Kennedy aide who provided the sixtieth Democrat vote until Massachusetts could hold a special election.

Chapter 44

1 To prove once again that Washington, DC, initiatives rarely expire, at this writing, nearly two decades later, the Senate Republican Conference chairman still shows videos at Tuesday lunches, hoping to cajole colleagues into singing off the same song sheet.

2 Edward Luce, "Defiant Obama Vows to Stay the Course," *Financial Times*, January 28,2010,https://www.ft.com/content/cf807cb2-0c3e-11df-8b81-00144feabdc0.

Chapter 45

1 Later in the day, I gave the president a letter showing that the nonpartisan Congressional Budget Office had estimated that "the average premium per person covered…for new nongroup policies would be about 10 percent to 13 percent higher in 2016 than the average in that same year under current law." See Tyler Cowen, "Is There ACA Rate Shock in California?" Marginal Revolution, June 5, 2013, https://marginalrevolution.com/marginalrevolution/2013/06/is-there-aca-rate-shock-in-california.html#:~:text=Still%2C%20the%20question%20having%20been,such%20policies%20under%20current%20law.

2 Frank H. Mackaman, "The Long, Hard Furrow: Everett Dirksen's Part in the Civil Rights Act of 1964," The Dirksen Congressional Center, January 2005, https://dirksencenter.org/wp-content/uploads/The-Long-Hard-Furrow.pdf.

Chapter 46

1 "Lamar Alexander to Resign from GOP Leadership Post to Pursue Senate Bipartisan Dealmaking," *The Denver Post*, September 20, 2011, https://www.denverpost.com/2011/09/20/lamar-alexander-to-resign-from-gop-leadership-post-to-pursue-senate-bipartisan-dealmaking/.

2 Ruth Marcus, "Lamar Alexander: Liberated from Orthodoxy," *The Washington Post*, September 22, 2011, https://www.washingtonpost.com/opinions/

lamar-alexander-liberated-from-orthodoxy/2011/09/22/gIQALPgtoK_story.html.

3 "The Liberation of Alexander," *Herald-Tribune*, September 24, 2011, https://www.heraldtribune.com/story/news/2011/09/24/the-liberation-of-alexander/29047099007/.

4 Bob Schieffer, "When Giving Up Power is Liberating," *Face the Nation*, September 25, 2011, https://www.cbsnews.com/news/when-giving-up-power-is-liberating/.

Chapter 47

1 Nour Rahal, "Former Gov. Rick Snyder, Sen. Debbie Stabenow honored for public service, call for unity," *Detroit Free Press*, September 18, 2025, https://www.freep.com/story/news/local/michigan/2025/09/18/rick-snyder-debbie-stabenow-public-service-bipartisanship-citizens-research-council-michigan/86189646007/.

2 I worked with Senators Schumer, Levin, McCain, and Barrasso to speed up confirmation of 272 presidential nominations and eliminate the need to confirm 163 others, as well as eliminating the need to confirm thousands of members of the health service corps. Senators Bingaman, Feinstein, and I made sure the world's fastest computer was funded. Feinstein, Graham, and I worked with Vice President Biden on waterways and ports. I helped Senators Murray, Blunt, and Feinstein increase funding for biomedical and energy research.

3 Alexander Bolton, "Senator Criticizes Obama's 'Audacity' in Using Republican Lawmakers as 'Props,'" *The Hill*, May 25, 2010, https://thehill.com/homenews/senate/161802-senator-criticizes-obamas-audacity-in-using-republican-lawmakers-as-props/.

4 The sponsors who met with the president were Senators Durbin, Manchin, Carper, Coburn, Burr, King, and me.

Chapter 48

1 "CBS' *Face the Nation* with Bob Schieffer," *Los Angeles Times*, April 10, 2010, https://www.latimes.com/archives/blogs/top-of-the-ticket/story/2010-04-10/opinion-sunday-shows-queen-noor-h-clinton-barbour-r-gates.

2 Sharron Angle in Nevada (who had said that a hypothetical thirteen-year-old rape/incest victim should steer clear of abortion and make "lemons into lemonade"); Christine O'Donnell in Delaware (who announced, "I am not a witch"); and Todd Akin in Missouri (who said, "If it's a legitimate rape, the female body has ways to try to shut that whole thing down").

3 Dan Balz, "In Tennessee, Consensus Politics Makes a Last Stand," *Washington Post*, July 29, 2014, https://www.washingtonpost.com/politics/for-tennessee-gop-its-the-tea-party-vs-the-legacy-of-howard-baker/2014/07/29/53403502-12a6-11e4-9285-4243a40ddc97_story.html.

4 Reid Epstein, "Tennessee GOP Challengers Struggle," *Wall Street Journal*, July 18, 2014, https://www.wsj.com/articles/tennessee-gop-challengers-struggle-1405724774?gaa_at=eafs&gaa_n=ASWzDAhjdgL46X9hr7iMFLI-5JZyPGeHgYNYnqAZFaX-xcrljs6LrsmMmL9pN-gqIFCY%3D&gaa_ts=68a0abe9&gaa_sig=oVITUwcHCcnMf90CE_qWLqhHCVnO4FsRxCK-tRpgOMZ07W-C1TenzfH657manTjI---dREO2yqqeBLCirscMo1w%3D%3D.

5 Michael Warren, "Lamar Alexander in the Crosshairs," *Washington Examiner*, August 4, 2014, https://www.washingtonexaminer.com/magazine/2403451/lamar-alexander-in-the-crosshairs/.

6 I had 49.6 percent. Carr was second with 40.6 percent.

Chapter 49

1 Dave Boucher, "Obama Returns to TN Friday for College Announcement," *Tennessean*, January 3, 2015, https://www.tennessean.com/story/insession/2015/01/03/obama-returns-to-tennessee/21231119/?gnt-cfr=1&gca-cat=p&gca-uir=true&gca-epti=z113532d00----v113532b0039xxd003965&gca-ft=221&gca-ds=sophi.

2 Emily Cadei, "The Education Law Everyone Wants to Fix," *Newsweek*, July 3, 2015, https://www.newsweek.com/education-law-everyone-wants-fix-349905.

Chapter 50

1 Haley Sweetland Edwards, "What the New Senate Education Chair Thinks About No Child Left Behind," *Time*, January 25, 2015, https://time.com/3681776/lamar-alexander-no-child-left-behind/.

2 "No Child Left Behind's Successor," *Wall Street Journal*, November 29, 2015, https://www.wsj.com/articles/no-child-left-behinds-successor-1448838727?gaa_at=eafs&gaa_n=AWEtsqcr2z7AOx90V4ppnmodWcIDzcF2Kn_pGLhQ3w-JamJOUw31bUtgGY15y6F--mLc%3D&gaa_ts=690833af&gaa_sig=oGM-MDY9HT8ME1lmJCGMjOYXc8Y2aGno2TEJ7QjWWNFkMDHReOkjf-bC56BqPnnfkxuGp_k7kGty_IKIUoeFUjLw%3D%3D.

Chapter 51

1 Please see the Appendix for my entire two-minute speech.

2 "New Education Law Shifts Federal Influence Over Public Schools," PBS News, December 10, 2015, https://www.pbs.org/newshour/show/new-education-law-shifts-federal-influence-over-public-schools.

3 The White House Office of the Press Secretary, "Remarks by the President at Every Student Succeeds Act Signing Ceremony," December 10, 2015, https://obamawhitehouse.archives.gov/the-press-office/2015/12/10/remarks-president-every-student-succeeds-act-signing-ceremony.

4 Stephen Sawchuk, "The NEA's Best Frenemy: Lamar Alexander," Education Week, July 7, 2016, https://www.edweek.org/teaching-learning/the-neas-best-frenemy-lamar-alexander/2016/07.
5 US Senate Committee on Health, Education, Labor, and Pensions, "Washington Post: Distinguished Pol of the Week," December 14, 2015, https://www.help.senate.gov/chair/newsroom/news/washington-post-distinguished-pol-of-the-week.

Chapter 52

1 Kelly Servick, "U.S. Senators Advance Biomedical Innovation Bills, but Key NIH Funding Issue Unresolved," *Science*, April 7, 2016, https://www.science.org/content/article/us-senators-advance-biomedical-innovation-bills-key-nih-funding-issue-unresolved.
2 Jennifer Steinhauer, "Another Chance for Bipartisan Achievement Slips Away," *New York Times*, April 29, 2016, https://www.nytimes.com/2016/04/30/us/politics/another-chance-for-bipartisan-achievement-slips-away.html.
3 Ibid.
4 The delegation included Senate Budget Committee Chairman Mike Enzi, Senate Democrat whip Dick Durbin, Senate Appropriations Committee Chairman Thad Cochran, and Representative Fred Upton, Chairman of the House Energy and Commerce Committee and the primary sponsor of the House bill.
5 The café owner, a retired foreign service officer, told us, "The movie piano was made smaller—it had fewer octaves—because both Sam and [Humphrey] Bogart were small men and Sam was a singer, not a piano player. That music was dubbed." She also said that if there had been a real Rick's Café in Morocco, it would have been in Tangier, on the coast.

Chapter 53

1 "Congress's Cures Breakthrough," *Wall Street Journal*, December 6, 2016, https://www.wsj.com/articles/congresss-cures-breakthrough-1481071114?gaa_at=eafs&gaa_n=AWEtsqcAFGoFB3Tb4zeYo2ohg1vSngVMMdm9JK8x-1HYczybX2nRwaL9r5_-YxcyFpW0%3D&gaa_ts=6930abb0&gaa_sig=P-1MctYzn-iA1hB3r6lDLs6df25mjlJUkMghzVwy4xatbBh_dWwX2Cmk3NG-7Mcf0VFOnLJFhOEaWSRAenVw-_Ow%3D%3D.
2 United States Senate, "Senate Fistfight," February 22, 1902, https://www.senate.gov/about/powers-procedures/rules-procedures/tillman-mclaurin-rule-xix.htm.

Chapter 54

1 Andrew Jackson, "First Annual Message," The American Presidency Project, December 8, 1829, https://www.presidency.ucsb.edu/documents/first-annual-message-3.

Chapter 55

1 Jennifer Haberkorn, "2 GOP Heavyweights Brawl Over Obamacare Bill," *Politico*, September 17, 2017, https://www.politico.com/story/2017/09/17/obamacare-hatch-alexander-health-care-242790.

2 Donald J. Trump (@realDonaldTrump), "I am supportive of Lamar as a person & also of the process, but I can never support bailing out ins co's who have made a fortune w/ O'Care." Twitter, October 18, 2017, 8:41 a.m., https://x.com/realdonaldtrump/status/920645935981613057?refsrc=email&s=11.

3 The "Hyde Amendment" barred the use of federal funds—but allowed state funds—to pay for most abortions.

4 That's due to high drug prices, overtreatment, administrative costs, fraud, and abuse.

Chapter 56

1 Seung Min Kim, et al, "Top Senate Republicans Reject Trump's Renewed Call for Immediate Dismissal of Impeachment Charges," *Washington Post*, January 13, 2020, https://www.washingtonpost.com/politics/top-senate-republicans-reject-trumps-renewed-call-for-immediate-dismissal-of-impeachment-charges/2020/01/13/f5cf4a86-3624-11ea-bb7b-265f4554af6d_story.html.

2 Siobhan Hughes, "As Senate Career Draws to End, Lamar Alexander Weighs Whether to Stick With Trump," *Wall Street Journal*, January 17, 2020, https://www.wsj.com/articles/as-senate-career-draws-to-end-lamar-alexander-weighs-whether-to-stick-with-trump-11579276293.

Chapter 57

1 Jon Meacham, et al, *Impeachment: An American History* (New York: Modern Library, 2018).

2 Senator Murkowski's vote still mattered. If she were to vote "yes" for more evidence, that would create a fifty-fifty tie, which still would not allow more witnesses. But then, the chief justice would have to decide whether to cast a tie-breaking vote, or to decide not to vote. Either way, his decision would drag the Supreme Court into the politics of the impeachment, which several Democrat senators were hoping for. The next day, Murkowski voted "no," resolving the chief justice's dilemma.

3 My entire statement can be found in Appendix B. Also see: "Alexander Statement on Impeachment Witness Vote," U.S. Senate Committee on Health, Education, Labor, and Pensions, January 30, 2020, https://www.help.senate.gov/rep/newsroom/press/alexander-statement-on-impeachment-witness-vote.

4 Peter Baker and Susan Glasser, *The Divider: Trump in the White House* (New York: Doubleday, 2022) 403.

Chapter 58

1 Editorial Board, "Lamar Alexander's Finest Hour," *Wall Street Journal*, February 2, 2020, https://www.wsj.com/articles/lamar-alexanders-finest-hour-11580680232.

2 "Opinion: Day 10 of Trump's Trial: The Anticlimax," *New York Times*, February 1, 2020, https://www.nytimes.com/2020/02/01/opinion/trump-impeachment-senate.html.

3 Lindsey Graham (@LindseyGrahamSC), "Long story short, @SenatorAlexander most likely expressed the sentiments of the country as a whole as well as any single Senator possibly could. Those who hate Trump and wish to take the voters choice away in an unfounded manner, Sen. Alexander rightly rejected their arguments." Twitter, January 31, 2020, 9:03 a.m., https://x.com/LindseyGrahamSC/status/1223260569702215681.

4 The Editors, "Lamar Alexander Gets It Right," *National Review*, February 3, 2020, https://www.nationalreview.com/2020/02/trump-impeachment-trial-lamar-alexander-gets-it-right/.

5 There were more:
"Lamar speaks for lots and lots of us." —Senator Ben Sasse
"Senator Alexander... said out loud what I think most Senate Republicans believe in private: That yes, the president did withhold military assistance to try to get Ukraine to help with his election." —Senator Chuck Schumer

Chapter 59

1 Among the then 417 National Park Service properties, the Smokies had the biggest problem. By law, it has no entrance fee because the citizens of Tennessee and North Carolina who gave it to the federal government in the 1930s didn't want to have to pay to visit it. While western parks add entrance fee revenue to their federal appropriation, the Smokies have to rely on 2,200 volunteers to maintain roads, bridges, trails, bathrooms, and campgrounds.

2 Donald J. Trump (@realDonaldTrump), "I am calling on Congress to send me a Bill that fully and permanently funds the LWCF and restores our National Parks. When I sign it into law, it will be HISTORIC for our beautiful public lands. ALL thanks to @SenCoryGardner and @SteveDaines, two GREAT Conservative Leaders!" Twitter, March 3, 2020, 3:10 p.m., https://x.com/realDonaldTrump/status/1234949358644289541.

3 Those attending were Senators Cantwell, Daines, Gardner, Manchin, Portman, Warner, and me.

Chapter 60

1 "Alexander Statement on the Presidential Election," Official Press Release from Office of Former Sen. Lamar Alexander (R-TN), November 20, 2020, https://www.legistorm.com/stormfeed/view_rss/1678464/member/2/title/alexander-statement-on-the-presidential-election.html.

Chapter 61

1 "In Farewell Speech, Lamar Alexander Pleads with Colleagues to Fix the Senate," *New York Times,* December 2, 2020, https://www.nytimes.com/live/2020/12/02/us/joe-biden-trump.

2 The final pieces of the FAFSA reform legislation had become law after fifteen years of hearings and negotiations. Then, the Biden administration bungled its implementation for four more years, until it provided relief to millions of students.

Chapter 62

1 *Knoxville News Sentinel,* January 6, 2025, p. 7a

2 NPR Staff, "A Timeline of How the Jan. 6 Attack Unfolded, Including Who Said What and When," *NPR,* January 5, 2022, https://www.npr.org/2022/01/05/1069977469/a-timeline-of-how-the-jan-6-attack-unfolded-including-who-said-what-and-when.

3 Ibid.

4 *Knoxville News Sentinel,* January 6, 2025, p. 7a; p. 4a, 5a, 7a

5 Ryan J. Reilly, "Reagan-appointed judge stresses lasting impact of Jan.6 while sentencing rioter banking on Trump pardon," NBC News, December 6, 2024. https://www.nbcnews.com/politics/justice-department/royce-lamberth-reagan-jan-6-phillip-grillo-trump-rcna183221

6 BBC News, August 3, 2023

7 *Final Report of the Select Committee to Investigate the January 6th Attack on the United States Capitol* (PDF) (Report). U.S. Government Publishing Office. December 22, 2022. pp. 210–213. Retrieved July 7, 2023.

8 Bloomberg News, Bloomberg, https://assets.bwbx.io/documents/users/iqjWHBFdfxIU/riQQQpy2t1sM/v0.

9 *Wall Street Journal,* Monday, January, 2025

10 *USA Today,* Monday January 6, 2025, p. 6a.

Chapter 63

1 Jannell Costa and April Davidson were Honey's primary helpers.

2 The six friends were Nicky Cheek, Carol Hagan, Carole Sergent, Dana Sherrard, Mary Jane Smith, and Marcella Zimmerman.

Epilogue

1 ABC News, "Former Capitol Police Officer Seeks to End Falsehoods About Jan. 6," *ABC News,* https://abcnews.go.com/Politics/former-capitol-police-officer-end-falsehoods-jan-6/story?id=114464816.
2 Nashville Business Journal, April 15, 2025.
3 "The Shutdown of USAID Has Already Killed Hundreds of Thousands," *The New Yorker,* https://www.newyorker.com/culture/the-new-yorker-documentary/the-shutdown-of-usaid-has-already-killed-hundreds-of-thousands.
4 *New York Times,* August 14, 2025, p 21.
5 Author's conversation with Collins.
6 Emily Anthes, "Trump Science Funding Cuts Shake U.S. Research," *The New York Times,* December 2, 2025, https://www.nytimes.com/interactive/2025/12/02/upshot/trump-science-funding-cuts.html.
7 Dr. Don Ingber, *Knoxville News Sentinel,* Sunday April 20, 2025, p 17A.
8 NIH's budget was $48.2 billion in net spending for FY 2024 and the total federal budget was approximately $6.8 trillion
9 *Wall Street Journal,* Dec 6, 2025, p A11
10 "The average U.S. tariff on imported goods over the past six months had soared from 2.4 percent in 2024 to nearly 18 percent as of May 27, 2025—the highest level since 1934." *Wall Street Journal,* Friday, May 30, 2025, A15.
11 *The Wall Street Journal,* October 27 2025.
12 October 25, 2025 interview with Politico.
13 *New York Times,* September 14, 2025, p. 21.
14 On this I worked with Senators Blunt, Murray, and Durbin.
15 Scalia conversation with Justice Ruth Bader Ginsburg at The National Press Club, April 17, 2014.
16 BBC broadcast, September, 2025.
17 CNN, October 28, 2025.
18 *New York Times,* September 8, 2025, p. A13.
19 Ibid.
20 *New York Times,* November 25, 2025.
21 *Washington Post,* November 29, 2025.
22 Politico, December 2, 2025.
23 *The Daily Beast,* November 26, 2025.
24 Perhaps Republicans had remembered not only the wisdom of Justice Scaila but of James Madison who wrote in Federalist 47, "The accumulation of all powers, legislative, executive, and judiciary in the same hands ... may justly be pronounced the very definition of tyranny."
25 Conversation with author, April 2025.
26 From the author's conversation with former Sen. Ben Sasse, July 2024.

Photo Insert

1 Guy Tallent and Kent Russ ran the 100-yard dash in 9.7 seconds at a time when the world record was 9.2. Lynn Mayhan also was fast.

Index

Index

C

G

H

LAMAR
ALEXANDER
Concord
to
Nashua
to
The Sea